# DUBL

## 800 things to do in and around Dublin for all the family

JANE SUITER is a writer with the *Sunday Times* in Dublin. She was previously economics editor at the *Irish Times*, and has worked at a number of other newspapers and magazines, both in Ireland and in the UK. She lives in Dublin with her husband and three children.

LOUISE TREHY was brought up on the northside of Dublin. She has three children and works in online publishing. She still likes to watch the fishing boats in Howth harbour while eating a big bag of chips.

# Dublin for Kids

## JANE SUITER · LOUISE TREHY

THE O'BRIEN PRESS
DUBLIN

*This book is dedicated to*
*Nicky, Chen, Caoilfhionn, Cillian, Emer,*
*Colm, Blathnaid and Chloe.*

*With thanks to all our friends and family for their*
*support and help, and special thanks to Anita*
*Schwartz, Alison Dempsey, Aideen Quigley*
*and all at O'Brien Press.*

First published 2003 by
The O'Brien Press Ltd,
20 Victoria Road, Dublin 6, Ireland.
Tel: +353 1 4923333; Fax: +353 1 4922777
E-mail: books@obrien.ie
Website: www.obrien.ie

**ISBN: 0-86278-814-5**

British Library Cataloguing-in-Publication Data:
Suiter, Jane
Dublin for kids
1.Family recreation - Ireland - Dublin - Guidebooks
2.Dublin (Ireland) - Guidebooks
I.Title II.Trehy, Louise
914.1'835'04824

1 2 3 4 5
03 04 05 06 07

Editing, typesetting, layout and design:
The O'Brien Press Ltd
Printing: Nørhaven Paperback A/S, Denmark

# CONTENTS

**Dublin Area Map**                page 6

**Introduction**                         8

**How to Use this Book**          9

**City Centre**
    Things to Do                       13
    Places to Eat                       61

**North Dublin**
    Things to Do                       72
    Places to Eat                     130

**West Dublin**
    Things to Do                     136
    Places to Eat                     177

**South Dublin**
    Things to Do                     183
    Places to Eat                     265

**Party Services**                    271

**Organisations**                     275

**Festivals**                             287

**Emergencies**                       291

**Car parks**                           292

**Indexes**
    List of Indexes                   294
    General                             295
    Sports                               312
    Top Choices                       322

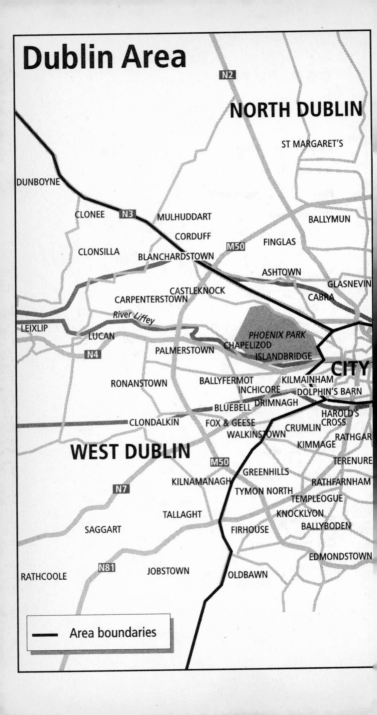

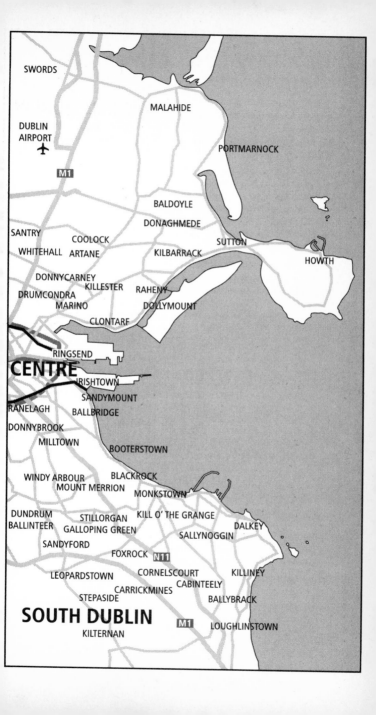

# Introduction

Hello and welcome to *Dublin for Kids*, your one-stop guide to entertainment and leisure activities for children in the Dublin area. There are over 800 entries in this book – you can find something different to do every weekend of the year, without visiting the same place twice!

As working parents, we are fully aware of the pressures of entertaining children, especially during Ireland's long summer holidays. As well as being packed full of activities for children and ideas for family days out, half of this book is dedicated to finding a group, hobby or sporting activity suitable for any child up to 16 years of age. We have provided information on holiday camps and courses in well over 100 different places. So, whether you have a disco diva or a Roy Keane wannabe, there's something to suit everyone.

We have carefully considered the many things that you need to know when planning a day out or activity with your children. There can be nothing as disappointing or frustrating as arranging a trip, only to arrive and discover that the event must be pre-booked, or that the venue is being refurbished, or that there is no buggy access. Not only do you end up with bored children, but very cranky ones too! This book allows you to make informed decisions on where to go and what to do, whether it is raining buckets or you are strapped for cash. We have listed prices, opening hours, age suitability, baby friendliness, public transport, availability of parking, contact names and numbers, and written our own comments on each activity or place. The information supplied has been independently researched, by parents, to a strict set of criteria, and is correct at the time of going to print.

Whether you live in Dublin or are visiting Ireland on holidays, Dublin is a great place for kids. There is plenty to see and do and it offers very good value for money. Irish people welcome families especially, and we are sure you will find plenty to keep your child amused and entertained.

We hope this book is a useful tool for anyone with children. We welcome your comments and suggestions, especially if there is anything you would like to see in future editions, or if there is any organisation we have left out.

Please write to us at:
18 Grosvenor Square,
Rathmines, Dublin 6
Or send us an email to:
info@dublinforkids.com

# How to Use this Book

Dublin for Kids is designed for ease of use, and has a simple refer-encing system. We have divided Dublin into four areas – City Centre, North, West and South (see map, pp. 6–7). The entries in each of these areas have been split into two parts: Things to Do and Places to Eat. Within each of these divisions, entries are listed alphabetically. There are also sections on Party Services, Organi-sations, Festivals, Emergencies and Car Parks.

Each entry has been given an individual number like this: **397**. These numbers run consecutively throughout the book.

If you want to look for a specific activity or type of place, go to the indexes at the back of the book. Here we have listed activities under various categories, eg, drama classes, museums, swimming pools. The reference numbers will refer you to the entries in the body of the book. There are also several indexes of our Top Choices of various kinds, our personal favourites in various cate-gories, eg, child-friendly restaurants/cafés, playgrounds, summer camps. We have made recommendations for various age groups and personality types, eg, recommended activities for 2–5-year-olds, or for inquisitive kids. Again, the entries can be found by their reference numbers.

Within each entry, you will find the following information:

- Name of place, business, or individual, followed by the ad-dress (or, in some cases, several addresses). In some cases we have not given a full address because the venue is liable to change, eg, in the case of music teachers, who may cover a certain area.
- Contact name: In some entries, this may refer to the indi-vidual who organises specific children's events, eg, work-shops in a museum, but throughout most of the book it refers to the organiser of a group, sport or hobby.
- Telephone numbers: There are a few entries listed that are outside the Dublin area, and here we have listed regional prefixes. The prefix to Dublin, when calling from outside the Dublin area, is 01, and the international code for dial-ling Ireland is +353.
- Fax numbers, e-mail addresses and website addresses are included when available.
- Open: Some activities only run at particular times of the year, while some run all year, and we will indicate this here. Although we have done our very best to be accurate with dates and times, please check before you venture out. Sports

clubs, classes, groups and hobbies are particularly likely to change their timetables, and it is worth checking with them to see if they have a time or venue that is more suitable for you.

- Charge: We have given the average charges into venues. While these are correct at the time of going to print, they may, of course, vary over time. The prices quoted should serve as a rough guide to what you will be charged.

- Suitable for ages: Again, this is usually a rough guide to what age group an activity is suitable for – for example, cinemas are listed as suitable for over-3s, but you may have a 2-and-a-half-year-old who will sit through and enjoy a movie. The ages given are intended as a guide to venues, but are specific when it comes to workshops, groups, sports and hobbies.

- Car parking: When a venue has its own designated parking area we have said so, and we have indicated if there is a charge. We know how difficult it is when making a trip with children (especially into the city centre), so, where appropriate, we have indicated the car park nearest to the venue which you will be visiting. The addresses and opening hours of these car parks can be found in the Car Parks chapter.

- Bus routes: We have listed the buses that stop nearest to each venue, as a guide only. Please check with Dublin Bus (Tel: 8734222) for further information.

- Rail station/DART station: Again, we have listed the stations which are nearest to the venues. When listed, a station is usually within 5–10 minutes' walk of your destination. The telephone number for Irish Rail (Íarnród Éireann), including suburban and DART services, is 8366222.

- Comment/review: Here we have tried to stick to the facts, and supply family-friendly information about an activity. When there is somewhere or something we think is really worth getting excited about, we say so, and when there is something negative about a place, or something else that we feel you should be aware of, we try to point it out.

# Symbols

Beside the name of each entry, you may see one or more symbols, which indicate various facilities available at a venue.

The symbol for Baby-Friendly is:

In most instances, this means you can push a buggy or pram around, and there is somewhere to change/feed a baby. In some cases, there may not a designated baby-change area or you may have to lift a buggy up one or two steps but, because of the nature of the venue or activity, we still would recommend it as baby-friendly. For specific ideas on where to bring under-2s, check out the Top Choices: For Ages 0–2 index.

The symbol for Birthday Party Bookings is:

There are four types of entry that fall in to this category: Firstly, a venue or activity that is all-inclusive, where you can book a private party and food will be supplied, with special birthday activities, and possibly a room decorated. Secondly, an activity or trip which would be a great treat for a small group, where you would arrange your own food. Thirdly, venues, particularly restaurants, where the birthday child may get a bit of a fuss made of them, for example where the staff would sing 'Happy Birthday' to them. Finally, party services – entertainers who will come to your home, or party equipment to hire, for example, bouncy castles. It is a good idea to book well in advance when planning a party, especially around the Holy Communion and confirmation season in April–May.

The symbol for Arts and Crafts is:

This indicates that a venue holds classes or workshops in arts and crafts, which may include painting, drawing, sculpture, drama, music or dance.

The symbol for Blue Flag is:

The award of European blue flag status to a beach is based on compliance with 27 criteria, including water quality, environmental education and information, environmental management, safety and services. A beach with blue flag status should be clean and unpolluted, and the water should be safe for swimming.

The symbol for Café is:

this means that there is somewhere to get refreshments – at least tea and a bun.

The symbol for Crêche is:

This indicates that there is a supervised drop-in crêche for children. Charges, age groups and maximum length of stay are given where available, but are liable to change.

The symbol for Playground is:

This indicates that there is an indoor or outdoor children's playground. We have also listed the best of these.

The symbol for Computers is:

This means that there are computer facilities specifically for children. This will usually be in libraries and information centres.

The symbol for Shop is:

This will be appropriate to the venue, eg, a museum shop will sell souvenirs, books, toys and knick-knacks; a cinema shop will sell snacks and sweets.

The symbol for Wheelchair Access is:

Where wheelchair access is restricted, we have said so. However, in most cases, even in venues with no wheelchair access, staff have said they would try to accommodate. It is always a good idea to ring in advance.

# City Centre

## Things to do

### 1  Abbey School of Music and Drama

9b Lwr Abbey St, Dublin 1; Contact: Kathleen Yeates (drama);
Tel: 8747908 (school), 086 8244826 (drama).
**Open:** All year; class times arranged to suit the individual ■
**Charge:** Cost will vary according to individual circumstances ■
**Suitable for ages:** 4+ ■ **Bus routes:** All city centre buses ■ **Rail
station:** Connolly ■ **DART station:** Connolly.
Individual music tuition for all ages (depending on instrument),
with instruments available to hire during courses. The school also
runs 10-week drama classes (you can try a sample class – ring for
details). Music teachers will assess each individual and teach
according to their needs, whether for exam preparation,
performance or just learning for fun.

### 2  Abbey Theatre ♿

26 Lwr Abbey St, Dublin 1; Tel: 8787222 (no booking fee);
Fax: 8729177; Website: www.abbeytheatre.ie
**Open:** All year; Performances Mon–Sun, matinee and evening
performances, ring for times; Tours Thur 11am ■ **Charge:** Tickets
for performances from €15 (adult/child matinee) ■ **Suitable for
ages:** 13+ ■ **Car parking:** Irish Life Centre car park ■ **Bus routes:**
All city centre buses ■ **Rail station:** Connolly ■ **DART station:**
Connolly.
Part of the National Theatre, the Abbey usually shows well-known
plays by established Irish playwrights. Together with the Peacock
Theatre, the Abbey runs a theatre club for 15–19-yr-olds, and are
introducing one for 13–15-yr-olds. There are weekly Thursday
morning tours of the Peacock and Abbey theatres, at 11am. There
is also an outreach programme, available to put on workshops and
activities for schools or groups.
**✱ TOP CHOICES: FOR AGES 10+ ✱ TOP CHOICES: FOR IMAGINATIVE
KIDS ✱**

### 3  African Cultural Project

Matt Talbot Hall, Dominick Place, Granby Lane, Dublin 1 (off

Granby Row/Parnell Sq); Contact: Melanie Jacobs; Tel: 8780613; E-mail: acp@indigo.ie

**Open:** All year, Sat 10.30am–3.30pm; call for details of this year's summer course ▪ **Charge:** Small charge payable weekly ▪ **Suitable for ages:** 9–19 ▪ **Bus routes:** All city centre buses ▪ **Rail station:** Connolly ▪ **DART station:** Connolly.

This project runs courses in drama, art, music and writing for 9–13-yr-olds and 14–18-yr-olds on Saturdays. They also run a summer project – call for this year's details.

✱ **TOP CHOICES: SUMMER CAMPS** ✱

## 4    Alliance Française

1 Kildare St, Dublin 2; Tel: 6761732; Fax: 6764077; E-mail: info@alliance-francaise.ie Website: www.alliance-francaise.ie

**Open:** All year except Aug; Tue–Thur 10am–7.30pm; Fri 10am–5.30pm; Sat 10am–1pm ▪ **Charge:** Free ▪ **Suitable for ages:** 6+ ▪ **Car parking:** Metered parking on street; otherwise Setanta car park or Dawson St car park ▪ **Bus routes:** All city centre buses ▪ **Rail station:** Pearse St ▪ **DART station:** Pearse St.

This institute promotes the language and culture of France. It has an extensive library open to the public, containing books, journals, film and music tapes (you need to become a member to borrow). It hosts occasional art exhibitions, and runs language classes, including classes for children. These classes aim to offer children an enjoyable introduction to the French language, through fun and lively activities – call for dates and times.

## 5    The Ark: Children's Cultural Centre

11a Eustace St, Dublin 2; Tel: 8721111; E-mail: info@ark.ie; Website: www.ark.ie

**Open:** All year; Ring for times of events and performances or call in Mon–Sun 10am–5pm ▪ **Charge:** Performances are approximately €8 ▪ **Suitable for ages:** 3–13 ▪ **Car parking:** Temple Bar car park ▪ **Bus routes:** All city centre buses ▪ **Rail station:** Tara St ▪ **DART station:** Tara St.

The Ark Children's Cultural Centre is a not-for-profit company presenting plays, exhibitions, workshops, concerts, readings and performances, for children aged between 3 and 13 years. There's no permanent programme or exhibition, so ring before you visit to see what's on. The theatre has terraced bench seating, which can be uncomfortable for adults. Make sure to get in to performances early to get seating with a clear view. No food or drink are allowed during performances, so leave the treats until later.

**★ TOP CHOICES: BIRTHDAY PARTY IDEAS ★ TOP CHOICES: CHRISTMAS VISITS ★ TOP CHOICES: FOR AGES 2–5 ★ TOP CHOICES: FOR AGES 5–10 ★**

## 6  Arnott's Department Store 🛒 🍴 ♿

12 Henry St, Dublin 1; Tel: 8050400, 8050413 (Schoolwear), 8050412 (Sports Dept.); Website: www.arnotts.ie
**Open:** All year; Mon–Fri 9am–6.30pm (Thur 9pm); Sat 9pm–6.30pm; Sun 12pm–6pm ■ **Suitable for ages:** All ■ **Car parking:** Arnott's car park ■ **Bus routes:** All city centre buses ■ **Rail station:** Connolly/Tara St ■ **DART station:** Connolly/Tara St.
A big department store, where you'll find everything from Barbie bed linen to school uniforms. Holy Communion and confirmation outfits come in after Christmas, and there's a host of designer babies' and kids' clothes on the second floor, including Tommy Hilfiger and DKNY. There is also a big sportswear department, a restaurant and a coffee shop. Older children and teenagers will adore Cody's Emporium on the ground floor – full of gadgets, Hello Kitty make-up bags and lovely smelly candles and soaps.

**★ TOP CHOICES: FOR TRENDY KIDS ★**

## 7  A Start in the Arts

Dublin Writers Museum, 18 Parnell Sq N, Dublin 1; Contact: Grainne; Tel: 8305090, 087 6395249.
**Open:** Sep–Jun; Sat 10–10.30am/10.40–11.20am/ 11.30am–12.10pm ■ **Charge:** 2–3 yrs €120 per term (16 x 30-minute classes); 3–5 yrs €160 per term (16 x 40-minute classes) ■ **Suitable for ages:** 2–5 years ■ **Bus routes:** All city centre buses ■ **Rail station:** Connolly ■ **DART station:** Connolly.
Saturday morning classes are held here, including song, story, dance and pre-instrumental musical activities for 2–5-yr-olds.

**★ TOP CHOICES: FOR AGES 2–5 ★**

## 8  Aughrim St Dance Classes

Aughrim St Parish Centre, 13 Prussia St, Dublin 7 (Phoenix Park end of North Circular Rd); Tel: 085 7103255.
**Open:** Call for new term dates and times ■ **Charge:** €55 per term ■ **Suitable for ages:** 7+ ■ **Car parking:** On-street parking ■ **Bus**

**routes:** 39, 39A/B/X, 70.
Hip hop and jazz dance classes are given for over-7s and teenagers.

## 9 Bank of Ireland Arts Centre ♿

Foster Place, Dublin 2; Tel: 6711488, 6707555.
**Open:** All year; Tue–Fri 10am–4pm ▪ **Charge:** Children free;
Adult €1.50; Students €1; Pre-booked groups free; Guided tours
free ▪ **Suitable for ages:** 5+ ▪ **Car parking:** Temple Bar car park
▪ **Bus routes:** All city centre buses ▪ **Rail station:** Tara St ▪ **DART
station:** Tara St.
The history of Irish banking, in an interactive museum. Guided
tours show you the old House of Lords – you can take a seat and
find out who used to sit in it. The centre hosts a variety of events,
including lunchtime and evening classical concerts, small theatre
performances and art exhibitions.

## 10 Basketball

Irish Basketball Association, National Basketball Arena, Tymon,
Dublin 24; Tel: 4590211; Fax: 4590212; Website: www.iba.ie
**Open:** Oct–Mar; Call for individual clubs' meeting days and times
▪ **Charge:** Annual fees range from €45 to €200; Basketball strip
approx. €50 ▪ **Suitable for ages:** 10+.
Most basketball clubs run junior teams and leagues; call for details.
Venues can change, so always check. The association also runs a
primary school programme. Competitive teams start at under-11.
Most teams require that you buy a strip to begin with, which can
cost around €50.

## 11 Tridents Basketball Club

Ard Scoil Ris, Aughrim Street, Dublin 7; Contact: John Cusack;
Tel: 8217172.
**Open:** All year; Call for meeting days and times ▪ **Charge:**
Membership fees and basketball strip price on request ▪ **Suitable
for ages:** 10+ ▪ **Bus routes:** 10, 37, 38, 39.

## 12 Behan, Sylvia, School of Ballet

30 Gardiner Pl, Dublin 1; Tel: 8749536.
**Open:** Call for new term times ▪ **Charge:** Fees on request ▪
**Suitable for ages:** 4+ ▪ **Bus routes:** All city centre buses ▪ **Rail
station:** Connolly ▪ **DART station:** Connolly.
Contact the teacher for times and availability.
✱ **TOP CHOICES: HOBBIES/ARTS AND CRAFTS** ✱

## 13   Bel Canto School of Singing

21 North Great George's St, Dublin 1; Tel: 8742460;
Fax: 8745139; E-mail: reception@thesingingschool.com;
Website: www.thesingingschool.com

**Open:** All year; Times arranged to suit individual ■ **Charge:** €50
for initial assessments and then fees according to circumstances ■
**Suitable for ages:** 5+ ■ **Bus routes:** All city centre buses ■ **Rail
station:** Connolly ■ **DART station:** Connolly.

This school provides voice assessment and coaching for ages 5+.

## 14   Boxing

Irish Amateur Boxing Association, National Stadium, South
Circular Rd, Dublin 8; Tel: 4733192; E-mail: iaba@eircom.net
**Open:** All year ■ **Charge:** Most clubs charge €1 or €2 per week ■
**Suitable for ages:** 11+.

Boxing clubs usually take children from 11 years old. Parents must
sign for permission for them to join, and all children must undergo
a medical examination and wear protective headgear. All boxing
clubs listed have Leinster Council IABA affiliation for 2002/2003.
Call for locations, as these can change.

## 15   Corinthians Boxing Club

Call for locations as these can change; Contact: James Dunne;
Tel: 8365876.

**Open:** All year; call for current meeting times ■ **Suitable for ages:**
11 years and over.

## 16   Inner City Boxing Club

Call for locations, as these can change; Contact: Olive Keogh;
Tel: 8470572.

**Open:** All year; Call for current meeting times ■ **Suitable for
ages:** 11+.

## 17   Brown Thomas/BT2 📦 ♿

92 Grafton St, Dublin 2, Tel: 6795666 (main store); 28 Grafton St,
Dublin 2, Tel: 6056666 (BT2) (shops are opposite each other on
Grafton St); Fax: 6056750.

**Open:** All year; Main store: Mon–Fri 9am–6.30pm (Thur 8pm);
Sat 9am–7pm; Sun 11am–6pm; BT2: Mon–Sat 10am–6.30pm;
Sun 12–6pm ■ **Suitable for ages:** 5+ ■ **Car parking:** Brown
Thomas car park ■ **Bus routes:** All city centre buses ■ **Rail**

**station:** Pearse St ■ **DART station:** Pearse St.

Brown Thomas is the main outlet for designer labels in the capital. It has a huge cosmetics section on the ground floor, plus shoes, bags and women's clothes from Irish and international designers throughout the store. There is a household section, with electrical goods and designer household items. It's a very hot shop and, unless you're buying a teenager some MAC make-up (they wish), for children's wear you're better off across the road in BT2 (Brown Thomas 2).

## 18 Central Library ♿ 🖳

ILAC Centre, Henry St, Dublin 1 (go up the stairs in the centre of the shopping centre. If you need to use the lift, ring in advance to check that it's working); Tel: 8734333; Fax: 8721451.
**Open:** All year; Mon–Thur 10am–8pm; Fri–Sat 10am–5pm; Closed Sat–Mon on bank holiday weekends ■ **Charge:** Free ■ **Suitable for ages:** All ■ **Car parking:** ILAC centre car park ■ **Bus routes:** All city centre buses ■ **Rail station:** Tara St/Connolly ■ **DART station:** Tara St/Connolly.

The Central Library includes a music library – a huge resource for music students and music lovers. There is also a children's library, where special activities and events are run throughout the year.

## 19 Charleville Mall Library 🚼 ♿ ✏ 🖳

North Strand, Dublin 1 (by the banks of the Royal Canal); Tel: 8749619; Website: www.iol.ie/dublincitylibrary
**Open:** All year; Mon/Wed/Fri 10am–1pm, 2–5pm; Tue/Thur 12.45–4pm, 4.45–8pm ■ **Charge:** Free ■ **Suitable for ages:** All ■ **Car parking:** Free ■ **Bus routes:** 20A/B, 27, 27A/B, 28, 29A, 30, 31, 31A/B, 32, 32A/B, 42B/C ■ **Rail station:** Connolly ■ **DART station:** Connolly.

Charleville Mall Library was one of the first municipal public libraries to be opened in Dublin. Regular activities include storytelling and arts-and-crafts (for 4–6-yr-olds, Mon and Wed 11am–12pm – booking is necessary). Seasonal arts-and-crafts activities, plus reading events, are organised throughout the year.
★ **TOP CHOICES: FOR AGES 2–5** ★

## 20 The Chester Beatty Library 🚼 🎒 ♿ ✏ €

Dublin Castle, Castle St, Dublin 2 (access via Ship St or Dublin Castle); Tel: 4070750; Fax: 4070760; E-mail: info@cbl.ie;

Website: www.cbl.ie
**Open:** All year; Oct–Apr: Tue–Fri 10am–5pm; May–Sep: Mon–Fri 10am–5pm; Sat 11am–5pm; Sun 1–5pm ■ **Charge:** Free ■ **Suitable for ages:** 7+ ■ **Car parking:** Christ Church car park ■ **Bus routes:** 50, 51B, 54A, 56A, 77, 77A, 78A, 123 ■ **DART station:** Tara St.

Named as European Museum of the Year 2002, the Chester Beatty Library is both an art museum and a library, housing an outstanding collection of Islamic manuscripts as well as Chinese, Japanese, Indian and other oriental art. The library hosts a series of monthly workshops for 7–11-yr-olds, on Saturdays at 3pm – book in advance. These explore a wide range of exciting topics, such as making lanterns to celebrate the Chinese New Year or following the travels of explorers through the collection. You can also learn about a host of different cultures and religions represented in the library. The Silk Road Café here is recommended.

✱ **TOP CHOICES: CHILD FRIENDLY RESTAURANTS** ✱ **TOP CHOICES: FOR INQUISITIVE KIDS** ✱ **TOP CHOICES: FOR IMAGINATIVE KIDS** ✱

## 21   The Chimney ♿

Smithfield Village, Smithfield, Dublin 7 (Smithfield is off Arran Quay); Tel: 8173800.
**Open:** All year; Mon–Sat 10am–6pm; Sun/bank holidays 11am–6pm ■ **Charge:** Child €3.50; Adult €5; Student/OAP €3.50 ■ **Suitable for ages:** 5+ ■ **Car parking:** Some disc parking on street, ring to arrange disabled parking ■ **Bus routes:** 70, 70X, 172.

If you have a good head for heights, the ride in this glass elevator is just how you imagine it to be from *Charlie and the Chocolate Factory*. You are rewarded with a fabulous 360-degree view of Dublin in an enclosed viewing platform.

✱ **TOP CHOICES: FOR AGES 5–10** ✱

## 22   Christ Church Cathedral ♿

Christ Church Pl, Dublin 8 (from Trinity College, head west down Dame St); Tel: 6778099; Fax: 6798991; Website: www.cccdub.ie
**Open:** All year; Mon–Fri 9.45am–5pm; Sat–Sun 10am–5pm; closed 26 Dec ■ **Charge:** Children free; €3 recommended donation ■ **Suitable for ages:** 5+ ■ **Car parking:** Some on-street parking outside, or Christ Church car park ■ **Bus routes:** 78A, 50.
Built on the edge of Dublin's original Viking settlement, the early wooden church was built in 1038. It was rebuilt in stone by

Norman knight Strongbow in 1172. However, most of the imposing structure you see today was built in the 19th century. As with most churches, it's the gory stuff that will interest children, especially older children: tombs, effigies, embalmed hearts, mummified cats – they're all in here, and if that's not enough, take them to the Dublinia exhibition in the Church's old Synod Hall.

✱ TOP CHOICES: CHRISTMAS VISITS ✱ TOP CHOICES: FOR AGES 10+
✱ TOP CHOICES: FOR INQUISITIVE KIDS ✱

## 23 City Hall 🚻 ✏

Dame St, Dublin 2 (towards Christ Church from Trinity College);
Tel: 6722204; Fax: 6722620; E-mail: cityhall@dublincorp.ie;
Website: www.dublincorp.ie/cityhall
**Open:** All year; Mon–Sat 10am–5.15pm; Sun 2–5pm ▪ **Charge:**
Child €1.50; Adult €4; Student/unwaged/senior citizens €1.50;
Family €9.50 ▪ **Suitable for ages:** 7+ ▪ **Car parking:** Drury St car park ▪ **Bus routes:** 50, 50A, 54, 56A, 77, 77A/B, 123, 150.
Pop your head in the door just for a gawk at the recently refurbished Rotunda, the circular entrance hall. It's like a fairytale ballroom, decorated in gold and marble. This was not its purpose, of course – it was the Royal Exchange, which you can learn all about, including its part in Irish nationalism, in the multimedia exhibition 'The Story of the Capital'. See the Lord Mayor of Dublin's chains of office, the Dublin Freedom Rolls and the Dublin City Council's seal. Classical music concerts are held here sometimes, as are children's mosaic workshops, for over-7s. Ring for details, as booking is necessary.

✱ TOP CHOICES: CHRISTMAS VISITS ✱ TOP CHOICES: FOR AGES 5–10 ✱

## 24 Clery's Department Store 🚼 📖 🚻

18/27 Lwr O'Connell St, Dublin 1 (opposite the GPO);
Tel: 8786000; Website: www.clerys.ie
**Open:** All year; Mon–Wed 9.30am–6pm; Thur 9am–9pm; Fri 9am–8pm; Sat 9am–6.30pm; ▪ **Suitable for ages:** 2+ ▪ **Car parking:** Arnott's car park ▪ **Bus routes:** All city centre buses ▪ **Rail station:** Connolly/Tara St ▪ **DART station:** Connolly/Tara St.
A lovely old department store, where you'd expect to see Mrs Slocombe from 'Are You Being Served' behind the counter. Children's clothes are on the second floor, but it's all gone a bit posh, with brands like French Connection and Osh Kosh. Holy Communion and confirmation outfits come into the store after Christmas. The ground floor more than caters for teenage girls,

with Miss Selfridge, Top Shop and the Bay Trading Company. You can treat your little madams to a manicure in the Nail Bar. The Rooftop Café has a great view. The days of the Santa's Grotto and big festive windows at Christmas are gone, and the Santa in 2002 was very disappointing.

**✱ TOP CHOICES: CHILD FRIENDLY RESTAURANTS ✱**

## 25  Community & Youth Information Centre

Sackville Place, Dublin 1 (just off O'Connell St, behind Clery's department store); Tel: 8786844; Fax: 8786610; E-mail: ycinfo@iol.ie; Website: www.iol.ie/dublincitylibrary
**Open:** All year; Mon–Wed 9.30am–1pm, 2–6pm; Thur–Fri 9.30am–1pm, 2–5pm; Sat 9.30am–1.30pm, 2.30–5pm ▪ **Charge:** Free ▪ **Suitable for ages:** 12+ ▪ **Car parking:** Irish Life Centre car park ▪ **Bus routes:** All city centre buses ▪ **Rail station:** Tara St/Connolly ▪ **DART station:** Tara St/Connolly.
An information centre providing a wide range of general information and advice, including welfare rights and entitlements, travel and accommodation, sports and leisure activities.

## 26  The Contemporary Music Centre

19 Fishamble St, Temple Bar, Dublin 8; Tel: 6731922; Fax: 6489100; E-mail: info@cmc.ie
**Open:** All year; Mon–Fri 10am–5.30pm; closed on bank holidays ▪ **Suitable for ages:** 10+ ▪ **Car parking:** Drury St car park ▪ **Bus routes:** All city centre buses ▪ **Rail station:** Tara St ▪ **DART station:** Tara St.
The Contemporary Music Centre is an archive of Irish 20th-century concert music. It contains a reference library with information on Irish composers, including concert programmes, biographical data, photos and press clippings, as well as specialist periodicals and books. The sound archive has rare recordings of radio broadcasts and live concerts, and also records, cassettes and CDs of 20th- and 21st-century concert music.

## 27  Corbett, Tom (Music Teacher)

Classes held at the Abbey Church, Parnell Sq, Dublin 1; Tel: 6265001.
**Open:** All year; Class times on request ▪ **Charge:** €90 for 9-week term ▪ **Suitable for ages:** 7+.
Individual or group lessons are available in soprano saxophone,

alto saxophone, concert flute, clarinet and recorder. Classical and jazz methods are taught, and students are prepared for ABRSM exams.

## 28 Croppies' Memorial Park 🚼 ♿

Wolfe Tone Quay, Dublin 8 (opposite Frank Sherwin Bridge at Wolfe Tone Quay); Tel: 6612369;
Website: www.dublincity.ie/parks
**Open:** All year; Mon–Fri 8.30am–dusk; Sat–Sun 9.30am–dusk ▪
**Charge:** Free ▪ **Suitable for ages:** All ▪ **Car parking:** Metered on-street parking ▪ **Bus routes:** 25, 25A, 66, 67, 90.
There is a lot of history in this little park, which was once known as the Crimean Trophy Plot due to the presence of Russian artillery guns captured during the 1854–56 Crimean War. The park was named in 1983 after the 'croppies' of the 1798 Rebellion, who were executed in the area. There's an ornamental pond here, featuring sections of Wicklow granite mounted on columns from the former Guinness Mansion at St Anne's Park.

## 29 Custom House Visitor Centre ♿

Custom House Quay, Dublin 1 (5 minutes' walk west of O'Connell Bridge, along the quays); Tel: 8787660; Fax: 8788013.
**Open:** All year; Mar–Oct: Mon–Fri 10am–5pm; Sat–Sun/bank holidays 2–5pm; Nov–mid-March: Wed–Fri 10am–5pm; Sun 2–5pm ▪ **Charge:** Children free; Adult €1; Family €3; Group €0.50 per person ▪ **Suitable for ages:** 10+ ▪ **Car parking:** Irish Life Centre car park ▪ **Bus routes:** All city centre buses ▪ **Rail station:** Tara St ▪ **DART station:** Tara St.
Though the river view and the architecture are nice, the visitor centre itself won't hold much interest for children. The Custom House was designed by Huguenot architect James Gandon (who also designed the Four Courts) and opened in 1791. There's an exhibition about his life and work in the centre. The Custom House was burned down in 1921 during the War of Independence, and rebuilt in the 1980s. The visitor centre occupies a small part of the building, and has audio-visual tours on tax collection and the like.

## 30 Debenham's Department Store 🚼 ☕ ♿

Jervis Centre, Henry St, Dublin 1; Tel: 8781222.
**Open:** All year; Mon–Sat 9am–6.30pm (Thur 9pm); Sun 12–6pm ▪ **Suitable for ages:** All ▪ **Car parking:** Jervis Centre car park ▪

**Bus routes:** All city centre buses ▪ **Rail station:** Connolly/Tara St ▪ **DART station:** Connolly/Tara St.

A British department store, which is eerily quiet compared to the rest of the Jervis Centre. There's a small range of children's and babies' wear downstairs, as well as an Early Learning Centre outlet. The best thing in here is the café, which has a small play area, plenty of seating – including high chairs – and good choices for kids.

✱ **TOP CHOICES: CHILD FRIENDLY RESTAURANTS** ✱

## 31 Diamond Park ♿

Gardiner St, Dublin 1; Tel: 6612369;
Website: www.dublincity.ie/parks
**Open:** All year; Mon–Fri 8.30am–dusk; Sat–Sun 9.30am–dusk ▪ **Charge:** Free ▪ **Suitable for ages:** All ▪ **Car parking:** Metered on-street parking ▪ **Bus routes:** All city centre buses ▪ **Rail station:** Connolly ▪ **DART station:** Connolly.
**Sports:** gaelic football, hurling, soccer
A small park with a floodlit football pitch.

## 32 The Dublin Bus City Tour

Dublin Bus, 59 Upr O'Connell St, Dublin 1 (tour starts at a marked bus stop at the upper end of O'Connell St (near McDonalds), and there are hop-on, hop-off points marked around the city); Tel: 8734222; Fax: 7033031;
Website: www.dublinbus.ie
**Open:** All year; Mon–Sun 9.30am–5pm every 10 minutes, 5–6.30pm every 30 minutes ▪ **Charge:** Child €5; Adult €10; Tickets from Dublin Bus or from Dublin Tourism Centre, Suffolk St, Dublin 2 ▪ **Suitable for ages:** 3+ ▪ **Car parking:** Marlborough St car park ▪ **Bus routes:** All city centre buses ▪ **Rail station:** Tara St/Connolly ▪ **DART station:** Tara St/Connolly.
A 90-minute 'official' tour in an open-top bus, but you can hop on and off, as your ticket is valid all day. The bus goes from O'Connell St to the Phoenix Park, passing Trinity College, St Stephen's Green, Dublin Castle, Christ Church Cathedral and Collins Barracks.

## 33 The Dublin Bus Coast and Castle Tour

Dublin Bus, 59 Upr O'Connell St, Dublin 1 (tour starts at a marked bus stop at the upper end of O'Connell St (near McDonalds), and there are hop-on, hop-off points marked around

the city); Tel: 8734222; Fax: 7033031;
Website: www.dublinbus.ie

**Open:** All year; Mon–Sun 10am ▪ **Charge:** Child €8.50; Adult
€17; Tickets from Dublin Bus or from Dublin Tourism Centre,
Suffolk St, Dublin 2 ▪ **Suitable for ages:** 5+ ▪ **Car parking:**
Marlborough St car park ▪ **Bus routes:** All city centre buses ▪ **Rail
station:** Tara St/Connolly ▪ **DART station:** Tara St/Connolly.
A tour of the north coast of Dublin in a double-decker bus, lasting
3 hours. The tour passes the National Botanic Gardens and the
Casino at Marino in Clontarf and takes a break in Malahide Castle.
Entrance to the castle is included in the price. The bus takes off
again around Howth Head, and returns to the city centre via
Dollymount Strand.

## 34 The Dublin Bus South Coast Tour

Dublin Bus, 59 Upr O'Connell St, Dublin 1 (tour starts at a
marked bus stop at the upper end of O'Connell St (near
McDonalds), and there are hop-on, hop-off points marked around
the city); Tel: 8734222; Fax: 7033031;
Website: www.dublinbus.ie

**Open:** All year; Mon–Sun 11am and 2pm ▪ **Charge:** Child €8.50;
Adult €17; Tickets from Dublin Bus or from Dublin Tourism
Centre, Suffolk St, Dublin 2 ▪ **Suitable for ages:** 5+ ▪ **Car
parking:** Marlborough St car park ▪ **Bus routes:** All city centre
buses ▪ **Rail station:** Tara St/Connolly ▪ **DART station:** Tara
St/Connolly.
A tour of the south coast of Dublin in a double-decker bus, lasting
3 hours 45 minutes. The tour really only starts as it reaches Dún
Laoghaire harbour, passing Joyce's Martello tower, Bray and
Greystones, and stopping at the Avoca Handweavers craft shop. It
then goes through the Glen of the Downs and Enniskerry, before
returning to the city centre.

## 35 Dublin Castle 🛒 📷 ♿ €

Dame St, Dublin 2 (behind City Hall); Tel: 6777129;
Fax: 6797831; E-mail: info@dublincastle.ie;
Website: www.dublincastle.ie

**Open:** All year; Mon–Fri 10am–5pm; Sat–Sun/bank holidays
2–5pm ▪ **Charge:** Free ▪ **Suitable for ages:** 2+ ▪ **Car parking:**
Christ Church car park ▪ **Bus routes:** 50, 54A, 56, 77 ▪ **Rail
station:** Tara St ▪ **DART station:** Tara St.
Dublin Castle began as a medieval castle, built by King John in

1204 on the River Poddle, possibly on the site of an early Gaelic ring fort. It was the centre of British rule in Ireland for over 750 years, and was extensively rebuilt in the 17th and 18th centuries. Today, the castle is used mostly for state functions and EU meetings. You can walk into the courtyard and see the Record Tower (the only remaining visible feature of the original Norman castle), the Chapel Royal and the Dubh Linn Gardens for free. There's a really nice café in the Castle Vaults, serving cheap lunches and lovely cakes. Guided tours of the State Apartments will take you to many of the magnificent rooms inside the castle, including the ornate St Patrick's Hall, where the presidents of Ireland are inaugurated.

★ TOP CHOICES: CHILD FRIENDLY RESTAURANTS ★

## 36 Dublin City on Ice

Smithfield, Dublin 7; Tel: 1850 423423 (Ice Line), 1890 925100 (Ticketmaster); Website: www.dublincity.ie/iceskating
**Open:** Dec–mid-Jan; Call for this year's exact dates; Mon–Sun 10am–10pm ■ **Charge:** Child €7; Adult €10; Fee is for one-hour skating and boot hire ■ **Suitable for ages:** 5+ ■ **Car parking:** On-street parking ■ **Bus routes:** 39, 90, 134 ■ **Rail station:** Heuston.
**Sports:** ice-skating

Dublin City on Ice, sponsored by BUPA, is only open for two months of the year. Skating is on real ice, which is frozen every night over a medium-sized (700 square metres) rink. The rink is generally very busy, and tickets are only sold by phone, well in advance. Skates are hired as part of the deal. Arrive 20 minutes early, to allow time to get your boots on. There are plenty of skate marshals to pick you up when you fall. There is also a small café where you can get soft drinks, hot chocolate and snacks. They say if you can walk you can skate.

★ TOP CHOICES: BIRTHDAY PARTY IDEAS ★ TOP CHOICES: SPORTS FACILITIES ★ TOP CHOICES: CHRISTMAS VISITS ★ TOP CHOICES: FOR AGES 10+ ★ TOP CHOICES: FOR ENERGETIC KIDS ★

## 37 Dublin City Quay Youth Samba Project

Christian Brothers School, Westland Row, Dublin 2; Tel: 8723638; E-mail: WhizKids@maSamba.com
**Open:** All year; Wed eves ■ **Charge:** Call for details ■ **Suitable for ages:** 5+ ■ **Bus routes:** All city centre buses ■ **Rail station:** Pearse St ■ **DART station:** Pearse St.

The Dublin City Quay Youth Samba Project holds weekly music workshops, as well as study visits and performances, in the local area, for 5–13-yr-olds. Projects involve music, song and movement. There's an open-door policy, and new members are always welcome. Rehearsals are held on Wednesday evenings.

## 38 Dublin Civic Museum

City Assembly House, 58 South William St, Dublin 2;
Tel: 6794260; Fax: 6775954;
Website: www.iol.ie/dublincitylibrary
**Open:** All year; Tue–Sat 10am–6pm; Sun 11am–2pm ■ **Charge:** Free ■ **Suitable for ages:** 5+ ■ **Car parking:** Drury St car park ■ **Bus routes:** 10, 11, 13 ■ **Rail station:** Pearse St/Tara St ■ **DART station:** Pearse St/Tara St.
This is where Nelson's head ended up – that is, the top of the statue from the column blown up by the IRA in 1966. The Civic Museum houses an interesting collection of artefacts, from a model of a Howth tram to Viking coins, and the exhibitions change constantly. The subjects covered in the permanent collection are: Streets and Buildings of Dublin, Traders, Industry, Transport, Political History, Maps and Views of Dublin.

## 39 The Dublin Ghost Bus Tour

Dublin Bus, 59 Upr O'Connell St, Dublin 1 (meeting point at Dublin Bus, near McDonalds on O'Connell St); Tel: 8734222; Fax: 7033031; Website: www.dublinbus.ie
**Open:** All year; Tue–Fri 8pm; Sat–Sun 7pm and 9.30pm ■ **Charge:** Child €20; Adult €20; Tickets from Dublin Bus or from Dublin Tourism Centre, Suffolk St, Dublin 2 ■ **Suitable for ages:** 14+ ■ **Car parking:** Marlborough St car park ■ **Bus routes:** All city centre buses ■ **Rail station:** Tara St/Connolly ■ **DART station:** Tara St/Connolly.
This is good fun for teenagers, but not for the faint-hearted! The bus tour lasts 2 hours 15 minutes, and brings you around some of Dublin's haunted houses, telling you all about Bram Stoker (the creator of Dracula) and body snatching in St Kevin's graveyard. Wear warm clothes and meet 15 minutes before departure.
✱ **TOP CHOICES: BIRTHDAY PARTY IDEAS** ✱ **TOP CHOICES: FOR AGES 10+** ✱

## 40 Dublinia 🖻 ♿ €

Christ Church, St. Michael's Hill, Dublin 2 (in the old Synod Hall,

Christ Church Cathedral. From Trinity College, go west down Dame St); Tel: 6794611; E-mail: info @dublinia.com; Website: www.dublinia.com

**Open:** All year; Apr–Sep: Mon–Sun 10am–5pm; Oct–Mar: Mon–Sat 11am–4pm; Sun/bank holidays 10am–4.30pm ■ **Charge:** Child €4.25; Adult €5.75; Under-5s free; Family ticket €15; Concessions €4.50 ■ **Suitable for ages:** 2+ ■ **Car parking:** Christ Church car park ■ **Bus routes:** 50, 54A, 56A.

Step into medieval Dublin! Stand on a ship in Wood Quay or walk down a market street. This exhibition is quite gory: there are rats and fleas, and people in the stocks getting a public flogging – all models of course! A fun and exciting way to learn about the Middle Ages. Dublinia also offers workshops, outreach visits and membership of the Irish Young Archaeologists Club. While you're here, take the opportunity to have a look around Christ Church itself.

✱ TOP CHOICES: FOR AGES 5–10 ✱ TOP CHOICES: FOR AGES 10+ ✱

## 41 Dublin School of Classical & Contemporary Dance

13 Stamer St, Portobello, Dublin 8; Tel: 4755451.

**Open:** Call for class times available ■ **Charge:** Child €6; Group class ■ **Suitable for ages:** 4+ ■ **Car parking:** On-street parking ■ **Bus routes:** 14, 14A, 16, 16A, 19, 19A, 122.

Comprehensive courses in ballet and jazz for ages 4+. Classes lead towards a yearly production, and RAD exams can be taken when the student is ready.

✱ TOP CHOICES: HOBBIES/ARTS AND CRAFTS ✱

## 42 Dublin School of Guitar

27 Drury St, Dublin 2 (above Musican Inc. shop); Tel: 6714732; Fax: 6796049.

**Open:** All year; Mon–Fri 2–9pm; Sat 9am–5.30pm ■ **Charge:** Prices given on request ■ **Suitable for ages:** 8+ ■ **Bus routes:** All city centre buses ■ **Rail station:** Tara St ■ **DART station:** Tara St.

Acoustic and electric guitar classes are given here, for ages 8+. Students can be prepared for exams or learn just for fun. All classes are on a one-to-one basis.

## 43 Dublin Writers' Museum

18 Parnell Sq N, Dublin 1 (opposite the Garden of Remembrance); Tel: 8722077; Fax: 8722231;

E-mail: writers@dublintourism.ie;

Website: www.writersmuseum.com

**Open:** All year; Mon–Fri 10am–5pm; Sun/bank holidays 11am–5pm (Jun–Aug late opening until 6pm) ▪ **Charge:** Under-11s €3.50; Concessions and under-18s €5.00; Adult €6; Family ticket (2 adults and 3/4 children) €16.50; Free entrance to café and bookshop ▪ **Suitable for ages:** 2+ ▪ **Car parking:** Marlborough St car park ▪ **Bus routes:** All city centre buses ▪ **Rail station:** Connolly ▪ **DART station:** Connolly.

The history of Irish literature is displayed in this magnificent 18th-century mansion, featuring the best in Irish writing from the past 300 years. It includes books, letters, portraits and personal items, and there's a special *Seómra na nÓg* (children's room) devoted to children's literature, though there's not much to see unless there's a workshop on. 'A Start in the Arts' runs here on Saturday mornings. The café here is well worth a visit on its own, as it's part of Chapters restaurant. Wheelchair and buggy access is limited to the ground floor only.

✱ **TOP CHOICES: CHILD FRIENDLY RESTAURANTS** ✱ **TOP CHOICES: FOR AGES 2–5** ✱

## 44   Dunnes Stores 🛒 🍴 ♿

St. Stephen's Green Shopping Centre, St. Stephen's Green, Dublin 2, Tel: 6714629; ILAC Centre, Henry St, Dublin 1, Tel: 8730211; Customer Services, Tel: 4751111; E-mail: www.dunnesstores.com

**Open:** All year; call Customer Services for local branch opening hours ▪ **Suitable for ages:** All ▪ **Car parking:** St. Stephen's Green Shopping Centre car park and ILAC Centre car park ▪ **Bus routes:** All city centre buses.

Dunnes Stores are a big Irish chain of supermarkets and shops, which can be found in most areas and nearly all shopping centres. The St. Stephen's Green and ILAC Centre stores both have wheelchair access, and the staff in the St. Stephen's Green store's café are very nice. Both stores have big children's departments, with good-quality clothing and footwear and a small range of children's bed linen and accessories, which are great value for money.

## 45   ENFO (Information on the Environment) ♿

17 St. Andrew St, Dublin 2; Tel: 8882001; Fax: 8883946; E-mail: info@enfo.ie; Website: www.enfo.ie

**Open:** All year; Mon–Sat 10am–5pm; closed on bank holidays ■
**Charge:** Free ■ **Suitable for ages:** 2+ ■ **Car parking:** Temple Bar
car park ■ **Bus routes:** All city centre buses ■ **Rail station:** Tara St
■ **DART station:** Tara St.

ENFO is a public service which provides information on the
environment. It includes a drop-in centre, with a children's corner
featuring floor games and puzzles, video, colouring activities, and
a PC with interactive games. ENFO puts on occasional workshops
and lectures – call for upcoming events. There is also a children's
club to join, which will keep you informed of upcoming activities
and events.

**✱ TOP CHOICES: FOR INQUISITIVE KIDS ✱**

## 46 Flagship Scuba Diving

*Naomh Eanna*, Charlotte Quay, Dublin 2; Tel: 6670988;
E-mail: info@flagshipscuba.com;
Website: www.flagshipscuba.com
**Open:** Feb–Nov, weather permitting; Discover Scuba is held on
Wed evenings 6.30–11pm ■ **Charge:** From €75 to €595 a course
■ **Suitable for ages:** 12+ ■ **Bus routes:** 2, 3.
**Sports:** scuba diving

Flagship is a dive centre which is PADI approved. It is based on a
ship called the *Naomh Eanna*, in the Grand Canal Basin. Courses
begin with a classroom lesson and introduction to the basics, and
then move on to a pool session, where you can get a taste of what
diving is about. After another four classes and pool sessions, the
course can lead you directly to becoming an open water scuba
diver. Prices range form €75 a day for 'Discover Scuba' to €595
for the most popular open-water certificate.

**✱ TOP CHOICES: SPORTS FACILITIES ✱ TOP CHOICES: HOBBIES/ARTS
AND CRAFTS ✱**

## 47 Flamenco y Más 📷 👤

B-Famous studios, 5 Wolfe Tone St, Dublin 1 (off Abbey St,
between Capel St and Jervis St); Contact: Ana Castellanos;
Tel: 8749070; E-mail: flamencoymas@hotmail.com;
Website: www.geocities.com/flamencoymas
**Open:** Aug–May; Pre-school Sat 10–11am; Flamenco classes for
ages 8+ Fri 4.30–5.30pm, 5.30–6.30pm ■ **Charge:** Pre-school
workshops €30 per child per month; Flamenco classes €110 per
child per 10-week term; Party bookings €400– €600 for a one-hour
workshop ■ **Suitable for ages:** 3–5, 8+ ■ **Bus routes:** All city

centre buses ▪ **Rail station:** Connolly ▪ **DART station:** Connolly.
Click a castanet, flick a fan, stamp your feet! Flamenco dance
classes allow you to make a lot of noise, so wear hard-soled shoes
(ie not trainers). There is also a pre-school workshop, teaching
world dance to 3–5-yr-olds, and flamenco classes for over-8s on
Fridays. Parents can go to the café in the studios during the class.
Ana (and a guitarist) will give a one-hour performance and
workshop in your home as a birthday party event.
★ TOP CHOICES: BIRTHDAY PARTY IDEAS ★

## 48 · Gaiety School of Acting

Sycamore St, Temple Bar, Dublin 2; Tel: 6799277; Fax: 6799568;
E-mail: gaiety.school@indigo.ie; Website: www.gaietyschool.com
**Open:** All year; Course 1: Oct–Dec; Course 2: Jan–Mar; Course
3: Apr–Jun; Classes run on Sat, times vary according to age and
experience; Easter Course: 4 days over Easter, 10am–5pm;
Summer Drama Course: Jul, Mon–Fri 10am–1pm; Summer 'Make
A Play' Course: Aug, Mon–Fri 10am–5pm ▪ **Charge:** 3-term
drama course, 90 minutes per week: 6–7-yr-olds €120; All other
age groups €150; Easter course: Make-A-Movie €190; Summer
1-week drama course €190; Summer 1-week Make-A-Play course
€190 ▪ **Suitable for ages:** 6–16 ▪ **Bus routes:** All city centre buses
▪ **Rail station:** Tara St ▪ **DART station:** Tara St.
The Young Gaiety School of Acting offers a three-course
programme, introducing children to drama. Classes are grouped
according to age and experience, and are staffed by trained
theatre professionals. The classes aim to build confidence, and to
develop imagination and self-expression. A production is given by
students who have completed the second and third courses at the
end of course three. The Easter Make-a-Movie course is for
11–15-yr-olds – students make, and act in, their own film and
receive a copy each to take home. A two-week drama summer
school for 8–10-year-olds, 11–13-year-olds and 14–16-year-olds
runs in July. A one-week Make-a-Play course runs in August, for
11–16-year-olds. The students perform an original production at
the end of the week.

## 49 Gaiety Theatre 🚼 📷 ♿ 👥

South King St, Dublin 2; Tel: 6771717 (box office); Fax: 6771921;
E-mail: info@gaietytheatre.net; Website: www.gaietytheatre.net
**Open:** All year; Mon–Sun matinee and evening performances;
Call for times ▪ **Charge:** Performance tickets from €13.50– €24.50

- **Suitable for ages:** All - **Car parking:** Royal College of Surgeons car park - **Bus routes:** All city centre buses - **Rail station:** Pearse St - **DART station:** Pearse St.

Famous for its Christmas panto, the Gaiety also hosts musicals and opera throughout the year. A nice idea for a birthday treat is to rent a private box for 2–6 people, with sandwiches and choccies as an added extra. The theatre's Plaza Café includes a heated outdoor plaza.

✱ TOP CHOICES: BIRTHDAY PARTY IDEAS ✱ TOP CHOICES: CHRISTMAS VISITS ✱

## 50 Gallery of Photography 🦽 ⬛

Meeting House Sq, Temple Bar, Dublin 2; Tel: 6714654; Fax: 6709293.

**Open:** All year; the gallery, bookshop and darkrooms are open Tue–Sat 11am–6pm; Sun 1–6pm; closed Good Friday and 24–26 December - **Charge:** Child €5 - **Suitable for ages:** 7–12 - **Car parking:** Temple Bar car park - **Bus routes:** All city centre buses - **Rail station:** Tara St - **DART station:** Tara St.

The gallery runs Family Days on Sundays – programmes of activities specially designed for parents and children aged 7–12. These are structured to provide a fun and accessible way of learning the basic principles of photography. Participants are helped to make photographs and to try different creative printing techniques. All children must be accompanied by an adult.

✱ TOP CHOICES: FOR AGES 10+ ✱

## 51 The Garda Museum and Archives

Dublin Castle, Dame St, Dublin 2 (behind City Hall);
Tel: 6719597; Fax: 6669992;
Website: www.garda.ie/angarda/museum.html

**Open:** All year; Mon–Fri 9am–4pm - **Charge:** Free - **Suitable for ages:** 2+ - **Car parking:** Christ Church car park - **Bus routes:** 50, 54A, 56, 77 - **Rail station:** Tara St - **DART station:** Tara St.

This is a police museum, housed in the 13th-century Norman 'Record Tower', the last intact tower of medieval Dublin. The museum contains a large amount of archival and artefactual material, relating not only to the Garda Síochána, but also to the Irish Constabulary, the Royal Irish Constabulary, the Dublin Police, and the Dublin Metropolitan Police.

CITY CENTRE

31

## 52 Garden of Remembrance

Parnell Sq E, Dublin 1 (opposite the Dublin Writers Museum);
Tel: 8743074.

**Open:** All year; Jan–Feb/Nov–Dec: Mon–Sun 11am–4pm;
Mar–Apr/Oct: Mon–Sun 11am–7pm; May–Sep: Mon–Sun
9.30am–8pm; Christmas Day 11am–1pm; Opening times are
subject to change ■ **Charge:** Free ■ **Suitable for ages:** 2+ ■ **Car
parking:** Marlborough St car park ■ **Bus routes:** All city centre
buses ■ **Rail station:** Connolly/Tara St ■ **DART station:**
Connolly/Tara St.

This is a small sunken garden with a lot of steps, largely occupied
by a square with seating around a large pool. There's a large
sculpture of the Children of Lir, which children love to hear about.
It's a nice place to sit on a sunny day with an ice cream, after a
visit to the Hugh Lane Gallery or the Dublin Writers Museum. The
garden is dedicated to the memory of those who gave their lives to
the cause of Irish freedom.

✱ **TOP CHOICES: FOR AGES 5–10** ✱

## 53 The Gate Theatre ♿

Cavendish Row, Dublin 1 (beside the Rotunda Hospital, at the
north end of O'Connell St); Tel: 8744045, 8746042;
Website: www.gate-theatre.ie

**Open:** All year; Mon–Sun, evening and matinee performances;
call for times ■ **Charge:** Performance tickets from €16 ■ **Suitable
for ages:** 5+ ■ **Car parking:** Limited parking, pay for a space
when you book your ticket ■ **Bus routes:** All city centre buses ■
**Rail station:** Connolly ■ **DART station:** Connolly.

Founded in 1928, the Gate soon established itself as the Irish
home of European and experimental drama. A very useful theatre
for secondary school students, it is home to productions of classics
from Samuel Beckett to Tennessee Williams. The Gate stages *A
Christmas Carol* every year at Christmas, which young and old will
enjoy.

✱ **TOP CHOICES: CHRISTMAS VISITS** ✱

## 54 General Post Office ♿

O'Connell St, Dublin 1; Tel: 7057000; Fax: 8723553;
Website: www.anpost.ie

**Open:** All year; Mon–Sat 8am–8pm (some services close at 7pm);
Sun/bank holidays 10am–6.30pm (open for stamps and *bureau de*

*change* only) ▪ **Charge:** Free ▪ **Suitable for ages:** 5+ ▪ **Car parking:** Jervis St car park or Arnott's car park ▪ **Bus routes:** All city centre buses ▪ **Rail station:** Connolly/Tara St ▪ **DART station:** Connolly/Tara St.

The GPO, built in 1814, is the headquarters building for An Post, the Irish postal service. Look out for the bullet holes in the stonework outside, from shots fired against the rebels who occupied the building during the 1916 Rising. Kids who collect stamps can join the Voyagers' Club, An Post's youth section of the Philatelic Service.

## 55  Glenans Sailing

5 Lwr Mount St, Dublin 2; Tel: 6611481; Fax: 6764249;
E-mail: info@glenans–ireland.com;
Website: www.glenans–ireland.com
**Open:** July; Call for this year's dates and times ▪ **Charge:** €499 all-inclusive for a week-long residential course ▪ **Suitable for ages:** 14+.
**Sports:** sailing

Glenans is a well known sailing school, with locations in Clew Bay, Co. Mayo, and Baltimore, Co. Cork. It offers residential sailing courses for over-14s – in Clew Bay for dinghies, and in Baltimore for dayboats. One-week and two-week courses are run in July. Pick-up is provided from Dublin and Cork airports and from Cork railway station. The bars in the centres are closed and the clubs are for under-18s only on these dates.

**✱ TOP CHOICES: SPORTS FACILITIES ✱ TOP CHOICES: SUMMER CAMPS ✱**

## 56  Goethe-Institut ♿

37 Merrion Sq E, Dublin 2; Tel: 6611155; Fax: 6611358;
E-mail: library@goethe.iol.ie;
Website: www.goethe.de/gr/dub/enindex.htm
**Open:** All year; Tue–Thur 12–8pm; Fri 10am–2.30pm; Sat 10am–1.30pm; Closed bank holiday weekends ▪ **Charge:** Free ▪
**Suitable for ages:** 12+ ▪ **Car parking:** Some meter parking or Royal college of Surgeons car park ▪ **Bus routes:** 5, 7, 7A, 45 ▪
**Rail station:** Pearse St ▪ **DART station:** Pearse St.

This is a German library and information service, providing information on all aspects of German language and culture. They will point you in the right direction if you need resources for a child learning the language. Post-primary students can request information (in writing only) on topics relating to Germany for project assignments. You will need to send a self-addressed A4 envelope, with stamps to the value of €0.92.

## 57 Guinness Storehouse ☕ ♿ €

St James's Gate, Dublin 8 (from Christ Church Cathedral, go down Thomas St towards St. James's Hospital); Tel: 4084800; Fax: 4084965; E-mail: guinness-storehouse@guinness.com; Website: www.guinness-storehouse.com
**Open:** All year; Mon–Sun 9.30am–5pm ▪ **Charge:** Child €2.50; Adult €12; under-6s free; Family (2 adults and 4 children under 12) €26; Concessions €5.30; Student over 18 €8 ▪ **Suitable for ages:** 5+ ▪ **Car parking:** Free ▪ **Bus routes:** 51B, 78A, 123 ▪ **Rail station:** Heuston.
This museum tells the story of Guinness and brewing. It's really quite interesting for older children, as there are interactive, hands-on experiences. Apart from brewing, they can learn about barrel-making, transporting the black stuff, marketing and advertising. At the end of the experience, there's a drink for everyone (soft drinks available too!) in the Sky Bar, where there are great views of Dublin City. This building also houses art exhibitions.
**✱ TOP CHOICES: FOR AGES 10+ ✱**

## 58 Heraldic Museum ♿

2 Kildare St, Dublin 2; Tel: 6030311; Fax: 6621062; E-mail: herald@nli.ie; Website: www.nli.ie
**Open:** All year; Mon–Wed 10am–8pm; Thur–Fri 10am–4.30pm; Sat 10am–2.30pm ▪ **Charge:** Free ▪ **Suitable for ages:** 8+ ▪ **Car parking:** Royal College of Surgeons car park ▪ **Bus routes:** All city centre buses.
This is another place to go, aside from the National Library, to get advice on genealogy. The museum houses a permanent exhibition of heraldry and heraldic insignia, including shields, banners, paintings, coins, porcelain and stamps depicting coats of arms. All very Harry Potter indeed.
**✱ TOP CHOICES: FOR AGES 5–10 ✱ TOP CHOICES: FOR INQUISITIVE KIDS ✱**

## 59 Hugh Lane Gallery 🚼 ♿ ✏ €

Charlemont House, Parnell Sq N, Dublin 1; Tel: 8741903; Fax: 8722182; E-mail: info@hughlane.ie; Website: www.hughlane.ie
**Open:** All year; Tue–Thur 9.30am–6 pm; Fri–Sat 9.30am–5pm;

Sun 11am–5pm ■ **Charge:** Free ■ **Suitable for ages:** 2+ ■ **Car parking:** 2 disabled spaces at the gallery, or Marlborough St car park ■ **Bus routes:** 3, 10, 11, 13, 16, 19 ■ **Rail station:** Connolly ■ **DART station:** Connolly.

A modern art gallery with a fantastic collection of works by artists such as Claude Monet, Auguste Renoir, Edgar Degas and Jack B Yeats. Visit the reconstructed Francis Bacon studio, and see if it compares to your child's bedroom! On Saturdays from 2–3pm there are workshops for children by visiting artists (for under-6s and 6–10s, €3.50 per child). Numbers are limited and booking is essential. There is also a kids' club, and activity sheets to complete as you go around the gallery. Lunchtime concerts are held here, and last about an hour. All age groups are welcome and all musical tastes are catered for, with attention being focused on particular anniversaries and new music.

★ TOP CHOICES: FOR AGES 5–10 ★ TOP CHOICES: FOR AGES 10+ ★
TOP CHOICES: FOR INQUISITIVE KIDS ★

## 60 Ice@IFSC 🍴 €

IFSC, Dublin 1; Tel: 4294004 (Ticket Lord);
Website: www.dublindocklands.ie/www.ticketlord.ie
**Open:** Mid-Nov–mid-Jan; ring for this year's exact dates;
Mon–Sun 10am–9pm; Call to check 2003/2004 times ■ **Charge:**
Child €7.50; Adult €9.50; Fee is for one hour's skating and boot hire ■ **Suitable for ages:** 5+ ■ **Car parking:** IFSC car park ■ **Bus routes:** 127, 129, 130, 20B, 27C, 748, 90, 90A ■ **Rail station:** Connolly ■ **DART station:** Connolly.
**Sports:** ice-skating

Ice@IFSC opened for the first time in 2002, and many people were disappointed by what they felt was a very small rink. The synthetic ice was also unpopular, although the clear awning over the rink meant that skaters kept dry in the rain. You must book by phone or online through Ticket Lord. Boots are provided as part of the deal. There are a number of food outlets overlooking the rink.

★ TOP CHOICES: FOR AGES 5–10 ★ TOP CHOICES: FOR AGES 10+ ★
TOP CHOICES: FOR ENERGETIC KIDS ★

## 61 ILAC Shopping Centre 🛒 🍴 ♿

Henry St, Dublin 1 (access from Moore St or Henry St);
Tel: 7041460, 6714629 (Dunnes Stores).
**Open:** All year; Mon–Sat 9am–6pm (Thur 9pm); Sun 12–6pm ■
**Suitable for ages:** All ■ **Car parking:** Free ■ **Bus routes:** All city

centre buses.

The central library is housed here, and also a big Dunnes Stores. Otherwise, there are plenty of cheap women's clothes shops for the young and size 8–10s. The main shops are Roches Stores and Dunnes Stores. Dunnes Stores, at the Moore St end (all homeware), has a restaurant which does a kids' hot or cold lunchbox.

## 62    Independent Theatre Workshop

Findlater's Studio, Abbey Presbyterian Church, North Frederick St, Dublin 1; Tel: 4968808; Fax: 4968808;
Website: www.independent-theatre-workshop.com
**Open:** All year; Wed 4–6pm, 6–8pm ■ **Charge:** Dance/Drama €140 per term ■ **Suitable for ages:** 7+ ■ **Bus routes:** All city centre buses ■ **Rail station:** Connolly ■ **DART station:** Connolly.
In association with the Helen Jordan Stage School, this course consists of one hour of drama and one hour of dance per week. Places in these classes (for ages 7+) are limited, and entry is by audition only. The course is run on Wednesday evenings and can lead to roles in television, film and theatre. Students in these classes also get an opportunity to perform in the School Show at the Olympia Theatre every second year, and perform regularly in pantomimes at Mosney and Holiday World.
**✱ TOP CHOICES: HOBBIES/ARTS AND CRAFTS ✱**

## 63    Irish City Coast and Garden Tour ♿

33–34 Bachelor's Walk, Dublin 1 (tour leaves the Gresham Hotel, Lwr O'Connell St, at 9.30am; call for other city departure points); Tel: 8729010, 4580054 (after office hours);
E-mail: linda@irishcitytours.com;
Website: www.irishcitytours.com
**Open:** All year; Mon–Sun, departs 9.30am, returns 1.30pm ■ **Charge:** Child €10; Adult €20; Tickets from the Tourist Info. Office, 12 Upr O'Connell St, or from Dublin Tourism Centre, Suffolk St, Dublin 2 ■ **Suitable for ages:** 5+ ■ **Car parking:** Marlborough St car park ■ **Bus routes:** All city centre buses ■ **Rail station:** Tara St/Connolly ■ **DART station:** Tara St/Connolly.
A bus tour of the south Dublin coast, stopping at Dún Laoghaire Harbour, James Joyce Tower, Dalkey Castle and Powerscourt Gardens (there is a separate admission fee to Powerscourt). It's quite a long drive from the city centre to Dún Laoghaire before you see anything worthwhile, but the guides are amusing.

## 64 Irish City, Dublin Bay and Castle Tour

33–34 Bachelor's Walk, Dublin 1 (tour leaves the Gresham Hotel, Lwr O'Connell St, at 2pm; call for other city departure points); Tel: 8729010, 4580054 (after office hours); E-mail: linda@irishcitytours.com; Website: www.irishcitytours.com

**Open:** All year; Mon–Sun, departs 2pm, returns 5.30pm ▪ **Charge:** Child €10; Adult €20; Tickets from the Tourist Info. Office, 12 Upr O'Connell St, or from Dublin Tourism Centre, Suffolk St, Dublin 2 ▪ **Suitable for ages:** All ▪ **Car parking:** Marlborough St car park ▪ **Bus routes:** All city centre buses ▪ **Rail station:** Tara St/Connolly ▪ **DART station:** Tara St/Connolly.

A bus tour of the north Dublin coast, including a stop at Malahide Castle (admission is included in the tour price). The castle is great for kids, so all ages will enjoy this trip. The tour carries on to Howth Head, where there's a harbour with fishing boats, and continues to Howth Summit, from where you can look out over Dublin Bay.

## 65 Irish City Dublin Bus Tour

33–34 Bachelor's Walk, Dublin 1 (tour starts at a marked bus stop at the upper end of O'Connell St (Savoy Cinema side), and there are hop–on, hop–off points around the city centre); Tel: 8729010, 4580054 (after office hours); E-mail: linda@irishcitytours.com; Website: www.irishcitytours.com

**Open:** All year; Apr–14 Jul: Mon–Sun 9.30am–5pm, every 15 minutes; 15 Jul–30 Sep: Mon–Sun 9.30am–5.30pm, every 10 minutes; Oct: Mon–Sun 9.30am–5pm, every 15 minutes; 1 Nov–31 Mar: Mon–Sun 9.30am–4pm, every 15 minutes; No tours 16–27 Dec or 17 Mar ▪ **Charge:** Child €4; Adult €12; Concessions €10; Family (2 adults and 4 children) €28; Tickets from the Tourist Info. Office, 12 Upr O'Connell St, or from Dublin Tourism Centre, Suffolk St, Dublin 2 ▪ **Suitable for ages:** All ▪ **Car parking:** Marlborough St car park ▪ **Bus routes:** All city centre buses ▪ **Rail station:** Tara St/Connolly ▪ **DART station:** Tara St/Connolly.

A hop-on, hop-off guided bus tour of the city centre. The double-decker bus is half open-topped upstairs, and there is wheelchair/buggy space on the bus. It goes from O'Connell St to the Phoenix Park, passing the GPO, Merrion Sq, Dublin Castle,

Christ Church Cathedral and Collins Barracks. The ticket is valid
for 24 hours.

## 66 Irish Film Centre 📷 ♿ €

6 Eustace St, Dublin 2; Tel: 6793477; E-mail: info@ifc.ie;
Website: www.fii.ie/ifc/index.html
**Open:** All year; Bookshop and café: Mon–Thur 11am–8.30pm;
Fri–Sat 11am–7pm; Sun 2–7pm; Films: cinema times vary ▪
**Charge:** Child €6; Adult €6; €1.30 temporary IFC membership for
a week or €10 annual membership ▪ **Suitable for ages:** 9+ ▪ **Car
parking:** Temple Bar car park ▪ **Bus routes:** All city centre buses ▪
**Rail station:** Tara St ▪ **DART station:** Tara St.
You are extremely unlikely to see the latest Disney movie at the
IFC – they usually show arty films or classic black-and-whites.
However, they do participate in the annual Junior Dublin Film
Festival, showing films made by and for 9–18-yr-olds, and hosting
seminars, workshops and presentations. The festival is usually
around Nov/Dec. Otherwise, the IFC is worth a visit with older
children, as they have a good bookshop where you can pick up a
film poster for their bedroom. There's a nice café too.
**✻ TOP CHOICES: CHILD FRIENDLY RESTAURANTS ✻ TOP CHOICES:
FOR AGES 10+ ✻ TOP CHOICES: FOR TRENDY KIDS ✻**

## 67 Irish Jewish Museum ♿

Walworth Rd, South Circular Rd, Dublin 8 (off Victoria St);
Tel: 4531797, 4901857.
**Open:** All year; May–Sep: Sun/Tue/Thur 11am–3.30pm;
Oct–Apr: Sun 10.30am–2.30pm ▪ **Charge:** Free ▪ **Suitable for
ages:** 5+ ▪ **Car parking:** Some on-street parking available ▪ **Bus
routes:** 16, 16A, 19, 19A, 22, 22A, 14, 14A, 15, 15A/B/C, 65,
65B, 83, 155.
An interesting little museum, and worth a visit no matter what
your beliefs are. Housed in a former synagogue, it contains a
collection of photographs, paintings, certificates, books and
artefacts concerning all aspects of Jewish life. The original
kitchen recreates a typical Sabbath meal setting of the early
1900s. Upstairs is the original synagogue, with displays of
religious articles in the back.

## 68 Irish Museum of Modern Art
🍴 ☕ ♿ ✏ €

Royal Hospital, Military Rd, Kilmainham, Dublin 8 (entrance is on

Military Road, 8 minutes walk from Heuston Station);
Tel: 6129900; Fax: 6129999; E-mail: info@modernart.ie;
Website: www.modernart.ie

**Open:** All year; Tue–Fri 10am–5.30pm; Sun 12–5.30pm ▪
**Charge:** Free ▪ **Suitable for ages:** 2+ ▪ **Car parking:** Free ▪ **Bus routes:** 68, 68A, 69, 78A, 79, 90, 123.

Housed in a restored 17th-century building, complete with baroque ceiling, which was once used as a home for retired soldiers, IMMA contains works by 20th-century Irish and non-Irish artists. There is hands-on art experience for all the family on Sunday afternoons from 2–5pm (Oct–Nov and Feb–end Jul), with the Explorer 1 programme. No booking is required, and it's free. There are also free guided tours available on Wed, Fri and Sun at 2.30pm, and formal gardens to explore.

✱ **TOP CHOICES: CHILD FRIENDLY RESTAURANTS** ✱ **TOP CHOICES: FOR AGES 2–5** ✱ **TOP CHOICES: FOR AGES 5–10** ✱

## 69  Irish National Youth Ballet Company

13 Stamer St, Portobello, Dublin 8; Tel: 4755451; Fax: 4755451; E-mail: inybco@inybco.com; Website: www.inybco.com

**Open:** All year; Sat for classes, or rehearsals when required for productions ▪ **Suitable for ages:** 10+ ▪ **Car parking:** On-street parking ▪ **Bus routes:** 14, 14A, 16, 16A, 19, 19A, 122 ▪ **DART station:** Salthill and Monkstown.

This is a company for Irish ballet dancers aged 10–21, aiming towards a professional career on stage. Entrance is by audition only. The dancers train as a company, with internationally trained teachers and visiting choreographers. They stage two seasons of performances a year, in professional theatres.

## 70  Irishtown Nature Park ♿

Poolbeg, Dublin 2; Tel: 6684364;
E-mail: parks.parks@dublincity.ie;
Website: www.dublincity.ie/parks

**Open:** All year; Mon–Fri 8.30am–dusk; Sat–Sun 9.30am–dusk ▪
**Charge:** Free ▪ **Suitable for ages:** All ▪ **Car parking:** On-street parking ▪ **Bus routes:** 1, 2, 3.

This park is on the Poolbeg peninsula and provides a bracing coastal walk, with a backdrop of the two ESB cooling towers. The park was a landfill site until 1977, and as such is deemed unsuitable for active recreation, but it won a Ford Conservation Award in 1987.

## 71  James Joyce Centre &#9855; &euro;

35 North Great George's St, Dublin 1 (10 minutes walk from
O'Connell Bridge, towards Parnell Sq); Tel: 8788547;
Fax: 8788488; E-mail: joycecen@iol.ie;
Website: www.jamesjoyce.ie
**Open:** All year; Mon–Sat 9.30am–5pm; Sun/bank holidays
12.30–5pm ▪ **Charge:** Under-12s free; Adults €4.50;
Students/seniors €3.50 ▪ **Suitable for ages:** 10+ ▪ **Car parking:**
Marlborough St car park ▪ **Bus routes:** 3, 10, 11, 13, 16, 19, 22,
123 ▪ **Rail station:** Connolly ▪ **DART station:** Connolly.
Set in a restored Georgian house, the centre contains a library,
Joyce family portraits and exhibitions exploring Joyce's
background and inspiration. There are guided tours and walks of
Joyce's Dublin available for a charge (booking necessary). The
centre has a good schools programme for Junior Cert and Leaving
Cert students.

## 72  Jervis St Shopping Centre

Henry St, Dublin 1 (at the Mary St end of Henry St);
Tel: 8781323.
**Open:** All year; Mon–Fri 9am–6pm (Thur 9pm); Sat
9am–6.30pm; Sun/bank holidays 12–6pm ▪ **Suitable for ages:** All
▪ **Car parking:** Jervis Centre car park ▪ **Bus routes:** All city centre
buses.
An overheated shopping centre with quite a few good shops for
children and babies. UK high-street fashion stores make it a
teenager's paradise. Eat in Debenham's, who do free babyfood
and a cold pick-and-mix lunchbox for kids. They also have a small
play area.
✱ TOP CHOICES: FOR AGES 10+ ✱ TOP CHOICES: FOR TRENDY KIDS ✱

## 73  Kevin Street Library

18 Lwr Kevin St, Dublin 8 (a short walk west of St. Stephen's
Green); Tel: 4753794; Website: www.iol.ie/dublincitylibrary
**Open:** All year; Mon/Wed/Fri 10am–1pm, 2–5pm; Tue/Thur
12.45–4pm, 4.45–8pm ▪ **Charge:** Free ▪ **Suitable for ages:** All ▪
**Car parking:** St. Stephen's Green Shopping Centre car park ▪ **Bus
routes:** 16, 16A, 19, 19A, 22, 22A, 83 ▪ **Rail station:** Pearse St ▪
**DART station:** Pearse St.
Kevin St Library holds a Children's Art Class for 5–12-yr-olds on
Tue 5.30–7pm. Other seasonal arts-and-crafts and reading events

for children are organised throughout the year.

## 74 Leinster School of Music and Drama

Griffith College Dublin Campus, South Circular Rd, Dublin 8 (1km from the centre of Dublin, at the junction of Parnell Rd and the South Circular Rd); Tel: 4150467; E-mail: leinster-school@gcd.ie; Website: www.gcd.ie
**Open:** All year; Call for individual course times ■ **Charge:** Fees for individual courses or tuition on request ■ **Suitable for ages:** 5+ ■ **Bus routes:** 16, 16A, 19, 49, 49A, 56A, 65, 65A/B, 122, 155, 210.
A 100-year-old school, with over 600 independent music and drama teachers affiliated to it. The emphasis is on learning through enjoyment, and while exams are encouraged they are not compulsory. A diverse range of styles is on offer – from classical to modern and popular to traditional. The school also runs courses in speech and drama, including public speaking, choral speaking and solo, duologue and group acting.
✱ TOP CHOICES: HOBBIES/ARTS AND CRAFTS ✱ TOP CHOICES: FOR IMAGINATIVE KIDS ✱

## 75 Liberty Hall Theatre ♿

Eden Quay, Dublin 1 (approx. 5 minutes' walk from O'Connell Bridge, on the quays before the Custom House – the theatre is in the Old Union Hall, next door to the main building);
Tel: 8721122 (no booking fee).
**Open:** All year; Mon–Sun, evening and matinee performances, call for times ■ **Charge:** Tickets (adult/child) from approx €18 ■ **Suitable for ages:** 2+ ■ **Car parking:** Irish Life Centre car park ■ **Bus routes:** All city centre buses ■ **Rail station:** Tara St ■ **DART station:** Tara St.
A venue on the quays with a varied programme, including plays by Roddy Doyle and pantomime at Christmas. It is now home to Poetry Ireland and the Dublin Theatre Festival Club.
✱ TOP CHOICES: CHRISTMAS VISITS ✱ TOP CHOICES: FOR TRENDY KIDS ✱

## 76 Liberty Park 🚼 ♿ 🧗

Foley St, Dublin 1 (near Busáras); Tel: 6612369;
Website: www.dublincity.ie/parks
**Open:** All year; Mon–Fri 8.30am–dusk; Sat–Sun 9.30am–dusk ■ **Suitable for ages:** All ■ **Car parking:** Metered street parking ■

**Bus routes:** All city centre buses ▪ **Rail station:** Connolly ▪ **DART station:** Connolly.
**Sports:** soccer
A small park with an all-weather soccer pitch. Sited in what was once the notorious 'Monto' area, the red-light district made famous by James Joyce in *Ulysses*.

## 77 Markiewicz Leisure Centre ♿ 🛈

Townsend St, Dublin 2 (just down from the Screen cinema, parallel to the south quays); Tel: 6729121; Fax: 6719120.
**Open:** All year; Mon–Fri 2–5pm; Sat 9am–5.45pm; Sun 10am–3.45pm ▪ **Charge:** Child €2.50; Adult €4.40; Fee is for entrance to swimming pool ▪ **Suitable for ages:** All ▪ **Bus routes:** All city centre buses.
**Sports:** swimming, gymnasium
A modern swimming pool run by Dublin City Council, with public sessions only – there are no lessons on offer.

## 78 Marks & Spencer 🛒 ☕ ♿

24/29 Mary St, Dublin 1, Tel: 8728833; 15–20 Grafton St, Dublin 1, Tel: 6797855.
**Open:** Mary St: Mon–Fri 9am–7pm (Thur 9pm); Sat 8.30am–7pm; Sun 12–6.60pm; Grafton St: Same as Mary St, except store opens Mon–Sat at 8.30am ▪ **Suitable for ages:** All ▪ **Car parking:** Jervis Centre car park or St. Stephen's Green Shopping Centre car park ▪ **Bus routes:** All city centre buses ▪ **Rail station:** Tara St ▪ **DART station:** Tara St.
A UK chain store which does good-quality babies' and children's wear. Both city-centre stores have an unsupervised soft seating area, with video screens showing cartoons, but they are both near escalators. M&S carries a small range of books and toys, novelty birthday cakes and very nice cards. The Mary St store has a small café for tea and cake.

## 79 Marsh's Library ♿ €

St. Patrick's Close, Dublin 8 (behind St. Patrick's Cathedral); Tel: 4543511; Fax: 4543511; Website: www.marshlibrary.ie
**Open:** All year; Mon/Wed–Fri 10am–1pm, 2–5pm; Sat 10.30am–1pm ▪ **Charge:** Children free; Adult €2.50; Students €1.25 ▪ **Suitable for ages:** 5+ ▪ **Car parking:** Christ Church car park ▪ **Bus routes:** 49, 49A, 50, 54A, 77, 77A, 150.
This is Ireland's oldest public library, opened in 1701. It contains

over 25,000 books relating to the 16th, 17th and 18th centuries and covering medicine, law, science, travel, navigation, mathematics, music, surveying and classical literature. The museum puts on yearly exhibitions where books are displayed according to a theme, eg the smallest and largest books in the library. There's some great gory stuff in here, including Foxe's *Book of Martyrs*, with detailed descriptions of torture; and a volume of plates to accompany Captain Cook's voyages – lots of people in the nip! The library is sometimes used as a venue for classical music concerts.

**✱ TOP CHOICES: FOR AGES 5–10 ✱ TOP CHOICES: FOR AGES 10+ ✱ TOP CHOICES: FOR INQUISITIVE KIDS ✱**

## 80 The Merriman School Of Singing and Music

21 North Great Georges St, Dublin 1; Tel: 8742034; Fax: 8745139. **Open:** All year; Call for an appointment ▪ **Charge:** €50 for voice assessment and then fees will be discussed ▪ **Suitable for ages:** 5+ ▪ **Bus routes:** All city centre buses ▪ **Rail station:** Connolly ▪ **DART station:** Connolly.

Singing lessons from one of the best voice teachers in the country. Voice assessments are held for children from the age of five, with advice on how to proceed from there.

**✱ TOP CHOICES: HOBBIES/ARTS AND CRAFTS ✱ TOP CHOICES: FOR IMAGINATIVE KIDS ✱**

## 81 Merrion Square

Merrion Sq, Dublin 2; Tel: 8346973;
E-mail: parks.parks@dublincity.ie;
Website: www.dublincity.ie/parks

**Open:** All year; Mon–Fri 8.30am–dusk; Sat–Sun 9.30am–dusk ▪ **Charge:** Free ▪ **Suitable for ages:** All ▪ **Car parking:** On-street parking ▪ **Bus routes:** 5, 7, 7A, 44, 45, 46 ▪ **Rail station:** Pearse St ▪ **DART station:** Pearse St.

Merrion Square, or Archbishop Ryan Park, is a typical Georgian square. Once the preserve of well-heeled key owners, it is now open to the public. Opposite Government buildings, it contains the Rutland Memorial, a collection of old Dublin lamp posts, a central floral garden, a heather garden, a playground and many sculptures. Lunchtime concerts are held here during the summer.

**✱ TOP CHOICES: PICNIC SPOTS ✱ TOP CHOICES: FOR AGES 0–2 ✱ TOP CHOICES: FOR AGES 2–5 ✱**

CITY CENTRE

43

## 82　Flora Millar Dance Centres

54 Parnell Sq, Dublin 1 (opposite Rotunda Hospital);
Tel: 2888455; Fax: 2888309; E-mail: floramillar@ireland.com;
Website: www.floramillar.com
**Open:** All year; Under-8s and newcomers classes
10.30–11.30am; Competitor practice class 11.30am–1pm ▪
**Charge:** Courses run for 10 weeks and must be pre-paid; Prices
given on request ▪ **Suitable for ages:** 3+ ▪ **Bus routes:** All city
centre buses ▪ **Rail station:** Connolly ▪ **DART station:** Connolly.
Flora Millar is one of Ireland's best-known dance teachers, and has
received international recognition for her contribution to ballroom
dancing. These ballroom and Latin dancing classes can progress to
competition level, for children from ages three-and-a-half onwards.
**✱ TOP CHOICES: HOBBIES/ARTS AND CRAFTS ✱ TOP CHOICES: FOR
IMAGINATIVE KIDS ✱**

## 83　Mountjoy Square Park 🚼 ♿ 🧗

Mountjoy Sq, Dublin 1 (at the top of Gardiner St); Tel: 6612369,
8554030; Website: www.dublincity.ie/parks
**Open:** All year; Mon–Fri 8.30am–dusk; Sat–Sun 9.30am–dusk ▪
**Suitable for ages:** All ▪ **Car parking:** Metered on-street parking ▪
**Bus routes:** 41B/C ▪ **Rail station:** Connolly ▪ **DART station:**
Connolly.
**Sports:** soccer, tennis
Set in the middle of the Georgian Mountjoy Square, this park has
an all-weather, floodlit football pitch.
**✱ TOP CHOICES: SPORTS FACILITIES ✱**

## 84　The Moving Crib

St Martin's Apostolate, 42 Parnell Sq, Dublin 1 (ILAC centre side
of Parnell Sq); Tel: 8370147, 8745456.
**Open:** Christmas; 1 Dec–15 Jan; closed 24–26/31 Dec and 1 Jan;
Mon–Fri 2–6pm; Sat–Sun/bank holidays 11.30am–6pm ▪ **Charge:**
Free ▪ **Suitable for ages:** All ▪ **Car parking:** Marlborough St car
park ▪ **Bus routes:** All city centre buses ▪ **Rail station:** Connolly ▪
**DART station:** Connolly.
The Moving Crib is a series of animated figures depicting scenes
from the Bible, including the Nativity. It has been going for nearly
50 years and, even though some of the figures are a bit worn, it
hasn't lost its charm. There is also a large doll's house to see. All
children will enjoy this, especially now that Dublin department

stores no longer bother with a children's Christmas window display. The exhibition is down a few steps and you are asked to leave your buggy upstairs.

**★ TOP CHOICES: CHRISTMAS VISITS ★**

## 85 National Concert Hall

Earlsfort Terrace, Dublin 2 (beside St. Stephen's Green);
Tel: 4751666, 4751572 (box office); Fax: 4783797;
Website: www.nch.ie
**Open:** All year; Mon–Sun daytime and evening performances; call for times ▪ **Charge:** Tickets from €5 concessions to €35 full adult price, depending on the performance ▪ **Suitable for ages:** All ▪ **Car parking:** Some on-street parking or Royal College of Surgeons car park ▪ **Bus routes:** All city centre buses ▪ **Rail station:** Pearse St ▪ **DART station:** Pearse St.
The NCH shows a wide variety of musical concerts throughout the year, including Irish Youth Orchestra performances. They host really good workshops, including Parent-and-Toddler Workshops, Musical Puppet Making, Sound Sculpture (music from household objects!), Music and Illustration, and a children's summer workshop series.

**★ TOP CHOICES: CHRISTMAS VISITS ★ TOP CHOICES: FOR AGES 5–10 ★ TOP CHOICES: FOR SHY KIDS ★**

## 86 National Gallery of Ireland

Merrion Sq W, Dublin 2; Tel: 6615133; Fax: 6615372;
E-mail: info@ngi.ie; Website: www.nationalgallery.ie
**Open:** All year; Mon–Sat 9.30am–5.30pm ▪ **Charge:** Free ▪ **Suitable for ages:** 5+ ▪ **Car parking:** Royal College of Surgeons car park ▪ **Bus routes:** All city centre buses ▪ **Rail station:** Pearse St ▪ **DART station:** Pearse St.
The National Gallery of Ireland houses the national collection of Irish art and European master paintings, and includes the National Portrait Gallery and the Yeats Museum. It is huge, with 54 galleries. The new Millennium Wing is very space-age, all minimalist white concrete. At weekends there are talks for children. Family workshops with artists run throughout the year – bring your pencils and crayons, no booking is necessary. Decent food is provided by Fitzer's restaurant upstairs.

**★ TOP CHOICES: CHILD FRIENDLY RESTAURANTS ★ TOP CHOICES: FOR AGES 5–10 ★ TOP CHOICES: FOR INQUISITIVE KIDS ★**

## 87 The National Library of Ireland ♿ €

Kildare St, Dublin 2; Tel: 6618811; E-mail: info@nli.ie;
Website: www.nli.ie
**Open:** All year; Main Reading Room: Mon–Wed 10am–9pm;
Thur–Fri 10am–5pm; Sat 10am–1pm; Manuscripts Reading:
Mon–Wed 10am–8.30pm; Thur–Fri 10am–4.30pm; Sat
10am–12.30pm; Readers' Ticket Office: Mon–Wed
10am–12.30pm, 2–5pm; Thur–Fri 10am–12.30pm, 2–4.30pm;
Sat 10am–12.30pm ■ **Charge:** Free ■ **Suitable for ages:** 10+ ■
**Car parking:** Some disc parking; otherwise Setanta car park or
Dawson St car park ■ **Bus routes:** All city centre buses ■ **Rail
station:** Pearse St ■ **DART station:** Pearse St.
This is a reference library only, containing books and periodicals –
including first editions of famous Irish writers. You need a reader's
ticket to do research, and these are not likely to be given to the
under-16s. However, adults can get a day pass and bring children
along, to learn how to go about researching their family tree.

## 88 National Museum of Ireland (History and Archaeology) ☕ ♿ ✎ €

Kildare St, Dublin 2; Tel: 6777444; Fax: 6619199;
E-mail: education.nmi@indigo.ie
**Open:** All year; Tue–Sat 10am–5pm; Sun 2–5pm ■ **Charge:** Free
■ **Suitable for ages:** 4+ ■ **Car parking:** Some on-street parking;
otherwise Setanta car park or Dawson St car park ■ **Bus routes:** 7,
7A, 8, 10, 11, 13 ■ **Rail station:** Pearse St ■ **DART station:** Pearse
St.
Opened in 1890, the National Museum of Ireland contains
artefacts from 7000BC. This is the place to learn about Egyptian
mummies, Vikings and Ireland's Stone and Bronze Ages.
Workshops are held at the weekend (Sundays 3–4pm, occasional
Saturdays), and include storytelling, jewellery-making, exploring
burial rites, and much more besides. Some workshops have
limited places, so book in advance. They are usually for ages 4+
and are free. Fantastic! Wheelchair access is limited to the ground
floor only.
**✱ TOP CHOICES: FOR AGES 10+ ✱ TOP CHOICES: FOR INQUISITIVE
KIDS ✱ TOP CHOICES: FOR TRENDY KIDS ✱**

## 89 National Museum of Ireland (History and Decorative Arts) 🖼️ ♿ ✏️ €

Benburb St, Collins Barracks, Dublin 7 (from the city centre, go along the quays towards Heuston Station. Benburb St is off Wolfe Tone Quay); Tel: 6777444; Fax: 6619199;
E-mail: education.nmi@indigo.ie
**Open:** All year; Tue–Sat 10am–5pm; Sun 2–5pm ▪ **Charge:** Free
▪ **Suitable for ages:** 4+ ▪ **Car parking:** Free ▪ **Bus routes:** 25, 25A, 66, 67, 90.

This museum is gorgeous, and totally worth the short hop from the city centre! The restored Collins Barracks contains weaponry, furniture, costumes, silver, ceramics and glassware. Workshops are held at the weekend (Sundays 3–4pm, occasional Saturdays), and include poster design, song and dance, mask-making, storytelling, and much more. Some workshops have limited places, so book in advance. They are usually for ages 4+ and are free!
★ **TOP CHOICES: FOR AGES 5–10** ★ **TOP CHOICES: FOR INQUISITIVE KIDS** ★

## 90 National Museum of Ireland (Natural History) ♿ ✏️ €

Merrion St, Dublin 2 (west of Merrion Sq); Tel: 6777444; Fax: 6619199.
**Open:** All year; Tue–Sat 10am–5pm; Sun 2–5pm ▪ **Charge:** Free
▪ **Suitable for ages:** All ▪ **Car parking:** Some on-street parking; otherwise Setanta car park or Dawson St car park ▪ **Bus routes:** 7, 7A, 8, 10, 11, 13 ▪ **Rail station:** Pearse St ▪ **DART station:** Pearse St.

This museum is packed to the gills with all kinds of creepy-crawlies, sea life, birds and mammals. From the giant Donegal sunfish to the skeleton of the extinct Irish elk, there is loads to see – you'll be entertained for hours. There are worksheets available for different age groups, to be completed as you go around (bring pencils). Even a baby will enjoy pointing out the animals, some cute and some in scary poses. The museum also houses an intricate and beautiful collection of glass models of marine animals by Leopold Blaschka. Workshops are held at weekends (Sundays 3–4pm, occasional Saturdays), and include looking at camouflage, animal hunting habits, evolution, and much more. Some workshops have limited places, so book in advance. They are usually for ages 6+ and are free! Wheelchair

and buggy access is limited to the ground floor only, though there
are another 3 floors of exhibits.

**✱ TOP CHOICES: FOR AGES 5–10 ✱ TOP CHOICES: FOR INQUISITIVE KIDS ✱**

## 91 National Photographic Archive ♿ €

Meeting House Sq, Temple Bar, Dublin 2; Tel: 6030200;
Fax: 6777451; E-mail: photoarchive@nli.ie; Website: www.nli.ie
**Open:** All year; Mon–Fri 10am–5pm; Sat 10am–2pm (exhibition
area only) ▪ **Charge:** Free ▪ **Suitable for ages:** 10+ ▪ **Car
parking:** Temple Bar car park ▪ **Bus routes:** All city centre buses ▪
**Rail station:** Tara St ▪ **DART station:** Tara St.
The photographic collections of the National Library of Ireland
are all housed here. Early sepia photographs are displayed, along
with the work of more contemporary photographers. There is a
reading room, an exhibition area and a small shop. Prints of
photographs that particularly catch your eye can be ordered
from the archives.

## 92 The National Wax Museum ♿ 👶 €

Granby Row, Parnell Sq W, Dublin 1 (near Dorset St Upr);
Tel: 8726340.
**Open:** All year; Mon–Sat 10am–5.30pm; Sun 12–5.30pm ▪
**Charge:** Child €4; Adult €7 ▪ **Suitable for ages:** 2+ ▪ **Car
parking:** Marlborough St car park ▪ **Bus routes:** All city centre
buses ▪ **Rail station:** Connolly ▪ **DART station:** Connolly.
Wax models of Irish and international celebrities are housed here,
including politicians and film, music, television and sports stars.
There is a Chamber of Horrors (a little scary for under-5s), a
children's cinema and even figures from the latest Star Wars
movie. No booking is necessary for birthday parties, and the
birthday child goes free (minimum 20 kids). You'll have to take
them somewhere else for food though. Wheelchair access is
limited to the ground floor only (one-third of the exhibition), and
there are steps to negotiate at the front too.

**✱ TOP CHOICES: BIRTHDAY PARTY IDEAS ✱ TOP CHOICES: FOR AGES
5–10 ✱ TOP CHOICES: FOR TRENDY KIDS ✱**

## 93 National Youth Orchestra of Ireland

37 Molesworth St, Dublin 2; Tel: 6628735; Fax: 6613642;
E-mail: info@nyoi.ie; Website: www.nyoi.ie
**Open:** All year; Call for audition and workshop dates ▪ **Charge:**

Residential weekend string training courses €280 ▪ **Suitable for ages:** 12–18.
An under-18s youth orchestra, with entrance by audition only. They hold residential weekend string training courses for €280. The orchestra stages public performances, including some at the National Concert Hall.

## 94 Newman House

85–86 St. Stephen's Green, Dublin 2 (south side of St. Stephen's Green); Tel: 7067422; Fax: 7067211;
E-mail: ruth.ferguson@ucd.ie
**Open:** 2 Apr–31 Aug; Access by guided tour only; Tue–Fri: Tours at 12pm, 2pm, 3pm and 4pm; Sat: tours at 2pm, 3pm and 4pm ▪
**Charge:** Child €3; Adult €4; Concessions €3; Admission to Newman House includes the guided tour and an exhibition on the restoration project ▪ **Suitable for ages:** 10+ ▪ **Car parking:** Royal College of Surgeons car park ▪ **Bus routes:** All city centre buses.
Newman House is made up of two Georgian houses. Fully restored to their former glory, they are famous mainly for their brilliant Palladian and rococo plasterwork. Newman House was the first home of University College, Dublin, and many famous people have studied there, including Gerard Manley Hopkins, James Joyce and Flann O'Brien.

## 95 Norton, Betty Ann, Theatre School, Harcourt St

Clonbrock House, 11 Harcourt St, Dublin 2; Tel: 4751913;
Fax: 4751140; E-mail: bettyann.norton@iegateway.net;
Website: www.bettyann-nortontheatreschool.com
**Open:** Sep–Jun; 3 x 10-week terms; also summer course; Courses vary from 1 hour–90 minutes weekly ▪ **Charge:** Summer courses from €115; Other course prices on request ▪ **Suitable for ages:** 4+ ▪ **Bus routes:** All city centre buses ▪ **Rail station:** Tara St ▪ **DART station:** Tara St.
One of the best theatre schools in Dublin, it offers speech and drama for the very young, as well as music, mime, movement, puppetry and storytelling. Older children participate in *feiseanna* and are auditioned for radio, television, theatre and films when suitable parts appear. Teenagers can join the drama workshop, designed as an aid to personality development and confidence building. There are also introduction to stage craft and theatre studies courses. The school runs classes and courses in speech

therapy, aiming to build confidence and creativity.
**✱ TOP CHOICES: HOBBIES/ARTS AND CRAFTS ✱ TOP CHOICES: SUMMER CAMPS ✱**

## 96   Number Twenty Nine 🏠 €

29 Lwr Fitzwilliam St, Dublin 2; Tel: 7026165; Fax: 7027796;
E-mail: numbertwentynine@mail.esb.ie;
Website: www.esb.ie/education
**Open:** All year except 2 weeks before Christmas; Tue–Sat
10am–5pm; Sun 2–5pm ▪ **Charge:** Children free; Adult €3.15;
Concessions €1.25 ▪ **Suitable for ages:** 3+ ▪ **Car parking:** Royal
College of Surgeons car park ▪ **Bus routes:** 6, 7, 8, 10, 45 ▪ **Rail
station:** Pearse St ▪ **DART station:** Pearse St.
A great place for nosey-parkers! This is an exhibition of home life
in Dublin around 1790–1820, in a completely restored
middle-class house of the late 18th century. At the top of the
house are the children's bedrooms, governess's room and play
room, complete with toys and doll's house. Below are the
mistress's boudoir and the family drawing room, with the kitchen
in the basement. Most children love to learn about how people
lived in the past, and this is a fun way to learn about 18th-century
domestic life.
**✱ TOP CHOICES: FOR AGES 5–10 ✱ TOP CHOICES: FOR INQUISITIVE
KIDS ✱**

## 97   Olympia Theatre ♿

72 Dame St, Dublin 2; Tel: 6777744; Fax: 6777124;
Website: www.mcd.ie/venues/olympia
**Open:** All year; Mon–Sun matinee and evening performances;
call for times ▪ **Charge:** Child €20; Adult €20; Approx. ticket
prices for large scale productions, eg pantomime ▪ **Suitable for
ages:** All ▪ **Car parking:** Temple Bar car park ▪ **Bus routes:** All
city centre buses ▪ **Rail station:** Tara St ▪ **DART station:** Tara
St.
The Olympia stages a range of shows throughout the year,
including musicals, theatre and performances from children
attending Dublin stage schools. They also show special visiting
productions for children, usually during school holidays.
**✱ TOP CHOICES: CHRISTMAS VISITS ✱**

## 98   Peacock Theatre

26 Lwr Abbey St, Dublin 1 (downstairs, in the same building as the

Abbey Theatre); Tel: 8787222 (No booking fee); Fax: 8729177; Website: www.abbeytheatre.ie

**Open:** All year; Performances: Mon–Sun matinee and evening performances; call for times; Tours: Thur 11am ▪ **Charge:** Child €5; Adult €10; Average ticket prices for performance suitable for children ▪ **Suitable for ages:** 13+ ▪ **Car parking:** Irish Life Centre car park ▪ **Bus routes:** All city centre buses ▪ **Rail station:** Connolly ▪ **DART station:** Connolly.

Part of the National Theatre, the Peacock usually shows contemporary plays by newer Irish playwrights, occasionally suitable for children. Together with the Abbey Theatre, it runs a theatre club for 15–19-yr-olds, and is introducing one for 13–15-yr-olds. There are weekly Thursday morning tours of the Peacock and Abbey theatres, at 11am. There is also an outreach programme.

## 99 Penney's Stores 🛒 ♿

47 Mary St, Dublin 1, Tel: 8727788; O'Connell St, Dublin 1, Tel: 8720466; Website: www.primark.co.uk

**Open:** All year; O'Connell St: Mon–Wed 8.30am–6pm; Thur–Fri 8.30am–9pm; Sat 8.30am–6pm; Sun 12–6.30pm; Mary St: Mon–Wed 9am–6.30pm; Thur 9am–9pm; Fri 9am–7pm; Sat 9am–6.30pm; Sun 12–6pm ▪ **Suitable for ages:** All ▪ **Car parking:** Jervis Centre car park ▪ **Bus routes:** All city centre buses ▪ **Rail station:** Tara St ▪ **DART station:** Tara St.

Babies' and children's wear can be got at bargain prices from this Irish chain of clothing shops. You can buy a whole outfit, including shoes, for well under €50.

## 100 Point Theatre ♿

East Link Bridge, North Wall Quay, Dublin 1 (approx. 30 minutes' walk from O'Connell Bridge, on the north quays past the Custom House); Tel: 8363633; Fax: 8366422.

**Open:** All year; Mon–Sun evening and matinee performances; call for times ▪ **Charge:** Performances from €12 (adult/child matinee price) to approx. €30 for evening concert ▪ **Suitable for ages:** 5+ ▪ **Car parking:** €5 – limited parking available so get there half-an-hour early ▪ **Bus routes:** 53, 53A.

A large music and theatre venue, the Point is the place to take young teenagers to scream at Westlife and the like (earplugs not supplied). It is also host to touring dance companies, American wrestlers and other special events. No entry to children under 5 to this venue (except when Disney on Ice is on). All children under 16 must be accompanied by an adult.

✱ TOP CHOICES: BIRTHDAY PARTY IDEAS ✱ TOP CHOICES: CHRISTMAS VISITS ✱ TOP CHOICES: FOR AGES 10+ ✱ TOP CHOICES: FOR TRENDY KIDS ✱

## 101 Project Arts Centre 🛒 📺 ♿

39 East Essex St, Dublin 2; Tel: 1850 260027 (booking), 8819613, 6796622; Fax: 6792310; E-mail: info@project.ie; Website: www.project.ie

**Open:** All year; Performance and exhibition times vary ▪ **Charge:** Child €12; Adult €15; Family Ticket €45 (4 persons); Average price for a family production ▪ **Suitable for ages:** All ▪ **Car parking:** Temple Bar car park ▪ **Bus routes:** All city centre buses ▪ **Rail station:** Tara St ▪ **DART station:** Tara St.

The Project presents contemporary artwork by Irish and international artists, including exhibitions, theatre, dance and workshops, which are occasionally suitable for children. The new centre has four floors, with very good facilities.

## 102 Roches Stores 🛒 📺 ♿

54/62 Henry St, Dublin 1; Tel: 8730044; Fax: 8730791.

**Open:** All year; Mon–Sat 9am–6pm (Thur 9pm); Sun 12–6pm ▪ **Suitable for ages:** All ▪ **Car parking:** Jervis Centre car park ▪ **Bus routes:** All city centre buses.

Roches Stores is one of the best places in Dublin for baby equipment. It has a big range of prams, buggies, cots, etc., and rows of frilly baby dresses and sailor suits. It also stocks school uniforms, Holy Communion and confirmation wear, as well as children's clothes.

## 103 Royal Irish Academy of Music

36 Westland Row, Dublin 2; Tel: 6764412; Fax: 6622798; E-mail: info@riam.ie; Website: www.riam.ie

**Open:** Sep–Jun; Classes available daily ▪ **Charge:** Instrument classes approx. €200 a year for 30-minute lesson each week; Pre-instrumental classes €333 a year for 45-minute lesson each week; Speech and drama €117 a semester for 45-minute lesson each week ▪ **Suitable for ages:** 4+ ▪ **Bus routes:** All city centre buses ▪ **Rail station:** Pearse St ▪ **DART station:** Pearse St.

Tuition is available here at all levels and ages in most instruments. There is a pre-instrumental class for small children (ages 4–9)

under the Kodály method of teaching, which includes: listening, singing, body movement, playing percussion instruments and an introduction to the instruments of the orchestra. No beginners over the age of 12 for pianoforte and violin, and no singing students under the age of 16. There are also speech and drama classes available from kindergarten level up.

**✱ TOP CHOICES: HOBBIES/ARTS AND CRAFTS ✱**

## 104 St. Audeon's Church ♿

High St, Dublin 8 (near Christ Church Cathedral); Tel: 6770088; Fax: 6709431; Website: www.heritageireland.ie
**Open:** 1 Jun–Sep; Mon–Sun 9.30am–5.30pm; last admission 45 minutes before closing ▪ **Charge:** Child €0.70; Adult €1.90; Group/OAP €1.20; Student €0.70; Family €5.00 ▪ **Suitable for ages:** 5+ ▪ **Car parking:** Christ Church car park ▪ **Bus routes:** 50, 54A, 56A.

This is the only remaining medieval parish church in Dublin, and part of it is still in use by the Church of Ireland. St. Audeon's contains an exhibition on its importance in medieval Dublin, as well as recently restored 17th-century memorials to the Sparke and Duff families, and the 15th-century effigial tomb of Baron Portlester and his wife. The church incorporates the first stone city wall, dating from about 1100AD, and St. Audeon's Arch, the last surviving entrance to the old city.

## 105 St. Mary's Pro-Cathedral

Marlborough St, Dublin 1 (off the north end of O'Connell St); Tel: 8745441; Fax: 8742406; Website: www.procathedral.ie
**Open:** All year; Mon–Sun 8am–6pm ▪ **Charge:** Free ▪ **Suitable for ages:** 5+ ▪ **Car parking:** Marlborough St car park ▪ **Bus routes:** All city centre buses ▪ **Rail station:** Connolly ▪ **DART station:** Connolly.

St. Mary's was built in 1816–1825, and is Dublin's principal Catholic cathedral. It's a pity it has its back to O'Connell St, as it has six impressive-looking Doric columns, modelled on the Temple of Theseus in Athens. The Palestrina Choir sing at the Latin Mass here each Sunday at 11am and there's a Mass for young adults at St. Kevin's Oratory on Saturdays at 8pm.

## 106 St. Michan's Church

Church St, Dublin 7 (off Arran Quay, up from the Four Courts); Tel: 8724154; Fax: 8782615; E-mail: stmichan@iol.ie

**Open:** All year except Christmas, bank holidays and some days in Holy Week; Mar–Oct: Mon–Fri 10am–12.30pm, 2–4.30pm; Nov–Mar: Mon–Fri 12.30–3.30pm; Jan–Dec: Sat 10am–12.45pm ■ **Charge:** Child €2.50; Adult €3.30; Students/OAPs €3; Group rates available ■ **Suitable for ages:** 7+ ■ **Car parking:** Metered on-street parking ■ **Bus routes:** 37, 39, 51, 51X, 70, 70X, 134, 172.

Coffins, death masks, mummies – it doesn't get much more macabre than this. Founded in 1095, St. Michan's Church was, until 1686, the only church on the north side of Dublin city. The dry atmospheric conditions in the vaults have resulted in the mummification of corpses, which are on display. Also to be seen in the vaults are the death mask of Wolfe Tone and the coffins of the 1798 rebels John and Henry Sheares. Wheelchair access is limited to the church only.

✱ TOP CHOICES: FOR AGES 10+ ✱ TOP CHOICES: FOR INQUISITIVE KIDS ✱

## 107 St. Patrick's Cathedral ♿ €

Patrick St, Dublin 2 (from Trinity College, go down Dame St, then turn left down Patrick St, opposite Christ Church Cathedral); Tel: 4539472 (office), 4754817 (cathedral); Fax: 4546374; E-mail: admin@stpatrickscathedral.ie; Website: www.stpatrickscathedral.ie

**Open:** All year; Apr–Oct: Mon–Sun 9am–6pm; Nov–Mar: Mon–Fri 9am–6pm; Sat 9am–5pm; Sun 10am–3pm; Evensong: Mon–Fri 5.35pm; Sun 3.15pm; Sung matins: Sun 11.15am; No sung services Sat/Wed in Jul/Aug; closed to visitors 24 and 26 Dec, 1 Jan ■ **Charge:** Child €2.50; Adult €4; Unwaged (OAP, student, unemployed) €3; Family (2 adults and 2 children) €9.00 ■ **Suitable for ages:** 2+ ■ **Car parking:** Christ Church car park ■ **Bus routes:** 50, 54A, 56A.

A majestic cathedral, built on the site of a well where St. Patrick is said to have baptized converts to Christianity. Along with other notables, Jonathan Swift, author of *Gulliver's Travels* and dean of the cathedral for 32 years, is buried here. Children will probably show no interest in the grand mosaic floor or the hanging medieval banners. However, they'll enjoy 'chancing their arm' through the chapter house door – a door with a hole it, through which two Norman earls shook hands after a feud. Music lovers will enjoy the evensong and the sung matins. At Advent and Christmas, there are special events, including candlelight processions and carol singing.

✱ TOP CHOICES: CHRISTMAS VISITS ✱ TOP CHOICES: FOR AGES 5–10 ✱

## 108 St. Stephen's Green ⛹ ♿ 🤸

St. Stephen's Green, Dublin 2; Tel: 6723305;
E-mail: parks.parks@dublincity.ie;
Website: www.dublincity.ie/parks
**Open:** All year; Mon–Fri 8.30am–dusk; Sat–Sun 9.30am–dusk ▪
**Charge:** Free ▪ **Suitable for ages:** All ▪ **Car parking:** On-street
parking ▪ **Bus routes:** All city centre buses ▪ **Rail station:** Pearse
St/Tara St ▪ **DART station:** Pearse St/Tara St.
St. Stephen's Green, or 'the Green' as it is usually known, is a
27-acre park right in the heart of Dublin city. It is a very popular
lunchtime retreat for many office workers in the area. Children
enjoy feeding the ducks and geese, and there is also a largish
playground. The park has many statues, including memorials to
WB Yeats and James Joyce. Lunchtime concerts are held here in
the summer.
**✱ TOP CHOICES: PICNIC SPOTS ✱ TOP CHOICES: PARKS ✱ TOP
CHOICES: PLAYGROUNDS ✱ TOP CHOICES: FOR AGES 0–2 ✱ TOP
CHOICES: FOR AGES 2–5 ✱ TOP CHOICES: FOR ENERGETIC KIDS ✱**

## 109 St. Stephen's Green Shopping Centre ⛹ ☕ ♿

St. Stephen's Green, Dublin 2; Tel: 4780888, 6714629 (Dunnes
Stores); E-mail: thegreen@indigo.ie
**Open:** All year; Mon–Sat 9am–6pm (Thur 9pm); Dunnes Stores:
Mon–Sat 9am–7pm (Thur 9pm); Sun/bank holidays 12–6pm ▪
**Suitable for ages:** All ▪ **Car parking:** St. Stephen's Green
Shopping Centre ▪ **Bus routes:** All city centre buses ▪ **Rail
station:** Pearse St ▪ **DART station:** Pearse St.
An airy shopping centre on three levels, mainly filled with fashion
outlets. Dunnes Stores has a decent café, which does cheap kids'
hot or cold lunchboxes. The Dome Café upstairs has a great view
of Grafton Street and St. Stephen's Green, but it can get very busy.
**✱ TOP CHOICES: CHILD FRIENDLY RESTAURANTS ✱**

## 110 Savoy Cinema ♿ €

O'Connell St Upr, Dublin 1 (next to the Gresham Hotel);
Tel: 8748487 (programme info.), 8746000 (advance booking).
**Open:** All year; Mon–Sun; children's programmes before 7pm ▪
**Charge:** Child €5; Adult €6; Off-peak prices given; family ticket
€20 ▪ **Suitable for ages:** 3+ ▪ **Car parking:** Marlborough St car
park ▪ **Bus routes:** All city centre buses ▪ **Rail station:** Connolly ▪

**DART station:** Connolly.

The Savoy is Dublin's largest old-style cinema. It has a big screen and plush red velvet seats, but no kids' club.

**★ TOP CHOICES: FOR AGES 5–10 ★ TOP CHOICES: FOR AGES 10+ ★ TOP CHOICES: FOR TRENDY KIDS ★**

## 111 Screen Cinema ♿ €

D'Olier St, Dublin 2; Tel: 6725500.

**Open:** All year; Mon–Sun matinee and evening performances ■
**Charge:** Child €4.50; Adult €5; Off-peak prices given ■ **Suitable for ages:** 12+ ■ **Car parking:** Temple Bar car park ■ **Bus routes:** All city centre buses.

A classy, old-style cinema, complete with double seats! You can catch the odd blockbuster here, but they don't usually show films for the under-12s.

## 112 Sea Safari ♿ 👶

Dublin City Moorings (opposite Jury's Inn Hotel) on Custom House Quay; Tel: 8061626, 086 3855011; Fax: 8168078; Website: www.seasafari.ie

**Open:** All year; Call for sailing times ■ **Charge:** Child €25; Adult €25; Family €80 (4 persons) ■ **Suitable for ages:** 8+ ■ **Car parking:** Irish Life Centre car park ■ **Bus routes:** All city centre buses ■ **Rail station:** Connolly ■ **DART station:** Connolly.

There are three safaris available, in all-weather rigid inflatable lifeboats with seating: the Eco Safari lasts 90 minutes and explores birds and wildlife around Skerries, Lambay Island and Ireland's Eye; the Thrill Seeker is a one-hour, high-speed ride around Ireland's Eye, Howth, the Baily Lighthouse and Dublin Bay; the Leisure Safari is more relaxed, and is concerned more with culture and heritage from the River Liffey to Malahide. The boats all meet the necessary safety standards and have handrails. Life jackets and waterproof clothing are supplied, but you are advised to wear flat shoes and warm clothing. Under-15s must be accompanied by an adult. You can book the whole boat (a 7-seater for €150, or an 11-seater for €250) as a special birthday treat. For children with disabilities, ring in advance.

**★ TOP CHOICES: PICNIC SPOTS ★ TOP CHOICES: BIRTHDAY PARTY IDEAS ★ TOP CHOICES: FOR AGES 10+ ★ TOP CHOICES: FOR TRENDY KIDS ★**

## 113 Shaw Birthplace €

33 Synge St, Dublin 8 (a short walk from St. Stephen's Green, off

the South Circular Rd); Tel: 4750854; Fax: 8722231;
E-mail: shawhouse@dublintourism.ie;
Website: www.visitdublin.com

**Open:** May–Sep; Mon–Sat 10am–5pm; Sun/bank holidays
11am–5pm; Closed lunchtimes 1–2pm ▪ **Charge:** Child €5; Adult
€5.50; Concessions €8; Family (2 adults and 3/4 children) €15 ▪
**Suitable for ages:** 5+ ▪ **Car parking:** Disk parking on street ▪ **Bus
routes:** 16, 19, 122.

This was the home of George Bernard Shaw, 'author of many
plays'. A restored Victorian house, full of atmosphere and charm,
it includes a drawing room, parlour and children's bedroom, with
Shaw's photographs, letters and documents scattered throughout
the house.

## 114 Smyth's Toys & Computer Games 🛒 ♿

Jervis St, Dublin 1 (around the corner from Penney's, opposite the
Jervis Centre); Tel: 8782878 (store), 1550226677 (info. – 73c per
minute); E-mail: cs@toys.ie; Website: www.toys.ie

**Open:** All year; Mon–Wed 9am–6pm; Thur 9am–9pm; Fri–Sat
9am–6pm; Sun 1–6pm ▪ **Suitable for ages:** All ▪ **Car parking:**
ILAC Centre car park ▪ **Bus routes:** All city centre buses ▪ **Rail
station:** Tara St/Connolly ▪ **DART station:** Tara St/Connolly.

Smyth's are a large chain of toy shops in Ireland. The big
branches, including the Jervis Street one, have huge aisles of toys,
computer games, bicycles, swings, slides and baby equipment.
There are always plenty of toys on display to try out. The Jervis
Street branch has giant Lego *Star Wars* and Harry Potter figures –
the shop is worth visiting for them alone. You can ring the
(premium rate) product information line to check stock
availability, or look it up on the internet.

✱ **TOP CHOICES: FOR AGES 0–2** ✱ **TOP CHOICES: FOR AGES 2–5** ✱

## 115 Taekwon–Do Centre

10 Exchequer St, Dublin 2; Tel: 6710705; E-mail: inta@iol.ie

**Open:** All year; Mon–Fri 6–8pm; Sat 10am–12pm ▪ **Charge:** €13
weekly; €40 monthly for three classes a week ▪ **Suitable for ages:**
7+ ▪ **Bus routes:** All city centre buses.

**Sports:** martial arts

Classes for children are held every evening at 6pm or 7pm, and
also on Saturday mornings.

✱ **TOP CHOICES: HOBBIES/ARTS AND CRAFTS** ✱

## 116 Tivoli Theatre ♿

135 Francis St, Dublin 8 (from Trinity College, go down Dame St towards Christ Church Cathedral. Continue past the cathedral on Cornmarket High St, and turn left for Francis St); Tel: 1890 925100 (Ticketmaster), 4544472.

**Open:** All year; Mon–Sun matinee and evening performances; call for times ■ **Charge:** Child €20; Adult €18.50; Approx. price for performances ■ **Suitable for ages:** 2+ ■ **Car parking:** Pay-per-hour car park beside the theatre ■ **Bus routes:** 51B, 121.

Theatre performances here range from Shakespeare to comedy. There are special productions suitable for children at Christmas, and occasionally during school holiday periods.

## 117 Trinity College (The Dublin Experience and the Book of Kells) 📷 ♿

Trinity College, Dublin 2 (opposite the Central Bank, facing Dame St. The Book of Kells is in the Old Library – go through the main entrance into Parliament Square. The Dublin Experience is in the Arts and Social Sciences Dept., on the right-hand side near the Provost's garden. The Old Library is towards the right of Parliament Square); Tel: 6082320; Website: www.tcd.ie/Library

**Open:** All year; Mon–Sat 9.30am–5.30pm; Sun Oct–May: 12–4.30pm; Sun Jun–Sep: 9.30am–4.30pm; Sunday opening hours also apply on bank holidays, except those falling between May–August, when weekday opening hours apply ■ **Charge:** Entrance to college grounds is free; The Dublin Experience: Under-12s free; Adults €7.50; Concessions €6.50; Family €15; The Book of Kells: Under-12s free; Adults €4.20; Concessions €3.50; Family (2 adults and 4 children) €8.40; Combined tickets to both attractions: Under-12s free; Adults €10.50; Concessions €8.50; Family (2 adults and 4 children) €21 ■ **Suitable for ages:** 7+ ■ **Car parking:** Temple Bar car park ■ **Bus routes:** All city centre buses ■ **Rail station:** Tara St/Pearse St ■ **DART station:** Tara St/Pearse St.

Trinity College, Dublin, is Ireland's premier university. It opened in 1592, and is still used for its original purpose today. There are two main visitor attractions: the Book of Kells, housed in the Old Library, and an audio-visual show, The Dublin Experience. You can get tickets to see them separately or a combined ticket for both.

## 118 UGC Cinemas ♿ €

Parnell Centre, Parnell St, Dublin 1 (behind the ILAC shopping centre); Tel: 8728444; Fax: 8728875;
Website: www.ugccinemas.co.uk
**Open:** All year; Children's programmes: Mon–Sun before 7pm; Kids' Club: Sat 10am ▪ **Charge:** Child €4.25; Adult €5.25; Prices given are for shows before 5pm ▪ **Suitable for ages:** 3+ ▪ **Car parking:** Car park on Parnell St, behind cinemas: pay per hour, Mon–Sat 7.30am–after midnight; Sun 11am–12.30am ▪ **Bus routes:** All city centre buses ▪ **Rail station:** Connolly ▪ **DART station:** Connolly.

A multiplex cinema, including a kids' club at 10am every Saturday, where adults go free when you pay for a full-price children's (under-15) ticket. Booster seats are available, as are infrared receivers to boost the sound to hearing aids.
**✱ TOP CHOICES: BIRTHDAY PARTY IDEAS ✱ TOP CHOICES: FOR TRENDY KIDS ✱**

## 119 Vicar St (Music Venue) ♿

58–59 Thomas St, Dublin 8 (from Trinity College, head straight up Dame St past Christ Church Cathedral, and keep going until you reach Thomas St. Vicar St is opposite the National College of Art and Design); Tel: 1890 925150 (booking info), 4546656; Fax: 4546787; E-mail: office@aikenpromotions.ie;
Website: www.vicarstreet.com
**Open:** All year; Mon–Sun, evening performances usually ▪ **Charge:** Tickets about €33 for a chart-topping band ▪ **Suitable for ages:** 10+ ▪ **Car parking:** Some on street parking outside, or Christ Church car park ▪ **Bus routes:** 78A, 123.

Mainly a venue for larger rock, pop and jazz bands, very occasionally they have concerts suitable for under-18s (check before you book). If you share the same music taste as your teenager (don't cod yourself), this is a good place to bring them to see their favourite band. It is spaciously seated, with state-of-the-art sound and light systems and a licensed bar.
**✱ TOP CHOICES: FOR AGES 10+ ✱ TOP CHOICES: FOR TRENDY KIDS ✱**

## 120 Viking Splash Tour 👤

Bull Alley St, Dublin 2 (beside St. Patrick's Cathedral);
Tel: 8553000; E-mail: viking@esatclear.ie;
Website: www.vikingsplashtours.com

**Open:** Feb–Nov; Mon–Sun, 10 tours a day; call for details ▪
**Charge:** Children (under-13s) €7.50; Adults €13.50; Family ticket
€45 ▪ **Suitable for ages:** 2+ ▪ **Car parking:** Christ Church car
park ▪ **Bus routes:** 50, 54A, 56A.

A great fun tour in a Second-World-War amphibious 'duck' (a
truck that goes in the water), lasting about 90 minutes.
Good-natured drivers give you a commentary (and opinions!) of
sights en route, before you end up in the Grand Canal Harbour.
You have to give a Viking roar as you pass by gobsmacked
pedestrians. Seats are limited and the front ones are the best, so
it's a good idea to book in advance or you may have to wait. No
under-2s, and no buggies are allowed – they're not insured to take
them. You can book up all the seats for a birthday party treat.
✱ TOP CHOICES: BIRTHDAY PARTY IDEAS ✱ TOP CHOICES: FOR AGES
5–10 ✱ TOP CHOICES: FOR AGES 10+ ✱ TOP CHOICES: FOR
ENERGETIC KIDS ✱

## 121 Walton's New School of Music

69 South Great George's St, Dublin 2; Tel: 4781884;
Fax: 4751346; E-mail: info@newschool.ie;
Website: www.newschool.ie
**Open:** Sep–Jun Summer Term June 30–Aug 2; Mon–Thur
10am–10pm; Fri 10am–8pm; Sat 10am–6pm ▪ **Charge:** Music
For Me: 10-week course or 5-week summer course €100;
Beginners Group courses: 10 hours over 10 weeks €125; Guitar
for Teens: 5- or 10-week summer course €125; Ring for details of
private tuition and Leaving Cert courses ▪ **Suitable for ages:** 5+ ▪
**Bus routes:** All city centre buses ▪ **Rail station:** Tara St ▪ **DART
station:** Tara St.

Individual or group lessons are available for ages 5+ in traditional
and modern instruments, and also voice. Music For Me gives
5–7-yr-olds and 7–9-yr-olds a fun introduction to music before
choosing an instrument – it runs during the year and also as an
intensive summer course. For teenagers there are guitar and
singing courses, lasting 10 weeks (one hour per week) during the
year and again with a condensed course (two hours per week for
five weeks) in the summer. The school also offers prizes and
scholarships, and runs instrument hire schemes. The building is
very badly laid out for wheelchair access.
✱ TOP CHOICES: SUMMER CAMPS ✱

## 122 Waterways Visitor Centre ♿

Grand Canal Quay, Dublin 2 (off Ringsend end of Pearse St);
Tel: 6777510; Fax: 6777514; Website: www.heritageireland.ie
**Open:** All year; Jun–Sep: Mon–Sun 9.30am–5.30pm; Oct–May:
Wed–Sun 12.30am–5.30pm ▪ **Charge:** Child €1.27; Adult €2.54;
Senior/group (20+) €1.90; Student €1.27; Family €6.35 ▪
**Suitable for ages:** 5+ ▪ **Car parking:** Free ▪ **Bus routes:** 1, 2 ▪
**Rail station:** Pearse St ▪ **DART station:** Pearse St.
An exhibition exploring Ireland's inland waterways, housed in a
modern building overlooking the canal. Attractions include an
interactive audio-visual show and working models showing various
engineering features. Guided tours are available on request.
Wheelchair access is limited to the ground floor.
**✱ TOP CHOICES: FOR INQUISITIVE KIDS ✱**

# Places to eat

## 123 Bad Ass Café 🎱

Crown Alley, Temple Bar, Dublin 2; Tel: 6712596; Fax: 6712596;
E-mail: bad_ass_café@hotmail.com;
Website: www.badasscafe.com
**Open:** All year; Mon–Fri 11.30am until late ▪ **Charge:** Kids eat
from €6; adults €10 ▪ **Suitable for ages:** All ▪ **Car parking:**
Temple Bar car park ▪ **Bus routes:** All city centre buses.
A good, fun pizza place in the heart of Temple Bar, where you
can see your pizza being made in the open kitchen. The burgers
are good too, and for dessert, the ice creams come with lighted
sparklers. Toilets are upstairs. The Bad Ass Café has a bar licence,
and a kids' menu is available. For birthday parties you pay per
person and bring your own cake.
**✱ TOP CHOICES: FOR AGES 5–10 ✱**

## 124 Bewley's Oriental Café, Grafton St 🚼 ♿

78 Grafton St, Dublin 2; Tel: 6776761;
E-mail: manager@graftonst.bewleys.ie; Website: www.bewleys.ie
**Open:** All year; Mon–Thur 7.30am–11pm; Fri–Sat
7.30am–1am; Sun 8am–11pm ▪ **Charge:** Lunch for kids €5;
Adults €7 incl. drinks ▪ **Suitable for ages:** All ▪ **Bus routes:** All
city centre buses ▪ **Rail station:** Tara St/Pearse St ▪ **DART
station:** Tara St/Pearse St.

CITY CENTRE

If you abandoned Bewley's years ago for cooler coffee houses, and places that offer better than bland sausages and lumpy mash, it's time to get re-acquainted. There is now a choice of sandwiches, pannini and wraps (from €5), and even a children's bowl of soup for under €3. Kids' eyes will pop out when they see the size of the cream cakes! Classic and comfy, this branch has waiter service. All branches of Bewley's have spacious seating, easy to negotiate with your buggy, shopping and kids.

## 125 Bewley's Oriental Café, Mary St 🚼 ♿

40 Mary St, Dublin 1 (at the bottom of Henry St); Tel: 6776761; Fax: 6774021; Website: www.bewleys.ie
**Open:** All year; Mon–Sat 7.30am–6pm (Thur 7pm); Sun 12–5pm ■ **Charge:** Lunch for kids €5; Adults €7 incl. drinks ■ **Suitable for ages:** All ■ **Bus routes:** All city centre buses ■ **Rail station:** Connolly ■ **DART station:** Connolly.
Rejoice! This branch of Bewley's has a specially designed children's play area. Gossip with your friends while the children watch a video! The food's not bad either.
✱ TOP CHOICES: FOR AGES 0–2 ✱ TOP CHOICES: FOR AGES 2–5 ✱

## 126 Bewley's Oriental Café, Westmoreland St 🚼 ♿

10/12 Westmoreland St, Dublin 2; Tel: 6776761; Fax: 6774021; E-mail: manager@westst.bewleys.ie; Website: www.bewleys.ie
**Open:** All year; Mon/Wed/Fri/Sat 7.30am–7pm; Thur 7.30am–8.30pm; Sun 8.30am–7pm ■ **Charge:** Lunch for kids €5; Adults €7 incl. drinks ■ **Suitable for ages:** All ■ **Bus routes:** All city centre buses ■ **Rail station:** Tara St ■ **DART station:** Tara St.
An oasis in a strip of fast-food places.

## 127 Butler's Chocolate Café 🔲 €

51a Grafton St, Dublin 2, Tel: 6710599; 24 Wicklow St, Dublin 2, Tel: 6710591; 9 Chatham St, Dublin 2, Tel: 6726333; 18 Nassau St, Dublin 2, Tel: 6710772.
**Open:** All year; Mon–Fri 8am–7pm (Thur 9pm); Sat 9am–7pm; Sun 11am–6pm ■ **Charge:** Coffee from €2.50, Sundaes €4.55 ■ **Suitable for ages:** 4+ ■ **Car parking:** Drury St car park ■ **Bus routes:** All city centre buses ■ **Rail station:** Tara St ■ **DART station:** Tara St.
If you need a quick coffee break while you're shopping in the city centre, a Butler's café is the place to go. They are all quite small,

drink-up-and-go places, but good for a pit stop. Children can have a fabulous hot chocolate or chocolate sundae, and adults get a gorgeous chocolate with their coffee. It's brilliant for Easter eggs too.

**★ TOP CHOICES: FOR TRENDY KIDS ★**

## 128 Captain America's

44 Grafton St, Dublin 2 (at the St. Stephen's Green end of Grafton St); Tel: 6715266; Fax: 6715213;
Website: www.captainamericas.com
**Open:** All year; Mon–Sun 12pm–12am ▪ **Charge:** Main courses under €5 for kids; Adults from €10 ▪ **Suitable for ages:** All ▪ **Car parking:** St. Stephen's Green Shopping Centre car park or Royal College of Surgeons car park ▪ **Bus routes:** All city centre buses ▪ **Rail station:** Pearse St ▪ **DART station:** Pearse St.
Apparently Brad Pitt and Showaddywaddy have eaten here! A 30-year-old establishment, up a steep staircase, serving steaks, burgers, chicken, seafood and veggie food, all served with fries, and big portions at that. If you're being a goody-goody, you can get an okay salad. There's a children's menu available, and clowns may even appear on a Sunday. Licensed to sell alcohol. For birthday parties, you pay per child and a cake can be arranged.

**★ TOP CHOICES: CHILD FRIENDLY RESTAURANTS ★**

## 129 Clery's Rooftop Café

Clery's Department Store, 18/27 Lwr O'Connell St, Dublin 1; Tel: 8786000.
**Open:** All year; Mon–Wed 9am–5pm; Thur 9am–6pm; Fri 9am–5.30pm; Sat 9am–5pm ▪ **Charge:** Kids eat for €5; Adults about €10, incl. drink ▪ **Suitable for ages:** All ▪ **Car parking:** Arnott's car park ▪ **Bus routes:** All city centre buses ▪ **Rail station:** Connolly/Tara St ▪ **DART station:** Connolly/Tara St.
If your little ones enjoyed the movie *Mary Poppins*, they'll love this restaurant, with its rooftop view of Dublin. The food is standard department-store fare, with just one option for kids, but it's very cheap, and good for a hot breakfast if you have to come into town early.

**★ TOP CHOICES: FOR AGES 2–5 ★**

## 130 Eddie Rockets Diner

7 Sth Anne St, Dublin 2, Tel: 6797340; 77/78 Dame St, Dublin 2, Tel: 6703893; 52 Lwr O'Connell St, Tel: 8730611; Wexford St,

Tel: 4752077; Contact: Valerie Crowley for party bookings, Tel: 6797340; Website: www.eddierockets.ie

**Open:** All year; Sun–Wed 9am–1am; Thur–Sat 9am–4am ▪ **Charge:** Kids from €5 for meal and drink; adults €10 for burger, fries and drink ▪ **Suitable for ages:** All ▪ **Bus routes:** All city centre buses ▪ **Rail station:** Tara St ▪ **DART station:** Tara St.

Eddie Rockets is a chain of American-diner-style cafés, famous for their burgers and fries and serving much better milkshakes and malts than the bigger fast-food chains. There's a kids' menu, and kids get a free goodie bag with their meal. All of these branches have booths for sitting in, but they also have high chairs. Kids love it. Special arrangements can be made for birthday parties – call for details.

✶ **TOP CHOICES: BIRTHDAY PARTY IDEAS** ✶ **TOP CHOICES: FOR AGES 10+** ✶

## 131 Epicurean Food Hall

Lwr Liffey St, Dublin 1.

**Open:** All year; Mon–Wed 9.30am–5.30pm; Thur–Fri 9.30am–7pm; Sat 9.30am–5pm ▪ **Charge:** Lunch, including a drink, from €5 per person ▪ **Suitable for ages:** All ▪ **Car parking:** Jervis Centre car park ▪ **Bus routes:** All city centre buses ▪ **Rail station:** Tara St ▪ **DART station:** Tara St.

The Epicurean Food Hall has a selection of take-away counters, with a seating area in the middle. Even a small child will love the choice – from Greek kebabs to Mexican tortillas, Indian samosas and even Irish soup and soda bread. If all else fails, there's Southern Fried Chicken boxes. There is great food to be had here, but this is not a place to hang about, as the tables are small and seat only four, and it can get very crowded at lunchtime. You can ask for a high chair. The service is quick (except the Mexican stall) and the food is very cheap too. The toilets have a baby-change facility, but they can be quite scruffy.

✶ **TOP CHOICES: FOR AGES 10+** ✶ **TOP CHOICES: FOR TRENDY KIDS** ✶

## 132 Lemon Café

66 South William St, Dublin 2; Tel: 6729044; Fax: 6729044; E-mail: info@lemonco.com; Website: www.lemonco.com

**Open:** All year; Mon/Wed/Fri 8am–7.30pm; Thur 8am–9.30pm; Sat 9am–7.30pm; Sun 10am–6pm ▪ **Charge:** Crêpes under €4 ▪ **Suitable for ages:** 3+ ▪ **Bus routes:** All city centre buses ▪ **Rail station:** Tara St ▪ **DART station:** Tara St.

Super pancakes, savoury or sweet. Kids go for the Smartie-filled ones. The only drawback is that this is a small place – too small to bring an overloaded buggy. This is so simple, and yet a great alternative to where kids usually want to go.

**★ TOP CHOICES: CHILD FRIENDLY RESTAURANTS ★ TOP CHOICES: FOR AGES 5–10 ★ TOP CHOICES: FOR AGES 10+ ★**

## 133 Milano 🛒 ♿

18 Essex St E, Temple Bar, Dublin 2, Tel: 6707744; 38/39 Lr Ormond Quay, Dublin 2, Tel: 6703384; 38 Dawson St, Dublin 2, Tel: 6707744.

**Open:** All year; Mon–Sun 12pm–12am ▪ **Charge:** Main course €10–15 ▪ **Suitable for ages:** All ▪ **Car parking:** Temple Bar car park ▪ **Bus routes:** All city centre buses ▪ **Rail station:** Pearse St/Tara St ▪ **DART station:** Pearse St/Tara St.

A popular Italian restaurant, which kids will enjoy. The menu is child-friendly – there are pizzas and dough balls, which babies love. The Dawson Street branch has a free crêche on Sundays from 12–5pm. Bliss!

**★ TOP CHOICES: CHILD FRIENDLY RESTAURANTS ★ TOP CHOICES: FOR AGES 0–2 ★ TOP CHOICES: FOR AGES 2–5 ★**

## 134 Odessa Lounge & Grill

13/14 Dame Court, Dublin 2 (near the Stag's Head pub); Tel: 6707634; Fax: 6704195; Website: www.odessa.ie

**Open:** All year; Mon–Thur 5.30–11pm; Fri 7pm–12am; Sat–Sun 12pm–12am ▪ **Charge:** Sunday brunch €15; Homemade burger and fries €12 ▪ **Suitable for ages:** 10+ ▪ **Car parking:** Drury St car park ▪ **Bus routes:** All city centre buses ▪ **Rail station:** Tara St ▪ **DART station:** Tara St.

Not really a child-friendly place at all, but that doesn't stop young couples with small kids turning up, particularly for Sunday brunch. The big sofas downstairs are great for a big crowd getting together, even if the interiors make you feel like you're in a David Lynch movie. The food is really nice, but expensive for what you get.

## 135 TGI Friday 🛒 ♿ 🖼

St. Stephen's Green, Dublin 2 (beside Stephen's Green Shopping Centre); Tel: 4781233; Fax: 4781550.

**Open:** All year; Mon–Sat 12–11.30pm; Sun 12–11pm ▪ **Charge:** Child menu approx. €5.95 incl. drink; Adults from €10 ▪ **Suitable for ages:** All ▪ **Car parking:** Royal College of Surgeons car park ▪

**Bus routes:** All city centre buses ▪ **Rail station:** Pearse St ▪ **DART station:** Pearse St.

An American-style restaurant, serving burgers, steak, fries, etc., but also pasta, wraps and vegetarian options. The staff are brilliant with kids, and are happy to sing 'Happy Birthday' and bring the birthday child a special ice cream sundae with a lighted candle in it.

✱ TOP CHOICES: CHILD FRIENDLY RESTAURANTS ✱ TOP CHOICES: BIRTHDAY PARTY IDEAS ✱ TOP CHOICES: FOR AGES 10+ ✱

## 136 Thunder Road Café 🚼 ♿ 🎈

Fleet St, Dublin 2 (just off Westmoreland St, in Temple Bar);
Tel: 6794057; Fax: 6794057;
Website: www.thunderroadcafe.com
**Open:** All year; Sun–Wed 12–11pm; Thur–Sat 12pm–12am ▪
**Charge:** Kids' menu €5.70 for chips, drink, pizza/burger plus a free gift; Adults eat from €15.50 ▪ **Suitable for ages:** All ▪ **Car parking:** Drury St car park ▪ **Bus routes:** All city centre buses ▪ **Rail station:** Tara St ▪ **DART station:** Tara St.

For little Hell's Angels. A biker-themed restaurant which is so popular, you need to book a week in advance for a table at weekends and a day in advance during the week. The menu has chicken, steak, burgers, and so on. For birthday children, the staff will bring a dessert with a lighted candle and sing 'Happy Birthday'.

✱ TOP CHOICES: CHILD FRIENDLY RESTAURANTS ✱ TOP CHOICES: BIRTHDAY PARTY IDEAS ✱ TOP CHOICES: FOR AGES 10+ ✱ TOP CHOICES: FOR TRENDY KIDS ✱

## 137 Trentuno 🚼 ♿

Wicklow St, Dublin 2; Tel: 6774190.
**Open:** All year; Mon–Wed 12–11pm; Thur–Sat 12pm–12am; Sun 1–9pm ▪ **Charge:** Child menu from €6.25 for pizza; Adult from €10 for pizza/pasta ▪ **Suitable for ages:** All ▪ **Car parking:** Drury St car park ▪ **Bus routes:** All city centre buses ▪ **Rail station:** Tara St ▪ **DART station:** Tara St.

A family-friendly Italian restaurant, with good food and lovely staff. The menu includes pizza, pasta and steak. Children's portions are available.

✱ TOP CHOICES: CHILD FRIENDLY RESTAURANTS ✱

## 138 Wagamama

South King St, Dublin 2; Tel: 4782152;
Website: www.wagamama.com
**Open:** All year; Mon–Sat 12–11pm; Sun 12–10pm ▪ **Charge:**
Main courses about €10– €15 ▪ **Suitable for ages:** 3+ ▪ **Car
parking:** Royal College of Surgeons car park ▪ **Bus routes:** All city
centre buses.

A Japanese noodle bar, which offers plain noodles or side dishes
for children. They give out crayons and colouring paper for kids
before the food arrives. There's no wheelchair access, as it is
downstairs.

**★ TOP CHOICES: CHILD FRIENDLY RESTAURANTS ★**

## 139 Yamamori Noodles 🛒 ♿

71/72 South Great George's St, Dublin 2 (across the road from
George's St Arcade); Tel: 4755001; Fax: 4755001.
**Open:** All year; Sun–Wed 12.30–11pm; Thur–Sat
12.30–11.30pm ▪ **Charge:** Main courses approx. €15 ▪ **Suitable
for ages:** All ▪ **Car parking:** Drury St car park ▪ **Bus routes:** All
city centre buses.

The staff here are just great and the food – Japanese noodle and
rice dishes – is just as good. There is no kids' menu, but they can
get a small portion or share a plate.

# St Michan's Church
## CHURCH ST, DUBLIN 7

Founded in 1095, St Michan's Church is one of Dublin's most popular sights. Its many features include: a beautiful organ, windows and penitents' pew.
It is mostly renowned for the mummified bodies in the vaults whose preservation has been attributed to the dry atmosphere in the crypt.

Tours available every day (except Sunday)
Nov - Mar, 12.30 - 3.30pm
Apr - Oct, 10.00 - 12.30pm & 2.00 - 4.45pm
Saturday, 10.00 - 1.00pm
Phone: (01) 872 4154

# National Concert Hall
**Education & Community
Outreach Programme**

**Bank of Scotland (Ireland)
"Creation Station"
music, art and dance for children**

**A series of workshops for children, taking place
in August at the National Concert Hall.**

**A whole host of activities for children from 18
months up to 12 years.  On selected workshops
parents are invited to take part too!**

**Activities include:
Music Making
Mask Making
Instrument Making
Creative Dance
Storytelling
Parent & Toddler Workshops**

**From Saturday 9 August to Saturday 30 August**

**To obtain a brochure with further details contact:
Lucy Champion - National Concert Hall
Tel: 01-417 0077
or via email: lucy.champion@nch.ie
or check www.nch.ie/education.htm**

**✳ BANK OF SCOTLAND**
Ireland

**the business people**

# THE NATIONAL
# Wax Museum

Granby Row, Parnell Square. Dublin 1

# The Children's World of Fairytale & Fantasy

Visit the Children's World of Fairytale and Fantasy. This display is truly a joy from children as they wander through the Kingdom of Fairytales to find the magic lamp and the all-powerful genie!

Meet such favourites as Jack and the Beanstalk, Snow White and the Seven Dwarfs, Sleeping Beauty, Robin Hood, Cinderella, Harry Potter, The Simpsons and Star Wars.

Opening hours:
Monday to Saturday - 10am-5:30pm
Sunday - 12pm-5:30pm

THE NATIONAL
PERFORMING
ARTS SCHOOL

# Performing Arts Classes for 2-20 yrs

- Drama
- Funk
- Hip Hop
- Street Dance
- Street Tap
- Musical Theatre
- Singing
- Tap
- Jazz
- Ballet
- Song n' Dance
- Funky Jazz
- Singing for Toddlers

## Phone (01) 668 4035 for a brochure

MON-FRI DURING OFFICE HOURS

NPAS, PO BOX 8943, DUBLIN 4.

Web: www.npas.ie
Email: info@npas.ie

# North Dublin

## Things to do

**140 Ardgillan Castle**

Balbriggan, Co. Dublin (take the N1, Dublin–Belfast road, to Balbriggan. Turn right at Balrothery onto a minor road. Ardgillan main car park is signposted); Tel: 8492212; Fax: 8492194.
**Open:** All year; Apr–Sep: Tue–Sun and bank holidays 11am–6pm; Jul–Aug: Mon–Sun 11am–6pm; Oct–Mar: Tue–Sun and bank holidays 11am–4.30pm ■ **Charge:** Free ■ **Suitable for ages:** All ■ **Car parking:** Free ■ **Bus routes:** 33 ■ **Rail station:** Balbriggan.
Formerly the residence of the Taylor family, this stately home was built in 1738. Set against a coastal background, the house itself is stunning, but it is the gardens that are the real attraction. There are two gardens – the fragrant, walled Rose Garden with its Victorian conservatory, and the large kitchen garden, which supplied cut flowers, herbs, fruit, vegetables and even plants for dyeing and pot-pourri. The house has recently been restored, and two floors are open to the public. The rooms are furnished in the Victorian style, and in the Library there's a secret passageway hidden in the bookshelves. On a nice day, bring a flask and sandwiches, as there are plenty of wild woodland walks with sheltered picnic areas.
✱ TOP CHOICES: PICNIC SPOTS ✱ TOP CHOICES: PARKS ✱ TOP CHOICES: PLAYGROUNDS ✱ TOP CHOICES: FOR AGES 0–2 ✱ TOP CHOICES: FOR AGES 2–5 ✱ TOP CHOICES: FOR ENERGETIC KIDS ✱

**141 AutoDefence Wing Tchun**

Oakwood Community Hall, Jamestown Rd, Finglas East, Co. Dublin; Tel: 8347895.
**Open:** All year; Tue/Thur eves, call for times ■ **Charge:** Child €4 ■ **Suitable for ages:** 6+ ■ **Bus routes:** 19, 19A.
**Sports:** martial arts
Kung Fu classes for children are held on Tuesday and Thursday evenings.

**142 Axis Arts Centre**

Town Centre, Ballymun, Dublin 9 (off the Ballymun Rd, opposite

the Garda station, behind the shopping centre); Tel: 8832100;
Website: www.axis-ballymun.ie
**Open:** All year; Mon–Sun matinee and evening performances; call
for times ▪ **Charge:** Child €5; Adult €8; Approx. price for theatre
performances ▪ **Suitable for ages:** All ▪ **Car parking:** Free ▪ **Bus
routes:** 13, 13A, 17A, 46X, 58X, 103, 104, 220.
A modern arts centre with a fully integrated range of cultural and
social facilities, including training rooms, a theatre, conference
rooms, workshops and performance areas. The theatre stages
seasonal shows suitable for children (panto, dance, etc.). Ballet
and drama classes are available for children, call for details.
★ TOP CHOICES: CHRISTMAS VISITS ★ TOP CHOICES: FOR AGES 5–10
★ TOP CHOICES: FOR IMAGINATIVE KIDS ★

## 143 Balbriggan Beach 🏖

Balbriggan, Co. Dublin (from the city centre, take the M1. Go past
Swords and continue until you see the signs for Balbriggan).
**Open:** Lifeguard: Jun–Sep; Mon–Sun 10am–8pm ▪ **Charge:** Free
▪ **Suitable for ages:** All ▪ **Rail station:** Balbriggan.
**Sports:** swimming
Balbriggan has a traditional fishing harbour, overlooked by a
Martello tower. Its lovely sandy beach is popular with all age
groups. There's a large colony of seals who inhabit the coastline
and can be seen regularly around the harbour.

## 144 Balbriggan Public Library 📝 🖥

George's Sq, Balbriggan, Co. Dublin; Tel: 8411128;
Fax: 8412101; E-mail: balbrigganlibrary@yahoo.co.uk;
Website: www.iol.ie/~fincolib/la.htm
**Open:** All year; Mon/Wed 10am–1pm, 2–5pm; Tue/Thur
2–8.30pm; alternate Fri and Sat 10am–1pm, 2–5pm; bank
holiday weekends closed Sat and Mon ▪ **Charge:** Free ▪ **Suitable
for ages:** All ▪ **Car parking:** Free ▪ **Bus routes:** 33 ▪ **Rail station:**
Ballbriggan.
Regular activities here include a Junior Creative Writers Group, on
Thursdays at 7pm. Storytime and various arts-and-crafts activities
are held throughout the year. Call for times and book in advance.
★ TOP CHOICES: FOR AGES 5–10 ★

## 145 Baldoyle Badminton Centre

Unit 4, Baldoyle Industrial Estate, Dublin 13; Tel: 8393355
(Margaret Corcoran); E-mail: margaretcorcoran2@eircom.net

**Open:** All year; Wed 6–8pm, Sat am ▪ **Charge:** Prices given on request ▪ **Suitable for ages:** 8+ ▪ **Bus routes:** 102, 105, 129, 32, 32A, 32B.
**Sports:** badminton
Children's badminton classes are held on Wednesday evenings from 6–8pm, and also on Saturday mornings.

## 146 The Ballet School, Raheny

238 Howth Rd, Dublin 5; Tel: 8339697.
**Open:** Call for new term times ▪ **Charge:** Fees on request ▪ **Suitable for ages:** 4+ ▪ **Bus routes:** 31, 31A/B, 32, 32A/B/X ▪ **DART station:** Raheny.
Contact the teacher for times and availability.

## 147 Ballymun Library

Ballymun Rd, Dublin 9 (after the junction with Glasnevin Ave); Tel: 8421890; Website: www.iol.ie/dublincitylibrary
**Open:** All year; Mon–Thur 10am–8pm; Fri–Sat 10am–5pm ▪ **Charge:** Free ▪ **Suitable for ages:** All ▪ **Car parking:** Free ▪ **Bus routes:** 13, 13A, 17A, 19A, 103, 220.
A children's art class is held on Saturdays at 2.30pm. Seasonal arts-and-crafts activities, plus reading events, are organised throughout the year.
**✷ TOP CHOICES: FOR AGES 5–10 ✷**

## 148 Ballymun Swimming Pool

Ballymun Shopping Centre, Dublin 11 (the pool is on the far side of the car park from the Garda station); Tel: 8421368.
**Open:** All year; Summer: Mon/Wed–Thur 4–7.40pm; Sat 10am–12.30pm, 2–5.30pm; Sun 10.30am–1pm; Rest of year: Mon–Fri 11am–7.30pm ▪ **Charge:** Child €1.80; Adult €3.60 ▪ **Suitable for ages:** All ▪ **Car parking:** Free ▪ **Bus routes:** 13, 13A, 17A.
**Sports:** swimming
A Dublin City Council pool, which is hired out to schools for most of the year. It is open to the public on weekends and weekday afternoons, and has long opening hours during the holidays. The pool has a hoist for disabled swimmers, but you need to call in advance for it to be set up.

## 149 Barrington, Marie, Speech and Drama

26 Iona Crescent, Glasnevin, Dublin 9; Tel: 8305389.
**Open:** Contact the teacher to arrange times ▪ **Charge:** Fees vary
for individual circumstances ▪ **Suitable for ages:** 7+.
Speech-and-drama classes for ages 7+, with exams taken.

## 150 Barry, Billie, Stage School

CYMC, Philibsborough Ave, Fairview, Dublin 3 (opposite Fairview
Church); Tel: 8332522.
**Open:** New students intake Sep and Jan; Daily classes available
outside school hours depending on age group ▪ **Charge:** €25 for
4-week trial period (45 minutes/1 hour per week) ▪ **Suitable for
ages:** 4+ ▪ **Car parking:** Free ▪ **Bus routes:** 20B, 27, 27B/C/X,
29A, 31, 31A/B, 32, 32A/B/X, 42A ▪ **DART station:** Clontarf Rd.
Samantha Mumba, Bryan McFadden (of Westlife) and Mikey
Graham (of Boyzone) all trained at this well-known stage school,
famous for supplying talent to the Christmas pantomime at the
Gaiety Theatre. Children do a four-week trial period, to see if they
enjoy the experience. They learn drama, dance, musical theatre
and voice training (for over-8s). One of the longest-established
stage schools in Dublin.
**✱ TOP CHOICES: FOR IMAGINATIVE KIDS ✱**

## 151 Basketball

Irish Basketball Association, National Basketball Arena, Tymon,
Dublin 24; Tel: 4590211; Fax: 4590212; Website: www.iba.ie
**Open:** Oct–Mar; Call for individual clubs' meeting days and times
▪ **Charge:** Annual fees range from €45 to €200; Basketball strip
approx. €50 ▪ **Suitable for ages:** 10+.
Most of the clubs listed below run junior teams and leagues; call
for details. Where available, the venues have been listed, but
these can change, so always check. The association also runs a
primary school programme. Competitive teams start at under-11.
Most teams require that you buy a strip to begin with, which can
cost around €50.

## 152 ABFRC Basketball Club

ABFRC Centre, Artane, Dublin 5; Contact: Bernie; Tel: 8379094.
**Open:** All year; Call for club's meeting days and times ▪ **Charge:**
Membership fees and basketball strip price on request ▪ **Suitable
for ages:** 10+ ▪ **Bus routes:** 27, 42, 42B, 127, 129.

## 153 Corinthians Basketball Club

Mount Temple School, Malahide Rd, Dublin 3; Contact: Comets Basketball Club (Paul Ryan); Tel: 8830630.
**Open:** All year; Call for meeting days and times ▪ **Charge:** Membership fees and basketball strip price on request ▪ **Suitable for ages:** 11+ ▪ **Bus routes:** 20B, 27, 27B/C, 42, 42B, 43, 103, 104, 127, 129.

## 154 Crusaders Basketball Club

Kilmore West, Coolock, Dublin 17 (opposite Northside Shopping Centre); Contact: Michelle O'Rourke; Tel: 8476383.
**Open:** All year; Call for meeting days and times ▪ **Charge:** Child €2; Membership fees and basketball strip price on request ▪ **Suitable for ages:** 11+ ▪ **Bus routes:** 17A, 27.

## 155 Killester Basketball Club

St. Finan's, Dublin Rd, Sutton, Co. Dublin; Trinity Sports Centre, Donaghmede, Co. Dublin; Contact: Mary Keogh; Tel: 8327664; E-mail: killesterbc@hotmail.com; Website: www.killester.com
**Open:** All year; Call for meeting days and times ▪ **Charge:** Membership fees and basketball strip price on request ▪ **Suitable for ages:** 10+ ▪ **Bus routes:** 29A, 31, 31A/B, 127 ▪ **DART station:** Sutton.

## 156 Kilsaran Basketball Club

Gormanston College, Gormanston, Co. Meath; Contact: Anne Caldwell; Tel: (042) 937·2012 (Anne Caldwell), (042) 9336892 (Terry Doherty).
**Open:** All year; Call for meeting days and times ▪ **Charge:** Membership fees and basketball strip price on request ▪ **Suitable for ages:** 10+ ▪ **Rail station:** Gormanston.

## 157 Malahide Basketball Club

Malahide Community School, Broomfield, Malahide, Co. Dublin; Contact: Jean Craddock; Tel: 8408755.
**Open:** All year; Call for meeting days and times ▪ **Charge:** Membership fees and basketball strip price on request ▪ **Suitable for ages:** 10+ ▪ **Bus routes:** 32A, 42, 102, 105, 230 ▪ **Rail station:** Malahide ▪ **DART station:** Malahide.

## 156 Mercy College Basketball Club

Mercy College, Coolock, Dublin 17; Contact: Annette Ingle;

Tel: 8318328.
**Open:** All year; Call for meeting days and times ▪ **Charge:**
Membership fees and basketball strip price on request ▪ **Suitable for ages:** 10+ ▪ **Bus routes:** 17A, 27.

## 157 Rangers Basketball Club

Portmarknock Sports & Leisure Centre, Blackwood Lane,
Carrickhill, Portmarnock, Co. Dublin; Contact: Donald Robinson;
Tel: 8453072.
**Open:** All year; Call for meeting days and times ▪ **Charge:**
Membership fees and basketball strip price on request ▪ **Suitable for ages:** 10+ ▪ **Bus routes:** 32, 32A, 102, 230 ▪ **Rail station:**
Portmarnock.

## 158 Swords/Fingal Basketball Club

St. Finian's Community College, Swords, Co. Dublin; Contact:
Marie Crummy; Tel: 8402488.
**Open:** All year; Call for meeting days and times ▪ **Charge:**
Membership fees and basketball strip price on request ▪ **Suitable for ages:** 11+ ▪ **Bus routes:** 33A/B, 41, 41A/B, 230.

## 159 Tolka Rovers Basketball Club

Tolka Rovers Complex, Glasnevin, Dublin 9; Contact: Geraldine
Elliot; Tel: 8201382.
**Open:** All year; Call for meeting days and times ▪ **Charge:**
Membership fees and basketball strip price on request ▪ **Suitable for ages:** 10+ ▪ **Bus routes:** 13A, 19, 134.

## 160 Belcamp Park 🚼 ♿ 🧎 🚻

Coolock, Dublin 17 (between the Clonshaugh Rd and the M50
link road in Clonshaugh); Tel: 8336262, 8483739;
Website: www.dublincity.ie/parks
**Open:** All year; Mon–Fri 8.30am–dusk; Sat–Sun 9.30am–dusk ▪
**Charge:** Free ▪ **Suitable for ages:** All ▪ **Car parking:** On-street
parking ▪ **Bus routes:** 748.
**Sports:** basketball, cycling, gaelic football, golf, hurling, soccer,
tennis, pitch-and-putt
A 25-hectare park with a significant range of mature trees. There is
plenty of space here for walking, and a number of playing fields.
Dublin Public Parks Tennis runs here during the summer months.

## 161 Belgrove Football Club

Mount Prospect Ave, Clontarf, Dublin 3; Tel: 8331296.
**Open:** Sep–May ▪ **Suitable for ages:** 7+ ▪ **Bus routes:** 130.
**Sports:** soccer

## 162 Birmingham, Audrey, Irish Dancing

Cabra West Parish Youth Service, St. Finbarr's National School,
Kilkieran Rd, Cabra, Dublin 7; Tel: 8380734.
**Open:** All year; Thur 7–8.30pm; Sat 11am–12.30pm ▪ **Charge:**
€5 per 90-minute group class ▪ **Suitable for ages:** 4+ ▪ **Car
parking:** Free ▪ **Bus routes:** 120, 121, 122.
Irish dancing classes for all ages. Children take part in competitions
and can take exams when they are ready.

## 163 Blackheath Archers

Indoor: Irish Wheelchair Association, Sports Hall, Blackheath Ave,
Clontarf, Dublin 3; Outdoor: Sportslink, Furry Park, Cloughran,
Co. Dublin; Contact: Pauline Conroy; Tel: 4057453.
**Open:** All year; Call for current meeting times ▪ **Suitable for
ages:** 10+.
**Sports:** archery
✱ **TOP CHOICES: HOBBIES/ARTS AND CRAFTS** ✱

## 164 Bohemians Football Club

Dalymount Park, Dublin 7; Tel: 8680923; Fax: 8686460;
E-mail: bohemians@eircom.net; Website: www.bohemians.ie
**Open:** Sep–May ▪ **Suitable for ages:** 7+ ▪ **Bus routes:** 10, 120,
134, 19, 19A, 38.
**Sports:** soccer

## 165 The Botanic Art School ✎

28a Prospect Ave, Glasnevin, Dublin 9 (off Botanic Rd, near the
Botanic Gardens); Tel: 8304720.
**Open:** School holidays; Mon–Fri ▪ **Charge:** €120 for a 5-day
course ▪ **Suitable for ages:** 7–12 ▪ **Bus routes:** 13, 19, 19A, 134.
Five-day art and drama workshops for 7–12-yr-olds, costing €120,
run during school holidays.
✱ **TOP CHOICES: HOBBIES/ARTS AND CRAFTS** ✱

## 166 Boxing

Irish Amateur Boxing Association, National Stadium, South
Circular Rd, Dublin 8; Tel: 4733192; E-mail: iaba@eircom.net
**Open:** All year ▪ **Charge:** Most clubs charge €1 or €2 per week ▪
**Suitable for ages:** 11+.
Boxing clubs usually take children from 11 years old. Parents must
sign for permission for them to join, and all children must undergo
a medical examination and wear protective headgear. All boxing
clubs listed have Leinster Council IABA affiliation for 2002/2003.
Call for locations, as these can change.

### 167 Arbour Hill Boxing Club

Call for locations as these can change; Contact: Ronnie Woods;
Tel: 8382210.
**Open:** All year; Call for current meeting times ▪ **Suitable for
ages:** 11+ ▪ **Bus routes:** 120.

### 168 Baldoyle Boxing Club

Call for locations as these can change; Contact: Bert Wade;
Tel: 086 4096420.
**Open:** All year; Call for current meeting times ▪ **Suitable for
ages:** 11+ ▪ **Bus routes:** 127, 29A.

### 169 Ballymun Boxing Club

Call for locations as these can change; Contact: Noel Doran;
Tel: 8424115.
**Open:** All year; Call for current meeting times ▪ **Suitable for
ages:** 11+ ▪ **Bus routes:** 13, 13A, 17A, 220.

### 170 Baycity Boxing Club

Call for locations as these can change; Contact: Patrick Morrissey;
Tel: 8471863.
**Open:** All year; Call for current meeting times ▪ **Suitable for
ages:** 11+.

### 171 Bracken Boxing Club, Balbriggan

Call for locations as these can change; Contact: Brendan Purtill;
Tel: 8412815.
**Open:** All year; Call for current meeting times ▪ **Suitable for
ages:** 11+ ▪ **Bus routes:** 33, 33A.

### 172 Cabra Panthers Boxing Club

Call for locations as these can change; Contact: Maureen Reid;
Tel: 8743439.

**Open:** All year; Call for current meeting times ▪ **Suitable for
ages:** 11+.

### 173 Darndale Boxing Club

Call for locations as these can change; Contact: Joe Lawlor;
Tel: 8486618.

**Open:** All year; Call for current meeting times ▪ **Suitable for
ages:** 11+.

### 174 Dublin City Vocational Schools Boxing Club

Call for locations as these can change; Contact: Jayne McGoworn;
Tel: 8373866 (Joe Vaughan).

**Open:** All year; Call for current meeting times ▪ **Suitable for
ages:** 11+.

### 175 Fingal Boxing Academy

Call for locations as these can change; Contact: Noel Coady;
Tel: 8405372.

**Open:** All year; Call for current meeting times ▪ **Suitable for
ages:** 11+.

### 176 Glasnevin Boxing Club

Call for locations as these can change; Contact: Donal Quinn;
Tel: 8346094.

**Open:** All year; Call for current meeting times ▪ **Suitable for
ages:** 11+.

### 177 Glin Amateur Boxing Club

Call for locations as these can change; Contact: John Moore;
Tel: 8375790.

**Open:** All year; Call for current meeting times ▪ **Suitable for
ages:** 11+.

### 178 Phibsboro Boxing Club

Call for locations as these can change; Contact: Paddy Delaney;
Tel: 8783373.

DUBLIN FOR KIDS

**Open:** All year; Call for current meeting times ▪ **Suitable for ages:** 11+.

### 179 Portmarnock Boxing Club

Call for locations as these can change; Contact: Robert Redmond; Tel: 8460760.

**Open:** All year; Call for current meeting times ▪ **Suitable for ages:** 11+.

### 180 St. Brigid's Boxing Club, Bettystown

Call for locations as these can change; Contact: Gary Keegan; Tel: (041) 9827719, 087 2758906.

**Open:** All year; Call for current meeting times ▪ **Suitable for ages:** 11+.

### 181 St. Luke's Boxing Club, Coolock

Call for locations as these can change; Contact: John Mohan; Tel: 8478535.

**Open:** All year; Call for current meeting times ▪ **Suitable for ages:** 11+.

### 182 St. Pappin's Boxing Club, Poppintree

Call for locations as these can change; Contact: Jimmy Flynn; Tel: 8427176.

**Open:** All year; Call for current meeting times ▪ **Suitable for ages:** 11+.

### 183 St. Saviour's Olympic Boxing Club, Santry

Call for locations as these can change; Contact: Jimmy Flynn; Tel: 8423458 (Martin Power).

**Open:** All year; Call for current meeting times ▪ **Suitable for ages:** 11+.

### 184 Swords Boxing Club

Call for locations as these can change; Contact: Nicky O'Callaghan; Tel: 8406225.

**Open:** All year; Call for current meeting times ▪ **Suitable for ages:** 11+.

## 185 Browne, Lorraine (Music Teacher)

Swords, Co. Dublin; Tel: 8900143.
**Open:** All year; Class times on request ▪ **Charge:** Fees on request
▪ **Suitable for ages:** 5+.
Lorraine Browne gives tuition in piano and electric keyboards. She teaches a variety of styles, including classical, jazz, traditional, world and pop music. Exam preparation is provided for RIAM, ABRSM, GSMD, LCM, TLC, LSM and Junior and Leaving certificates.

## 186 Brushstrokes Art School

7 Marino Mart, Fairview, Dublin 3; Tel: 8335955;
E-mail: brushstrokes@eircom.net
**Open:** 10-week terms of 1 hour per week, plus all-day workshops during the year; Mon–Fri afternoons; Sat daytime ▪ **Charge:** €63.40 per 10-week term ▪ **Suitable for ages:** 6–12 ▪ **Bus routes:** 20B, 29A, 31, 32, 130 ▪ **DART station:** Clontarf.
Brushstrokes Art School hosts art classes designed to encourage creativity while introducing more structured techniques. Children start off on water-based materials (included in the fees) before moving on to using oils (at an extra cost).
✸ TOP CHOICES: HOBBIES/ARTS AND CRAFTS ✸ TOP CHOICES: FOR IMAGINATIVE KIDS ✸

## 187 Cabra Library

Navan Rd, Dublin 7 (near McDonalds); Tel: 8691414;
Fax: 8691412; Website: www.iol.ie/dublincitylibrary
**Open:** All year; Mon–Thur 10am–8pm; Fri–Sat 10am–5pm ▪
**Suitable for ages:** All ▪ **Car parking:** Free ▪ **Bus routes:** 37, 38, 38A, 39, 39A, 70, 70X, 122.
Regular activities include a Junior Book Club and Storytelling (call for days and times). The Parents and Toddlers Group meets on Tuesday and Thursday mornings, 10.30–11.30am. Seasonal arts-and-crafts activities, plus reading events, are organised throughout the year.
✸ TOP CHOICES: FOR AGES 0–2 ✸ TOP CHOICES: FOR AGES 2–5 ✸

## 188 Cadwell, Cora, School Of Dancing

Annagh, 607 Howth Rd, Raheny, Dublin 5; Tel: 8313752.
**Open:** All year; Classes are held outside school hours and at the weekends, according to age/experience ▪ **Charge:** €4 for 1-hour

group class ■ **Suitable for ages:** 3+ ■ **Car parking:** On-street parking ■ **Bus routes:** 31, 31A, 32, 32A, 32B.
Irish dancing classes from ages 3+, including participation in exams and competitions.

✱ **TOP CHOICES: HOBBIES/ARTS AND CRAFTS** ✱

## 189 Casino Marino

Malahide Rd, Dublin 3 (5km from the city centre, off the Malahide Rd, first turn left after Griffith Avenue); Tel: 8331618; Fax: 8332636.
**Open:** Guided tours Feb–Nov; Feb–Mar: Sun–Thur 12–4pm; Apr: Sun–Thur 12–5pm; May: Mon–Sun 10am–5pm; Jun–Oct: Mon–Sun 10am–5.00pm; Nov: Sun–Thur 12–4pm ■ **Charge:** Child €1.25; Adult €2.75; Group/senior citizen €2; Student €1.25; Family €7 ■ **Suitable for ages:** 2+ ■ **Car parking:** Free ■ **Bus routes:** 20A/B, 27, 27A/B, 42, 42C, 123 ■ **Rail station:** Clontarf Rd.
All children will enjoy exploring this Dr Who's 'tardis' of a building. The Casino is considered to be one of the finest 18th-century neoclassical buildings in Europe. It's a true folly, with 16 finely decorated rooms, including a Zodiac Room – so called because the domed ceiling has the signs of the zodiac arranged around it. Outside there are smiling stone lions, kitchen and ornamental gardens, and inside there is a secret tunnel. Access is by guided tour only, and there are stairs to climb.

✱ **TOP CHOICES: FOR AGES 5–10** ✱ **TOP CHOICES: FOR INQUISITIVE KIDS** ✱

## 190 Charleville Lawn Tennis Club

Whitworth Rd, Dublin 9; Contact: Marie MacCumhaill; Tel: 8304149.
**Open:** All year; Mon–Sun 10am–10pm; Children must be off courts by 7pm; Call for details of this year's summer camp dates ■ **Charge:** €350 family membership or €70 per child; Tennis coaching fees are extra; Summer camp fees on request ■ **Suitable for ages:** 6+ ■ **Car parking:** Free ■ **Bus routes:** 13A, 40, 40A/B/C.
**Sports:** tennis
This club has new Savannah (or sand) tennis courts. It has an active children's section, with tennis coaching camps during most school holidays. Membership is required, and coaching costs extra.

✱ **TOP CHOICES: SPORTS FACILITIES** ✱ **TOP CHOICES: ART/CRAFT ACTIVITIES** ✱

## 191 Clontarf Lawn Tennis Club

Oulton Rd, Clontarf Rd, Dublin 3 (off Clontarf Rd); Contact: Jean Strange; Tel: 8339782.

**Open:** All year; Mon–Sun 9am–10pm; Children allowed up to 6pm; Call for details of this year's summer camp dates ▪ **Charge:** Junior membership €100; Tennis coaching fees are extra; Summer camp fees on request ▪ **Suitable for ages:** 5+ ▪ **Car parking:** Free ▪ **Bus routes:** 130, 29A ▪ **DART station:** Killester.

**Sports:** tennis

This club has a very active children's section. They do 'round robins' (where players are challenged by other players until they are beaten and then the winner takes over) and short tennis (tennis played within the serving lines) for little ones. Inter-club tennis is run for the more competitive player. They also run summer camps. Membership is required, and coaching costs extra.

★ TOP CHOICES: HOBBIES/ARTS AND CRAFTS ★ TOP CHOICES: SUMMER CAMPS ★

## 192 Clontarf Rugby Football Club

Clontarf, Dublin 5; Contact: Ronan McCoy; Tel: 4961600, 8332621 (office); E-mail: mccoyclan@eircom.net

**Open:** Sep–Apr ▪ **Suitable for ages:** 6+ ▪ **Bus routes:** 103, 104, 130 ▪ **DART station:** Clontarf.

**Sports:** rugby

## 193 Clontarf School of Music

6 Marino Mart, Fairview, Dublin 3; Tel: 8330936.

**Open:** Sep–Jun; Classes on weekdays until 10pm; Sat all day ▪ **Charge:** Costs vary from term to term; Call for details ▪ **Suitable for ages:** 3+ ▪ **Car parking:** On-street parking ▪ **Bus routes:** 20B, 27, 27B/C/X, 29A, 31, 31A/B, 32, 32A/B/X, 42A ▪ **DART station:** Clontarf.

Individual and group lessons are given here in traditional instruments. The school also runs an Introduction to Music course for 3–6-yr-olds.

## 194 Coláiste Íde Sports Complex ♿

Cardiffsbridge Rd, Finglas, Dublin 11 (follow the dual carriageway past Glasnevin cemetery. After you pass the pub Gleeson the Finglas on the right, take the next left. Follow the road through

two sets of traffic lights, turn left and the centre is on your left);
Tel: 8362340; Fax: 8347242; E-mail: leisurepoint@ide.cdvec.ie
**Open:** All Year; Mon–Sun 10am–5pm ▪ **Charge:** Child €2; Entry
fee to classes and Saturday morning kids' club ▪ **Suitable for ages:**
5+ ▪ **Car parking:** Free ▪ **Bus routes:** 40, 17A.
**Sports:** basketball, gymnastics
This is mainly an adult complex, but children's classes are run
during the week and on Saturday mornings in gymnastics and
dance. There is also a two-hour Saturday morning kids' club, 'Club
Active', for 5–12-yr-olds, which is mostly fun and games.

## 195 Conaghan, Dorothy (Music Teacher)

Malahide, Co. Dublin; Tel: 8451666;
E-mail: ydsymposium@eircom.net
**Open:** All year; Class times on request ▪ **Charge:** Fees on request
▪ **Suitable for ages:** 12+.
Violin, viola and cello tuition are on offer from Dorothy
Conaghan. Classical and Suzuki methods are taught, alongside
conventional teaching methods. Woodwind is also taught, and
students can be prepared for ABRSM and LCM exams.

## 196 Coolock Library 🛒 ♿ ✎ 🖥

Barryscourt Rd, Dublin 17 (near the Stardust Memorial Park);
Tel: 8477781; Website: www.iol.ie/dublincitylibrary
**Open:** All year; Mon–Thur 10am–8pm; Fri–Sat 10am–5pm ▪
**Charge:** Free ▪ **Suitable for ages:** All ▪ **Car parking:** Free ▪ **Bus
routes:** 17A, 27, 27A/B, 101.
Regular activities include: Children's Art Class (Sat 11.30am),
Happy Hour (play and storytelling for 3–5-yr-olds, Thur
10.15–11.15am), Magic Wardrobe Bookclub (first Wed of every
month, 3.30pm). Other seasonal arts-and-crafts and reading
events for children are organised throughout the year.
**★ TOP CHOICES: FOR AGES 2–5 ★**

## 197 Daniels, Nicola (Music Teacher)

Skerries, Co. Dublin; Tel: 8492654, 086 8140689.
**Open:** All year; Class times on request ▪ **Charge:** Fees on request
▪ **Suitable for ages:** 6+.
Nicola Daniels gives tuition in classical, world and jazz piano and
electric organ. She also teaches music theory, and prepares
students for RIAM exams.

## 198 Dean Swift Sports Club ♿

Belcamp Park, Coolock, Dublin 17 (in Belcamp Park in Prizewood); Tel: 8482283.
**Open:** All year; Mon–Sun 9am–5pm ▪ **Charge:** Child €0.60; Annual membership €10 plus €0.60 per activity, or pay as you go ▪ **Suitable for ages:** 2+ ▪ **Bus routes:** 27.
**Sports:** basketball, golf, soccer, tennis, pitch-and-putt
A Dublin City Council sports club, with tennis and basketball courts. The pitch-and-putt course is very popular. The club runs a sports day in summer.
**✱ TOP CHOICES: SPORTS FACILITIES ✱**

## 199 Donabate/Portrane Beach 🌊 🏰

Donabate, Fingal, Co. Dublin (from the city centre, take the M1 past Swords. Stay on the N1 until you see the signs for Donabate).
**Open:** Lifeguard: Jun–Sep; Daily 10am–8pm ▪ **Charge:** Free ▪ **Suitable for ages:** All ▪ **Car parking:** Park on the hard sand on the beach ▪ **Bus routes:** 33B ▪ **Rail station:** Donabate.
**Sports:** swimming
Donabate is a gorgeous, clean, sandy beach. Portrane is just beyond, and has blue flag status. There are caves at the Martello tower end, which are great for exploring when the tide is out – make sure children are supervised. There is also a cliff-path walk – this has a safety warning, and is not suitable for children. Both beaches are close to Rogerstown Estuary, an internationally important waterfowl site.
**✱ TOP CHOICES: BEACHES ✱ TOP CHOICES: FOR AGES 0–2 ✱ TOP CHOICES: FOR AGES 2–5 ✱**

## 200 Donaghmede Library 🚼 ♿ ✎ 🖥

Donaghmede Shopping Centre, Grange Rd, Dublin 15; Tel: 8482833; Website: www.iol.ie/dublincitylibrary
**Open:** All year; Mon/Thur 1–8pm; Tue/Wed/Fri/Sat 10.30am–5pm ▪ **Charge:** Free ▪ **Suitable for ages:** All ▪ **Car parking:** Free ▪ **Bus routes:** 29A ▪ **Rail station:** Howth Junction ▪ **DART station:** Howth Junction.
This library has a children's art class on Saturdays at 10.30am. Seasonal arts-and-crafts and reading events for children are organised throughout the year.
**✱ TOP CHOICES: FOR AGES 5–10 ✱**

## 201 Donaghmede Shopping Centre ♘ 🗄 ♿

Grange Rd, Donaghmede, Co. Dublin; Tel: 8481819.
**Open:** All year; Mon–Wed 9am–6pm; Thur–Fri 9am–9pm; Sat
9am–6pm; Sun 12–6pm ▪ **Suitable for ages:** All ▪ **Car parking:**
Free ▪ **Bus routes:** 29A, 129.
This small shopping centre was revamped a few years ago, with a
flat escalator to the upstairs part that will accommodate buggies
and wheelchairs. There's a big Dunnes Stores, Kay's Restaurant
and the excellent Pride and Joy toyshop, which has a wide range
of Barbie and Action Man dolls and accessories.

## 202 Drumcondra Library ✎ 🖥

Millmount Ave, Dublin 9 (beside Griffith Park); Tel: 8377206;
Website: www.iol.ie/dublincitylibrary
**Open:** All year; Mon/Wed/Fri 10am–1pm, 2–5pm; Tue/Thur
12.45–4pm, 4.45–8pm ▪ **Charge:** Free ▪ **Suitable for ages:** All ▪
**Car parking:** Free ▪ **Bus routes:** 3, 11, 11A.
A small children's section, with no wheelchair access. Special
seasonal arts-and-crafts and reading events for children are
organised throughout the year.

## 203 Dublin Archers

Indoor: St. Paul's School, Sybil Hill Rd, Raheny, Dublin 5;
Outdoor: Plunkett College, Swords Rd, Whitehall, Dublin 9;
Contact: Sinead Cuthbert; Tel: 8671693;
E-mail: sin_cuthbert@hotmail.com
**Open:** All year; Call for current meeting times ▪ **Suitable for
ages:** 10+ ▪ **Bus routes:** 29A, 31A/B, 32A/B ▪ **DART station:**
Raheny.
**Sports:** archery

## 204 Dublin Ballet School Ltd

U5, All Saints Pk, Raheny, Co. Dublin; Tel: 8512571.
**Open:** Call for new term times ▪ **Charge:** Fees on request ▪
**Suitable for ages:** 4+ ▪ **Bus routes:** 31, 31B, 32, 32A/B/X, 29A,
105 ▪ **Rail station:** Raheny ▪ **DART station:** Raheny.
Contact the teacher for times and availability.

## 205 Dublin Butterfly House ♘ 🗄 ♿ 🚻

Harap Farm, Magillstown, Swords, Co. Dublin (signposted from

the Estuary roundabout, Swords (R125)); Tel: 087 6686235;
E-mail: mj@iol.ie; Website: www.dublinbutterfly.com
**Open:** Apr–Sep; Tue–Sun 10am–5.30pm; Open on bank holidays
■ **Charge:** Child €2.50; Adult €5; Concessions €4; Family €12 ■
**Suitable for ages:** All ■ **Car parking:** Free.
Many species of beautiful butterflies are kept here. There are also
spiders and stick insects, and aviaries with plenty of birds on show.
You can buy a hot drink here or bring a picnic.
**✱ TOP CHOICES: PICNIC SPOTS ✱ TOP CHOICES: BIRTHDAY PARTY
IDEAS ✱ TOP CHOICES: FOR AGES 2–5 ✱**

## 206 Dublin Youth Symphonia

Malahide, Co. Dublin (call for rehearsal venues); Contact: Dorothy
Conaghan; Tel: 8451666; Fax: 8451666.
**Open:** All year for concerts; Meetings held once a month on
Sunday afternoons ■ **Charge:** Membership fee may be required ■
**Suitable for ages:** 13+ ■ **Bus routes:** 32, 32A, 42, 102, 230 ■
**Rail station:** Malahide ■ **DART station:** Malahide.
Youth Dublin Symphonia is a chamber orchestra for children and
young people aged 13–20 years. It gives students the opportunity
to play in a large ensemble. Entrance is by audition only. The
orchestra performs at *feiseanna ceoil* and the NCH Festival of
Youth Orchestras.
**✱ TOP CHOICES: HOBBIES/ARTS AND CRAFTS ✱**

## 207 Dymphna's Equestrian Centre

Surgalstown, Swords, Co. Dublin; Tel: 8900710, 086 8650095.
**Open:** All year; Tue–Sun 9am–6pm; Call for dates of this year's
summer camps ■ **Charge:** €12 per hourly lesson; Prices on
request for summer camps ■ **Suitable for ages:** 6+ ■ **Car
parking:** Free ■ **Bus routes:** 41B.
**Sports:** horse-riding
Dymphna's has an outdoor arena where riding lessons are given.
Children are only brought on the road occasionally, but generally
get a 'hack', or ride out, in pony camp during the summer.
**✱ TOP CHOICES: SPORTS FACILITIES ✱**

## 208 Edenmore Park ♿

Raheny, Dublin 5 (between Raheny Rd and Edenmore Crescent);
Tel: 8336262, 8482114; Website: www.dublincity.ie/parks
**Open:** All year; Mon–Fri 8.30am–dusk; Sat–Sun 9.30am–dusk ■
**Charge:** Free ■ **Suitable for ages:** All ■ **Car parking:** On-street

parking ▪ **Bus routes:** 29A ▪ **DART station:** Raheny.
**Sports:** cycling, gaelic football, golf, hockey, hurling, rugby,
soccer, pitch-and-putt
A 10-hectare park, which was once a landfill site. It has a good
pitch-and-putt course, and playing fields.
**✱ TOP CHOICES: SPORTS FACILITIES ✱**

## 209 Ellenfield Park 🚼 ♿ 🏃

Whitehall, Dublin 9 (off the Swords Rd, before the junction with
the M1); Tel: 8336262, 8421182;
Website: www.dublincity.ie/parks
**Open:** All year; Mon–Fri 8.30am–dusk; Sat–Sun 9.30am–dusk ▪
**Charge:** Free ▪ **Suitable for ages:** All ▪ **Car parking:** On-street
parking ▪ **Bus routes:** 16, 16A, 33, 41, 41B/C, 103.
**Sports:** cycling, gaelic football, hurling, soccer, tennis
A 10-hectare park with playing fields, Ellenfield Park is the main
sports ground in the Whitehall area. Dublin Public Parks Tennis
runs here during the summer months.
**✱ TOP CHOICES: SPORTS FACILITIES ✱**

## 210 Fairview Park 🚼 ♿ 🏃 🚉

Fairview, Dublin 3 (in the heart of Fairview, between the DART
line and the River Tolka); Tel: 8336262;
Website: www.dublincity.ie/parks
**Open:** All year; Mon–Fri 8.30am–dusk; Sat–Sun 9.30am–dusk ▪
**Charge:** Free ▪ **Suitable for ages:** All ▪ **Car parking:** Metered
on-street parking ▪ **Bus routes:** 20B, 27, 27B/C/X, 29A, 31,
31A/B, 32, 32A/B, 42A.
**Sports:** cycling, gaelic football, hurling, soccer, athletics
A sprawling, urban 20-hectare park, Fairview Park has pretty
flower displays along the Fairview Road to cheer you up when
you're stuck in traffic. It also contains playing fields, a children's
playground and tree-lined walks. Across the railway line is the
Traffic School, an all-weather 400-metre athletic track and
five-a-side football pitches.
**✱ TOP CHOICES: SPORTS FACILITIES ✱ TOP CHOICES: FOR AGES 0–2**
**✱ TOP CHOICES: FOR AGES 2–5 ✱**

## 211 Father Collins Park ♿

Donaghmede, Co. Dublin (between the Hole in the Wall Rd and
the Mayne River in Donaghmede); Tel: 8336262;
Website: www.dublincity.ie/parks

**Open:** All year; Mon–Fri 8.30am–dusk; Sat–Sun 9.30am–dusk ▪
**Suitable for ages:** All ▪ **Car parking:** On-street parking ▪ **Bus routes:** 27, 27C/X, 129.
**Sports:** cycling, gaelic football, hurling, soccer
A 26-hectare park, mainly taken up with sports grounds.

## 212 Fingall Sailing School, Malahide

Upper Strand, Malahide, Co. Dublin; Tel: 8451979;
Fax: 8453689; E-mail: fingall.maritime@indigo.ie
**Open:** All year; Mon–Sun 10am–5pm; Summer camp Mon–Fri
9.30am–4.30pm – call for details ▪ **Charge:** €180 for a 1-week
course; €45 per child for a minimum of three people for a 3-hour
course ▪ **Suitable for ages:** 8+ ▪ **Car parking:** Free ▪ **Bus routes:**
102, 105, 230, 32A, 42.
**Sports:** sailing, windsurfing
Fingall offers courses all year in sailing and windsurfing for groups of
children (with a minimum of three children in a group, which you
have to organise). In the summer months, week-long multi-activity
courses are held. Wetsuits, windsurfers and boats are supplied.
✱ **TOP CHOICES: SPORTS FACILITIES** ✱

## 213 Finglas Library 🛒 ♿ ✑ 🖥

Finglas Shopping Centre, Jamestown Rd, Dublin 11;
Tel: 8344906; Fax: 8642085;
Website: www.iol.ie/dublincitylibrary
**Open:** All year; Mon/Wed 1–8pm; Tue/Thur/Fri/Sat
10.30am–5pm ▪ **Charge:** Free ▪ **Suitable for ages:** All ▪ **Car
parking:** Free ▪ **Bus routes:** 134, 37, 38, 39, 40, 40A, 120.
Regular activities include: Story-time for toddlers (Tue 11.30am),
art classes for children (Sat 10.30am), Quidditch junior readers
group (9–12-yr-olds, every second Wed 3pm), Mother and
Toddlers group (Thur 11.15am). New members are very welcome
to join in. Call in advance for help with wheelchair access. Other
seasonal arts-and-crafts and reading events for children are
organised throughout the year.
✱ **TOP CHOICES: FOR AGES 2–5** ✱ **TOP CHOICES: FOR AGES 5–10** ✱

## 214 Forrest Equestrian Centre

Cloghran, Co. Dublin; Tel: 8402388;
E-mail: forestequestrian@online.ie
**Open:** All year; Tue–Sun 10am–5pm; Call for dates of this year's
summer camps ▪ **Charge:** €12.50 per hourly lesson; Livery and

summer camp prices on request ■ **Suitable for ages:** 5+.
**Sports:** horse-riding
Forrest has one outdoor sand arena. Lessons are available six days
a week. Forrest also does livery, where they keep horses and
ponies for others. Pony camps are run in the summer.

## 215 Freestyle Disco

WFTA Club, Mellowes Rd, Finglas West, Dublin 9; Tel: 8770758,
087 2847213.
**Open:** All year, but check to see if classes are still running in July;
Fri 6–7.45pm; Sat 3–5.30pm ■ **Charge:** €32 per month for 4
hours of classes ■ **Suitable for ages:** 7–18 ■ **Car parking:**
On-street parking ■ **Bus routes:** 17, 17A, 40, 40A, 104.
Freestyle disco classes for children aged 7–18 years, including
participation in competitions.

## 216 Fry Model Railway Museum 🚼 🍼 ♿ €

Malahide Castle and Demesne, Malahide, Co. Dublin (take the
Dublin–Belfast road (N1). Take the right turn at Swords bypass
roundabout, headed for Malahide. The main car park is via the
back road to Malahide, signposted. Another car park is provided
by the railway station on the Dublin road); Tel: 8463779
(Apr–Sep), 8462184 (Oct–Mar); Fax: 8462537;
Website: www.visitdublin.com
**Open:** Apr–Dec; Mon–Sat 10am–1pm, 2–5pm; Sun/bank
holidays 2–6pm ■ **Charge:** Children (ages 3–11) €3.50; Adults €6;
Concessions and under-18s €5.00; Family ticket (2 adults and 3/4
children) €16.50; Combined tickets available with Malahide Castle
■ **Suitable for ages:** All ■ **Car parking:** Free ■ **Bus routes:** 32A,
42, 102, 230 ■ **Rail station:** Malahide ■ **DART station:** Malahide.
This is a display of Irish trains and railways in Lilliputian scale.
Younger children especially will enjoy this museum. It includes
replicas of Dublin's Heuston and Cork stations, with working
model trains, from 1920s models to modern machines. This
museum is set in the grounds of Malahide Castle. While you're
here, you can also visit Tara's Palace.
✱ TOP CHOICES: FOR AGES 2–5 ✱ TOP CHOICES: FOR AGES 5–10 ✱
TOP CHOICES: FOR INQUISITIVE KIDS ✱

## 217 Cumann Luthchleas Gael/GAA

Croke Park, Dublin 3; Tel: 8363222; Fax: 8366420;
E-mail: info@gaa.ie; Website: www.gaa.ie

**Open:** All year ■ **Charge:** Weekly charge ■ **Suitable for ages:** 5+.
**Sports:** gaelic football, hurling, camogie, handball
Clubs in north Dublin are listed below. See the Organisations
chapter for more information on the GAA.
★ **TOP CHOICES: HOBBIES/ARTS AND CRAFTS** ★

## 218 Beann Eadair GAA Club

Balkill Rd, Howth, Co. Dublin; Contact: Pat Minogue;
Tel: 8323738.
**Open:** All year ■ **Suitable for ages:** 5+ ■ **Bus routes:** 31, 31A/B
■ **DART station:** Howth.
**Sports:** gaelic football, hurling

## 219 Clontarf GAA Club

Seafield Rd, Clontarf, Dublin 3; Contact: Kieran McMahon;
Tel: 8530454.
**Open:** All year ■ **Suitable for ages:** 5+ ■ **Bus routes:** 103, 104,
130.
**Sports:** gaelic football, hurling

## 220 Craobh Chiarain GAA Club

Parnell Park, Doneycarney, Dublin 5; Tel: 8311050;
Fax: 8510650.
**Open:** All year ■ **Suitable for ages:** 5+ ■ **Bus routes:** 20B, 27,
28, 42A/B.
**Sports:** gaelic football, hurling

## 221 Erin's Isle GAA Club

Farnham Drive, Finglas, Dublin 11; Tel: 8342556;
Website: www.erinsisle.cgb.net
**Open:** All year ■ **Suitable for ages:** 5+ ■ **Bus routes:** 40, 40A/C.
**Sports:** gaelic football, hurling

## 222 Fingallians GAA Club

Lawless Memorial Pk, Swords, Co. Dublin; Contact: Dara Ó
Murchú; Tel: 8400125.
**Open:** All year ■ **Suitable for ages:** 5+ ■ **Bus routes:** 33, 33A/B,
41, 41A/B, 230.
**Sports:** gaelic football, hurling

## 223 Innisfáil GAA Club

Carr's Lane, Balgriffin, Dublin 5; Tel: 8463627.

**Open:** All year ▪ **Charge:** Small weekly fee ▪ **Suitable for ages:** 5+ ▪ **Bus routes:** 42, 43.
**Sports:** gaelic football, hurling

### 224 Naomh Barrog GAA Club

Kilbarrack Rd, Raheny, Dublin 5; Contact: Larry McCarthy; Tel: 8396963.
**Open:** All year ▪ **Suitable for ages:** 5+ ▪ **Bus routes:** 29A, 31A/B, 32A/B.
**Sports:** gaelic football, hurling

### 225 Naomh Fionnbarra GAA Club

Recreation Centre, Fassaugh Ave, Dublin 7; Contact: Ailish Uí Longain; Tel: 8384881; Fax: 8686209.
**Open:** All year ▪ **Suitable for ages:** 5+ ▪ **Bus routes:** 120, 121, 122.
**Sports:** gaelic football, hurling

### 226 Naomh Mearnog GAA Club

St Helen's, Portmarnock, Co. Dublin; Contact: Dan Linehan; Tel: 8464266.
**Open:** All year ▪ **Suitable for ages:** 5+ ▪ **Bus routes:** 32, 32A, 102, 105, 230.
**Sports:** gaelic football, hurling

### 227 O'Dwyer's GAA Club

Bremore, Balbriggan, Co. Dublin; Tel: 8413820.
**Open:** All year ▪ **Suitable for ages:** 5+ ▪ **Bus routes:** 33, 33A.
**Sports:** gaelic football, hurling

### 228 Parnell's GAA Club

The Clubhouse, Coolock, Dublin 5; Contact: Brendan Conlon; Tel: 8486166.
**Open:** All year ▪ **Suitable for ages:** 5+ ▪ **Bus routes:** 17A, 27.
**Sports:** gaelic football, hurling

### 229 Raheny GAA Club

2 All Saints Dr, Raheny, Dublin 5; Contact: Tony Lee; Tel: 8313530.
**Open:** All year ▪ **Suitable for ages:** 5+ ▪ **Bus routes:** 29A, 31A/B, 32A/B.
**Sports:** gaelic football, hurling

## 230 St. Monica's GAA Club

Edenmore Pk, Raheny, Dublin 5; Contact: Paul Kelly;
Tel: 8486818.
**Open:** All year ■ **Suitable for ages:** 5+ ■ **Bus routes:** 42A/B.
**Sports:** gaelic football, hurling

## 231 St. Oliver Plunkett's GAA Club

Spur Rd, Glenarriff Rd, Dublin 7; Tel: 8389316.
**Open:** All year ■ **Charge:** Small weekly fee ■ **Suitable for ages:**
5+ ■ **Bus routes:** 19, 19A, 38, 38A/B.
**Sports:** gaelic football, hurling

## 232 St. Sylvester's GAA Club

2 Church Rd, Malahide, Co. Dublin; Tel: 8453879.
**Open:** All year ■ **Charge:** Small weekly fee ■ **Suitable for ages:**
5+ ■ **Bus routes:** 32A, 42, 102, 105, 230.
**Sports:** gaelic football, hurling

## 233 St. Vincent's GAA Club

Malahide Rd, Dublin 3; Contact: Martin O'Hora; Tel: 8335722.
**Open:** All year ■ **Suitable for ages:** 5+ ■ **Bus routes:** 20B, 27,
27B, 42, 42B, 43, 103, 104, 127, 129.
**Sports:** gaelic football, hurling

## 234 Scoil Uí Chonaill GAA Club

Clontarf Rd, Dublin 3; Contact: Susan Naughton; Tel: 8333729.
**Open:** All year ■ **Suitable for ages:** 5+ ■ **Bus routes:** 103, 104,
130.
**Sports:** gaelic football, hurling

## 235 Skerries Harps GAA Club

Dublin Rd, Skerries, Co. Dublin; Contact: Denis Murphy;
Tel: 8494420.
**Open:** All year ■ **Suitable for ages:** 5+ ■ **Bus routes:** 33, 33A.
**Sports:** gaelic football, hurling

## 236 Whitehall Colmcille GAA Club

Collins Ave, Dublin 9; Contact: Eamonn Bryce; Tel: 8375330.
**Open:** All year ■ **Suitable for ages:** 5+ ■ **Bus routes:** 3, 16, 20B,
42A, 77B, 103, 105.
**Sports:** gaelic football, hurling

## 237 GAA Museum 🚼 🎫 ♿ €

New Stand, Croke Park, Dublin 3 (access from Clonliffe Rd, using
St. Joseph's Ave); Tel: 8558176; Fax: 8558104;
E-mail: gaamuseum@crokepark.ie; Website: www.gaa.ie/museum
**Open:** All year; May–Sep: Mon–Sat 10am–5pm; Sun 12–5pm;
Oct–Apr: Tue–Sat 10am–5pm; Sun 12–5pm; Closed on match
days ▪ **Charge:** Child €3; Adult €5; Student/OAP €3.50; Family (2
adults and 2 children) €13.00; Museum entrance with Stadium
Tour: Adult €8.50; Student/OAP €6.00; Child (under 12) €5.00;
Family (2 adults and 2 children) €21.00 ▪ **Suitable for ages:** 3+ ▪
**Car parking:** Free ▪ **Bus routes:** 3, 11, 11A, 16, 16A, 123 ▪ **Rail
station:** Connolly ▪ **DART station:** Connolly.
**Sports:** gaelic football, hurling
This is an interactive museum, chronicling the history of the Gaelic
Athletic Association at home and abroad. You can spend hours
here – there's loads of stuff to see and do. You can learn all about
Ireland's national sporting heroes, as well as testing your own
game skills on touch-screen computers, and even hear the roar of
the crowd at a big match. The stadium tour is a must for sports
fans, giving access into the players' entrance, team dressing rooms,
the media area and the tunnel up to the pitch. You are advised to
bring walking shoes and wear warm clothing.
★ TOP CHOICES: BIRTHDAY PARTY IDEAS ★ TOP CHOICES: SPORTS
FACILITIES ★ TOP CHOICES: FOR AGES 5–10 ★ TOP CHOICES: FOR
AGES 10+ ★ TOP CHOICES: FOR INQUISITIVE KIDS ★ TOP CHOICES:
FOR ENERGETIC KIDS ★

## 238 Gaiety School of Acting

Scoil Mhuire, Howth Village, Co. Dublin; Tel: 1890 256356;
Fax: 6799568; E-mail: gaiety.school@indigo.ie;
Website: www.gaietyschool.com
**Open:** All year; Three terms: Oct–Dec, Jan–Mar and Apr–Jun; Sat,
class times vary according to age and experience, phone for
details; Also, Easter course: 4 days 10am–5pm, call for dates;
Summer course: Jul, Mon–Fri 10am–5pm, call for dates ▪ **Charge:**
3-term drama course, 90 minutes per week: 6–7-yr-olds €120; All
other age groups €150; Easter course: Make-A-Movie €190;
Summer 1-week drama course: €190 ▪ **Suitable for ages:**
6–15/16 ▪ **Car parking:** On-street parking ▪ **Bus routes:** 31, 31B
▪ **DART station:** Howth.
The Young Gaiety School of Acting offers a three-course
programme, introducing children to drama. Classes are grouped

NORTH DUBLIN

according to age and experience, and are staffed by trained theatre professionals. The classes aim to build confidence, and to develop imagination and self-expression. A production is given by students who have completed the second and third courses at the end of course three. Easter Course: Make-a-Movie for 11–15-yr-olds – students make, and act in, their own film, and receive a copy each to take home. A one-week drama summer school for 7–10-yr-olds, 11–13-yr-olds and 14–16-yr-olds runs in July.

✱ TOP CHOICES: SUMMER CAMPS ✱ TOP CHOICES: FOR IMAGINATIVE KIDS ✱

## 239 Glasnevin Lawn Tennis Club

Ballymun Rd, Glasnevin, Dublin 9; Contact: Shay Dolan; Tel: 8371042.
**Open:** All year; Mon–Sun 8am–5pm for juniors ▪ **Charge:** €59 annual membership ▪ **Suitable for ages:** 6+ ▪ **Bus routes:** 11, 11A/B, 13, 13A, 19A, 103.
**Sports:** tennis
Eight synthetic courts are available. A tennis coach from outside the club comes three days a week during the winter, and he/she also runs summer camps.

## 240 Griffith Park

Glasnevin, Dublin 9 (on theTolka River, southeast of the National Botanic Gardens); Tel: 8373891, 8373290;
Website: www.dublincity.ie/parks
**Open:** All year; Mon–Fri 8.30am–dusk; Sat–Sun 9.30am–dusk ▪ **Charge:** Free ▪ **Suitable for ages:** All ▪ **Car parking:** On-street parking ▪ **Bus routes:** 11, 11A/B, 13A, 16, 16A, 33, 41, 41A/B/C/X, 51A, 58X.
A pretty park with trees, flower gardens and a riverside walk (the park is either side of the river Tolka). There's also a small playground best suited to under-6s.

✱ TOP CHOICES: FOR AGES 0–2 ✱ TOP CHOICES: FOR AGES 2–5 ✱

## 241 Gymboree Music on the Go

Base Community Centre, Brackenstown, Swords, Co. Dublin; Holmpatrick Parish Hall, Skerries, Co. Dublin; Tel: 2789069 (info), 4905880 (parties at home); Website: www.playandmusic.ie
**Open:** All year; Swords: Tue 11am, 12pm; Skerries: Sat 10am, 11am, 12pm ▪ **Charge:** €5– €7.50 per class (with reduction for

booking a block session) ▪ **Suitable for ages:** 0–5 years ▪ **Car parking:** Free.

Gymboree Music on the Go is a range of creative programmes for children from birth to 5 years old. The children can play percussion instruments, and sing and dance with an instructor. The musical themes vary from reggae to polka. Parents are involved in sessions and must be present. There are also Gymboree party plans (see Gymboree main entry).

**★ TOP CHOICES: FOR AGES 0–2 ★ TOP CHOICES: FOR AGES 2–5 ★**

## 242 Hampstead Park (Albert College Park)

Glasnevin, Dublin 9 (beside DCU campus, off the Ballymun Rd); Tel: 8373891; Website: www.dublincity.ie/parks
**Open:** All year; Mon–Fri 8.30am–dusk; Sat–Sun 9.30am–dusk ▪ **Charge:** Free ▪ **Suitable for ages:** All ▪ **Car parking:** On-street parking ▪ **Bus routes:** 11, 13A, 16, 16A, 19A, 46X, 58X, 103, 116.

**Sports:** basketball, cycling, gaelic football, hurling, soccer, tennis
Originally called Albert College Park because of its history with UCD, Hampstead Park was once a centre for agricultural and horticultural education and research – it was here that the potato blight fungus was first identified. It became a public park in 1978, and now includes playing fields, tennis courts and walks. There's a well laid-out playground with a soft surface and loads of equipment, including climbing walls, roundabouts, swings, climbing ropes and a large spider's web for older kids. A toddlers' area is separated by a small fence. Dublin Public Parks Tennis runs here during the summer months.

**★ TOP CHOICES: PLAYGROUNDS ★ TOP CHOICES: FOR AGES 0–2 ★ TOP CHOICES: FOR AGES 2–5 ★**

## 243 The Helix (Theatre)

DCU campus, Collins Ave, Glasnevin, Dublin 9 (from city centre: Drive towards Drumcondra along the N1. Just before the M1, turn left on to Collins Ave. From M50 Northbound: Leave the M50 at the Ballymun exit, and drive through Ballymun; Go straight through the roundabout in Ballymun (second exit), and take the second turn on the left onto Collins Ave); Tel: 7007000 (box office); Fax: 7007110; E-mail: info@thehelix.ie; Website: www.thehelix.ie
**Open:** All year; Mon–Sun matinee and evening performances;

Call for times ▪ **Charge:** Ticket prices range from €7 to €32, depending on the scale of the production, eg. jazz gig to ice show. Family special: Up to two children for half price with each full paying adult ▪ **Suitable for ages:** All ▪ **Car parking:** €1 per hour (max €4) ▪ **Bus routes:** 11, 13A, 16, 16A, 19A, 46X, 58X, 103, 116.

The Helix at Dublin City University is a modern, multi-performance venue space, which hosts concerts, dance, ballet, plays, opera and even an ice show. The RTÉ Concert Orchestra and the National Youth Orchestra of Ireland play here. There is also gallery space, with changing exhibitions, and an education programme proposed for 2003 (call for details).

**✷ TOP CHOICES: CHRISTMAS VISITS ✷**

## 244 Hills Cricket Club

Milverton, Skerries, Co. Dublin; Tel: 8492233.
**Open:** May–Sep; Mon–Fri approx. 10am–4pm ▪ **Charge:** Small weekly charge; Summer camp fees on request ▪ **Suitable for ages:** 6+ ▪ **Bus routes:** 33, 33A.
**Sports:** cricket

Nearly all Dublin clubs offer summer camps for children, and most will also do schools cricket during school terms. The camps are often run from Mon to Fri, for several hours a day. Ordinary sportswear is fine. Pads, etc., are supplied by the club.

**✷ TOP CHOICES: HOBBIES/ARTS AND CRAFTS ✷**

## 245 Hip Hop Dance Classes

Portmarnock Sports and Leisure Club, Portmarnock, Co. Dublin (beside Portmarnock Community School, on the Carrickhill Rd); Tel: 087 7983391, 8462122.
**Open:** During school term times; Sat 4.30pm ▪ **Charge:** Child €3 ▪ **Suitable for ages:** 12+ ▪ **Car parking:** Free ▪ **Bus routes:** 32, 32A/B/X, 102.

Hip hop classes are taught here for girls and boys over 12 years old.

**✷ TOP CHOICES: FOR TRENDY KIDS ✷**

## 246 Hockey

Irish Hockey Association, 6A Woodbine Park, Blackrock, Co. Dublin; Tel: 2600028; Fax: 2600087;
E-mail: joanmorgan@hockey.ie; Website: www.hockey.ie
**Open:** Sep–Apr; Call for meeting dates and times ▪ **Charge:** Annual membership around €45 ▪ **Suitable for ages:** 6+.

The Irish Hockey Association oversees all Irish hockey clubs.
Children's teams usually start at under-8s and go up to under-16s.
Coaching is often on Sat mornings and Fri nights – call for details.

## 247 Clontarf Hockey Club

DCU Astro Turf, St. Clare's, Ballymun Rd, Dublin 1; Contact:
Walter Mc Connell; Tel: 087 2394996;
E-mail: info@clontarfhc.com; Website: www.clontarfhc.com
**Open:** Sep–Apr; Call for meeting dates and times ▪ **Suitable for ages:** 6+ ▪ **Bus routes:** 13, 13A, 19A, 11, 11A/B.

## 248 Portrane Hockey Club

RCSI Sports Grounds, Dardistown, Swords, Co. Dublin; Contact:
Percy Henchy; Tel: 8436608, 087 6791853.
**Open:** Sep–Apr; Call for meeting dates and times ▪ **Suitable for ages:** 6+ ▪ **Bus routes:** 33, 33B, 41, 41B/C.

## 249 Skerries Hockey Club

Skerries Community Centre AWP, Dublin Rd, Skerries, Co.
Dublin; Contact: Janice Dowling; Tel: 8494029;
E-mail: skerrieshc@hotmail.com
**Open:** Sep–Apr; Call for meeting dates and times ▪ **Suitable for ages:** 6+ ▪ **Bus routes:** 33.

## 250 Sportslink Eastern Health Hockey Club

Sportslink, Furry Park, Cloughran, Co. Dublin (go through Santry
on the Old Airport Rd. Take a left after the Texaco garage into the
grounds); Contact: Patrick Ennis; Tel: 6210981, 086 2471705;
E-mail: pat.ennis@anpost.ie
**Open:** Sep–Apr; Call for meeting dates and times ▪ **Suitable for ages:** 6+ ▪ **Bus routes:** 41, 41B/C.

## 251 Suttonians Hockey Club

Sutton Park School, St. Fintan's Road, Sutton, Dublin 13; Contact:
Aedin Scully; Tel: 8463426, 087 2395601;
E-mail: aedinscully@hotmail.com
**Open:** Sep–Apr; Call for meeting dates and times ▪ **Suitable for ages:** 6+ ▪ **Bus routes:** 31B ▪ **DART station:** Sutton.

## 252 Howth Castle Gardens

Howth, Co. Dublin; Tel: 8400077 (tourist info).

**Open:** All year, but best in May and June; Mon–Sun ▪ **Charge:**
Free ▪ **Suitable for ages:** All ▪ **Bus routes:** 31, 31B ▪ **DART
station:** Howth.

Howth Castle was built in 1464, and was the seat of the Earl of
Howth until 1909. The castle isn't open to the public, but you can
visit the lovely gardens. There are magnificent rhododendron
displays, best seen in May and June, and lovely views of Dublin
Bay and the Mourne Mountains. For children these are hardly
worth a visit on their own, so take the opportunity to visit the Fry
Model Railway at the same time.

## 253 Howth Head 🚉

Ballygreen Rd, Howth, Co. Dublin (go past the harbour front, then
turn right up the hill to the Summit car park).
**Open:** All year; Mon–Sun 24 hours ▪ **Charge:** Free ▪ **Suitable for
ages:** 5+ ▪ **Car parking:** Free ▪ **Bus routes:** 31 ▪ **DART station:**
Howth.

Start at the Summit car park and follow the path over the east
mountain area. As you approach Cliff Road, at the other end of
the path, there are fantastic views to Ireland's Eye and sometimes
the Mountains of Mourne. If you prefer a longer walk, take one of
the paths leading off the main path from the Summit to the lower
cliff path. Be careful though – the path is often narrow; this is not
buggy territory! It is also quite dangerous for young children, as
the cliffs are steep. You'll go past Casana Rock, with its nesting
birds – particularly kittiwakes and fulmar petrels. The path then
dips steeply and heads onto Ballycadden Road, before heading
back to the Summit.
★ **TOP CHOICES: WALKS** ★

## 254 Howth Library 🚼 ✒️ 🖥️

Main St, Howth, Co. Dublin; Tel: 8322130; Fax: 8322277;
E-mail: howthlibrary@hotmail.com;
Website: www.iol.ie/~fincolib/ss.htm
**Open:** All year; Mon/Wed 2–8.30pm; Tue/Thur 10am–1pm,
2–5.15pm; Fri–Sat 10am–1pm, 2–5.15pm; Closed on the Sat and
Mon of a bank holiday weekend ▪ **Charge:** Free ▪ **Suitable for
ages:** All ▪ **Car parking:** Free ▪ **Bus routes:** 31, 31B ▪ **DART
station:** Howth.

Howth Library includes a children's library on the ground floor,
although there's only a small door, not suited to double buggies or

wheelchairs. Holiday activities are organised during the year –
watch the noticeboard and book in advance.

## 255 Howth Rock Guitar and Songwriting School

2 Dunbo Hill, Howth, Co. Dublin; Contact: Frank Kearns;
Tel: 8324430; E-mail: frankkearns@hotmail.com
**Open:** Call for course dates and times ▪ **Charge:** Fees on request
▪ **Suitable for ages:** 12+.
Courses are held here for pop wannabes in rock music and
songwriting, including summer schools.
✱ TOP CHOICES: HOBBIES/ARTS AND CRAFTS ✱ TOP CHOICES:
SUMMER CAMPS ✱ TOP CHOICES: FOR TRENDY KIDS ✱ TOP
CHOICES: FOR IMAGINATIVE KIDS ✱

## 256 Howth Yacht Club 🍴 ♿

Harbour Rd, Howth, Co. Dublin; Tel: 8322141; Fax: 8392430;
E-mail: admin@hyc.iol.ie; Website: www.hyc.ie
**Open:** All year; Mon–Fri 10am–4pm for weekly courses; Call for
times and dates of weekend courses ▪ **Charge:** €53 annual
membership for juniors. 4-week courses €250 ▪ **Suitable for ages:**
8+ ▪ **Car parking:** Free ▪ **Bus routes:** 33 ▪ **DART station:**
Howth.
**Sports:** sailing
A well-known yacht club, with popular courses for children on
weekends and during school holidays. There is also club racing for
all standards. You must join as a member, and either own or share
a dinghy. The summer courses usually last four weeks.
✱ TOP CHOICES: SUMMER CAMPS ✱

## 257 Johnstown Park 🚼 ♿ 🏃

Ballygall, Glasnevin, Dublin 9 (between Glasanaon Rd and
Ballygall Rd E); Tel: 8343656; Website: www.dublincity.ie/parks
**Open:** All year; Mon–Fri 8.30am–dusk; Sat–Sun 9.30am–dusk ▪
**Suitable for ages:** All ▪ **Car parking:** On-street parking ▪ **Bus
routes:** 19, 19A, 134.
**Sports:** gaelic football, hockey, hurling, rugby, soccer, tennis
A popular 13-hectare park with good playing fields. Dublin Public
Parks Tennis runs here during the summer months.
✱ TOP CHOICES: SPORTS FACILITIES ✱

NORTH DUBLIN

## 258 Kart City Ltd (Indoor Karting and Skate Park) 📺 ⛸️

Old Airport Rd (Swords Rd), Santry, Dublin 9 (from Dublin, travel on the Swords Rd, turn left before Dublin Airport); Tel: 8426322; Fax: 8426185; E-mail: info@kartcity.net;
Website: www.kartcity.net

**Open:** All year; Mon–Sun 10am–12am ▪ **Charge:** Prices start at €20 for 15 minutes; €46 for full Grand Prix; Skating from €6.50 per child; Junior Karting on Sat from €12 per child ▪ **Suitable for ages:** 6+ ▪ **Car parking:** Free ▪ **Bus routes:** 16A, 33, 33X, 41, 41A/B/C, 46, 58X.

**Sports:** karting, rollerskating

There is a special track available for children aged 6–16. On Saturday afternoons at 12, 1, 2 and 3pm, 15-minute races are run especially for children, costing €12 per child. There's also a skate park, with helmet hire available (bring your own skates, and arm and knee pads). There are two supervised sessions on a Saturday, from 10am–12pm for smaller children and 12–2pm for older kids. You can book a group in for a birthday treat for activities, but no special party facilities are available in the restaurant.

✱ TOP CHOICES: BIRTHDAY PARTY IDEAS ✱ TOP CHOICES: SPORTS FACILITIES ✱ TOP CHOICES: FOR AGES 5–10 ✱ TOP CHOICES: FOR AGES 10+ ✱ TOP CHOICES: FOR TRENDY KIDS ✱

## 259 Kiddie Kuts 🛒 ♿ 🎈

U14 Omni Park Centre, Santry, Dublin 9 (off the M1, junction 3); Tel: 2836566.

**Open:** All year; Mon–Sat 9am–6pm; Sun 1–5pm ▪ **Charge:** Parties from €17/ €18 per child ▪ **Suitable for ages:** All ▪ **Car parking:** Free ▪ **Bus routes:** 16, 16A, 33, 41, 41B/C, 103, 104, 746.

Brilliant! A hair salon especially for children. There are little cars for reluctant toddlers to sit in while they are getting their hair done, and a range of products and accessories to thrill any little princess. Kiddie Kuts also hold parties in the salon, popular with 7/8-year-old girls, where food is supplied and the girls get a hairstyle with braids and accessories.

✱ TOP CHOICES: BIRTHDAY PARTY IDEAS ✱

## 260 Kidzone Play and Party Centre 🛒 📺 ♿ 🎈 🏃

Feltrim Rd, Swords, Co. Dublin (on Feltrim Rd, between Kinsealy

Court and Melrose Park); Contact: Tom/Mellissa; Tel: 8401195; Fax: 8401195.

**Open:** All year; Mon–Sun 10am–7pm ■ **Charge:** Child 1–3yrs €4.50 per hour; Child 4–11yrs €6 per hour; Birthday parties from €8.57 per child (minimum 10) ■ **Suitable for ages:** 1–11 ■ **Car parking:** Free ■ **Bus routes:** 43.

A fun house for children aged 1–11 years. Parents must be present, but you can enjoy a coffee and let the staff do all the hard work. There's a toddlers' soft play area (for under-4s), a bouncy castle, walkways, slides, ball pools and a play house. For birthday boys or girls you can have a themed party: Barbie, Football, Karaoke and Disco, or Wild West, which last two hours. Food is supplied, but bring your own cake.

✱ TOP CHOICES: BIRTHDAY PARTY IDEAS ✱ TOP CHOICES: PLAYGROUNDS ✱ TOP CHOICES: FOR AGES 0–2 ✱ TOP CHOICES: FOR AGES 2–5 ✱ TOP CHOICES: FOR AGES 5–10 ✱

## 261 Kilronan Equestrian Centre

Kilronan, Swords, Co. Dublin; Tel: 8403499; Fax: 8400028.
**Open:** All year; Tue–Sun 9.30am–5pm; Ring for dates of this year's summer camps ■ **Charge:** €13.90 per hourly lesson; Pony camp prices on request ■ **Suitable for ages:** 5+ ■ **Bus routes:** 33, 41.

**Sports:** horse-riding

Kilronan has large indoor and outdoor arenas, and lessons are available six days a week. Pony camps are organised in the summer.

✱ TOP CHOICES: SPORTS FACILITIES ✱

## 262 Leisureplex, Coolock 🎪 📷 ♿ 🎈 🎿

Malahide Rd, Coolock, Dublin 17 (on the Malahide Rd, opposite Tayto and Cadbury factories); Tel: 8485722; Fax: 8485729; E-mail: coolock@leisureplex.ie; Website: www.leisureplex.ie
**Open:** All year; Mon–Sun 24 hours ■ **Charge:** Activities from about €5, Birthday parties from €11 per child, including: activities, food, cake, balloons, party bags and a photo ■ **Suitable for ages:** All ■ **Car parking:** Free ■ **Bus routes:** 17A, 27, 42, 43.

**Sports:** Snooker, pool, 10 pin bowling

Fun for all: for little ones there's The Zoo – a huge, soft play area with slides and balls, including space for under-3s. Snooker, pool and Quazar are available for ages 7/8+, as well as bowling with ball walls, which give small children a chance of hitting the pins by bouncing the ball back into the bowling lane (there is a junior bowling club on Saturday mornings at 10am). Young teens can hang out in the games area, complete with the ever popular dance machine. Great for birthday parties, especially for the under-8s, who have theirs hosted by Plexy the dinosaur. Caution is advised in this neighbourhood after dark.

✱ TOP CHOICES: PLAYGROUNDS ✱ TOP CHOICES: FOR AGES 2–5 ✱ TOP CHOICES: FOR AGES 5–10 ✱ TOP CHOICES: FOR AGES 10+ ✱ TOP CHOICES: FOR TRENDY KIDS ✱ TOP CHOICES: FOR ENERGETIC KIDS ✱

## 263 Loughshinny Beach 🚻

Loughshinny, Fingal, Co. Dublin (from the city centre, take the M1 past Swords. Stay on the N1 until you are past Lusk. Loughshinny is between Rush and Skerries).

**Open:** Lifeguard: Jun–Sep; Mon–Sun 10am–8pm ▪ **Charge:** Free ▪ **Suitable for ages:** All ▪ **Car parking:** On-street parking ▪ **Bus routes:** 33.

**Sports:** swimming

Loughshinny is a picturesque fishing village with a small, sandy beach. It has a small harbour and lovely views of Lambay Island. It is popular with little children.

✱ TOP CHOICES: FOR AGES 0–2 ✱ TOP CHOICES: FOR AGES 2–5 ✱

## 264 Lusk Heritage Centre

Lusk, Co. Dublin (in the centre of Lusk Village, off the N1 towards Skerries); Tel: 8437683; Fax: 6616764.

**Open:** Mid-Jun–mid-Sep; Mon–Fri 10am–5pm ▪ **Charge:** Child €0.50; Adult €1.25; Group/Senior Citizen €0.80; Child/student €0.50; Family €3.80 ▪ **Suitable for ages:** 5+ ▪ **Car parking:** Free ▪ **Bus routes:** 33.

Built over 1,000 years ago, Lusk Heritage Centre consists of a round tower, a medieval belfry and a 19th-century church. There's an exhibition on the medieval churches of north County Dublin in the belfry, and the 16th-century effigy tomb of Sir Christopher Barnewall and his wife Marion Sharl.

## 265 Malahide Castle and Demesne
🛒 ☕ ♿ € 🧷 🚉

Malahide, Co. Dublin (take the N1 Dublin–Belfast road. Turn right at Swords bypass roundabout, heading for Malahide. Main car park is reached via back road to Malahide, signposted. Another car park is available at the railway station on the Dublin road);

Tel: 8462184; Fax: 8462537; E-mail: malahidecastle@
dublintourism.ie; Website: www.visitdublin.ie
**Open:** All year; Mon–Sat 10am–5pm; Sun and bank holidays
Apr–Oct 11am–6pm; Sun and bank holidays Nov–Mar
11am–5pm; Closed daily for tours 12.45–2pm ▪ **Charge:** Children
(ages 3–11) €3.50; Adults €6; Concessions and under-18s €5.00;
Family (2 adults and 3/4 children) €16.50; Combined tickets
available with Fry Model Railway Museum ▪ **Suitable for ages:** All
▪ **Car parking:** Free ▪ **Bus routes:** 32A, 42, 102, 230 ▪ **Rail
station:** Malahide ▪ **DART station:** Malahide.
A fairytale 12th-century castle. The beautiful grounds also house
the famous Talbot Botanic Gardens, containing over 5,000 species
of plants. The castle itself is a bit too formal to interest under-10s,
though they'll enjoy the dungeon feel of the excellent café.
There's a great playground, made from reclaimed materials, set in
the woods. The only drawback of this is the gravel flooring – not
great for pushing a buggy across. The castle's facilities are
excellent, so why not make a day of it and visit the Fry Model
Railway Museum next-door, or Tara's Palace?
✱ **TOP CHOICES: CHILD FRIENDLY RESTAURANTS** ✱ **TOP CHOICES:
PICNIC SPOTS** ✱ **TOP CHOICES: PARKS** ✱ **TOP CHOICES:
PLAYGROUNDS** ✱ **TOP CHOICES: FOR AGES 0–2** ✱ **TOP CHOICES: FOR
AGES 2–5** ✱ **TOP CHOICES: FOR AGES 5–10** ✱ **TOP CHOICES: FOR
ENERGETIC KIDS** ✱

## 266 Malahide Library

Main St, Malahide, Co. Dublin; Tel: 8452026; Fax: 8452199;
Website: www.iol.ie/~fincolib/ma.htm
**Open:** All year; Mon–Wed 10am–1pm, 2–8.30pm; Fri–Sat
10am–1pm, 2–5pm; Closed on the Sat and Mon of a bank
holiday weekend ▪ **Charge:** Free ▪ **Suitable for ages:** All ▪ **Car
parking:** Free ▪ **Bus routes:** 32A, 42, 102, 230 ▪ **Rail station:**
Malahide ▪ **DART station:** Malahide.
The children's library is upstairs. Arts-and-crafts activities and
seasonal events are held throughout the year.

## 267 Malahide Rugby Football Club

Broomfield, Malahide, Co. Dublin; Contact: Eddie Mullin;
Tel: 8461672, 8867700; E-mail: eddie@uefl.ie
**Open:** Sep–Apr ▪ **Suitable for ages:** 6+ ▪ **Bus routes:** 32A, 42,
102, 105, 230 ▪ **Rail station:** Malahide ▪ **DART station:** Malahide.
**Sports:** rugby

## 268 Malahide Yacht Club

St. James's Terrace, Malahide, Co. Dublin; Tel: 8436767, 087 2367789 (Sean Colbert), 8454831 (Anna McGrath); Website: www.myc.ie
**Open:** Apr–Oct; Racing: Tue 6.30–9.30pm; Sat–Sun daylight hours; Summer camps during Jul–Aug; Call for dates ▪ **Charge:** Family membership €400 a year; Cadet membership (for those joining without their family) €120 ▪ **Suitable for ages:** 7+ ▪ **Bus routes:** 42, 102, 105, 230 ▪ **Rail station:** Malahide ▪ **DART station:** Malahide.
**Sports:** sailing
A medium-sized sailing club with a sizeable junior section. Racing is on Tue evenings, and Sat and Sun afternoons. Non-members can attend a four-week course in July and August, but you must own a boat. Courses cost extra.
**✱ TOP CHOICES: HOBBIES/ARTS AND CRAFTS ✱**

## 269 Mangan Yamaha Keyboard and Guitar School of Music ♿

210 Botanic Rd, Glasnevin, Dublin 9; Tel: 8370244.
**Open:** Sep–Jun; Mon–Sat afternoons until 6pm ▪ **Charge:** Approx €120 for a 10-week course ▪ **Suitable for ages:** 6+ ▪ **Car parking:** Use church car park across the road ▪ **Bus routes:** 13, 19, 19A, 134.
This school holds 10-week courses in guitar or keyboards for ages 6+ throughout the year. They also run various summer courses – call for details.

## 270 Marino Boys Soccer Club (Association Football Club)

79 Brian Avenue, Dublin 3; Contact: Patrick Donoghue; Tel: 8331033.
**Open:** Sep–May ▪ **Suitable for ages:** 12–17 ▪ **Bus routes:** 20B, 27, 27B, 42B, 43, 123.
**Sports:** soccer
Marino Boys AFC includes five teams, for 12–17-yr-olds, competing in the Dublin and District Schoolboys' League.
**✱ TOP CHOICES: HOBBIES/ARTS AND CRAFTS ✱**

## 271 Marino Library 🖊️ 🖥️

14–20 Marino Mart, Fairview, Dublin 3 (beside Marino College);
Tel: 8336297; Website: www.iol.ie/dublincitylibrary
**Open:** All year; Mon/Wed 12.45–4pm, 4.45–8pm; Tue/Thur/Sat
10am–1pm, 2–5pm ▪ **Charge:** Free ▪ **Suitable for ages:** All ▪ **Car
parking:** Metered parking on street ▪ **Bus routes:** 20A/B, 27,
27A/B, 28, 29A, 30, 31, 31A/B, 32, 32A/B, 42B/C ▪ **Rail station:**
Clontarf Rd.
Special seasonal arts-and-crafts activities, and reading events for
children, are organised throughout the year.

## 272 May Park (Doneycarney Park) 🚼 ♿ 🧍

Doneycarney, Dublin 3 (near Fairview, off the Malahide Rd);
Tel: 8336262; Website: www.dublincity.ie/parks
**Open:** All year; Mon–Fri 8.30am–dusk; Sat–Sun 9.30am–dusk ▪
**Suitable for ages:** All ▪ **Car parking:** On-street parking ▪ **Bus
routes:** 20B, 27, 27B/C, 42, 42A/B/X, 43, 129, 127.
**Sports:** cycling, gaelic football, hockey, hurling, soccer
A local park with playing fields.

## 273 Mellowes Park (Casement Park) 🚼 ♿ 🧍

Finglas, Dublin 9 (between the bypass and Casement Rd);
Tel: 8373891; Website: www.dublincity.ie/parks
**Open:** All year; Mon–Fri 8.30am–dusk; Sat–Sun 9.30am–dusk ▪
**Charge:** Free ▪ **Suitable for ages:** All ▪ **Car parking:** On-street
parking ▪ **Bus routes:** 17, 40, 104.
**Sports:** cycling, soccer, tennis
A 10.5-hectare park with soccer and tennis facilities. Dublin Public
Parks Tennis runs here during the summer months.

## 274 Morton Stadium ♿

Santry, Dublin 9 (take the N1 Dublin–Belfast road, then turn onto
the Old Airport Rd to Santry); Tel: 8620635.
**Open:** All year; Mon–Fri 12–10pm; Sat 9am–6pm; Sun 9am–1pm
▪ **Charge:** Child €6.50; Adult €6.50; Price is given for a training
session as part of a school or sports club ▪ **Suitable for ages:** 7+ ▪
**Car parking:** Free ▪ **Bus routes:** 33, 41, 41A, 16.
**Sports:** athletics
Morton Stadium is one of the venues for the 2003 Special

Olympics. The stadium is open to everyone, but is usually booked for groups and schools. The facilities here are fantastic – there are four outdoor long-jump pits, an all-weather shot-putt area, and state-of-the-art equipment for all track-and-field events. There is a 400-metre synthetic track, comprising an eight-lane circuit, with ten lanes on the finishing 100 metres.
**\* TOP CHOICES: SPORTS FACILITIES \***

## 275 Muldowney Beach (Malahide) 🚹

Malahide, Co. Dublin (from the City Centre, take the M1 to Swords, and then the R106 to Malahide, or take the coast road from Clontarf).
**Open:** Lifeguard: Jun–Sep; Mon–Sun 10am–8pm ■ **Charge:** Free ■ **Suitable for ages:** All ■ **Rail station:** Malahide ■ **DART station:** Malahide.
**Sports:** sailing, swimming, windsurfing
This sandy beach is south of Malahide village. There's a grassy bank to sit on, where you can watch sailing boats drift by. Watersports are popular, based at the marina in the village.

## 276 National Botanic Gardens 🚼 📷 ♿

Glasnevin, Dublin 9 (off Botanic Rd, north of Glasnevin Cemetery); Tel: 8374388; Fax: 8360080.
**Open:** Summer Gardens: Mon–Sat 9am–6pm; Sun 11am–6pm; Summer Glasshouses: Mon–Fri 9am–5.15pm (Thur 3pm); Sat 9am–5.45pm; Sun 2–5.45pm; Winter Gardens: Mon–Sat 10am–4.15pm (Thur 2–4.15pm); Winter Glasshouses: Mon–Sat 10am–4.30pm; Sun 11am–4.30pm; All-year Alpine Houses: Mon–Fri 10.45am–12.15pm, 2.15–3.15pm; Sun 2–5.45pm; Bank holidays 9am–5.45pm; Some glasshouses may close for lunch ■ **Charge:** Free ■ **Suitable for ages:** All ■ **Car parking:** Free ■ **Bus routes:** 13, 13A, 19, 19A, 134.
Gorgeous gardens, which are a treat to visit. There are around 20,000 species of plants here, with plenty to smell and admire. There are Victorian glasshouses, built by Richard Turner (of Kew and Belfast Gardens fame), and the world-famous curvilinear houses, which have been fully restored and now contain palms and giant lilies – a delight to children. Also on offer are herbaceous displays, a rose garden, a rockery, a vegetable garden, an arboretum, shrub borders and displays of wall plants.
**\* TOP CHOICES: PARKS \* TOP CHOICES: FOR AGES 2–5 \***

## 277 National Diving School

8 St. James Terrace, Malahide, Co. Dublin; Contact: Sarah
O'Mahony; Tel: 8452000; Fax: 8452920;
E-mail: ntdive@indigo.ie; Website: www.nds.ie
**Open:** All year; Wed evening ■ **Charge:** €400 for scuba course;
€600 for open water certificate ■ **Suitable for ages:** 12+ ■ **Bus
routes:** 32A, 42, 102, 105, 230 ■ **Rail station:** Malahide ■ **DART
station:** Malahide.
**Sports:** diving, scuba diving
To start diving, you must begin with the €40 'Try Dive' course,
which takes around two hours in a swimming pool. Here you
learn about the equipment, hand signals and safety. The next step
is to sign up for the 'Scuba Diver' or more advanced 'Open
Water' diving courses (the latter costs €600, including all
equipment and four sea dives).
**\* TOP CHOICES: SPORTS FACILITIES \* TOP CHOICES: HOBBIES/ARTS
AND CRAFTS \***

## 278 National Transport Museum

Heritage Depot, Howth Demesne, Howth, Dublin 13 (as you
approach Howth, turn right just past the DART station);
Tel: 8320427 (museum), 8480831 (outside opening hours);
Website: www.nationaltransportmuseum.org
**Open:** Jan–Aug: Mon–Fri 10am–5pm; Sat–Sun/bank holidays
2–5pm; Sep–May: Sat/Sun/bank holidays 2–5pm; Christmas (26
Dec–1 Jan): 2–5pm ■ **Charge:** Child €1.50; Adult €3; Family €8 ■
**Suitable for ages:** All ■ **Car parking:** Free ■ **Bus routes:** 31, 31B
■ **DART station:** Howth.
Military, commercial and domestic vehicles dating from
1883–1984 are all housed in a hangar in this friendly, no-frills
museum. Buses, tanks, trams and even bread vans are on display.
It will take about an hour to walk around and explore. There's a
nice café in the Deer Park Hotel, which is in the same grounds.
**\* TOP CHOICES: FOR AGES 2–5 \* TOP CHOICES: FOR AGES 5–10 \*
TOP CHOICES: FOR INQUISITIVE KIDS \* TOP CHOICES: FOR
ENERGETIC KIDS \***

## 279 Newbridge Demesne

Donabate, Co. Dublin (off the Dublin–Belfast road (N1), 3 miles
north of Dublin Airport on the road to Donabate); Tel: 8436534
(house), 8436064 (demesne); Fax: 8436535.

**Open:** Summer: Tue–Sat 10am–1pm, 2– 5pm; Sun/bank holidays 2–6pm; Oct–Mar: Sat/Sun/bank holidays 2–5pm ▪ **Charge:** Free ▪ **Suitable for ages:** All ▪ **Car parking:** Free ▪ **Bus routes:** 33B.
Newly opened in 2003 are the restored 4.5-acre Victorian Gardens. There are two glasshouses, a kitchen garden, a rose garden and a herbaceous border. The extensive 150-hectare demesne also has a wildlife and deer park, playing and walking areas and a 19th-century working farm, with old Irish breeds, a courtyard and, of course, the impressive Newbridge House. The playground is brilliant, one of the biggest and best on the northside. (See also Newbridge House)

★ TOP CHOICES: PICNIC SPOTS ★ TOP CHOICES: PARKS ★ TOP CHOICES: PLAYGROUNDS ★ TOP CHOICES: WALKS ★ TOP CHOICES: FOR AGES 0–2 ★ TOP CHOICES: FOR AGES 2–5 ★ TOP CHOICES: FOR ENERGETIC KIDS ★

## 280 Newbridge House 🛏 € ⛹

Donabate, Co. Dublin (off the Dublin–Belfast road (N1), 3 miles north of Dublin Airport on the road to Donabate); Tel: 8436534, 8436064; Fax: 8462537; E-mail: bd@dublintourism.ie
**Open:** Apr–Sep: Tue–Sat 10am–1pm, 2–5pm; Sun/bank holidays 2–6pm; Oct–Mar: Sat/Sun/bank holidays 2–5pm ▪ **Charge:** Child €3.50; Adult €6; OAPs/concessions €5; Family ticket €16.50; Traditional Farm only: Adults €2.50; Children €1.50; Family €6 ▪ **Suitable for ages:** All ▪ **Car parking:** Free ▪ **Bus routes:** 33B.
An 18th-century manor, set on 350 acres of parkland and with a farmyard full of animals which children will thoroughly enjoy. The Georgian interior is one of the best in Ireland, with a magnificent red drawing room in a wing which was added to the house by Lady Elizabeth Beresford, in order to display her husband's collection of 17th- and 18th-century paintings. There is also a courtyard, surrounded by a dairy, a blacksmith's forge, a carpenter's shop and an estate worker's house, all of which have been fitted out with original tools, implements and furniture. (See also Newbridge Demesne.)

## 281 Newgrange and Boyne Valley 🛏 ♿

Donore, Co. Meath (south of the River Boyne on the L21, 2km west of Donore. Signposted from Drogheda (off N1), and from Slane (off N2). Visitors cross the pedestrian bridge and are taken by coach to the sites); Tel: (041) 9880300, (041) 9823071.
**Open:** Visitor centre: Mar–Apr: Mon–Sun 9.30am–5.30pm; May:

Mon–Sun 9am–6pm; Jun–mid-Sep: Mon–Sun 9am–7pm; Mid-Sep–end Sep: Mon–Sun 9am–6.30pm; Oct: Mon–Sun 9.30am–5.30pm; Nov–Feb: Mon–Sun 9.30am–5pm; 45-minute tours set off roughly every 30 minutes ▪ **Charge:** Child €2.75; Adult €5.50; Concession €4.25; Family €13.75; Prices are given for Newgrange and the visitor centre ▪ **Suitable for ages:** 5+ ▪ **Car parking:** Free.

The megalithic (meaning made of big stones) sites of Newgrange, Dowth and Knowth are accessed by guided tours only, through the Brú na Bóinne visitor centre. The three passage tombs were built over 5,000 years ago, by Neolithic (New Stone Age) man, making them older than Stonehenge or the pyramids of Egypt. Newgrange is the greatest Celtic passage tomb in Europe, and it is the busiest of the three, as you can actually go inside. It is a huge grass-covered, kidney-shaped mound, surrounded by the remains of a circle of large standing stones. Inside the tomb is a cross-shaped central chamber, with stones hollowed out where the ashes of the dead were interred. The passageway to the tomb is illuminated by the sun at dawn during the winter solstice, but there's a lottery for the 20 tickets a year available to witness this. Dowth is still being excavated, and is not open to the public, but Knowth has wonderful stone carvings outside the tomb. Brú na Bóinne was designated a World Heritage Site by UNESCO in 1993. Everyone should visit it once in their lifetime.

**✱ TOP CHOICES: FOR AGES 10+ ✱**

## 282 North Bull Island and Dollymount Strand

Dollymount, Dublin 5 (take the coast road from the city centre, past St. Annes's Park, and turn right at the traffic lights onto the causeway); Tel: 8331859, 8338341; Website: www.dublincity.ie/parks
**Open:** All year; Mon–Sun 24 hours; Nov–Dec is the best time for bird watching ▪ **Charge:** Free ▪ **Suitable for ages:** All ▪ **Car parking:** Free ▪ **Bus routes:** 32X, 130.

The 5km-long Bull Island is a bird sanctuary, a nature reserve and a UNESCO biosphere reserve. If your children are interested in nature, this is a lovely walk. Remember to take wellies and binoculars. More than 20,000 birds visit Bull Island – up to 180 different bird species, including wild fowl and waders. After the first left turn from the roundabout, turn north, away from the hard sand on the beach, and continue alongside the dunes. There is plenty of flora behind the Marram grass here if you want to investigate further, otherwise continue until you reach the end of the Bull, where little ones can collect shells. Now turn left, go over the dunes and proceed down the inner shore until you reach the salt marsh. Here you will see ducks and geese, along with the mud-flat feeders, on the marsh. There are a few paths from here on, with gorgeous wild flowers (no picking!), going towards the golf club. Go back to the dunes and on to the beach. Dollymount Strand is 3 miles of sandy shore with sand dunes behind it. It's not great for swimming, but paddling is okay. Dollymount is ideal for many sports – especially when the tide is out – including surfing, windsurfing and kiting (either on the land or the water). Watch out for learner drivers, who practise here, and walkers.

**✱ TOP CHOICES: BEACHES ✱ TOP CHOICES: WALKS ✱ TOP CHOICES: FOR AGES 5–10 ✱ TOP CHOICES: FOR AGES 10+ ✱ TOP CHOICES: FOR INQUISITIVE KIDS ✱ TOP CHOICES: FOR ENERGETIC KIDS ✱**

## 283 Northside Shopping Centre

Coolock, Dublin 5 (off the Oscar Traynor Rd); Tel: 8486049 (centre), 8477743 (swimming pool); Fax: 8670154.
**Open:** All year; Mon–Wed 9am–6pm; Thur–Fri 9am–9pm; Sat 9am–6pm; Sun 12–6pm ▪ **Charge:** Crêche €2 per hour, for max. 90 minutes ▪ **Suitable for ages:** All ▪ **Car parking:** Free ▪ **Bus routes:** 17A, 27, 27B.
An older shopping centre, with 70 shops. There are good services here, including a Free Legal Advice Centre, a Dublin Well Woman Centre and even a swimming pool. Superquinn's crêche is open to all shoppers during the centre's opening hours (opening a half-hour later and closing a half-hour earlier than the shopping centre times given).

## 284 Norton, Betty Ann, Theatre School, Swords

BASE Resource Centre, Brackenstown, Swords, Co. Dublin; Tel: 4751913; Fax: 4751140;
E-mail: bettyann.norton@iegateway.net;
Website: www.bettyann-nortontheatreschool.com
**Open:** Sep–Jun: 3 x 10-week terms; Summer course: Courses vary from 1 hour to 90 minutes weekly ▪ **Charge:** Summer courses from €115; Other course prices on request ▪ **Suitable for ages:** 4+ ▪ **Bus routes:** 41, 41B/X.
Speech and drama classes for children from very young onwards, as

well as music, mime, movement, puppetry and storytelling. Older children participate in *feiseanna* and are auditioned for radio, television, theatre and films when suited to casting requirements. Teenagers can join the drama workshop, designed as an introduction to stagecraft and theatre studies as well as an aid to personality development and confidence-building. The school also runs classes and courses in speech therapy, aiming to build confidence and creativity. It is one of the best theatre schools in Dublin.

★ **TOP CHOICES: HOBBIES/ARTS AND CRAFTS** ★ **TOP CHOICES: SUMMER CAMPS** ★

## 285 Oldtown Riding Stables 

Wyestown, Oldtown, Co. Dublin; Tel: 8354755.

**Open:** All year; Tue–Sun 10am–4pm; Call for dates of this year's summer camps ▪ **Charge:** €15 per hourly lesson; Pony camp prices on request ▪ **Suitable for ages:** 3+.

**Sports:** horse-riding

Oldtown specialises in children's riding and offers lessons for all standards. Riding out is usually over farmland. Former clients have gone on to jump nationally. There is no indoor arena. Pony camps are run in the summer.

★ **TOP CHOICES: SPORTS FACILITIES** ★

## 286 Omni Park, Santry 

Swords Rd (Old Airport Rd), Santry, Dublin 9 (off the M1, Junction 3); Tel: 8421262.

**Open:** All year; Centre: Mon 9am–7pm; Wed–Fri 9am–9pm; Sat 9am–6pm; Sun 12–6pm; Crèche: Mon–Wed 10am–6pm; Thur–Fri 10am–7pm; Sat 10am–6pm ▪ **Charge:** Crèche: Drop-in €3.80 per hour, max 2-hour stay; Play School €32 per week ▪ **Suitable for ages:** All ▪ **Car parking:** Free ▪ **Bus routes:** 16, 16A, 33, 41, 41B/C, 103, 104, 746.

A good-sized shopping centre, beside cinemas. There are plenty of fast-food places here, and a Bewley's café. The crèche includes a playschool from 10am–12pm Mon–Fri, and a drop-in facility after that.

## 287 Omniplex Cinemas 

Old Airport Rd (Swords Rd), Santry, Dublin 9 (in Santry Omni Park, off the M1, Junction 3); Tel: 8428844.

**Open:** All year; Children's programmes: Mon–Sun, before 7pm; Kids' Club: Sat 12pm ▪ **Charge:** Child €4.50; Adult €5; Off-peak prices given ▪ **Suitable for ages:** 3+ ▪ **Car parking:** Free ▪ **Bus**

**routes:** 16, 16A, 33, 41, 41B/C, 103, 104, 746.

A multiplex with a Saturday kids' club at 12pm. Tickets are €2 per person. A discount is available for group bookings.

**★ TOP CHOICES: BIRTHDAY PARTY IDEAS ★ TOP CHOICES: FOR AGES 5–10 ★ TOP CHOICES: FOR AGES 10+ ★**

## 288 The Pavilion Shopping Centre

Swords, Co. Dublin (off the N1, near the Malahide roundabout); Tel: 8904580.

**Open:** All year; Mon–Wed 9am–9pm; Thur–Fri 9am–10pm; Sat 8.30am–7pm; Sun 10am–6pm ▪ **Charge:** Crèche €2 per hour, for max. 90 minutes ▪ **Suitable for ages:** All ▪ **Car parking:** Paying car park from €2 per hr ▪ **Bus routes:** 41, 41A/B/X, 43, 230.

A modern, space-age shopping centre, with a big Dunnes Stores and a very busy Kylemore Café. Superquinn runs a crèche during the centre's opening hours (closing a half-hour before the centre's closing time). Annoyingly, buses heading towards the city centre don't come right to the door.

**★ TOP CHOICES: SUMMER CAMPS ★**

## 289 Phibsboro Library

Blackquire Bridge, Dublin 7; Tel: 8304341; Website: www.iol.ie/dublincitylibrary

**Open:** All year; Mon/Wed 12.45–4pm, 4.45–8pm; Tue/Thur/Sat 10am–1pm, 2–5pm ▪ **Charge:** Free ▪ **Suitable for ages:** All ▪ **Car parking:** Metered parking on street ▪ **Bus routes:** 10, 19A, 22.

There is a small children's section here, where special seasonal arts-and-crafts and reading events for children are organised throughout the year.

## 290 Pope John Paul II Park

Cabra, Dublin 7 (between Nephin Rd and Ratoath Rd); Tel: 8373891, 8384233; Website: www.dublincity.ie/parks

**Open:** All year; Mon–Fri 8.30am–dusk; Sat–Sun 9.30am–dusk ▪ **Charge:** Free ▪ **Suitable for ages:** All ▪ **Car parking:** On-street parking ▪ **Bus routes:** 121, 122.

**Sports:** cycling, gaelic football, hurling, soccer, athletics

An 8.5-hectare park known locally as 'the Bogeys', it was originally named Nephin Park, but was renamed in 1980 to commemorate Pope John Paul II landing here by helicopter on his way to the nearby Papal Nunciature, during his historic visit to Ireland in

1979. There are pleasant walks around the flower gardens, as well as playing fields.

## 291 Poppintree Park ♿

Ballymun, Dublin 9 (between Ballymun, Poppintree and Glasnevin North); Tel: 8373891, 8428833;
Website: www.dublincity.ie/parks
**Open:** All year; Mon–Fri 8.30am–dusk; Sat–Sun 9.30am–dusk ■
**Charge:** Free ■ **Suitable for ages:** All ■ **Car parking:** On-street parking ■ **Bus routes:** 13, 40B, 220.
**Sports:** basketball, cycling, gaelic football, hurling, soccer, tennis
This park is mainly taken up with sports grounds for football, tennis and basketball, but there are pleasant walks also. Dublin Public Parks Tennis runs here during the summer months.

## 292 Portmarnock Beach ⊚

Strand Rd, Portmarnock, Co. Dublin (between Baldoyle and Malahide. From the city centre, take the M1 to Swords and then the R106 to Malahide, or take the coast road from Clontarf).
**Open:** Lifeguard: Jun–Sep; Mon–Sun 10am–8pm ■ **Charge:** Free
■ **Suitable for ages:** All ■ **Car parking:** On the seafront – can get very busy ■ **Bus routes:** 32, 32A/B, 102, 230.
**Sports:** horse-riding, swimming
A classic bucket-and-spade sandy beach, which is also good for a bracing walk in the winter. You can buy a decent picnic from the deli counter at the local Spar, and the kiosk sells crab hooks and nets for fishing in the rock pools. It's worth walking further up the beach, away from the toilets, where it's quieter. When the tide goes out, there's good hard sand for ball games.
**✱ TOP CHOICES: BEACHES ✱ TOP CHOICES: FOR AGES 0–2 ✱ TOP CHOICES: FOR AGES 2–5 ✱ TOP CHOICES: FOR AGES 5–10 ✱**

## 293 Portmarnock Sports and Leisure Club ☕♿⊚

Blackwood Lane, Carrickhill, Portmarnock, Co. Dublin (turn at the beach after Sands Hotel, go past Dunnes Stores, and then turn right); Tel: 8462122; Fax: 8461258; E-mail: pslc@eircom.net
**Open:** All year; Mon–Sun 10am–8pm; Call for details of this year's summer camp dates ■ **Charge:** €324 annual family membership; Junior membership €72 annually if the rest of the family does not want to join; Pool: 1 hour adult €2.25, child €1.20; Sports facilities from €1.50 adult, €0.90 child;

Non-members pay roughly double the prices given; Summer camp fees on request ▪ **Suitable for ages:** All ▪ **Car parking:** Free ▪ **Bus routes:** 32, 32A, 230, 102 ▪ **DART station:** Sutton.
**Sports:** badminton, basketball, soccer, squash, swimming, tennis
A private sports club, with swims on the hour. The shallow end of the pool is too deep for toddlers and for small children who aren't confident swimmers to stand up in. Swimming classes are available. Members get discounts on tennis and other coaching sessions. The weekly summer camps are open to non-members and are the best in this area, with loads of fun activities organised.
✱ TOP CHOICES: SPORTS FACILITIES ✱ TOP CHOICES: SUMMER CAMPS ✱

## 294 Raheny Library

Howth Rd, Raheny, Dublin 5; Tel: 8315521;
Website: www.iol.ie/dublincitylibrary
**Open:** All Year; Mon–Thur 10am–8pm; Fri–Sat 10am–5pm ▪
**Charge:** Free ▪ **Suitable for ages:** All ▪ **Car parking:** Free ▪ **Bus routes:** 29A, 31, 32, 32A/B ▪ **DART station:** Raheny.
Special seasonal arts-and-crafts and reading events for children.

## 295 Raheny United Football Club

All Saints Dr, Raheny, Dublin 5; Tel: 8510077.
**Open:** Sep–May ▪ **Suitable for ages:** 7+ ▪ **Bus routes:** 29A, 31, 31A, 32, 32A/B, 105, 129.
**Sports:** soccer

## 296 Ramp City

Old Airport Rd, Cloughran, Dublin 9; Tel: 8426322.
**Open:** All year; Mon 6–9pm; Tue–Fri 12–9pm; Sat–Sun 10am–9pm ▪ **Charge:** €6.50 for daytime sessions; €8 for evening session; All-day pass €15 ▪ **Suitable for ages:** 6+ ▪ **Bus routes:** 41, 41A, 46.
**Sports:** skateboarding, BMX biking
A large park filled with ramps and jumps, to allow blading or boarding in a safe and fun environment. Sessions usually last two hours, but are at intervals during the day, so call in advance. Monday evenings are reserved for BMX bikes only. You can bring kids for a party at the weekend and eat in the restaurant upstairs, but they can't offer any special arrangements.
✱ TOP CHOICES: BIRTHDAY PARTY IDEAS ✱ TOP CHOICES: SPORTS FACILITIES ✱ TOP CHOICES: FOR AGES 5–10 ✱ TOP CHOICES: FOR ENERGETIC KIDS ✱

## 297 Ramp N Rail Skatepark

Unit 3, 96A Drumcondra Rd Upr, Dublin 9; Tel: 8377533.
**Open:** All year; Tue–Sun 11am–9pm ▪ **Charge:** Membership is
€20 ▪ **Suitable for ages:** 6+ ▪ **Bus routes:** 3, 11, 11A/B, 13, 13A,
16, 16A, 41, 41A/B/C, 51A, 746.
**Sports:** skateboarding
A skate park for bladers and boarders. Membership is required –
you need to bring two passport-size photos, and a parent or
guardian must sign for permission to join.
✱ TOP CHOICES: SPORTS FACILITIES ✱ TOP CHOICES: FOR AGES 5–10
✱ TOP CHOICES: FOR AGES 10+ ✱ TOP CHOICES: FOR TRENDY KIDS
✱ TOP CHOICES: FOR ENERGETIC KIDS ✱

## 298 Rathbeale Public Library 🚼 ♿ ✏ 🖥

Swords Shopping Centre, Swords, Co. Dublin (down the road
from the Pavillion Shopping Centre); Tel: 8404179;
Fax: 8404417; E-mail: rathbealelib@eircom.net;
Website: www.iol.ie/~fincolib/me.htm
**Open:** All year; Mon–Thur 10am–1pm, 2–8.30pm; Fri–Sat
10am–5pm; Closed Sat–Mon of bank holiday weekends ▪
**Charge:** Free ▪ **Suitable for ages:** All ▪ **Car parking:** Free ▪ **Bus
routes:** 41, 41B/X.
Holiday activities for children are organised throughout the year.

## 299 Reynoldstown Victorian Country House and Farm 🚼 ♿ 🚻

Naul, Fingal, Co. Dublin (2 miles from Balbriggan, off the
Dublin–Belfast road (N1)); Tel: 8412615.
**Open:** Apr–Oct; Mon–Sun 12–5pm ▪ **Charge:** Child €5; Adult €5
▪ **Suitable for ages:** All ▪ **Car parking:** Free.
This is a working organic farm, with many rare species of farm
animals, including a miniature horse and rare fowl. The children
can have a hands-on experience, and can cuddle a rabbit or feed
a baby chick. Free tea and scones are included! Wear wellies and
old clothes. Birthday parties can be organised – if you bring your
own food, they will decorate some tables for you.
✱ TOP CHOICES: PICNIC SPOTS ✱ TOP CHOICES: BIRTHDAY PARTY
VENUES ✱ TOP CHOICES: FOR AGES 0–2 ✱ TOP CHOICES: FOR AGES
2–5 ✱ TOP CHOICES: FOR AGES 5–10 ✱ TOP CHOICES: FOR SHY KIDS
✱ TOP CHOICES: FOR ENERGETIC KIDS ✱

## 300 Rush Beach 🅰

Rush, Co. Dublin (from the city centre, take the M1 past Swords and follow signs for Donabate and Rush).
**Open:** Lifeguard: Jun–Sep; Mon–Sun 10am–8pm ▪ **Charge:** Free ▪ **Suitable for ages:** All ▪ **Car parking:** Free ▪ **Rail station:** Balbriggan.
**Sports:** sailing, swimming, windsurfing
This is a long, sandy beach, popular with Dubliners of all ages.

## 301 Rush Cricket Club

Rush, Co. Dublin; Tel: 8437189.
**Open:** May–Oct ▪ **Charge:** Small weekly charge; Summer camp fees on request ▪ **Suitable for ages:** 5+ ▪ **Car parking:** Free ▪ **Bus routes:** 33, 33A ▪ **Rail station:** Rush.
**Sports:** cricket
Nearly all Dublin clubs offer summer camps for children, and most also host schools cricket during term time. The camps are often run from Mon to Fri, for several hours a day. Ordinary sportswear is fine. Pads, etc., are supplied by the club.

## 302 St. Anne's Park 🚼 ♿ 🧒 🚻

Raheny, Dublin 5 (between the Clontarf Rd and the Howth Rd, Raheny); Tel: 8338898; Website: www.dublincity.ie/parks
**Open:** All year; Mon–Fri 8.30am–dusk; Sat–Sun 9.30am–dusk ▪ **Charge:** Free ▪ **Suitable for ages:** All ▪ **Car parking:** Free ▪ **Bus routes:** 29A, 31, 31A/B, 32, 32A/B, 130 ▪ **DART station:** Harmonstown.
**Sports:** cycling, gaelic football, hockey, hurling, soccer, tennis, golf, pitch-and-putt
The walk from the Howth Road end of St Anne's Park to Raheny is very pleasant. On the way, you pass through woodland, an old folly, the Rose Garden and the playing fields. The 270-acre park contains 35 playing pitches, 18 hard-surfaced tennis courts and a par-three golf course. There's also a good playground, with a rope bridge, swings and a maze. Dublin Public Parks Tennis runs here during the summer months.
✱ TOP CHOICES: PICNIC SPOTS ✱ TOP CHOICES: SPORTS FACILITIES ✱ TOP CHOICES: PARKS ✱ TOP CHOICES: PLAYGROUNDS ✱ TOP CHOICES: FOR AGES 0–2 ✱ TOP CHOICES: FOR AGES 2–5 ✱ TOP CHOICES: FOR AGES 10+ ✱ TOP CHOICES: FOR ENERGETIC KIDS ✱

## 303 St. Mary's Hospital Pool 🛒 ♿ ⊕

Willie Nolan Rd, Baldoyle, Co. Dublin (at the corner of the hospital, turn down the road beside Granger's Pub); Tel: 8323056 (hospital), 8392826 (pool).
**Open:** All year; Fri 7.30pm, Sun 2pm ▪ **Charge:** Child €3; Adult €4; lesson fees on request ▪ **Suitable for ages:** All ▪ **Car parking:** Free ▪ **Bus routes:** 32, 32A/B, 102.
**Sports:** swimming
This pool has facilities especially for children with physical disabilities. Children's swimming classes are held on Sat and Sun mornings and on Thur evenings. Parent-and-toddler sessions are on Tue at 9.30am.
★ TOP CHOICES: FOR AGES 0–2 ★ TOP CHOICES: FOR AGES 2–5 ★

## 304 St. Maur's Gaelic Football Club

South Shore, Rush, Co. Dublin; Contact: Ann Reynolds; Tel: 8438233.
**Open:** All year ▪ **Suitable for ages:** 5+ ▪ **Bus routes:** 33, 33A.
**Sports:** gaelic football

## 305 St. Vincent's CBS Pool

Finglas Rd, Glasnevin, Dublin 9; Tel: 8306716.
**Open:** All year; Tue–Wed 6–7pm; Sat 1–2pm; Sun 9–11am ▪ **Charge:** Child €2.50; Adult €3.50; Classes are extra ▪ **Suitable for ages:** All ▪ **Bus routes:** 13, 13A, 19.
**Sports:** swimming
There are open swims and classes available on Wed afternoons and at weekends in this small school's swimming pool.

## 306 Seamus Ennis Cultural Centre 📖 ♿ €

Naul, Fingal, Co. Dublin (2 miles from Balbriggan off the Dublin–Belfast Rd (N1)); Tel: 8020898; Fax: 8090899; Website: www.seamusennis.com
**Open:** All year; Musical events most evenings and weekends ▪ **Charge:** Child €6; Adult €12; Average price for events ▪ **Suitable for ages:** 5+ ▪ **Car parking:** On-street parking.
The story of Séamus Ennis, the famous Uilleann piper, storyteller and folk song collector. Traditional Irish music events are run most evenings and weekends in the thatched cottage.

NORTH DUBLIN

## 307 Sea Safari ♿ 👶

Malahide Marina, Malahide, Co. Dublin (take any of the side streets towards the sea from Malahide Main St); Tel: 8061626, 086 3855011 (mobile); Fax: 8168078; Website: www.seasafari.ie
**Open:** All year; Call for sailing times ▪ **Charge:** Child €25; Adult €25; Family €80 (4 persons) ▪ **Suitable for ages:** 8+ ▪ **Car parking:** Pay-and-display parking near departure point ▪ **Bus routes:** 32A, 42, 102, 105, 230.

There are three safaris available, in all-weather rigid inflatable lifeboats with seating: the Eco Safari lasts 90 minutes and explores birds and wildlife around Skerries, Lambay Island and Ireland's Eye; the Thrill Seeker is a one-hour, high-speed ride around Ireland's Eye, Howth, the Baily Lighthouse and Dublin Bay; the Leisure Safari is more relaxed, and is concerned more with culture and heritage from the River Liffey to Malahide. The boats all meet the necessary safety standards and have handrails. Life jackets and waterproof clothing are supplied, but you are advised to wear flat shoes and warm clothing. Under-15s must be accompanied by an adult. You can book the whole boat (a 7-seater for €150, or an 11-seater for €250) as a special birthday treat. For children with disabilities, ring in advance.

✱ TOP CHOICES: PICNIC SPOTS ✱ TOP CHOICES: BIRTHDAY PARTY IDEAS ✱ TOP CHOICES: FOR AGES 10+ ✱ TOP CHOICES: FOR TRENDY KIDS ✱ TOP CHOICES: FOR ENERGETIC KIDS ✱

## 308 Shoebridge, Kathleen (Music Teacher)

Artane, Dublin 5; Tel: 8311922.
**Open:** All year; Class times on request ▪ **Charge:** Fees on request ▪ **Suitable for ages:** 7+.

Kathleen Shoebridge gives classical piano lessons, from beginners to advanced students, with preparation for RIAM, ABRSM, and TCL exams.

## 309 Sillogue Park and Golf Course

Ballymun, Dublin 9 (off Junction 4, off the M50); Tel: 8429956 (park), 8429956 (golf reservations);
Website: www.dublincity.ie/parks
**Open:** All year; Mon–Fri 8.30am–dusk; Sat–Sun 9.30am–dusk ▪ **Charge:** Golf: Mon–Fri adult (9 holes) €8.80; Adult (18 holes) €13.90; Concession (9 holes, Mon–Fri 8.30am–1pm) €7.60; Concession (18 holes, Mon–Fri 8.30am–12pm) €8.80;

Sat/Sun/bank holidays adult/junior €15.20 (18-hole rounds available only) ▪ **Suitable for ages:** 10+ ▪ **Car parking:** On-street parking ▪ **Bus routes:** 40B.
**Sports:** golf
A demanding golf course, and very good value too.
**✻ TOP CHOICES: SPORTS FACILITIES ✻**

## 310 Sillybilly Learning Ltd 🛒 🖼️

St. Gabriel's Community Centre, St. Gabriel's Rd, Clontarf, Dublin 3; Malahide Seascouts' Hall, St. James's Terrace, Malahide, Co. Dublin; Tel: 8535353; Fax: 8535953;
E-mail: enquiries@sillybillylearning.com
**Open:** All year; Tue (Malahide); Fri (Clontarf); Call for times ▪
**Charge:** Music On The Go – you are asked to pre-book 6 sessions (approx. €60) in advance; Party plan prices on request (eg. Fairy Princess Party approx. €180 for 1 hr/ €250 for 2 hrs) ▪ **Suitable for ages:** 4 months to 4 years.
Sillybilly runs a programme of fun activities involving music, stories and play for children from four months to four-and-a-half years. All the play equipment is supplied and set up in a local centre. A parent/guardian must be present and is encouraged to get involved – this is a great way of meeting other parents/minders of small children. For wheelchair access, call for details on individual venues. Sillybilly will also hold parties in your own home. You just have to provide the food. Party Plans: 1. Sillybilly party (half-an-hour): An entertainer comes to your house with puppets, games, a magic show and a bubble disco. 2. Fairy Princess Party (1 or 2 hours): Songs and stories from a costumed fairy, with games and a bubble disco. 3. Soldiers Party (2 hours): Sergeant Sillybilly comes and tells soldier stories and provides fun challenges for a half-hour. If you pass them you get a certificate. The party includes a magic show, and kids get a model balloon to take home. 4. Sports Party (2 hours): Equipment is provided – tunnels, obstacle courses, etc. 5. Disco Party (half-an-hour): Disco, games, a magic show and balloon modelling. 6. Baby party: Activity play zone provided, alongside stories, songs and bubbles.
**✻ TOP CHOICES: BIRTHDAY PARTY IDEAS ✻ TOP CHOICES: FOR AGES 0–2 ✻ TOP CHOICES: FOR AGES 2–5 ✻**

## 311 Skerries Beach 🏃 🅰️

Skerries, Fingal, Co. Dublin (from the city centre, take the M1 past Swords. Stay on the N1 until you see the signs for Skerries).

**Open:** Lifeguard: Jun–Sep; Mon–Sun 10am–8pm ■ **Charge:** Free
■ **Suitable for ages:** All ■ **Rail station:** Skerries.
**Sports:** sailing, swimming, windsurfing

Skerries has a long, sandy beach, which is great for games and
swimming. It is joined by a grass promenade to Red Island Scenic
Park, which has a free children's playground. There's a pretty
harbour in Skerries, which has an amusement arcade and funfair
in the summer.

★ TOP CHOICES: BEACHES ★ TOP CHOICES: FOR AGES 0–2 ★ TOP
CHOICES: FOR AGES 2–5 ★

## 312 Skerries Library

Strand St, Skerries, Co. Dublin; Tel: 8491900; Fax: 8495142;
E-mail: skerrieslibrary@hotmail.com;
Website: www.iol.ie/~fincolib/md.htm
**Open:** All year; Mon/Wed/Fri–Sat 10am–1pm, 2–5pm; Tue/Thur
2–5pm ■ **Charge:** Free ■ **Suitable for ages:** All ■ **Car parking:**
On-street parking ■ **Rail station:** Skerries.

Seasonal arts-and-crafts activities, plus reading events for children,
are organised throughout the year.

## 313 Skerries Mills

Skerries, Co. Dublin (on the coast towards Drogheda);
Tel: 8495208; Fax: 8495213.
**Open:** All year; Apr–Oct: Daily 10.30am–6pm; Oct–Mar: Daily
10.30am–4.30pm ■ **Charge:** Free ■ **Suitable for ages:** 2+ ■ **Car
parking:** Free ■ **Bus routes:** 33 ■ **Rail station:** Skerries.

A delight for all ages, there are two fully restored, working
windmills here, and a museum dealing with the history and
traditions of milling. It's good to know that bread didn't always
come sliced, in a wrapper. Art exhibitions are sometimes
displayed in the tea rooms. Entry is free.

★ TOP CHOICES: FOR AGES 2–5 ★ TOP CHOICES: FOR AGES 5–10 ★
TOP CHOICES: FOR INQUISITIVE KIDS ★

## 314 Skerries Rugby Football Club

Holmpatrick, Skerries, Co. Dublin; Contact: Greg Robbins;
Tel: 8490066 (office); E-mail: greg@gregrobins.com
**Open:** Sep–Apr ■ **Suitable for ages:** 6+ ■ **Bus routes:** 33, 33A ■
**Rail station:** Skerries.
**Sports:** rugby

## 315 Skerries Sailing Club

Harbour Rd, Skerries, Co. Dublin; Tel: 8491233, 8490363 (Paul Hick – seniors), 8411190 (Conor Barn – juniors).
**Open:** All year; Holiday camps: 10am–6pm, depending on season and weather; Call for dates of this year's holiday camps ▪ **Charge:** €420 for annual family membership; €50 for individual junior membership; Fees for coaching and camps on request ▪ **Suitable for ages:** 8+ ▪ **Car parking:** Free ▪ **Bus routes:** 33, 33A ▪ **Rail station:** Skerries.
**Sports:** sailing
A private sailing club, with boats available to juniors for summer and other holiday camps. A one-week course teaches beginners the basics of how to sail a dinghy. Children need to have their own dinghy if they want to take up racing. However, boats and gear can be hired through the sailing school before you decide to invest.

## 316 Songschool Ltd

Unit 10, Sunlight Studios, Railway St, Balbriggan, Co. Dublin; Tel: 8417573; Fax: 8417573; Website: www.songschool.ie
**Open:** Workshops all year; Weekly summer schools in Jul/Aug, Mon–Fri 9.30am–5.30pm ▪ **Charge:** 1-day course €300; 2-day course €650 ▪ **Suitable for ages:** 12+.
Songschool holds one- and two-day workshops, offering a first-hand insight into life as a professional songwriter or musician, and an overview of songwriting and the music business. The one-day course includes songwriting and a performance of the new songs in the afternoon; the two-day course also includes recording and post-production. All participating students receive CDs of the work done on the course.
**★ TOP CHOICES: FOR IMAGINATIVE KIDS ★**

## 317 Sportslink Archery and Crossbow Club

Indoor/Outdoor: Sportslink, Furry Pk, Cloughran, Co. Dublin (go through Santry on the Old Airport Rd. Take a left after the Texaco garage into the grounds); Contact: Carmel Fields; Tel: 8901029; E-mail: sportslinkarchery@eircom.net
**Open:** All year; Call for current meeting times ▪ **Charge:** €152 for associate membership (you have to be proposed by an existing member) ▪ **Suitable for ages:** 10+ ▪ **Bus routes:** 41, 41B/C.
**Sports:** archery

You must be a member of the Sportslink Club to join this archery club and use the facilities. The club also has associate members.

## 318 Sportslink Club 🛒 🎲 ☕ ♿ 💁 ⓘ

PST Sports Club, Furry Pk, Cloughran, Co. Dublin (go through Santry on the Old Airport Rd. Take a left after the Texaco garage into the grounds); Tel: 8621200.
**Open:** All year; Mon–Fri 9am–10pm; Sat–Sun 9am–6pm ■
**Charge:** €152 for associate membership (you have to be proposed by an existing member) ■ **Suitable for ages:** All ■ **Car parking:** Free ■ **Bus routes:** 41, 41B/C.
**Sports:** archery, badminton, basketball, soccer, swimming, tennis
A sports club primarily for civil service and Telecom staff, although also open to the public as associate members. SportsLink offers a wide range of activities, from archery to basketball and tennis. Children must leave by 7pm.

## 319 Stanmullen Road Club (Cycling)

Stanmullen, Co. Meath; Contact: Kay Howard; Tel: 8411352.
**Open:** Mar–Sep ■ **Charge:** €15 membership fee ■ **Suitable for ages:** 10+.
**Sports:** cycling
A competitive cycling club with an active junior section. Training is tailored to suit individual requirements.
**✱ TOP CHOICES: HOBBIES/ARTS AND CRAFTS ✱**

## 320 Stardust Memorial Park 🛒 ♿ 🤸

Santry, Dublin 9 (between Greencastle Rd and Adare Rd, along the Santry River); Tel: 8331859, 8338341;
Website: www.dublincity.ie/parks
**Open:** All year; Mon–Fri 8.30am–dusk; Sat–Sun 9.30am–dusk ■
**Charge:** Free ■ **Suitable for ages:** All ■ **Car parking:** On-street parking ■ **Bus routes:** 27, 27C/X, 42.
**Sports:** cycling
This 8-hectare park was built in memory of those who died in the Stardust fire tragedy on St. Valentine's night, 1981. In the centre of the park is the Stardust Memorial, a life-size bronze sculpture of a dancing couple set in a pool with 48 fountain jets.

## 321 Starstruck Stage School, Clontarf

Westwood Health & Fitness Centre, Clontarf, Dublin 3 (near

Clontarf Rd DART station); Contact: Julian Benson; Tel: 6764377;
E-mail: starstruck@julian-benson.com;
Website: www.stageschool.com

**Open:** All year; 10 week terms; Sat, 1 hour per week, depending
on course taken ▪ **Charge:** €100 per 10-week term for 1 hour per
week; Private tuition fees on request ▪ **Suitable for ages:** 3+ ▪
**Bus routes:** 103, 104, 130.

A highly recommended performing arts school. Dance, voice and
drama coaching are offered for ages 3+. The course covers
modern, ballet, tap, jazz, Latin and hip hop dance, as well as
theatre acting and singing. The school has its own casting agency.
Call for details of this year's summer school.

✱ **TOP CHOICES: HOBBIES/ARTS AND CRAFTS** ✱ **TOP CHOICES:
SUMMER CAMPS** ✱ **TOP CHOICES: FOR IMAGINATIVE KIDS** ✱

## 322 Steele, Ann Marie (Music Teacher)

Fairview, Dublin 3; Tel: 086 3208295.

**Open:** All year; Class times on request ▪ **Charge:** €10 per
30-minute class ▪ **Suitable for ages:** 7+.

Ann Marie Steele teaches classical piano, and prepares students
for RIAM exams.

## 323 Sutton Beach 🚉

Howth, Co. Dublin (on the south side of Howth, facing Bull
Island).

**Open:** Lifeguard: Jun–Sep; Mon–Sun 10am–8pm ▪ **Charge:** Free
▪ **Suitable for ages:** All ▪ **Car parking:** On-street parking ▪ **Bus
routes:** 31, 31A/B ▪ **DART station:** Sutton.

**Sports:** swimming

A sandy beach with good rocks to jump off for swimming. The
water quality should improve once the new northside coastal
sewage pipe is built.

## 324 Sutton Dinghy Club

Strand Rd, Sutton, Dublin 13 (turn right going into Sutton village
onto Greenfield Rd, then veer right onto Strand Rd. The club is on
the right); Tel: 8393135; Fax: 8390174; E-mail: info@sdc.ie;
Website: www.sdc.ie

**Open:** All year; Mon–Sun 10am–4pm ▪ **Charge:** €85 annual
membership; classes are extra; No need to be a member for
summer camps, which cost about €160 a week ▪ **Suitable for
ages:** 7+ ▪ **Car parking:** Free ▪ **Bus routes:** 31A/B ▪ **DART**

**station:** Sutton.
**Sports:** sailing

Members can participate in all-year dinghy sailing, and enter all races and competitions. The club provides a range of boats and other sailing equipment, which can usually be availed of while you are doing courses. Non-members can participate in the summer camps, where all gear, including wetsuits and dinghies, is supplied.

✱ **TOP CHOICES: HOBBIES/ARTS AND CRAFTS** ✱ **TOP CHOICES: SUMMER CAMPS** ✱

## 325 Suttonians Rugby Football Club

Station Rd, Sutton, Dublin 13; Contact: Mick Reddin;
Tel: 8397490 (office), 8335088; E-mail: mickreddin@eircom.net
**Open:** Sep–Apr ▪ **Suitable for ages:** 6+ ▪ **Bus routes:** 31, 31A/B
▪ **DART station:** Sutton.
**Sports:** rugby

## 326 Sutton Lawn Tennis Club

176 Howth Rd, Sutton, Dublin 13; Tel: 8323035; Fax: 8392194;
E-mail: suttonltc@eircom.net
**Open:** All year; Mon–Sun 9am–6pm for children; Call for this year's holiday camp dates ▪ **Charge:** €195 annual membership; Summer camp and coaching fees on request ▪ **Suitable for ages:** 5+ ▪ **Bus routes:** 31, 31A/B ▪ **DART station:** Sutton.
**Sports:** squash, tennis

This is a very active tennis club for junior tennis players, especially in the summer. 'Round robins' (where players are challenged by other players until they are beaten, and then the winner takes over) are organised daily. There are competitions and league games most weeks. Children must be off the courts by 6pm. Summer camps and coaching are available to members only, at an extra cost.

## 327 Swords Cycling Club

Swords, Co. Dublin; Contact: Jason Kelly; Tel: 087 6492117.
**Open:** Mar–Sep; Sat–Sun, times vary ▪ **Charge:** €10 membership fee ▪ **Suitable for ages:** 10+.
**Sports:** cycling

Juniors meet on weekend mornings. Racing starts in May, and strips, etc., are provided.

## 328 Swords Lawn Tennis Club

Castle Grounds, Bridge St, Swords, Co. Dublin; Contact: Jim Dwane; Tel: 8400160.

**Open:** All year; Mon–Sun 10am–8pm ▪ **Charge:** Membership is €40 a year; Coaching is €20 for 10 weeks ▪ **Suitable for ages:** 7+ ▪ **Car parking:** Free ▪ **Bus routes:** 230, 33, 33A/B, 41C, 43.
**Sports:** tennis

A public tennis club with a big junior programme available. Coaching is held on Friday nights and parties are put on three times a year. Children can also take part in competitions. The Dublin Public Parks Tennis league runs in the summer, as well as two fun weeks in August.

## 329 Tara's Palace 🍴 ☕ ♿

Malahide Castle and Demesne, Malahide, Co. Dublin (take the Dublin–Belfast road (N1). Turn right at Swords bypass roundabout, heading for Malahide. The main car park is reached via the back road to Malahide, and is signposted. Another car park is provided by the railway station on the Dublin road); Tel: 8462184 (Oct–Mar), 8463779 (Apr–Sep); Fax: 8462537; Website: www.visitdublin.ie

**Open:** Apr–Sep; Mon–Sat 10am–1pm, 2–5pm; Sun/bank holidays 2–6pm ▪ **Charge:** Child €1; Adult €2; Price given is the recommended donation ▪ **Suitable for ages:** 2+ ▪ **Car parking:** Free ▪ **Bus routes:** 32A, 42, 102, 230.

A magnificent doll's house, Tara's Palace is influenced by the grandeur and elegance of Ireland's three great 18th-century mansions: Castletown House, Leinster House and Carton House. A delight for young and old alike, it has taken over 20 years to build and work is ongoing. There is also a collection of dolls, antique toys and other dolls' houses, including a doll's house from the family of Lady Wilde (Oscar's mother). (See also Malahide Castle and the Fry Model Railway Museum.)
**✹ TOP CHOICES: FOR AGES 5–10 ✹**

## 330 Thornton Park Riding

Kilsallaghan, The Ward, Co. Dublin; Tel: 8351164, 8352448; E-mail: info@thorntonpark.ie; Website: www.thorntonpark.ie
**Open:** All year; Mon–Sun 9am–6pm; Call for dates of this year's pony camps ▪ **Charge:** €15 per hour-long lesson; €20 for a half-hour private lesson; Pony camp prices on request ▪ **Suitable**

**for ages:** 7+ ▪ **Bus routes:** 103.
**Sports:** horse-riding
Thornton Park has two indoor and two outdoor arenas. Children must take private lessons until they can ride out in a group. There is no riding out during lessons. Pony camps are offered during the holidays.

## 331 Tolka Valley Park 🚼 ♿ 🧒 🚻

Finglas, Dublin 9 (off the Finglas Rd, north of the Botanic Gardens); Tel: 8373891, 8302689.
**Open:** All year; Mon–Fri 8.30am–dusk; Sat–Sun 9.30am–dusk ▪
**Charge:** Golf/pitch-and-putt: Adult per round €3.80; Concessions €1.50 ▪ **Suitable for ages:** All ▪ **Car parking:** On-street parking ▪
**Bus routes:** 40, 40A/B/C, 220.
**Sports:** gaelic football, hurling, soccer, fishing, pitch-and-putt
The River Tolka runs through this park, which is unrecognisable as a former landfill site. There are scenic walks and riverside trails here. You can go fishing along the river, or from the fine stone bridges at Finglaswood and Cardiffsbridge. There are also playing pitches and pitch-and-putt.
**✱ TOP CHOICES: PARKS ✱ TOP CHOICES: FOR AGES 0–2 ✱ TOP CHOICES: FOR AGES 2–5 ✱ TOP CHOICES: FOR ENERGETIC KIDS ✱**

## 332 UCI Coolock ♿ €

Malahide Rd, Dublin 17 (on the Malahide Rd, opposite Tayto and Cadbury factories); Tel: 8485122.
**Open:** All year; Children's programmes: Mon–Sun before 7pm; Kids' Club: Sat 11am ▪ **Charge:** Child €5.25; Adult €6.25; Adult price given is for before 5pm; Kids' Club €2.50 ▪ **Suitable for ages:** 3+ ▪ **Car parking:** Free ▪ **Bus routes:** 17A, 27, 42, 43.
A cinema multiplex with a Saturday morning kids' club. Adults go free, and kids' tickets are €2.50. There is often a kids' promotional snackbox available. Register your details on the website www.pigsback.com for offers and competitions.
**✱ TOP CHOICES: FOR AGES 10+ ✱ TOP CHOICES: FOR TRENDY KIDS ✱**

## 333 Ward River Valley Park 🚼 ♿ 🧒 🚻

Swords, Co. Dublin (take the Dublin–Belfast road (N1) to Swords. The park is signposted from Swords Main St); Tel: 8727777; Fax: 8727530.
**Open:** All year ▪ **Suitable for ages:** All ▪ **Car parking:** Free ▪ **Bus routes:** 31, 41, 41B.

**Sports:** gaelic football, hurling, soccer, tennis

An 89-hectare linear park, situated alongside the River Ward Valley. There are woodlands, wetlands, playing fields, tennis facilities and the remains of an Italian garden. Babies in their buggies and toddlers will enjoy the walk from the playground, which runs alongside the river, with woodland on one side and grassland on the other.

**✱ TOP CHOICES: PARKS ✱ TOP CHOICES: FOR AGES 0–2 ✱ TOP CHOICES: FOR AGES 2–5 ✱ TOP CHOICES: FOR ENERGETIC KIDS ✱**

## 334 Westwood Health and Fitness Centre, Clontarf 🏋 📷 ♿ 👶 🔞

Clontarf Rd, Dublin 3 (on the coast road next to Clontarf DART station); Tel: 8530353; Fax: 8530354; E-mail: info@westwood.ie; Website: www.westwood.ie

**Open:** All year; Mon–Fri 6am–11pm; Sat–Sun 8am–9pm ▪ **Charge:** Junior annual membership €398 if parent is not a member, €300 if parent is a member; All activities are included in membership; Classes and summer camps are additional; Birthday parties from €9 per child ▪ **Suitable for ages:** All ▪ **Car parking:** Free ▪ **Bus routes:** 103, 104, 130 ▪ **DART station:** Clontarf Rd.

**Sports:** badminton, martial arts, squash, swimming, tennis, gym, spinning, circuit, aerobics, gymnastics, step aerobics

Westwood Clontarf is a private, members-only club, which boasts Dublin's first 50-metre pool. There is also a smaller children's pool, with a slide. Swimming classes for children usually run for 12 weeks. Classes are held from complete beginner level to national competition level. FitZone has teen fitness classes, along with a teen gym. Other classes include spinning, circuit training and aerobics. Younger members can enjoy the special ball play room, where birthday parties are also held for around €9 a head. Over-13s can join as junior members, but parents must be members in order to bring younger children.

**✱ TOP CHOICES: BIRTHDAY PARTY IDEAS ✱ TOP CHOICES: SPORTS FACILITIES ✱**

## 335 White, Marianne (Music Teacher)

Portmarnock, Co. Dublin; Tel: 8460018, 086 8647276.

**Open:** All year; Class times on request ▪ **Charge:** Fees on request ▪ **Suitable for ages:** 8+.

Marianne White gives classical piano tuition to students at all levels, and preparation for RIAM and ABRSM exams.

# Places to eat

## 336 Bewley's Oriental Café, Omni Park Shopping Centre 🚼 ♿

Omni Park Shopping Centre, Swords Rd, Santry, Dublin 9 (on the ground floor of the shopping centre); Tel: 8424211;
Fax: 8424727; E-mail: manager@omnipark.bewleys.ie;
Website: www.bewleys.ie
**Open:** All year; Mon–Wed 9am–6pm; Thur–Fri 9am–8.30pm; Sat 8.30am–6pm; Balcony café: Mon–Wed 9am–6pm; Thur–Fri 6.30–8.30pm; Sat 12–6pm ▪ **Charge:** Lunch for kids €5; Adults €7 incl. drink ▪ **Suitable for ages:** All ▪ **Car parking:** Free ▪ **Bus routes:** 16, 16A, 33, 41, 41B/C, 103, 104, 746.
This branch of Bewley's is right beside the Omniplex cinemas, and there's a real fire in winter.

## 337 Big Blue Restaurant

30 Church St, Howth, Co. Dublin (Church St is on the right after the DART station); Tel: 8320565.
**Open:** All year; Tue–Sat 6–11pm; Sunday lunch from 12.30pm; dinner 6–11pm ▪ **Charge:** Child menu from €6.20; Adult main course average price €13 ▪ **Suitable for ages:** 2+ ▪ **Car parking:** On-street parking ▪ **Bus routes:** 31, 31B ▪ **DART station:** Howth.
Popular with families, especially for Sunday lunch. The main restaurant is upstairs, overlooking St Mary's Abbey and Howth Harbour, with the smaller Big Blue Café downstairs. Steak, chicken, fish and vegetarian food are on the menu. Colouring paper and pencils are available to keep hungry children amused.

## 338 Casa Pasta 🚼 ♿ 🍼

Clontarf Rd, Clontarf, Dublin 3 (Fairview end of the Clontarf Rd); Tel: 8331402.
**Open:** All year; Mon–Sun 12.30pm–1am ▪ **Charge:** Adult pizzas from €8.50, pasta €10; Individual child pizza €6 or half portions from the main menu ▪ **Suitable for ages:** All ▪ **Car parking:** Plenty of parking on the seafront ▪ **Bus routes:** 130 ▪ **DART station:** Clontarf Rd.
A very friendly Italian restaurant, offering freshly made pizza and pasta dishes. High chairs are available for babies, as are colouring sheets and crayons, and afterwards you can come back

and see your child's pictures displayed on the walls. For birthday parties, order off the normal menu, or special arrangements can be made – they know good local bakeries, and can organise a cake.

**\* TOP CHOICES: CHILD FRIENDLY RESTAURANTS \* TOP CHOICES: BIRTHDAY PARTY IDEAS \* TOP CHOICES: FOR AGES 10+ \***

## 339 Eddie Rockets Diner

Main St, Swords, Co. Dublin, Tel: 8405969; Phibsboro Shopping Centre, Dublin 7, Tel: 8309940; Contact: Valerie Crowley for party bookings; Tel: 6797340; Website: www.eddierockets.ie
**Open:** All year; Sun–Thur 11am–1am; Fri–Sat 11am–4am ▪
**Charge:** Kids from €5 for meal and drink; Adults €10 for burger, fries and drink ▪ **Suitable for ages:** All.

Eddie Rockets is a chain of American-diner-style cafés, famous for their burgers and fries. There's a kids menu, and kids get a free goodie bag with their meal. Both of these branches have booths for sitting in, but they do also have high chairs. They do much better milkshakes and malts than the bigger fast-food chains. Kids love them.

**\* TOP CHOICES: CHILD FRIENDLY RESTAURANTS \* TOP CHOICES: BIRTHDAY PARTY IDEAS \***

## 340 El Paso Restaurant

10 Harbour Rd, Howth, Co. Dublin (opposite the harbour); Tel: 8323334, 8395094; E-mail: elpaso@eircom.net; Website: www.elpasorestaurant.com
**Open:** All year; Lunch: Mon–Fri 12–3pm; Dinner: Mon–Sat 6–11pm; Sun 2–11pm ▪ **Charge:** Adults eat from €15 ▪ **Suitable for ages:** 2+ ▪ **Car parking:** On-street parking ▪ **Bus routes:** 31, 31B ▪ **DART station:** Howth.

A friendly Tex-Mex restaurant, which is very child-friendly. You can eat in the heated conservatory and have a view of the harbour. Small doors make it hard for wheelchair or buggy access. There is no special kids' menu, but they'll enjoy a mix of starters to share – especially the spicy chicken wings.

**\* TOP CHOICES: FOR AGES 10+ \***

## 341 Giovanni's Restaurant

3–4 Townyard House, Townyard Lane, Malahide, Co. Dublin. (just in front of Malahide's marina, in the centre of the village); Tel: 8451733; Fax: 8456128.

**Open:** All year; Mon–Sun 12.30pm–12am ▪ **Charge:** Pizzas from €9 ▪ **Suitable for ages:** All ▪ **Car parking:** Metered parking on street or free parking at the train station ▪ **Bus routes:** 32A, 42, 102, 105, 230 ▪ **Rail station:** Malahide ▪ **DART station:** Malahide.

A friendly Italian restaurant, which welcomes children. You can ask for smaller portions from the main menu for children, or they can share. A high chair is available.

✱ TOP CHOICES: CHILD FRIENDLY RESTAURANTS ✱

## 342 Wong's (Chinese Restaurant) 🚼 ♿

436 Clontarf Rd, Clontarf, Dublin 3 (big black building near St. Anne's Park); Tel: 8334400; Fax: 8337064.

**Open:** All year; Mon–Sat 12pm–12am; Sun 5–11pm ▪ **Charge:** Main courses about €20 ▪ **Suitable for ages:** 3+ ▪ **Car parking:** Free ▪ **Bus routes:** 130.

A very popular, but expensive, restaurant for family get-togethers. The food is great here and there's plenty of seating. Kids can share or have a mix of starters. High chairs are available.

✱ TOP CHOICES: CHILD FRIENDLY RESTAURANTS ✱ TOP CHOICES: FOR AGES 10+ ✱

# sea safari

## eel the adventure!

### *Discover our exciting coastline from the sea!!*

☞ The Rockabill Lighthouse, Lambay Island, Ireland's Eye, Dublin City Moorings, Daley Island, Killiney Bay. It's there for you to see!

☞ Seals, Porpoises, possibly a dolphin: Kittihawks, Guillemots, Shags, Fulmars, Puffins, Terns.

☞ Lifejackets and all-weather clothing are provided.

**Malahide Marina, Malahide, Co Dublin**

**Dublin City Moorings, Custom House Quay, Dublin 1**

# Get your kids to Draíocht fast or Michelle will have all the fun!

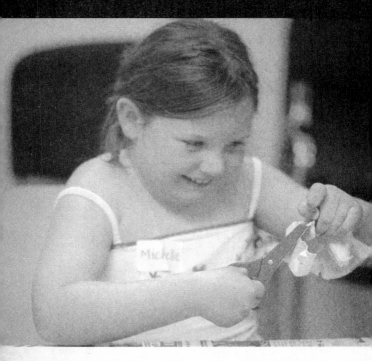

## Draíocht ... Discover the Magic!
www.magicinblanch.com    tel: 885 2622

# Dúchas Heritage Card

## ...the cost effective way to explore Ireland's heritage

Buy a Dúchas Heritage Card and enjoy unlimited admission for one year to the sites below and 55 more heritage sites throughout the country.

| | |
|---|---|
| **Adult** | **€20.00** |
| **Senior Citizen** | **€15.00** |
| **Child/Student** | **€7.50** |
| **Family** | **€50.00** |

**For information on our sites or to order a Heritage Card:**

**Web:** www.heritageireland.ie
**Email:** heritagecard@duchas.ie
**Tel:** 01 647 2461

*Available at all Dúchas sites; at the Waterways Ireland Visitor Centre, Tel. (01) 677 7510 and at Dublin Castle, Tel. (01) 677 7129*

**Dúchas**
The Heritage
Service

Heritage Week 7-14 September 2003

# West Dublin

## Things to do

### 343 Alternative Entertainment Community Art Group ♿ ✎

Tymon Bawn Community Centre, Firhouse Rd W, Tallaght, Dublin 24; Tel: 4520611, 4621029; E-mail: info@altents.ie; Website: www.altents.ie

**Open:** All year; Call for details of workshops and activities ■ **Charge:** Costs vary according to activities ■ **Suitable for ages:** All ■ **Bus routes:** 15F, 49X.

Loads of activities for children are run throughout the year, including arts and crafts, storytelling, music courses, reading and puppetry. In 2002 a very successful novel-writing group was run for teenagers, with author Larry O'Loughlin. In 2003 there are plans for a series of creative-writing workshops throughout the summer. Also for 2003, there will be drama workshops and two film courses for teenagers, the finished projects being shown at the Junior Dublin Film Festival.

✱ **TOP CHOICES: HOBBIES/ARTS AND CRAFTS** ✱ **TOP CHOICES: SUMMER CAMPS** ✱ **TOP CHOICES: FOR AGES 5–10** ✱ **TOP CHOICES: FOR AGES 10+** ✱ **TOP CHOICES: FOR TRENDY KIDS** ✱ **TOP CHOICES: FOR IMAGINATIVE KIDS** ✱

### 344 Áras an Úachtaráin

Phoenix Park, Dublin 8 (you have to meet at the Phoenix Park Visitor Centre – 20 mins walk from the Gate at Ashtown Cross – and a bus takes you to the building); Tel: 6171000, 1890 430430 (Lo-call); Fax: 6171001; Website: www.gov.ie/aras

**Open:** Guided tours only; Summer, 10am–5pm; Winter, 10.30am–4.30pm ■ **Charge:** Free ■ **Suitable for ages:** 5+ ■ **Car parking:** Free ■ **Bus routes:** 10, 37, 38, 39.

Built in 1751, Áras an Úachtaráin is the official residence of the president of Ireland, and is the setting for many public functions. The tour includes five state rooms and the president's study.

### 345 Ashbourne Rugby Football Club

Miltown, Ashbourne, Co. Meath; Contact: Shea Gallagher;

Tel: 8351568, 087 2687625 (Shea Gallagher).
**Open:** Sep–Apr ▪ **Suitable for ages:** 6+ ▪ **Car parking:** Free.
**Sports:** rugby

## 346 Ashtown Stables

Ashtown, Castleknock, Dublin 15; Tel: 8383807.
**Open:** All year; Sat–Sun 9.30am–2pm; Call for this year's pony
camp dates ▪ **Charge:** €15 per hour-long lesson; Summer camp
prices on request ▪ **Suitable for ages:** 8+ ▪ **Bus routes:** 37, 38,
39, 70 ▪ **Rail station:** Ashtown.
**Sports:** horse-riding
Ashtown has an outdoor, all-weather arena. There are ride outs in
the Phoenix Park for more experienced riders. Pony camps are
offered in the summer, as well as some jumping.
**✱ TOP CHOICES: SPORTS FACILITIES ✱ TOP CHOICES: HOBBIES/ARTS
AND CRAFTS ✱ TOP CHOICES: SUMMER CAMPS ✱**

## 347 Astro Park 🐾

Greenhills Rd, Tallaght, Dublin 24 (turn left at the T-junction in
Tallaght village by the Esso station. The park is about half a mile
down on the left-hand side); Tel: 4599822; Fax: 4599313;
E-mail: info@astropark.ie; Website: www.astropark.ie
**Open:** All year; Mon–Sun 9.30am–11.30pm ▪ **Charge:** €25 per
hour to book a pitch Mon–Fri to 4.30pm, and all day Sat and Sun;
€50 per hour Mon–Fri after 4.30pm ▪ **Suitable for ages:** 5+ ▪
**Car parking:** On-street parking ▪ **Bus routes:** 77, 77A/B, 54.
**Sports:** soccer
A great outing for soccer-mad boys and girls. Ten outdoor
AstroTurf all-weather, five-a-side soccer pitches are available to
rent by the hour. Book in advance. Changing, shower and locker
facilities are provided. A reserved area in the clubhouse caters for
birthday parties. Food is provided at an additional cost – ring for
details.
**✱ TOP CHOICES: BIRTHDAY PARTY IDEAS ✱ TOP CHOICES: SPORTS
FACILITIES ✱ TOP CHOICES: FOR AGES 5–10 ✱ TOP CHOICES: FOR
AGES 10+ ✱ TOP CHOICES: FOR ENERGETIC KIDS ✱**

## 348 Ballyfermot Library 🚼 ♿ ✎ 🖥

Ballyfermot Rd, Dublin 10 (beside Tesco near the roundabout);
Tel: 6269324, 6269325; Fax: 6237365;
Website: www.iol.ie/dublincitylibrary
**Open:** All year; Mon–Thur 10am–8pm; Fri–Sat 10am–5pm ▪

**Charge:** Free ▪ **Suitable for ages:** All ▪ **Car parking:** Free ▪ **Bus routes:** 18, 76, 78A, 79.

Regular activities include: Storytime for 3–7-yr-olds (Wed at 3pm), Children's Art Classes for over-6s and a Junior Book Discussion Group (ring for days and times). Seasonal arts-and-crafts activities, plus reading events, are organised throughout the year.

✱ **TOP CHOICES: FOR AGES 2–5** ✱ **TOP CHOICES: FOR AGES 5–10** ✱

## 349 Ballyfermot Swimming Pool

Blackditch Rd, Ballyfermot, Dublin 10 (go up Ballyfermot Rd, turn left after Tesco and the pool is in Le Fanu Park); Tel: 6266504.
**Open:** All year; Summer: Daily 12–7.30pm; Rest of Year: Sun 10.30am–1pm ▪ **Charge:** Child €1.80; Adult €3.60 ▪ **Suitable for ages:** All ▪ **Car parking:** Free ▪ **Bus routes:** 78.
**Sports:** swimming

A Dublin City Council pool, which is also hired out to schools and groups. It is only open for public swims on Sundays, except in the summer when it is open every day.

## 350 Barnhall Rugby Football Club

Barnhall, Leixlip, Co. Kildare; Contact: John Hughes;
Tel: 4570206, 6245420 (office); E-mail: john@pembroke.iol.ie
**Open:** Sep–Apr ▪ **Suitable for ages:** 6+ ▪ **Bus routes:** 66, 66A/B.
**Sports:** rugby

## 351 Basketball

Irish Basketball Association, National Basketball Arena, Tymon, Dublin 24; Tel: 4590211; Fax: 4590212; Website: www.iba.ie
**Open:** Oct–Mar; Call for individual clubs' meeting days and times ▪ **Charge:** Annual fees range from €45 to €200; Basketball strip approx. €50 ▪ **Suitable for ages:** 10+.

Most of the clubs listed below run junior teams and leagues; call for details. Where available, the venues have been listed, but these can change, so always check. The association also runs a primary school programme. Competitive teams start at under-11. Most teams require that you buy a strip to begin with, which can cost around €50.

✱ **TOP CHOICES: HOBBIES/ARTS AND CRAFTS** ✱

## 352 Drimnagh Basketball Club

Oblate Hall, Inchicore Roadstone Sports Centre, Naas Rd, Dublin 22; Contact: Louise O'Doherty; Tel: 4517086.

**Open:** All year; Call for meeting days and times ▪ **Charge:** Membership fees and basketball strip price on request ▪ **Suitable for ages:** 10+ ▪ **Bus routes:** 51, 51B, 68, 69.

## 353 Firhouse Basketball Club

Firhouse Community and Leisure Centre, Firhouse Rd, Dublin 24; Contact: Josephine Purcell; Tel: 4522239.
**Open:** All year; Call for meeting days and times ▪ **Charge:** Membership fees and basketball strip price on request ▪ **Suitable for ages:** 10+ ▪ **Bus routes:** 49, 49A, 75.

## 354 Kilcock Ladies' Basketball Club

Scoil Dara, Kilcock, Co. Kildare; Contact: Mary O'Brien; Tel: 6287349.
**Open:** All year; Call for meeting days and times ▪ **Charge:** Membership fees and basketball strip price on request ▪ **Suitable for ages:** 11+ ▪ **Bus routes:** 66.

## 355 Kilnamanagh Basketball Club

Kilnamanagh Family Rec. Centre, Treepark Rd, Kilnamanagh, Dublin 24; Contact: Paul Fagan; Tel: 2444756.
**Open:** All year; Call for meeting days and times ▪ **Charge:** Membership fees and basketball strip price on request ▪ **Suitable for ages:** 10+ ▪ **Bus routes:** 50, 202.

## 356 Leixlip Basketball Club

Leixlip Amenity Centre, Collintown, Maynooth Rd, Leixlip, Co. Kildare; Contact: Vincent Homan; Tel: 4557601.
**Open:** All year; Call for meeting days and times ▪ **Charge:** Membership fees and basketball strip price on request ▪ **Suitable for ages:** 10+ ▪ **Bus routes:** 66, 66A/B ▪ **Rail station:** Leixlip.

## 357 Moyle Park Basketball Club

Moyle Park College, Clondalkin, Dublin 22; Contact: Joy McCann; Tel: 6219030.
**Open:** All year; Call for meeting days and times ▪ **Charge:** Membership fees and basketball strip price on request ▪ **Suitable for ages:** 10+ ▪ **Bus routes:** 51, 51B/D, 68, 69, 76, 76A/B, 90, 210.

## 358 Rathcoole Rockets Basketball Club

Moyle Park, Clondalkin, Dublin 22; Contact: Mary Flanagan;

Tel: 4543818.
**Open:** All year; Call for meeting days and times ▪ **Charge:**
Membership fees and basketball strip price on request ▪ **Suitable
for ages:** 10+ ▪ **Bus routes:** 51, 51B, 68, 69, 76, 76A/B, 90, 210.

## 359 Belly Dance Ireland

Tymon Bawn Community Centre, Firhouse Rd W, Tallaght, Dublin
24; Tel: 2963856.
**Open:** Sep–Jun; Thur 8–9.30pm ▪ **Charge:** €90 for a 10-week
term ▪ **Suitable for ages:** 12+ ▪ **Bus routes:** 15F, 49X.
Over-12s can go to this mainly adult class with their
parents'/guardians' permission, or go along yourself! If you can
find a long Indian-type skirt, cropped top and head scarf, wear
them! Costumes can also be bought from the teacher.
✱ **TOP CHOICES: FOR TRENDY KIDS** ✱

## 360 Blanchardstown Library 🚼 ♿ ✎ 🖥

Civic Centre, Blanchardstown Centre, Dublin 15 (opposite the
Blue entrance of Blanchardstown Shopping Centre);
Tel: 8905560, 8905563; Fax: 8905563;
E-mail: blanchlib@fingalcoco.ie;
Website: www.iol.ie/~fincolib/ba.htm
**Open:** All year; Mon–Thur 10am–8.30pm; Fri–Sat 10am–5pm;
Closed on the Sat and Mon of a bank holiday weekend ▪ **Charge:**
Free ▪ **Suitable for ages:** All ▪ **Car parking:** Free ▪ **Bus routes:**
39, 220.
A huge, modern library. Regular activities include a Young Writers'
Group (for 9–12-yr-olds), which meets fortnightly; a Parent and
Toddler Group (Mon and Thur 10.30–11.30am) and a Junior
Chess Club (Wed) 4–5pm. Other activities are organised
throughout the year, around seasonal events.
✱ **TOP CHOICES: FOR AGES 2–5** ✱ **TOP CHOICES: FOR AGES 5–10** ✱
**TOP CHOICES: FOR AGES 10+** ✱

## 361 Blanchardstown Shopping Centre 🚼 🧩 ☕ ♿

Blanchardstown, Dublin 15 (on the Navan Road (N3), just off the
M50 ring road); Tel: 8221356 (centre), 8222668 (Heinz Farley
crêche).
**Open:** All year; Mon/Tue/Sat 9am–7pm; Wed–Fri 9am–9pm;
Sun/bank holidays 11am–6pm ▪ **Charge:** Crêche €6 per hour,
max 2 hours per day ▪ **Suitable for ages:** All ▪ **Car parking:** Free

- **Bus routes:** 39, 70, 76A, 220, 237, 238, 239, 270.

A monster of a shopping mall. All of the big names have an outlet here, including Dunnes Stores and Roches Stores. There's also a large UCI cinema and leisureplex and the Draíocht Theatre. Full crèche facilities are available during the centre's opening hours, catering for children from 2–7 years old. There are also many services, including a doctor, a dentist and a library. There's even an oratory for quiet prayer and reflection, if you need some time out.

**★ TOP CHOICES: FOR TRENDY KIDS ★**

## 362 Boxing

Irish Amateur Boxing Association, National Stadium, South Circular Rd, Dublin 8; Tel: 4733192; E-mail: iaba@eircom.net
**Open:** All year ■ **Charge:** Most clubs charge €1 or €2 per week ■ **Suitable for ages:** 11+.

Boxing clubs usually take children from 11 years old. Parents must sign for permission for them to join, and all children must undergo a medical examination and wear protective headgear. All boxing clubs listed have Leinster Council IABA affiliation for 2002/2003. Call for locations, as these can change.

## 363 Drimnagh Boxing Club

Call for locations as these can change; Contact: Austin Carruth; Tel: 4508083.
**Open:** All year; Call for current meeting times ■ **Suitable for ages:** 11+.

## 364 Golden Cobra Boxing Club

Call for locations as these can change; Contact: Patrick Hyland; Tel: 4624157.
**Open:** All year; Call for current meeting times ■ **Suitable for ages:** 11+.

## 365 Lucan Boxing Club

Call for locations as these can change; Contact: Terence Grey; Tel: 6241462.
**Open:** All year; Call for current meeting times ■ **Suitable for ages:** 11+.

## 366 Mulhuddart Boxing Club

Call for locations as these can change; Contact: John Farrell; Tel: 087 9617292.

**Open:** All year; Call for current meeting times ■ **Suitable for ages:** 11+.

### 367 Neilstown Boxing Club

Call for locations as these can change; Contact: Garrett Dunne, Gerry Fleming; Tel: 4576943 (Garrett Dunne), 085 7371636 (Gerry Fleming).
**Open:** All year; Call for current meeting times ■ **Suitable for ages:** 11+.

### 368 Quarryvale Boxing Club

Call for locations as these can change; Contact: Stephen Kelly; Tel: 4573934.
**Open:** All year; Call for current meeting times ■ **Suitable for ages:** 11+.

### 369 Sacred Heart Tallaght Boxing Club

Call for locations as these can change; Contact: Tommy Hanrahan; Tel: 4523220.
**Open:** All year; Call for current meeting times ■ **Suitable for ages:** 11+.

### 370 St. Mary's Boxing Club, Saggart

Call for locations as these can change; Contact: John Mohan; Tel: 4596062 (Derek Riordan).
**Open:** All year; Call for current meeting times ■ **Suitable for ages:** 11+.

### 371 St. Matthew's Boxing Club, Ballyfermot

Call for locations as these can change.; Contact: William Tyrrell; Tel: 6269689.
**Open:** All year; Call for current meeting times ■ **Suitable for ages:** 11+.

### 372 West Side Tallaght Boxing Club

Call for locations as these can change; Contact: William Stacey; Tel: 087 2067457.
**Open:** All year; Call for current meeting times ■ **Suitable for ages:** 11+.

### 373 Brady School of Dance

Lucan, Co. Dublin (call for venues); Tel: 2984819, 087 4152993.

**Open:** Call for new term times; Thur 3pm ▪ **Charge:** Fees on request ▪ **Suitable for ages:** 3+.
Brady School of Dance holds RAD ballet and modern dance classes for boys and girls from age 3+.

## 374 Buttner, Linda (Music Teacher)

Palmerstown, Dublin 20; Tel: 6265374.
**Open:** All year; Class times on request ▪ **Charge:** Fees on request ▪ **Suitable for ages:** 7+.
Linda Buttner gives tuition in classical piano, and prepares students for RIAM and ABRSM exams.

## 375 Carton Equestrian Centre

Kilcloone, Co. Meath (signposted from Maynooth and Dunboyne. About a 10-minute drive from Maynooth); Tel: 6290691; E-mail: cartonequestriancentre@eircom.net
**Open:** All year; Tues 8.30am–6.30pm; Wed–Sun 8.30am–7.30pm; Call for details of camps ▪ **Charge:** €13.50 per hourly lesson; Summer camp prices on request ▪ **Suitable for ages:** 4+.
**Sports:** horse-riding
Carton has a floodlit outdoor arena, and mainly specialises in showjumping and livery. It has a gallops track for exercising. There are pony camps during all school breaks, as well as shows on bank holidays. Lessons are available all week. For those without a car, a pick-up or taxi can be arranged from Maynooth railway station.

## 376 Castleknock Lawn Tennis Club

Navan Rd, Castleknock, Dublin 15; Tel: 8207591, 8217117 (Junior Developer); Fax: 8207591.
**Open:** Sep–May; Mon–Sun 10am–10pm ▪ **Charge:** Around €70 annual membership for juniors; Tennis coaching fees are extra ▪ **Suitable for ages:** 5+ ▪ **Car parking:** Free ▪ **Bus routes:** 37, 38, 38A, 39, 39A, 70, 122.
**Sports:** tennis
This club runs a junior development programme with group coaching from Sep to May. Membership is required, and coaching costs extra. In the summer the club runs social activities for all children, from beginners to advanced players, who take part in junior open competitions. There is mini tennis on short courts for under-10s.

## 377 Castletymon Library 🛒 ♿ ✍ 🖥

Tymon North Shopping Centre, Castletymon, Tallaght, Dublin 24;
Tel: 4524888; Fax: 4597873; E-mail: libraries@sdcc.ie;
Website: www.sdcc.ie/library
**Open:** All year; Mon–Thur 9.45am–5pm; Fri–Sat
9.45am–4.30pm; closed bank holidays ▪ **Charge:** Free ▪ **Suitable
for ages:** All ▪ **Car parking:** Free ▪ **Bus routes:** 77, 77A.
Story time for under-8s is on Wed afternoons, 3.30–4.30pm. Sat
afternoon art classes are held from 2.30–3.30pm (book in
advance). Other seasonal arts-and-crafts and reading events for
children are organised throughout the year.
✱ **TOP CHOICES: FOR AGES 5–10** ✱

## 378 Causey Farm ✍ 🎏

Girley, Fordstown, Navan, Co. Meath (from Kells, take the Athboy
Rd and travel for four miles to the village of Fordstown. Turn right
just before Bray's pub. The Causey Experience is located one mile
from this turn, on the left-hand side); Tel: 4634135;
E-mail: info@causeyexperience.com;
Website: www.causeyexperience.com
**Open:** All year; Be Irish For a Day: Mid-Apr–mid-Oct; Causey
Experience for School tours: May–Jun; Charity Open Day: last Sun
in Jul ▪ **Charge:** Child €35; Adult €50; Prices given for full day of
'Be Irish For A Day'; The Causey Experience €10 per child;
Charity Open Day €10 per child ▪ **Suitable for ages:** All ▪ **Car
parking:** Free.
Families can visit the farm for a day of Irish activities, with
afternoon tea, an evening meal and a céilí night. Activities include
cooking, turf-cutting and bogland visits, hurling lessons, sheepdog
demonstrations, céilí dancing workshops, súgán rope-making and
bodhrán classes. The Causey Experience is a three-and-a-half-hour
programme for school tours only, and includes: traditional turf
cutting, Causey Challenge course, forest nature walk, clay
modelling, treasure hunt, gardening, potting, graffiti art, súgán
rope-making, 'meet your farmyard friends', tractor and trailer ride
and giant bubble-blowing. Children should wear old clothes and
wellingtons if possible, and bring an old towel, a change of clothes
and a packed lunch. There is also a family Charity Open Day on
the last Sunday in July.
✱ **TOP CHOICES: FOR ENERGETIC KIDS** ✱

## 379 Celbridge Abbey Grounds

Clane Rd, Celbridge, Co. Kildare (20km from Dublin on the N4; cross the bridge in Celbridge and turn left); Tel: 6275062, 6275208; Fax: 6270790.

**Open:** All year; Mon–Sat 10am–6pm; Sun/bank holidays 12–6pm; Closed for a short period after Christmas ▪ **Charge:** Child €2.50; Adult €3.80; OAPs €2.50; Family day tickets €9.50; Family season ticket (2 adults and 3 children) €82.50 ▪ **Suitable for ages:** All ▪ **Car parking:** Free ▪ **Bus routes:** 67, 67A ▪ **Rail station:** Hazelhatch.

The grounds of Celbridge Abbey were planted by William of Orange's daughter Vanessa, in order to impress her friend and admirer Jonathon Swift. The magnificent grounds are situated on the River Liffey, and feature varied flora and fauna, natural woodland gardens and a garden centre. Children will love exploring the gardens, as there are alien and monster sculptures hidden amongst the trees. There are guided tours, nature walks and a model railway. The house is not open to the public, but sometimes special events are held in the grounds, e.g. vintage car shows. A visit to the restaurant is recommended.

✱ TOP CHOICES: PICNIC SPOTS ✱ TOP CHOICES: PARKS ✱ TOP CHOICES: PLAYGROUNDS ✱ TOP CHOICES: FOR AGES 0–2 ✱ TOP CHOICES: FOR AGES 2–5 ✱ TOP CHOICES: FOR AGES 5–10 ✱ TOP CHOICES: FOR ENERGETIC KIDS ✱

## 380 Cherry Orchard Football Club

Phoenix Ctr, Ballyfermot Rd Upr, Dublin 10; Tel: 6231963.
**Open:** Sep–May ▪ **Suitable for ages:** 7+ ▪ **Bus routes:** 18, 76, 76A/B, 78A, 79, 206.
**Sports:** soccer

## 381 Civic Theatre

Blessington Rd, Tallaght, Dublin 24 (Blessington Rd is between the Square Shopping Centre and Tallaght Hospital); Tel: 4627477 (box office); Fax: 4627478; E-mail: civictheatred24@eircom.net; Website: www.civictheatre.ie

**Open:** All year; Gallery: Mon–Sat 10am–6pm; Performances: Matinee and evening performances; call for times ▪ **Charge:** Performances approx. €12 per child, €15.50 per adult, €48 for family ticket (2 adults + 2 children). ▪ **Suitable for ages:** All ▪ **Car**

**parking:** Free ▪ **Bus routes:** 49, 50, 54A, 56A, 65, 65B, 75, 76, 76B, 77, 77A/X.

A modern community arts centre with a varied programme throughout the year. Performances include music, drama, ballet, dance and stage musicals, with seasonal shows for children. Alternative Entertainments, Tallaght, exhibit some of the work they do with children in the art gallery here from time to time.

✱ **TOP CHOICES: CHRISTMAS VISITS** ✱ **TOP CHOICES: FOR AGES 10+** ✱

## 382 Terence Clancy (Music Teacher)

Tallaght, Dublin 24; Tel: 4514373.

**Open:** All year; Class times on request ▪ **Charge:** Fees on request ▪ **Suitable for ages:** 6+.

Terence Clancy offers group and individual tuition in alto saxophone, tenor saxophone, concert flute, oboe, clarinet and recorder. Classical and jazz methods are taught, and students can be prepared for RIAM, ABRSM, LCM and TCL exams.

## 383 Clondalkin Library

Monastery Rd, Clondalkin, Dublin 22; Tel: 4593315;
Fax: 4595509; E-mail: libraries@sdcc.ie;
Website: www.sdcc.ie/library

**Open:** All year; Mon–Thur 9:45am–8pm; Fri–Sat 9:45am–4:30pm; closed bank holidays ▪ **Charge:** Free ▪ **Suitable for ages:** All ▪ **Car parking:** Parking on street ▪ **Bus routes:** 51, 51B, 68, 69, 76, 76A/B.

There is a children's section upstairs, but no lift. There is a Kids' Book Club, and exhibitions for children – ring for details. A Parent & Toddler Group meets on Wed mornings, 10am–12pm. A music keyboard is available. Other seasonal arts-and-crafts and reading events for children are organised throughout the year.

✱ **TOP CHOICES: FOR AGES 2–5** ✱

## 384 Clondalkin Rugby Football Club

Kingswood, Clondalkin, Dublin 22; Tel: 4516005.

**Open:** Sep–Apr ▪ **Suitable for ages:** 6+ ▪ **Bus routes:** 56, 76, 76A/B.

**Sports:** rugby

## 385 Clondalkin Sports and Leisure Centre

Nangor Rd, Clondalkin, Dublin 22 (head to the round tower from the village and take the first left. After McDonalds, take the first left and the centre is at the top of the lane); Tel: 4574858; Fax: 4576058; E-mail: scdls@eircom.net; Website: www.clondalkin.com/cslc

**Open:** All year; Mon–Sun 9.15am–4.30pm ▪ **Charge:** Child €1.75; Fee is for entry to swimming pool; Birthday party bookings from €6.50 per child; Prices for sports facilities on request ▪ **Suitable for ages:** 2+ ▪ **Car parking:** Free ▪ **Bus routes:** 76, 76B, 51, 51B.

**Sports:** archery, badminton, basketball, rowing/canoeing, soccer, swimming, climbing, orienteering, kayaking, gorge-walking
This is one of the best leisure centres run by South Dublin County Council. Swimming pool sessions last an hour. The centre also runs some minority sports for older kids, including canoeing, kayaking, archery, indoor climbing and gorge-walking. The indoor hall offers a huge variety of sports, from indoor football to basketball, and can be rented by the hour. You can have a great swimming birthday party here: You get an hour in the pool (another party may be in with you), followed by an hour in the coffee shop, where food, goody bags and drinks are supplied. Adults should get their togs on and supervise smaller children while swimming.
**✱ TOP CHOICES: BIRTHDAY PARTY IDEAS ✱ TOP CHOICES: SPORTS FACILITIES ✱ TOP CHOICES: SUMMER CAMPS ✱**

## 386 Commercial Rowing Club

Longmeadows, Islandbridge, Dublin 8 (turn off Ballyfermot Rd onto Sarsfield Rd and then onto Con Colbert Rd on south side of Liffey); Tel: 6711238, 4554246.

**Open:** All year; Weekend mornings for learning; training Tue/Thur 5pm ▪ **Charge:** Annual membership about €70, which covers all sessions ▪ **Suitable for ages:** 12+ ▪ **Car parking:** Free ▪ **Bus routes:** 25, 25A, 26, 51, 68, 69 ▪ **Rail station:** Heuston.

**Sports:** rowing/canoeing
One of Dublin's two private rowing clubs, which is very well known for its junior boys' programme. Kids need to be 12 years old to start rowing, as the equipment is adult-sized, although younger children can cox, or sit at the top of the boat. Racing does

WEST DUBLIN

not start until age 14. Kids begin on a Sat or Sun, but once they are experienced there is training on Tue and Thur evenings, at 5pm. They can also use the gym, which has rowing and running machines. Rowers will need a one-piece wetsuit (costs about €60), as well as a splash top in club colours (about €75). Boats, oars and coaching are provided.

**✱ TOP CHOICES: HOBBIES/ARTS AND CRAFTS ✱**

## 387 Paul Conway (Music Teacher)

Clondalkin, Dublin 22; Tel: 4593847.
**Open:** All year; Class times on request ■ **Charge:** Fees on request ■ **Suitable for ages:** 12+.
Paul Conway teaches classical, world and early music genres in piano, electric organ and electric keyboards, viol (an early string instrument) and recorder. Preparation is given for RIAM, ABRSM and TCL exams.

## 388 Coolmine Equestrian Centre

Coolmine House, Saggart, Co. Kildare; Tel: 4588447, 087 2220992.
**Open:** All year; Tue–Thur 9am–9pm; Fri 9am–6.30pm; Sat–Sun 9am–5.30pm; Call for this year's pony camp dates ■ **Charge:** €16 per hourly lesson; Pony camp and riding lesson fees on request ■ **Suitable for ages:** 4+ ■ **Bus routes:** 69 (2 miles out of village).
**Sports:** horse-riding
Coolmine has both indoor and outdoor arenas, and offers lessons for all levels, as well as showjumping. During the summer, there are cross-country rides out and treks in the forest. Pony camps are also offered during school holidays.

**✱ TOP CHOICES: SPORTS FACILITIES ✱ TOP CHOICES: HOBBIES/ARTS AND CRAFTS ✱**

## 390 Coolmine Rugby Football Club

Ashbrook, Castleknock, Dublin 15; Tel: 8385066.
**Open:** Sep–Apr ■ **Suitable for ages:** 6+ ■ **Bus routes:** 37, 38, 38B, 237.
**Sports:** rugby

## 391 Coolmine Sports and Leisure Centre

Clonsilla, Dublin 15 (between the town centre and the village.

After the fire station and Statoil station, turn left at small roundabout); Tel: 8214549, 8214344 (info on swim times).
**Open:** All year; Mon–Sun 9am–10pm ■ **Charge:** Family membership is €75 or children on their own pay €20 annual membership; Activities are approximately €1.50 for children; Small entry fee for pool for non-members ■ **Suitable for ages:** 2+ ■ **Car parking:** Free ■ **Bus routes:** 39.
**Sports:** gaelic football, hurling, martial arts, swimming, gymnastics, judo

A sports centre run by Dublin City Council, with a very popular 25-metre pool. Parent-and-child swims are on Wed and Sat. There is a long waiting list for swimming and gymnastics classes, for children over 4 years old. There are also outdoor activities on the GAA pitch. You need to join as a member to do any of the activities. Summer camps incorporate a range of activities and run from Mon–Fri for five weeks – you can attend as many weeks as you like. This year you may have to join as a member as well as paying the camp fee – details are available from the centre.
✱ **TOP CHOICES: SPORTS FACILITIES** ✱

## 392 County Library, Tallaght 🚼 ♿ ✒ 🖥

Town Centre, Tallaght, Dublin 24 (opposite Tesco and the Civic Theatre); Tel: 4620073; Fax: 4149207;
E-mail: talib@sdublincoco.ie; Website: www.sdcc.ie/library
**Open:** All year; Mon–Thur 9.45am–8pm; Fri–Sat 9.45am–4.30pm; closed bank holidays ■ **Charge:** Free ■ **Suitable for ages:** All ■ **Car parking:** Free ■ **Bus routes:** 49A/B, 50, 54A, 56A, 65B, 77, 77A.

A parent-and-toddler group is held on Wed, 10.30–11.30am, and there is a chess club for children on Wed, 6.30–7.30pm. The library also hosts storytelling, call for days and times. Other seasonal arts-and-crafts and reading events for children are organised throughout the year.
✱ **TOP CHOICES: FOR AGES 2–5** ✱ **TOP CHOICES: FOR AGES 5–10** ✱
**TOP CHOICES: FOR AGES 10+** ✱

## 393 Draíocht 🚼 ☕ ♿ ✒

Deanstown House, Main St, Blanchardstown, Dublin 15 (opposite the Blue entrance of Blanchardstown Shopping Centre);
Tel: 8852610, 8852622; Fax: 8243434.;
E-mail: admin@draiocht.ie;
Website: www.fingalarts.ie/info/draiocht.html

**Open:** All year; Call for course times or programmes ▪ **Charge:** Prices for performances, exhibitions or courses vary – call for details ▪ **Suitable for ages:** All ▪ **Car parking:** Free ▪ **Bus routes:** 39, 220.

Draíocht is a flexible, multi-purpose arts facility for all, with a special emphasis on the arts for children and young people. Classes and workshops are run for children throughout the year; call for details of current activities and exhibitions. Activities include dance, drama, comedy, 'battle of the bands', cabaret, popular entertainment, band rehearsal, a choral festival, youth theatre, puppetry, 'magic festival', community arts, poetry, sculpture, painting, pottery, circus skills, photography, radio, studio training, video, broadcasting, new media, outdoor work and TV recording. There are workshops, classes and lectures. Concerts and exhibitions are put on, and Draíocht also does outreach work.

✱ **TOP CHOICES: SUMMER CAMPS** ✱ **TOP CHOICES: CHRISTMAS VISITS** ✱ **TOP CHOICES: FOR AGES 5–10** ✱ **TOP CHOICES: FOR AGES 10+** ✱ **TOP CHOICES: FOR ENERGETIC KIDS** ✱ **TOP CHOICES: FOR IMAGINATIVE KIDS** ✱

## 394 Drimnagh Castle 🚼 ☕ ♿ 🚻

Drimnagh Castle, Longmile Rd, Dublin 12 (off the Long Mile Rd, off junction 9 off the M50, south of the Phoenix Park);
Tel: 4502530.

**Open:** All year; 1 Apr–31 Oct: Wed/Sat–Sun 12–5pm; Rest of year: Wed 10am–5pm; Sun 2–5pm ▪ **Charge:** Child €2.50; Adult €3 ▪ **Suitable for ages:** All ▪ **Car parking:** Free ▪ **Bus routes:** 50, 55, 56A.

This castle was built by the Anglo-Norman de Barnewall family around 1240, and was restored by An Taisce (the National Trust) and FÁS in the 1980s. There's a fully flooded moat, a great hall with hand-carved oak roof and balconies, and nine effigies carved in the likenesses of people associated with the restoration, by FÁS trainees. Apparently the castle is haunted by a ghost, de Barnewall's niece Eleanora, and there's a murder hole where boiling oil could be poured over would-be attackers. The formal 17th-century-style garden is striving for self-sufficiency, and includes a collection of interesting fowl belonging to the Christian Brothers secondary school next door.

✱ **TOP CHOICES: PARKS** ✱ **TOP CHOICES: FOR INQUISITIVE KIDS** ✱

## 395 Dublin Municipal Rowing Centre

Longmeadows, Islandbridge, Dublin 7 (beside the Garda Club);
Contact: Billy King; Tel: 6779746.
**Open:** Easter/Summer; Mon–Fri 10am–2pm; Call for this year's
dates ▪ **Charge:** €12 a week ▪ **Suitable for ages:** 12+ ▪ **Bus
routes:** 25, 25A, 26, 51, 66, 68, 69.
**Sports:** rowing/canoeing
A Dublin City Council-run club, offering a schools programme as
well as week-long courses during the summer and Easter holidays.
July is usually reserved for youth groups or clubs, while June and
August are for the public.
**✱ TOP CHOICES: SPORTS FACILITIES ✱ TOP CHOICES: SUMMER
CAMPS ✱**

## 396 Dublin Zoo

Phoenix Park, Dublin 8 (in the Phoenix Park, at the Park Gate
entrance (the nearest city centre entrance)); Tel: 4748900;
Fax: 6771660; E-mail: info@dublinzoo.ie;
Website: www.dublinzoo.ie
**Open:** All year; Mar–Oct: Mon–Sat 9.30am–6pm; Sun
10.30am–6pm; Nov–Feb: Mon–Sat 9.30am–dusk; Sun
10.30am–dusk; Last admission 1 hour before closing ▪ **Charge:**
Child €6.30; Adult €10.10; Concessions €7.70; Child price is for
under-16s; Under-3s free; Family €29.40; Annual family
membership €90 ▪ **Suitable for ages:** All ▪ **Car parking:** Free ▪
**Bus routes:** 10, 25, 26.
Dublin Zoo is spread out over 30 acres, with plenty of pit-stops for
refreshments. There are big cats, primates, penguins and a reptile
house – everything you'd expect to see in a large zoo. You can
meet the keeper and see the animals being fed. Family
memberships are good value, giving unlimited access for €90 a
year. For a birthday party, if you ring in advance, the birthday
child gets to feed the elephants. There is a discount for a group
booking, but no special arrangements can be made at the
restaurants. A word of warning – don't stand too near the hippos'
fence, especially if they haven't had a good meal in a few hours!
**✱ TOP CHOICES: BIRTHDAY PARTY IDEAS ✱ TOP CHOICES: FOR AGES
0–2 ✱ TOP CHOICES: FOR AGES 2–5 ✱ TOP CHOICES: FOR AGES 5–10
✱ TOP CHOICES: FOR AGES 10+ ✱ TOP CHOICES: FOR ENERGETIC
KIDS ✱**

WEST DUBLIN

## 397 Dunsink Observatory

Castleknock, Dublin 15 (8 kms northwest of Dublin city centre, in the suburb of Castleknock); Contact: Bill Dumpleton;
Tel: 8387911; Fax: 8387090; Website: www.dunsink.dias.ie
**Open:** Winter; Open Nights are held on the 1st and 3rd Wed of each month during the winter ▪ **Charge:** Free ▪ **Suitable for ages:** 10+ ▪ **Car parking:** Free ▪ **Bus routes:** 38, 39, 70.
Built in 1783, Dunsink Observatory houses the Astronomy section of the School of Cosmic Physics, part of the Dublin Institute for Advanced Studies. If your child likes stargazing, there are Open Nights during the winter – send a stamped, addressed envelope to the address given, marked 'Open Nights'.
✱ **TOP CHOICES: FOR AGES 10+** ✱ **TOP CHOICES: FOR INQUISITIVE KIDS** ✱

## 398 Eamon Ceannt Park

Sundrive Rd, Dublin 12 (between Sundrive Road and Clogher Road); Tel: 4540799; E-mail: parks.parks@dublincity.ie;
Website: www.dublincity.ie/parks
**Open:** All year; Mon–Fri 8.30am–dusk; Sat–Sun 9.30am–dusk ▪ **Charge:** Free ▪ **Suitable for ages:** All ▪ **Car parking:** On-street parking ▪ **Bus routes:** 17, 18, 50, 54A, 56A, 83, 150.
**Sports:** basketball, cycling, gaelic football, hurling, soccer, tennis, athletics
Dating from the 1960s, this park is mainly devoted to sport. It is one of the larger parks in Dublin, at 17 hectares (42 acres). It includes an athletics track, a banked cycle track, playing fields, tennis courts and a children's playground. There is no need to book. Dublin Public Parks Tennis runs here in the summer.
✱ **TOP CHOICES: SPORTS FACILITIES** ✱ **TOP CHOICES: FOR AGES 0–2**
✱ **TOP CHOICES: FOR AGES 2–5** ✱ **TOP CHOICES: FOR AGES 5–10** ✱

## 399 Farmleigh House

White's Gate, Phoenix Park, Castleknock, Dublin 8 (near Mountjoy Cross. Access is via any of the park gates except White's Gate, which is closed); Tel: 8155981.
**Open:** Easter weekend and May–Sep; Sat–Sun 11am–4pm; Call in advance to confirm times ▪ **Charge:** Free ▪ **Suitable for ages:** 5+ ▪ **Car parking:** Free ▪ **Bus routes:** 25, 25A, 66, 66A/B, 67A.
Farmleigh House is a very grand place altogether, and is the site of many state functions. The house's ground floor is open in the

summer for tours. It hosts occasional special events, like a Victorian Christmas. The house is very formal – not really the place for toddlers wiping their hands on the furniture. There are walled and sunken gardens, but the cows and donkeys in the nearby field would be far more interesting.

**✱ TOP CHOICES: CHRISTMAS VISITS ✱**

## 400 First Flight Balloons

The Pond House, Narraghmore, Co. Kildare (call for directions); Tel: 8079098; E-mail: info@firstflight.co.uk; Website: www.balloonflights.ie

**Open:** Apr–Sep; 2 flights a day, one at sunrise and another 2 hours before sunset ▪ **Charge:** Child €195; Adult €195; Fee is per person for a one-hour flight ▪ **Suitable for ages:** 7+ ▪ **Car parking:** Free.

This is a fantastic experience, but very weather-dependent. You book your flight in advance, and have to ring the day before to see what your chances are of going up in the balloon. Vouchers are valid for a year. The direction you travel in will depend on the wind. The balloon can take up to eight people at a time. Flights usually take place at either end of the day, meeting at sunrise or a few hours before sunset to allow flying in calmer breezes. Your flight will last approximately one hour, before setting down in a suitable field. On landing, the balloon will be packed up and you will be met by the retrieve team, who will return you to the original launch site. The whole experience takes approximately three hours. During the flight it is usually warmer in the basket than on the ground. Normal outdoor clothing is fine, but wear suitable footwear, bearing in mind the early morning dew and the likely landing out in the countryside. Children under 12 years must be accompanied by an adult.

**✱ TOP CHOICES: BIRTHDAY PARTY IDEAS ✱ TOP CHOICES: FOR AGES 10+ ✱**

## 401 Fort Lucan

Westmanstown, Lucan, Co. Dublin (signposted from Lwr Lucan Rd); Tel: 6280166.

**Open:** Mar–Nov; Daily 12–5pm ▪ **Charge:** Child €5 ▪ **Suitable for ages:** All ▪ **Car parking:** Free ▪ **Bus routes:** 37, 239.

**Sports:** golf, crazy golf, trampolining, assault course

Fort Lucan is an adventure playground, featuring crazy golf, trampolines and an assault course, and is a fun day out for under-10s. There are picnic tables and a café. However, it can be very overcrowded and is often quite dirty.

**★ TOP CHOICES: PLAYGROUNDS ★ TOP CHOICES: FOR AGES 2–5 ★ TOP CHOICES: FOR AGES 5–10 ★ TOP CHOICES: FOR AGES 10+ ★ TOP CHOICES: FOR ENERGETIC KIDS ★**

## 402 Futurekids, Lucan 🖳

11 Lwr Main St, Lucan, Co. Dublin; Tel: 6280301;
E-mail: lucan@futurekids.ie; Website: www.futurekids.ie
**Open:** 7-week terms and summer camp; Call for class times ▪
**Charge:** Prices start at €90 per 7-week term, with discount for members of the same family ▪ **Suitable for ages:** 4–16 ▪ **Bus routes:** 25, 66, 66A/B, 67, 67A/X, 239.

Basic computer literacy classes for children from ages of 4–16, in classes of one hour per week. Computer skills are taught using themes and projects, making learning relevant and fun. Subjects include word-processing, spreadsheets, databases, graphics, multimedia, desktop publishing, telecommunications, operating environments, applied technologies and programming. There are also one-week summer camps.

**★ TOP CHOICES: HOBBIES/ARTS AND CRAFTS ★ TOP CHOICES: SUMMER CAMPS ★ TOP CHOICES: FOR AGES 10+ ★ TOP CHOICES: FOR INQUISITIVE KIDS ★**

## 403 Cumann Luthchleas Gael/GAA

Croke Park, Dublin 3; Tel: 8363222; Fax: 8366420;
E-mail: info@gaa.ie; Website: www.gaa.ie
**Open:** All year ▪ **Charge:** Weekly charge ▪ **Suitable for ages:** 5+.
**Sports:** gaelic football, hurling, camogie, handball
Clubs in west Dublin are listed below. See the Organisations chapter for more information on the GAA.

**★ TOP CHOICES: HOBBIES/ARTS AND CRAFTS ★**

## 404 Ballyboden/St. Enda's GAA Club

Firhouse Rd, Dublin 18; Tel: 4947950; Fax: 4947051.
**Open:** All year ▪ **Suitable for ages:** 5+ ▪ **Bus routes:** 49, 49A.
**Sports:** gaelic football, hurling

## 405 Commercial Hurling Club

Naas Rd, Rathcoole, Co Dublin; Tel: 4588300.
**Open:** All year ▪ **Suitable for ages:** 5+ ▪ **Bus routes:** 69, 69X.
**Sports:** hurling

## 406 Liffey Gaels GAA Club

Sarsfield Rd, Inchicore, Dublin 8; Contact: Peter Kenny;
Tel: 6260875.
**Open:** All year ▪ **Suitable for ages:** 5+ ▪ **Bus routes:** 51, 51B,
68, 69.
**Sports:** gaelic football, hurling

## 407 Lucan Sarsfields GAA Club

12th Lock, Lucan, Co. Dublin; Contact: Michael Roche;
Tel: 6240744.
**Open:** All year ▪ **Suitable for ages:** 5+.
**Sports:** hurling

## 408 Round Tower GAA Club

Convent Rd, Clondalkin, Dublin 22; Contact: Bernie Cronin;
Tel: 4592960.
**Open:** All year ▪ **Suitable for ages:** 5+ ▪ **Bus routes:** 51, 51B,
68, 69, 76, 76A/B, 210.
**Sports:** gaelic football, hurling

## 409 St. Anne's GAA Club

St. Anne's, Bohernabreena, Tallaght, Dublin 24; Tel: 4510372.
**Open:** All year ▪ **Charge:** Small weekly fee ▪ **Suitable for ages:**
5+ ▪ **Bus routes:** 49, 201.
**Sports:** gaelic football, hurling

## 410 St. Brigid's GAA Club

Russel Pk, Navan Rd, Dublin 15; Contact: Tony Hegarty;
Tel: 8202484.
**Open:** All year ▪ **Suitable for ages:** 5+ ▪ **Bus routes:** 37, 38,
38A/C, 39, 39A, 70, 122.
**Sports:** gaelic football, hurling

## 411 St. Mark's GAA Club

Cookstown Rd, Tallaght, Dublin 24; Contact: Bill Ellison;
Tel: 4521609.
**Open:** All year ▪ **Suitable for ages:** 5+ ▪ **Bus routes:** 49, 49A,
50, 56A, 65, 75, 76, 77A/B, 201, 202.
**Sports:** gaelic football, hurling

## 412 St. Mary's GAA Club

Saggart, Co. Dublin; Contact: Michael Nugent; Tel: 4589099.

**Open:** All year ▪ **Suitable for ages:** 5+ ▪ **Bus routes:** 69.
**Sports:** gaelic football, hurling

## 413 St. Peregrine's GAA Club

Blackestown Rd, Dublin 15; Tel: 8223269.
**Open:** All year ▪ **Charge:** Small weekly fee ▪ **Suitable for ages:**
5+ ▪ **Bus routes:** 39, 76A, 220.
**Sports:** gaelic football, hurling

## 414 Thomas Davis GAA Sports Club

Kiltipper Rd, Tallaght, Dublin 24; Contact: Christopher
O'Donnell; Tel: 4525005.
**Open:** All year ▪ **Suitable for ages:** 5+ ▪ **Bus routes:** 75.
**Sports:** gaelic football, hurling

## 415 Giraffe's Play Centre

Unit 212, Coolmine Industrial Estate, Blanchardstown, Dublin 15
(around the corner from Blanchardstown Shopping Centre);
Tel: 8205526.
**Open:** All year; Mon–Fri 12–7pm; Sat–Sun 10am–7pm ▪ **Charge:**
€5 per hour's play; Birthday parties from €9.25 per person ▪
**Suitable for ages:** All ▪ **Car parking:** Free ▪ **Bus routes:** 39, 70,
220.
A big indoor play area, with bouncy castles, ball pools, swing
slides, aerial walkways, slides and climbing frames. Adults must
accompany children, but you can relax over a cup of coffee.
Birthday parties include play, food and a video recording of the
party.
✱ **TOP CHOICES: BIRTHDAY PARTY IDEAS** ✱ **TOP CHOICES:**
**PLAYGROUNDS** ✱ **TOP CHOICES: FOR AGES 2–5** ✱

## 416 Glenville Pitch-and-Putt Club

Kiltipper Rd, Tallaght, Dublin 24; Tel: 4519916.
**Open:** All year; Mon–Fri 2–5pm; Sat–Sun 10am–6pm ▪ **Charge:**
€30 annually, with no additional entrance charge ▪ **Suitable for**
**ages:** 10+ ▪ **Bus routes:** 75.
**Sports:** pitch-and-putt
A members-only pitch-and-putt club. Junior members must be at
least 10 years old, and can go unaccompanied. It takes about an
hour-and-a-half to complete the course.

## 417 Greenhills Archers

Indoor: Greenhills Scout Den, St James Road, Walkinstown, Dublin 12; Outdoor: Old Bawn Community School, Old Bawn, Tallaght, Dublin 24; Contact: Tom Moylan; Tel: 4532538.
**Open:** All year; Call for current meeting times ▪ **Suitable for ages:** 10+.
**Sports:** archery

## 418 Gymboree Music on the Go 🛒 📣

Methodist Church Hall, Lucan, Co. Dublin; Tel: 2789069 (info), 4905880 (parties at home); Website: www.playandmusic.ie
**Open:** All year; Wed 10am, 11.30am, 1pm ▪ **Charge:** €5– €7.50 per class (with reduction for booking a block session) ▪ **Suitable for ages:** 0–5 years ▪ **Car parking:** Free.
Gymboree Music on the Go is a range of creative programmes for children from birth to 5 years old. The children can play percussion instruments, sing and dance with an instructor. The musical themes vary from reggae to polka. Parents must be present and are involved in sessions. There are also Gymboree party plans (see Gymboree main entry).
✱ TOP CHOICES: FOR AGES 0–2 ✱ TOP CHOICES: FOR AGES 2–5 ✱

## 419 Hockey

Irish Hockey Association, 6A Woodbine Park, Blackrock, Co. Dublin; Tel: 2600028; Fax: 2600087;
E-mail: joanmorgan@hockey.ie; Website: www.hockey.ie
**Open:** Sep–Apr; Call for meeting dates and times ▪ **Charge:** Annual membership around €45 ▪ **Suitable for ages:** 6+.
The Irish Hockey Association oversees all Irish hockey clubs. Children's teams usually start at under-8s and go up to under-16s. Coaching is often on Saturday mornings and Friday nights – call for details.
✱ TOP CHOICES: HOBBIES/ARTS AND CRAFTS ✱

## 420 Glenanne Hockey Club

St. Mark's Community School, Fortunestown Lane, Tallaght, Dublin 24; Tel: 4620543 (Paul Bastable);
E-mail: paul.bastable@irishlife.ie
**Open:** Sep–Apr; Call for meeting dates and times ▪ **Suitable for ages:** 6+ ▪ **Bus routes:** 56A.
✱ TOP CHOICES: SPORTS FACILITIES ✱ TOP CHOICES: HOBBIES/ARTS AND CRAFTS ✱

## 421 Weston Hockey Club

Griffen Valley Park, Newcastle Rd, Lucan, Co. Dublin; Contact:
Jon Long; Tel: 6282040, 086 9881137;
E-mail: jonathan.long@puretelcom.ie;
Website: www.westonhockeyclub.com
**Open:** Sep–Apr; Call for meeting dates and times ▪ **Suitable for
ages:** 6+ ▪ **Bus routes:** 25A.

## 422 Inchicore Library 📝 🖫

34 Emmet Rd, Dublin 8; Tel: 4533793;
Website: www.iol.ie/dublincitylibrary
**Open:** All year; Mon/Wed 12.45–4pm, 4.45–8pm; Tue/Thur/Sat
10am–1pm, 2–5pm ▪ **Charge:** Free ▪ **Suitable for ages:** All ▪ **Car
parking:** Disc parking on Emmet Rd ▪ **Bus routes:** 51, 51B, 68A,
78A.
Inchicore Library has a Children's Art Class for 6–12-yr-olds on
Thursdays from 3–5pm. Other seasonal arts-and-crafts and reading
events for children are organised throughout the year.

## 423 Independent Theatre Workshop, Ballycullen Ave

Scoil Treasa, Ballycullen Ave, Tallaght, Dublin 24 (beside Firhouse
Shopping Centre and The Speaker Connolly pub); Tel: 4968808;
Fax: 4968808;
Website: www.independent-theatre-workshop.com
**Open:** All year; Thur 3.30pm, 4.30pm, 5.30pm ▪ **Charge:** €57 for
10-week term ▪ **Suitable for ages:** 7–15 ▪ **Bus routes:** 49, 49A/X.
Creative drama classes for ages 7+ are held on Thursday evenings.
See also main entry.
**★ TOP CHOICES: HOBBIES/ARTS AND CRAFTS ★**

## 424 Independent Theatre Workshop, Firhouse Rd W

Tymon Bawn Community Centre, Firhouse Rd W, Tallaght, Dublin
24; Tel: 4968808; Fax: 4968808;
Website: www.independent-theatre-workshop.com
**Open:** All year; Tue 4pm, 6pm, 7pm ▪ **Charge:** Creative drama
€57 per term ▪ **Suitable for ages:** 7–15 ▪ **Bus routes:** 15F, 49X.
The Independent Theatre Workshop holds creative drama classes
for ages 7+. See also main entry.

## 425 The Japanese Gardens and Irish National Stud ♨ 🍴 ♿ €

Tully, Co. Kildare (from Dublin, take the M7 and bypass Naas and Newbridge. On the way into Kildare Town, take a left at hotel, then take the first left. The Japanese Gardens are 1 mile down this road, on your left); Tel: (045) 522963, (045) 521251;
E-mail: tourism@irish-national-stud.ie;
Website: www.irish-national-stud.ie
**Open:** Mid-Feb–mid-Nov; Mon–Sun 9.30am–6pm ▪ **Charge:**
Child €4.50; Adult €8.50; Concessions €6.50; Family (2 adults and 4 children) €18.00; One ticket covers all three attractions (National Stud, Japanese gardens and St. Fiachra's Garden) ▪
**Suitable for ages:** All ▪ **Car parking:** Free ▪ **Bus routes:** Day Tours Unplugged, Tel: 8340941.
There are three attractions to see here – the Irish National Stud, the Japanese Gardens and St. Fiachra's Garden. The Irish National Stud is a government-sponsored horse farm and is home of some of Ireland's best breeding stock. There's a horse museum, where you can see the skeleton of Arkle, the 1960s champion racehorse. The Japanese Gardens were made by master gardener Tasso Eida in the years 1906–10, for a wealthy Scotsman. The gardens symbolise the progress of man from the Cave of Birth to the Gateway of Eternity. Finally, St. Fiachra's Garden was created to celebrate the Millennium. The entrance to the garden is via an underground stone passage, which leads you to lakes and woodlands, with a bronze statue of St. Fiachra sitting on the rocks. All in all, a nice day out in beautiful surroundings.
✱ TOP CHOICES: PICNIC SPOTS ✱ TOP CHOICES: PARKS ✱

## 426 Kill International ♿

Kill, Co. Kildare; Tel: (045) 877333, 1850 440330;
E-mail: killinternationalec@eircom.net
**Open:** All year; Tue–Sun 10am–4.30pm; Call for camp dates and times ▪ **Charge:** €15.50 per hourly lesson; Summer camp prices on request ▪ **Suitable for ages:** 4+ ▪ **Bus routes:** -.
**Sports:** horse-riding
Kill is the official equestrian venue for the 2003 Special Olympics. It has both indoor and outdoor arenas and offers lessons to beginners and advanced riders, specialising in livery and jumping. It does not offer riding out. Pony camps are run

during the summer and at Easter.

**✱ TOP CHOICES: SPORTS FACILITIES ✱ TOP CHOICES: HOBBIES/ARTS AND CRAFTS ✱**

## 427 Kilmainham Gaol 🚼 🍴 ♿

Inchicore Rd, Kilmainham, Dublin 8 (pass St. James's Hospital on James's St, and turn right up the South Circular Rd); Tel: 4535984; Fax: 4532037; Website: www.heritageireland.ie
**Open:** All year; Apr–Sep: Mon–Sun, 9:30am–6pm (last admission 4.45pm); Oct–Mar: Mon–Fri 9.30am–5pm (last admission 4pm); Sun 10am–6pm (last admission 4.45pm) ▪ **Charge:** Child €1.90; Adult €4.40; Student €1.90 Senior/Group €3.10 Family €10.10 ▪ **Suitable for ages:** 7+ ▪ **Car parking:** On-street parking ▪ **Bus routes:** 51, 51B, 78A, 79.

You can feel the history of Kilmainham Gaol oozing out of its walls. The prison opened in 1796 and closed in 1924, and is full of stories that even a small child will be both fascinated and chilled by – such as that of the 8-year-old famine victim convicted for stealing a cloak. On the guided tour you can see padded cells, a treadmill and the gallows. Finally, and most grisly of all, is the courtyard. Here prisoners – including many of those who fought for Ireland's independence – were shot. It's a bit like the last scene in *The Blair Witch Project*. You can also visit the church where Joseph Plunkett was married, hours before his execution. This is a museum for children who don't have nightmares about this kind of thing. Access is by guided tour only; wheelchair users should ring before visiting.

**✱ TOP CHOICES: FOR AGES 10+ ✱ TOP CHOICES: FOR INQUISITIVE KIDS ✱**

## 428 Kylemore Karting (Outdoor Karting) 🍴 ♺

Unit 1A, Kylemore Industrial Estate, Killeen Road, Kylemore, Dublin 10 (just off the Naas Rd); Tel: 6261444; Fax: 6261863; E-mail: info@kylemore-karting.com; Website: www.kylemore-karting.com
**Open:** All year; Mon–Fri 11am–late; Sat–Sun 10am–late ▪ **Charge:** Child €28; Adult €28; Prices range from €28–€32 per person; Junior race meetings from €20 per child ▪ **Suitable for ages:** 9+ ▪ **Car parking:** Free ▪ **Bus routes:** 18, 79. Minibus transport can be arranged.
**Sports:** karting

Before you start racing, you need to book a practice session, which can be on the same day that you want to race. This gives the driver an opportunity to sample driving a kart, with a computerised printout of his/her lap-times and average speeds achieved. All safety equipment is supplied. For children, it is recommended that you bring along your own group and book an exclusive race meeting (a €75 deposit is required). Groups from 6 to 60 are catered for. There are two types of race meetings – the Championship Race, at a cost of €32 per driver, and the Full Grand Prix race, from €36 per driver. Discounts are offered to groups of 20 and over. A Mini Endurance Race, for up to 8 drivers, costs €32 per driver. A junior version of Open Race nights is run every Sunday morning at 10am, limited to drivers between 9 and 14 years of age (and subject to a minimum height requirement of 54 inches). A great idea for an older child's birthday party, and food can be supplied.

✱ TOP CHOICES: BIRTHDAY PARTY IDEAS ✱ TOP CHOICES: SPORTS FACILITIES ✱ TOP CHOICES: FOR AGES 10+ ✱ TOP CHOICES: FOR TRENDY KIDS ✱ TOP CHOICES: FOR ENERGETIC KIDS ✱

## 429 Lansdowne Valley 

Slievebloom Rd, Drimnagh, Dublin 12 (located along the Cammock River between Slievebloom Road, Naas Road and Davitt Road); Tel: 4542555; E-mail: parks.parks@dublincity.ie; Website: www.dublincity.ie/parks
**Open:** All year; Mon–Fri 8.30am–dusk; Sat–Sun 9.30am–dusk ■ **Charge:** Free ■ **Suitable for ages:** All ■ **Car parking:** On-street parking.
**Sports:** pitch-and-putt
Lansdowne Valley is best known for its 18-hole pitch-and-putt course, which dominates its southern end. The rest of the park is mainly laid out in grass.

## 430 Larchill Arcadian Gardens 

Dunshaughlin Rd, Kilcock, Co. Kildare (30km west of Dublin, 5km from Kilcock on the Dunshaughlin Rd); Contact: Michael de Las Casas; Tel: 6287354, 6284580; E-mail: delascas@indigo.ie
**Open:** May/Sep: Sat–Sun 12–6pm; Jun–Aug: Mon–Sun 12–6pm (call to check – may close on Mon); Christmas: Santa sometimes comes 3 weeks before Christmas, but call to check ■ **Charge:** Child €5; Adult €7; Family ticket approx €20 ■ **Suitable for ages:**

All ▪ **Car parking:** Free.

This is the only example in Ireland, or indeed Europe, of a mid-18th-century Arcadian garden. There's a 40-minute walk through landscaped parkland, and plenty of wildlife to see around the lake. There's also a maze made of maize and a playground with old-fashioned games – giant skittles and the like. Larchill has the largest number of rare farm animal breeds in the State. No pesticides are used on the grounds. You can hold a birthday party here, and use the restaurant tables if you bring your own food. Santa sometimes visits for about 3 weeks before Christmas.

✸ **TOP CHOICES: PICNIC SPOTS** ✸ **TOP CHOICES: BIRTHDAY PARTY VENUES** ✸ **TOP CHOICES: PARKS** ✸ **TOP CHOICES: PLAYGROUNDS** ✸ **TOP CHOICES: WALKS** ✸ **TOP CHOICES: CHRISTMAS VISITS** ✸ **TOP CHOICES: FOR AGES 0–2** ✸ **TOP CHOICES: FOR AGES 2–5** ✸ **TOP CHOICES: FOR AGES 5–10** ✸ **TOP CHOICES: FOR ENERGETIC KIDS** ✸

## 431 Le Fanu Park

Blackditch Rd, Ballyfermot, Dublin 12 (bounded by Le Fanu, Clifden and Blackditch Roads); Tel: 6265064; E-mail: parks.parks@dublincity.ie; Website: www.dublincity.ie/parks

**Open:** All year; Mon–Fri 8.30am–dusk; Sat–Sun 9.30am–dusk ▪ **Charge:** Free ▪ **Suitable for ages:** All ▪ **Car parking:** On-street parking ▪ **Bus routes:** 18, 76, 76A, 78, 78A.

**Sports:** basketball, soccer, swimming, tennis

Le Fanu Park was developed primarily as a soccer sports ground, and is known locally as 'the Lawns'. It also includes tennis courts and a swimming pool. Dublin Public Parks Tennis runs here in the summer. There is a small playground for younger children.

## 432 Leisureplex, Blanchardstown

Blanchardstown Shopping Centre, Dublin 15 (from the M50 roundabout, head towards Navan on the Navan road. Take the second exit off the dual carriageway and then an immediate left); Tel: 8223030; E-mail: blanchardstown@leisureplex.ie; Website: www.leisureplex.ie

**Open:** All year; Mon–Sun 24 hours ▪ **Charge:** Activities from about €5; birthday parties from €11 per child, including: activity, food, cake, balloons, party bags and a photo ▪ **Suitable for ages:** All ▪ **Car parking:** Free ▪ **Bus routes:** 39, 220.

**Sports:** snooker, pool, 10-pin bowling

Fun for all! For little ones there's The Zoo – a huge, soft play area with slides and balls, including space for under-3s. Snooker, pool and Quazar are available for ages 7/8+, as well as bowling with ball walls (there is a junior bowling club on Saturday mornings at 10am). Young teens can hang out in the games area, complete with the ever-popular dance machine. Great for birthday parties, especially for the under-8s, who have theirs hosted by Plexy the dinosaur. This branch also has dodgem cars and Pompeii Paints – you can paint your own ceramics.

✱ TOP CHOICES: BIRTHDAY PARTY IDEAS ✱ TOP CHOICES: PLAYGROUNDS ✱ TOP CHOICES: FOR AGES 2–5 ✱ TOP CHOICES: FOR AGES 5–10 ✱ TOP CHOICES: FOR AGES 10+ ✱ TOP CHOICES: FOR ENERGETIC KIDS ✱

## 433 Leisureplex, Tallaght 🛒 🍵 ♿ 🎾 🧸

Village Green Ctr, Tallaght, Dublin 24 (Village Green is at the junction of the Naas Rd and the Old Bawn Rd); Tel: 4599411; E-mail: tallaght@leisureplex.ie; Website: www.leisureplex.ie
**Open:** All year; Mon–Sun 24 hours ■ **Charge:** Activities from about €5; birthday parties from €11 per child, including: activity, food, cake, balloons, party bags and a photo ■ **Suitable for ages:** All ■ **Car parking:** Free ■ **Bus routes:** 49, 50X, 54A, 65, 65B/X, 75, 77A/B/X, 201, 202.
**Sports:** snooker, pool, 10-pin bowling
Fun for all! For little ones there's The Zoo – a huge, soft play area with slides and balls, including space for under-3s. Snooker, pool and Quazar are available for ages 7/8+, as well as bowling with ball walls (there is a junior bowling club on Saturday mornings at 10am). Young teens can hang out in the games area, complete with the ever-popular dance machine. Great for birthday parties, especially for the under-8s, who have theirs hosted by Plexy the dinosaur.

✱ TOP CHOICES: BIRTHDAY PARTY IDEAS ✱ TOP CHOICES: PLAYGROUNDS ✱ TOP CHOICES: FOR ENERGETIC KIDS ✱

## 434 Liffey Valley Shopping Centre
🛒 🎲 🍵 ♿

Fonthill Rd, Clondalkin, Dublin 22 (Junction 7 off the M50, take the N4 towards Lucan/Galway); Tel: 6160200 (centre), 6239093 (crèche); Fax: 6233306; Website: www.liffeyvalley.ie
**Open:** All year; Centre: Mon–Tue 10am–7pm; Wed–Fri 10am–9pm; Sat 9.30am-7pm; Sun/bank holidays 11am–7pm;

Crèche: Mon–Tue 10am–5.45pm; Wed–Fri 10am–8.45pm; Sat 9.30am–5.45pm; Sun 12–5.45pm ▪ **Charge:** €6 per child for 2 hours crèche; €9.10 for 2 members of the same family ▪ **Suitable for ages:** All ▪ **Car parking:** Free ▪ **Bus routes:** 78A, 210, 239. A big, roomy shopping centre with plenty of shops for kidswear, including a big Marks & Spencer's and Dunnes Stores, plus a large Boots for baby stuff. This centre holds events such as fashion shows, E-Kara Search for a Star and competitions. You can hire 'kiddie cabs' for toddlers to peddle around in, or else take advantage of the crèche facilities.

## 435 Lodge Park Heritage Centre and Steam Museum 🚼 🍼 ♿ €

Straffan, Co. Kildare (16 miles from Dublin, off the N7, signposted from Kill); Tel: 6273155; Fax: 6273477;
Website: www.steam-museum.ie
**Open:** Jun–Aug; Jun–Jul: Tue–Fri Sun 2–6pm; Aug: Tue–Fri 2.30–5.30pm ▪ **Charge:** Child €3; Adult €4; Family €13; Concessions €3 ▪ **Suitable for ages:** All ▪ **Car parking:** Free. Lodge Park is a Palladian house, built in 1773, with a walled garden of 18th-century origin. This is divided into different sections, including a roserie – a must-see in the summer. Children will love the Steam Museum, which has working steam engines.
✱ TOP CHOICES: PARKS ✱ TOP CHOICES: FOR AGES 5–10 ✱

## 436 Longmeadows Ballyfermot Pitch & Putt Course

St. Laurence's Rd, Ballyfermot, Dublin 10; Tel: 6304380.
**Open:** All year; Winter: Mon–Sun 9.30am–3pm; Summer: Mon–Sun 9.30am–8.30pm ▪ **Charge:** €2 a round; Gear rental is €1.30, with a €5 deposit ▪ **Suitable for ages:** 7+ ▪ **Bus routes:** 78, 78A.
**Sports:** pitch-and-putt
Kids are welcome at this pitch-and-putt course during the day and on Saturday mornings. They need to bring their own golf balls, but clubs can be rented for a nominal fee, along with a €5 deposit.

## 437 Lucan Library 🚼 ♿ ✏ 🖥

Superquinn Shopping Centre, Newcastle Rd, Lucan, Co. Dublin; Tel: 6216422; Fax: 6216433; E-mail: libraries@sdcc.ie; Website: www.sdcc.ie/library

**Open:** All year; Mon–Thur 9:45am–8pm; Fri–Sat 9:45am–4:30pm; closed bank holidays ▪ **Charge:** Free ▪ **Suitable for ages:** All ▪ **Car parking:** Free ▪ **Bus routes:** 25A, 66, 66A/B, 67, 67A.

Art classes for 8–12-yr-olds are held here on Wed afternoons, and parent-and-toddler sessions on Mon and Wed. Other seasonal arts-and-crafts and reading events for children are organised throughout the year.

**✱ TOP CHOICES: FOR AGES 5–10 ✱**

## 438 Lucan Youth Dance/Drama Group

c/o Lucan Youth Service, The Life Centre, Esker Hill, Lucan, Co. Dublin; Contact: Helen Farmer; Tel: 6214202, 087 9732230.
**Open:** All year; Tue eves ▪ **Charge:** €3 per week ▪ **Suitable for ages:** 13–17 ▪ **Bus routes:** 25, 66, 66A/B, 67.

Mime, voice projection, acting, stage make-up and design, hip hop and street dance are just some of the activities on offer on Tue nights at St Mary's Boys' National School, for just €3 a week.

**✱ TOP CHOICES: HOBBIES/ARTS AND CRAFTS ✱ TOP CHOICES: FOR IMAGINATIVE KIDS ✱**

## 439 Markievicz Park 🚼 ♿ 🧒

Ballyfermot Rd, Dublin 10 (between Ballyfermot Rd and Decies Rd); Tel: 6265051; E-mail: parks.parks@dublincity.ie; Website: www.dublincity.ie/parks
**Open:** All year; Mon–Fri 8.30am–dusk; Sat–Sun 9.30am–dusk ▪ **Charge:** Free ▪ **Suitable for ages:** All ▪ **Car parking:** On-street parking ▪ **Bus routes:** 18, 76, 76A, 78A, 79, 206.
**Sports:** gaelic football, soccer

This 1960s park was redeveloped in the late 1990s. It now has an all-weather pitch for GAA and soccer. Younger children will enjoy the small playground.

## 440 Millennium Maze 🚼 ♿ 🚻

Ballinafagh Farm, Prosperous, Clane, Co. Kildare (north Kildare, on the R403 past Celbridge); Contact: Jim Wyse; Tel: (045) 861590; E-mail: enquiries@milleniummaze.com; Website: www.millenniummaze.com
**Open:** May–Oct; Mon–Sun 2–6pm ▪ **Charge:** Child €2.50; Adult €3.50 ▪ **Suitable for ages:** All ▪ **Car parking:** Free.
**Sports:** crazy golf

The Millennium Maze is designed in the shape of a St Brigid's cross. It covers almost an acre – there's more than a mile-and-a-half of paths, with 6-foot-high hedges. There's a paved maze for smaller children (and for those of us who still have nightmares after 1970s horror film *The Shining*). Other activities include crazy golf, pets' corner and a sandpit.

✱ TOP CHOICES: PARKS ✱ TOP CHOICES: PLAYGROUNDS ✱ TOP CHOICES: FOR AGES 2–5 ✱ TOP CHOICES: FOR AGES 5–10 ✱ TOP CHOICES: FOR ENERGETIC KIDS ✱

## 441 The Mill Shopping Centre

Clondalkin, Co. Dublin (off the new Nangor Rd); Tel: 4577144, 4577188 ext. 241 (crêche).
**Open:** All year; Centre: Mon–Tue 9am–7pm; Wed 9am–9pm; Thur–Fri 9am–10pm; Sat 9am–6.30pm; Sun 10am–6pm; Crêche: Mon–Wed 9.30am–5pm; Thur–Fri 9.30am–9pm; Sat 9.30am–6pm ■ **Charge:** Crêche €4.50 per child per hour, for max. 2-hour stay ■ **Suitable for ages:** All ■ **Car parking:** Free ■ **Bus routes:** 51, 76, 76A/B, 210.
A small shopping centre, all on one level, with a Dunnes Stores.

## 442 Morrell Farm

Turning, Straffan, Co. Kildare (16 miles from Dublin, off the N7); Contact: Edel Wilson; Tel: 6288636.
**Open:** All year, but call to check during the winter; Mon–Fri 10.30am–5.30pm ■ **Charge:** Child €3; Adult €4 ■ **Suitable for ages:** All ■ **Car parking:** Free.
This is absolutely brilliant for children. There are loads of animals to see, including foxes, deer, goats and some rare breeds of farm animals, and you can even pet a baby bunny rabbit in the barn. Take a picnic with you and eat it by the stream (there are no café facilities). For a birthday party there is a room (or alternatively a barn!) that can be hired, with decorations, food and a birthday cake at an extra charge.

✱ TOP CHOICES: PICNIC SPOTS ✱ TOP CHOICES: BIRTHDAY PARTY IDEAS ✱ TOP CHOICES: FOR AGES 0–2 ✱ TOP CHOICES: FOR AGES 2–5 ✱ TOP CHOICES: FOR AGES 5–10 ✱ TOP CHOICES: FOR ENERGETIC KIDS ✱

## 443 National Aquatic Centre

Snugborough Rd, Blanchardstown, Dublin 15 (The centre is off Junction 6 off the M50. Leave the Blanchardstown bypass (N3), take the third exit on the roundabout to Snugborough Rd);

Tel: 6464300; Fax: 6464325; E-mail: info@nac.ie;
Website: www.nac.ie

**Open:** All year; Competition Pools: Mon–Fri 6am–11pm; Sat–Sun
8am–8pm; Leisure Pool: Mon–Fri 11am–10pm; Sat–Sun
11am–8pm; Members admitted from 10am at weekends; Health
& Fitness Club (members only): Mon–Fri 7am–10pm ▪ **Charge:**
Pay-as-you-go prices: off-peak times (Mon–Fri, 11am–3pm):
Leisure Pool (including Competition Pool): Juniors/OAPs/students
€7; Adult €9; Family (2 adults and 2 children) €25.60; Peak times
(weekends and after 3pm Mon–Fri): Juniors/OAPs/students €8;
Adult €10; Family (2 Adults and 2 Children) €30.60; Membership,
swimming lesson and birthday party prices on request ▪ **Suitable
for ages:** All ▪ **Bus routes:** 38A, 238.

**Sports:** diving, swimming, water polo

A mega €62 million complex with a 50-metre Olympic-size
competition pool, top-class diving facilities and leisure pools.
There is a children's pool, complete with slides, a pirate ship and
other water features. There is a series of water activities to suit
everyone, from the exciting rollercoaster-style Master Blaster –
with hair-raising drops and curves – to the Lazy River, where you
float around the wave pool at two miles an hour. There is also a
scary Dark Hole ride, the Family Flume ride, the Flow Rider with
constant waves for surfing, and the Wave Pool. The centre also
offers full health and fitness facilities and a wet and dry café. There
are also mother-and-toddler swims and swimming lessons for
children. You can even have a birthday party here, call for details.

✱ **TOP CHOICES: BIRTHDAY PARTY IDEAS ✱ TOP CHOICES: SPORTS
FACILITIES ✱ TOP CHOICES: FOR AGES 2–5 ✱ TOP CHOICES: FOR
AGES 5–10 ✱ TOP CHOICES: FOR AGES 10+ ✱ TOP CHOICES: FOR
ENERGETIC KIDS ✱**

## 444 National Basketball Arena ♿

Tymon Park, Tallaght, Dublin 24 (head towards Tallaght from the
M50 exit and turn right at next roundabout onto Old Tallaght Rd.
Take the first right at a pedestrian crossing and the entrance is
opposite the Penny Black pub); Tel: 4590211; Fax: 4590212;
E-mail: information@iba.ie; Website: www.iba.ie

**Open:** All year; Mon–Sun 9.30am–4pm; Call for this year's
training camp dates ▪ **Charge:** Weekly camps from €50 ▪ **Suitable
for ages:** 7+ ▪ **Car parking:** Free ▪ **Bus routes:** 65, 76B, 77A.

**Sports:** basketball

The major arena for all basketball competitions, it also hosts
several basketball clubs. During school holidays there are weekly

training camps for different levels. Swimming is also provided during the course for the seniors (over-11s) in the Palace Sports Complex next door. An annual three-week course is held in Dungarvan, County Waterford, and is very popular with teenagers.

**✱ TOP CHOICES: SPORTS FACILITIES ✱ TOP CHOICES: SUMMER CAMPS ✱**

## 445 Neptune Rowing Club

Longmeadows, Islandbridge, Dublin 7; Tel: 6775079 (Terry Covey).

**Open:** All year; Sat–Sun 12pm (can vary); Training sometimes during the week; Times change depending on groups and coaches ▪ **Charge:** €70 annual membership ▪ **Suitable for ages:** 12+ ▪ **Car parking:** Free ▪ **Bus routes:** 25, 25A, 26, 51, 68, 69.
**Sports:** rowing/canoeing

This is a good club for more experienced rowers, and it is quite competitive. They have recently built a new clubhouse. Kids need to be 12 years old to start rowing, as the equipment is adult-sized, although younger children can cox. Racing does not start until age 14. Rowers will need a one-piece wetsuit (costs about €60), as well as a splash top in club colours (about €75). Boats, oars and coaching are provided.

**✱ TOP CHOICES: SPORTS FACILITIES ✱ TOP CHOICES: HOBBIES/ARTS AND CRAFTS ✱**

## 446 Nolan, Martin (Music Teacher)

Drimnagh, Dublin 12; Tel: 087 4121494.
**Open:** All year; Class times on request ▪ **Charge:** From €25 per hour ▪ **Suitable for ages:** 8+.

Martin Nolan gives individual or group tuition in tin whistle, low whistle and uilleann pipes. Beginners are welcome.

## 447 O'Boyle, Catherine (Music Teacher)

Lucan/Palmerstown, Co. Dublin; Tel: 6263058.
**Open:** All year; Class times on request ▪ **Charge:** €20 per 45-minute class ▪ **Suitable for ages:** 10+.

Catherine O'Boyle gives voice training for older children, in classical voice, jazz voice and traditional voice. Students can be prepared for TCL, ABRSM and LCM exams.

## 448 Worth, Orla, School of Irish Dance

The Old Library, Rathcoole, Co. Dublin (Rathcoole is off the Naas Rd; check in case the venue changes); Tel: 087 6374688; Website: www.worthacademy.com
**Open:** Call for new term times; Wed/Thur afternoons ▪ **Charge:** Fees on request ▪ **Suitable for ages:** 3+ ▪ **Car parking:** Free.
An Irish dancing school, whose students can participate in competitions.

## 449 Pelletstown Riding Centre

Pelletstown, Co. Meath (about a 10-minute drive from Blanchardstown Shopping Centre, signposted); Tel: 8259435.
**Open:** All year; Summer: Mon–Sun 10am–dark; Rest of year: Mon–Fri 3.30–7pm; Sat 10am–4pm; Sun 11am–1pm; Call for summer pony camp times ▪ **Charge:** €18 per hour-long lesson; Summer camp prices on request ▪ **Suitable for ages:** 5+.
**Sports:** horse-riding
Pelletstown has floodlit indoor and outdoor arenas. It specialises in cross-country riding and also offers hacking over farmland. Pony camps are available during the summer.
**✱ TOP CHOICES: SPORTS FACILITIES ✱ TOP CHOICES: SUMMER CAMPS ✱**

## 450 Phoenix Cricket Club

Phoenix Park, Dublin 8 (yellow house near Dublin Zoo); Tel: 6770121.
**Open:** Apr–Sep ▪ **Charge:** Small weekly charge; Summer camp fees on request ▪ **Suitable for ages:** 6+ ▪ **Car parking:** Free ▪ **Bus routes:** 10.
**Sports:** cricket
Nearly all Dublin cricket clubs offer summer camps for children, and most also host schools cricket during term time. The camps are often run from Mon to Fri, for several hours a day. Ordinary sportswear is fine. Pads, etc., are supplied by the club.
**✱ TOP CHOICES: HOBBIES/ARTS AND CRAFTS ✱**

## 451 Phoenix Park

Dublin 8 (west of the city centre. The Park Gate entrance is on the opposite side of the River Liffey from Heuston train station); Tel: 6770095; Fax: 6726454;
E-mail: phoenixparkvisitorcentre@ealga.ie

**Open:** All year; Park: Mon–Sun 24 hours; Ordnance Survey Centre: Mon–Thur 9am–4.45pm; Fri 9am–4.15pm; Closed for lunch 12.30–1.15pm ▪ **Charge:** Free ▪ **Suitable for ages:** All ▪ **Car parking:** Free ▪ **Bus routes:** 25, 25A, 66, 66A/B, 67A. **Sports:** cricket, cycling, gaelic football, horse-riding, hurling

The Phoenix Park is the biggest park in Europe, and contains the People's Gardens, the Zoological Gardens, Saint Mary's Hospital, the residence of the US Ambassador, Áras an Úachtaráin, the Wellington Monument and the Papal Cross. It's lovely for walking in. There is plenty of wildlife to see, including ponds full of ducks – bring your stale bread. Wild deer congregate around the Papal Cross, built to commemorate the Pope's 1979 visit to Ireland. There are also nature trails and walks to follow – information is given at the Knockmaroon Gate, at the Castleknock end of the park. Plenty of sports are played here, including polo, cricket, hurling and soccer. You can bring your skates or bicycle, or even a model airplane. There is an Ordnance Survey centre for children who like maps, and so many other things to do that we've listed them all separately – see entries on the Phoenix Park Visitor Centre, Áras an Úachtaráin, Farmleigh House and Dublin Zoo.

★ **TOP CHOICES: PICNIC SPOTS** ★ **TOP CHOICES: PARKS** ★ **TOP CHOICES: WALKS** ★ **TOP CHOICES: FOR AGES 0–2** ★ **TOP CHOICES: FOR AGES 2–5** ★ **TOP CHOICES: FOR ENERGETIC KIDS** ★

## 452 Phoenix Park Visitor Centre 🖼 ♿ €

Phoenix Park, Dublin 8 (in the Phoenix Park; Use the gate at Ashtown Cross – Visitor Centre is 20 minutes' walk from the gate. Or follow the signs after the Phoenix Monument from the Park Gate); Tel: 6770095, 6472461; Fax: 6726454; E-mail: phoenixparkvisitorcentre@ealga.ie; Website: www.heritageireland.ie

**Open:** Jan–mid-Mar: Sat–Sun 9.30am–4.30pm; Mid-Mar–May: Mon–Sun 9.30am–5pm; Jun–Sep: Mon–Sun 10am–6pm; Oct: Mon–Sun 9.30am–5pm; Nov–Dec: Sat–Sun 9.30am–4.30pm; Last Admission 45 minutes before closing ▪ **Charge:** Child €1.25; Adult €2.75; Group/Senior Citizen €2; Student €1.25; Family €7 ▪ **Suitable for ages:** All ▪ **Car parking:** Free ▪ **Bus routes:** 10, 37, 38, 39.

This centre has a fantastic exhibition on nature and wildlife in the park, which is great entertainment for kids. There's also an audio-visual presentation on the Phoenix Park through the ages, and a tomb containing two ancient skeletons found in the grounds. The fully restored Ashtown Castle – a 17th-century tower house – is also next door. Wheelchair access is limited to the ground floor of the centre only.

✱ TOP CHOICES: FOR AGES 2–5 ✱ TOP CHOICES: FOR AGES 5–10 ✱ TOP CHOICES: FOR INQUISITIVE KIDS ✱

## 453 Phoenix Riding Stables

Scibblestown Cross, Castleknock, Dublin 15; Tel: 8687000.
**Open:** All year; Mon–Sun 1–5pm; Call for dates of this year's summer camps ▪ **Charge:** €15 per hour-long lesson; Pony camp prices on request ▪ **Suitable for ages:** 6+ ▪ **Bus routes:** 37 ▪ **Rail station:** Ashtown (2 minutes).
**Sports:** horse-riding
Phoenix offers an outdoor arena and teaches basic horse-riding. The more experienced can ride in the Phoenix Park. Jumping is also offered, and pony camps are run in the summer.

## 454 Piccolo Lasso Choir

Dublin Choral Foundation, 107 New Ireland Rd, Rialto, Dublin 8; Contact: Ite O'Donovan; Tel: 4539663, 087 2340151;
E-mail: iteod@iol.ie; Website: www.dublinchoralfoundation.ie
**Open:** 3 terms a year: Sep–Dec, Jan–Mar, Apr–Jun ▪ **Charge:** €90 per term ▪ **Suitable for ages:** 6+.
A mixed choir, in which children learn sight-singing and perform at the National Concert Hall. Entrance is by audition only. Probationers are taken on from age 6.

✱ TOP CHOICES: HOBBIES/ARTS AND CRAFTS ✱

## 455 Roadstone Archers

Outdoor: Roadstone Group Sports Complex, Kingswood, Naas Rd, Dublin 22; Contact: Brian O'Briain; Tel: 4592635;
E-mail: brianmpob@eircom.net
**Open:** All year; Call for current meeting times ▪ **Suitable for ages:** 10+.
**Sports:** archery

## 456 St. Patrick's Athletic Football Club

125 Emmet Rd, Inchicore, Dublin 8; Tel: 4546332;
Fax: 4546211.
**Open:** Sep–May ▪ **Charge:** Small weekly fee ▪ **Suitable for ages:** 7+ ▪ **Bus routes:** 51, 51B, 68, 69.
**Sports:** soccer

## 457 Sillybilly Learning Ltd 🛒 🎭

Castleknock Parish Centre, Castleknock Village, Dublin 15;
Tel: 8535353; Fax: 8535953;
E-mail: enquiries@sillybillylearning.com
**Open:** All year; Wed; Call for times ▪ **Charge:** Music on the Go:
You are asked to pre-book 6 sessions in advance (approx. €60);
Party plan prices on request, eg Fairy Princess Party approx. €180
for 1 hour/ €250 for 2 hours ▪ **Suitable for ages:** 4 months to 4
years.

Sillybilly runs a programme of fun activities involving music, stories
and play, for children from four months to four-and-a-half years.
All the play equipment is supplied and set up in a local centre. A
parent/guardian must be present and is encouraged to get
involved – this is a great way of meeting other parents/minders of
small children. For wheelchair access, call for details on individual
venues. Sillybilly will also hold parties in your own home. You just
have to provide the food. Party Plans: 1. Sillybilly Party
(half-an-hour): An entertainer comes to your house with puppets,
games, a magic show and a bubble disco. 2. Fairy Princess Party
(one or two hours): Songs and stories from a costumed fairy, with
games and a bubble disco. 3. Soldiers Party (two hours): Sergeant
Sillybilly tells soldier stories and provides fun challenges. If you
pass them you get a certificate. The party includes a magic show,
and kids get a model balloon to take home. 4. Sports Party (two
hours): Equipment is provided – tunnels, obstacle courses, etc. 5.
Disco Party (half-an-hour): Disco, games, a magic show and
balloon modelling. 6. Baby party (one or two hours): Activity play
zone provided, alongside stories, songs and bubbles.
**✸ TOP CHOICES: BIRTHDAY PARTY IDEAS ✸ TOP CHOICES: FOR AGES
0–2 ✸ TOP CHOICES: FOR AGES 2–5 ✸**

## 458 The Square Shopping Centre 🛒 🍼 ♿

The Town Centre, Tallaght, Dublin 24 (off the Tallaght bypass
(N81), past the intersection with the M50 motorway);
Tel: 4525944.
**Open:** All year; Mon–Tue 9am–6pm; Wed–Fri 9am–9pm; Sat
9am–6pm; Sun 12–6pm ▪ **Suitable for ages:** All ▪ **Car parking:**
Free ▪ **Bus routes:** 49, 50, 54A, 65B, 76, 77A.
A mammoth shopping centre with loads of shops and places to eat
– mainly fast food outlets. Tallaght library is here, as is the UCI
cinema complex.

## 459 Stageright

Firhouse Community & Leisure Centre, Ballycullen Ave, Dublin 24; Contact: Bernie Brophy; Tel: 4514455.
**Open:** All year; Sat 9.30am–12pm, 1–3pm ▪ **Charge:** Prices given on request ▪ **Suitable for ages:** 2+ ▪ **Bus routes:** 49, 49A/X. Informal music, drama, dance and singing sessions for all ages, including toddlers.

## 460 Ster Century Multiplex Cinemas ♿ €

Liffey Valley Shopping Centre, Dublin 22 (head west on the N4 and take the first left after the junction with the M50);
Tel: 6055700 (box office); E-mail: info4dublin@stercentury.net;
Website: www.stercentury.ie
**Open:** All year; Children's programmes: Mon–Sun before 7pm; Kids' Club: Sat–Sun 12pm ▪ **Charge:** Child €5.10; Adult €5.90; Adult price given for Mon–Fri before 5pm, and Sat–Sun before 3pm; Family ticket €21.50; Kids' Club €2.50 ▪ **Suitable for ages:** 3+ ▪ **Car parking:** Free ▪ **Bus routes:** 25, 25A, 66, 66A/X, 67, 67A/X, 76, 76A/B, 78A.
A modern multiplex with 14 screens, which houses a Ben and Gerry ice cream stall as well as the usual snacks you'd expect in a large cinema. A kids' club is run on Sat and Sun mornings.
✱ TOP CHOICES: BIRTHDAY PARTY IDEAS ✱ TOP CHOICES: FOR AGES 10+ ✱ TOP CHOICES: FOR TRENDY KIDS ✱

## 461 Straffan Butterfly Farm ♿ €

Straffan, Co. Kildare (16 miles from Dublin, off the N7); Contact: Des and Iris Fox; Tel: 6271109; Fax: 4544864;
Website: www.straffanbutterflyfarm.com
**Open:** Jun–Aug; Mon–Sun 12–5.30pm ▪ **Charge:** Child €3; Adult €4.50; Family (2 adults and 3 children) €12.00 ▪ **Suitable for ages:** All ▪ **Car parking:** Free.
This butterfly house is home to many species of moth and butterfly. There are lots of Irish butterflies and the centre will tell you how to attract them to your garden. There are also reptiles, tarantulas, bird-eating spiders and even a milk snake!
✱ TOP CHOICES: FOR AGES 5–10 ✱

## 462 Stynes, Philomena (Music Teacher)

Lucan, Co. Dublin; Tel: 6241954.
**Open:** All year; Class times on request ▪ **Charge:** Fees on request

- **Suitable for ages:** 6+.

Philomena Stynes gives tuition in classical piano, electric keyboards and music theory. Preparation is given for RIAM, ABRSM and LSM exams.

## 463 Superdome 🚼 🍵 ♿ 👶 🎿

Palmerstown Shopping Centre, Palmerstown, Dublin 20; Tel: 6260700; Fax: 6260733; E-mail: superdome@eircom.net

**Open:** All year; 9.30am–11.30pm ▪ **Charge:** Entrance to the play dome €5 for over-5s at the weekends and €4.40 during the week. Under-5s €4.40 at weekends and €3.80 during the week. Bowling €28 for family groups or €21 for up to 6 kids; At the weekend €35 for a lane ▪ **Suitable for ages:** All ▪ **Car parking:** Free ▪ **Bus routes:** 25, 26, 66.

**Sports:** bowling

The Superdome is good fun for all ages. Under-8s love the play area, with the ever-popular ball pits, slides and tunnels. There's a separate area for the under-3s, who you have to supervise. For older ones, there's a bowling alley (ball walls are available), with a league for real enthusiasts. Young teenagers hang about in the arcade area, but the games are expensive. You can book any combination of activities for a birthday party. They will decorate a table and supply food for about €10 per child.

✹ TOP CHOICES: BIRTHDAY PARTY IDEAS ✹ TOP CHOICES: PLAYGROUNDS ✹ TOP CHOICES: FOR AGES 0–2 ✹ TOP CHOICES: FOR AGES 2–5 ✹ TOP CHOICES: FOR AGES 5–10 ✹ TOP CHOICES: FOR AGES 10+ ✹ TOP CHOICES: FOR TRENDY KIDS ✹ TOP CHOICES: FOR ENERGETIC KIDS ✹

## 464 Tallaght Community School Sports Complex ♿ 🅰

Balrothery, Tallaght, Dublin 24 (head towards Tallaght from the M50 exit. Turn right at the next roundabout onto Old Tallaght Rd. Take the first right at a pedestrian crossing; the entrance is opposite the Penny Black pub); Tel: 4515882.

**Open:** Pool: All year, Mon–Fri afternoons and Sat mornings; Summer swimming camp: Summer school holidays, Mon–Fri mornings; Summer general camp: Summer school holidays, Mon–Fri 10am–3pm ▪ **Charge:** Child €1.50; Price given is for entry fee to swimming pool; Gym/swimming lessons and summer camp fees on request ▪ **Suitable for ages:** 5+ ▪ **Car parking:** Free ▪ **Bus routes:** 55, 77X.

**Sports:** swimming, gymnastics

The swimming pool attached to the school is open for lessons and public swims on weekday afternoons and on Saturdays. There are lessons on offer in both swimming and gymnastics; ring for dates and times. The centre runs two types of summer camps: The swimming camp comprises two hours of swimming and pool fun in the mornings; The general camp provides a mixture of sports and activities, and runs from around 10am–3pm; call for this year's dates and times. If you need the hoist for the pool for children with physical disabilities, call in advance.

## 465 UCI Blanchardstown ♿ 🎈 €

Blanchardstown Shopping Centre, Dublin 15 (from the M50 roundabout, heading towards Navan on the Navan road, take the second exit off the dual carriageway, then an immediate left); Tel: 8128383.

**Open:** All year; Children's programmes: Mon–Sun before 7pm; Kids' Club: Sat 11am ▪ **Charge:** Child €5.25; Adult €6.25; Adult price given is for before 5pm; Kids' Club €2.50 ▪ **Suitable for ages:** 3+ ▪ **Car parking:** Free ▪ **Bus routes:** 39, 70, 220.

A cinema multiplex with a Saturday morning kids' club. Adults go free; kids' tickets are €2.50. There is often a kids' promotional snackbox available. Register your details on the website www.pigsback.com for offers and competitions.

**✱ TOP CHOICES: BIRTHDAY PARTY IDEAS ✱ TOP CHOICES: FOR TRENDY KIDS ✱**

## 466 UCI Tallaght ♿ €

Level 3, The Square, Tallaght, Dublin 24 (off the M50, at the Square Shopping Centre); Tel: 4598400;
Website: www.pigsback.com

**Open:** All year; Children's programmes: Mon–Sun before 7pm; Kids' Club: Sat 11am ▪ **Charge:** Child €5.25; Adult €6.25; Adult price given is for before 5pm; Kids' Club €2.50 ▪ **Suitable for ages:** 3+ ▪ **Car parking:** Free ▪ **Bus routes:** 49, 50, 54A, 77A, 65B, 76.

A cinema multiplex with a Saturday morning kids' club. Adults go free, kids' tickets are €2.50. There is often a kids' promotional snackbox available. Register your details on the website www.pigsback.com for offers and competitions.

**✱ TOP CHOICES: BIRTHDAY PARTY IDEAS ✱**

## 467 Usher Irish Road Cycling Club

Tallaght, Dublin 24; Contact: Alice Sherrett; Tel: 8210286.
**Open:** Mar–Sep; Sat mornings ■ **Charge:** €10 annual charge ■
**Suitable for ages:** 12+.
**Sports:** cycling

Children learn cycling skills in car parks before being put on the
road. Then they are brought out on trips and for races. Racing
bikes can be borrowed for the very keen if you don't have one.

## 468 Verona Sports and Leisure Club ♿

Grove Rd, Coolmine, Dublin 15 (follow the Clonsilla Rd from
Blanchardstown. Take a right at the new apartments and head up
to the Renault garage. Turn right at the garage; the entrance is
straight ahead); Tel: 8208160.
**Open:** All year; Mon–Fri 7am–11.30pm; Sat–Sun 12–11.30pm ■
**Charge:** Child €1.50; €1.50 to play soccer or basketball in hall ■
**Suitable for ages:** 5+ ■ **Car parking:** Free ■ **Bus routes:** 39.
**Sports:** basketball, soccer

Verona is an adult social club with a bar. It also has a hall for hire,
which is used for soccer. Kids can use the basketball hoops if their
parents are on the premises.

## 469 War Memorial Gardens 🚼 ♿ 🎠

Islandbridge, Dublin 8 (on the opposite side of the River Liffey
from the Phoenix Park); Tel: 6770236 (gardens), 6472498 (head
office).
**Open:** All year; Mon–Fri 8am–dusk; Sat–Sun 10am–dusk ■
**Charge:** Free ■ **Suitable for ages:** All ■ **Car parking:** Free ■ **Bus
routes:** 51, 68, 69, 69X.
**Sports:** cycling

These gardens are really pretty and make a nice one-hour stroll.
They are always very quiet, even in summer. They are particularly
good for toddlers, as there are ducks and swans to feed in the
weir, and (not working) fountains to stick their hands in. It is one
of the most famous memorial gardens in Europe, dedicated to the
memory of the 49,400 Irish soldiers who died in the First World
War. The names of all the soldiers are contained in the granite
bookrooms in the Gardens. There are beautiful sunken rose
gardens, herbaceous borders and nice trees to look at.
**★ TOP CHOICES: PARKS ★ TOP CHOICES: FOR AGES 0–2 ★ TOP
CHOICES: FOR AGES 2–5 ★**

# Places to eat

## 470 Angler's Rest (Pub)

Strawberry Beds, Chapelizod, Dublin 20 (turn right at the
Chapelizod exit from Phoenix Park); Tel: 8204351.
**Open:** All year; Mon–Sun 11am–11.30pm ■ **Charge:** €4.95 for
kids; €10 on average for adults ■ **Suitable for ages:** 2+ ■ **Car
parking:** Free ■ **Bus routes:** 25, 25A, 26, 66, 66A/B, 67, 67A.
Good pub food is served here, and it's handy for the Phoenix Park
if you're having a day out. There are lots of tables outside, and on
a sunny summer weekend it can be very busy, with lots of
children on weekend afternoons until early evening. A kids' menu
and two high chairs are available.
**✱ TOP CHOICES: CHILD FRIENDLY RESTAURANTS ✱**

## 471 Eddie Rockets Diner 🚼 ♿ 🎈

Liffey Valley Shopping Centre, Dublin 22, Tel: 6215970; U303,
The Square Shopping Centre, Town Centre, Tallaght, Dublin 24,
Tel: 4510443; Blanchardstown Shopping Centre, Dublin 15, Tel:
8222876; Contact: Valerie Crowley for party bookings, Tel:
6797340; Website: www.eddierockets.ie
**Open:** All year; Sun–Thur 11am–1am; Fri–Sat 11am–2am ■
**Charge:** Kids from €5 for meal and drink; Adults €10 for burger,
fries and drink ■ **Suitable for ages:** All.
Eddie Rockets is a chain of American-diner-style cafés, famous for
their burgers and fries. There's a kids menu, and kids get a free
goodie bag with their meal. All of these branches have booths for
sitting in, but they do also have high chairs. They do much better
milkshakes and malts than the bigger fast-food chains. Kids love them.
**✱ TOP CHOICES: BIRTHDAY PARTY IDEAS ✱**

## 472 Joel's Restaurant 🚼 ♿ 🎈

Newlands Cross, Dublin 22 (on The Naas Rd before Rathcoole,
look out for a big Jetson-style glass building); Tel: 4592968.
**Open:** All year; Sun–Thur 12–10.30pm; Fri–Sat 12–11pm ■ **Charge:**
Child menu from €8 incl. drink; Adults from €28 incl. starter and
main course ■ **Suitable for ages:** All ■ **Car parking:** Free.
American-style food in a space-age-looking restaurant. There is
plenty of seating available, and Joel's is very popular with families.
For a birthday party, book a table in advance. They can supply a
cake, or you can bring your own.

## 473 Kay's Kitchen

Blanchardstown, Dublin 15 (on the Navan Road (N3), just off the M50 ring road); Tel: 8222401; Fax: 8222403; E-mail: btg@iol.ie
**Open:** All year; Mon–Tue 9am–6pm; Wed–Fri 9am–9pm; Sat–Sun 9am–6pm ▪ **Charge:** Lunch from €5 ▪ **Suitable for ages:** All ▪ **Car parking:** Free ▪ **Bus routes:** 39, 70, 76A, 220, 237, 238, 239, 270.
A good all-rounder, dishing up everything from freshly made sandwiches to bargain-priced roast dinners. The portions are big, and the home-made desserts are good too. If you're an early shopper, you can get a good full Irish breakfast.

## 474 Spur Steakhouse

Liffey Valley Shopping Centre, Dublin 22 (opposite Ster Century cinemas, inside main entrance); Tel: 6209100.
**Open:** All year; Mon–Wed 12–9pm; Thur–Fri 12–10pm ▪ **Charge:** Kids' menu from €4.95; Adults approx. €12.50 ▪ **Suitable for ages:** All ▪ **Car parking:** Free ▪ **Bus routes:** 210, 239, 78A.
A wild-west themed restaurant, offering burgers, steaks and Mexican food. This is one of the best places to bring children to eat. The staff are great and kids love it. There is an enclosed play area with a ball pool, climbing frames and slide. Colouring pages and crayons are also provided. For birthday boys and girls, sneak the birthday cake in beforehand and the staff will bring it down and sing 'Happy Birthday'. Combine it with a trip to the cinema at Ster Century, which is opposite.
★ TOP CHOICES: CHILD FRIENDLY RESTAURANTS ★ TOP CHOICES: BIRTHDAY PARTY IDEAS ★ TOP CHOICES: FOR AGES 2–5 ★

## 475 TGI Friday's

Blanchardstown Shopping Centre, Blanchardstown, Dublin 22 (near the main entrance and Leisureplex); Tel: 8225990.
**Open:** All year; Mon–Sun 12–11pm ▪ **Charge:** Child menu approx €5.95 incl. drink; Adults from €10 ▪ **Suitable for ages:** All ▪ **Car parking:** Free ▪ **Bus routes:** 39, 70, 76A, 220, 237, 238, 239, 270.
An American-style restaurant, serving burgers, steak, fries, etc., but also pasta, wraps and vegetarian options. The staff are brilliant with kids, and are happy to sing 'Happy Birthday' and bring the birthday child a special sundae with a lighted candle in it.
★ TOP CHOICES: BIRTHDAY PARTY IDEAS ★

# Girls Just Wanna Have Fun!

## In The Irish Girl Guides, you can do just that!

Our groups meet every week and girls, aged between 5 and 21, get to do things that they might otherwise never experience.

You can:
meet other girls from your area and from all over the country and world...go on day trips and overnight adventures...help other people and learn about your community...make crafts, play games and go to campfires... learn about the world and our place in it...

*the list of Things to do is endless!*

To find out more click on www.irishgirlguides.ie or to find out about the unit nearest you contact:

The Irish Girl Guides,
27 Pembroke Park, Dublin 4
Ph 01 668 3898
or email us at info@irishgirlguides.ie

# Books for Kids
## from  O'BRIEN

From toddlers to teens, the O'Brien Press
publishes books suitable for children of all ages.
Look for the flag at the top right-hand corner of
our books. The colour will tell you the reading
age suitable for your child.

**Black Flag Books**
*Picture books*

**Orange Flag Books**
Age 4+
*Boo Series for Starter Readers*

**Purple Flag Books**
Age 5+
*Panda Series for Beginner Readers*

## Yellow Flag Books
Age 6+
*Flyers for Confident Readers*

## Red Flag Books
Age 8+

## lue Flag Books
Age 10+

## Green Flag Books
Age 12+

For a complete list of O'Brien books
➤ Visit www.obrien.ie
➤ E-mail marketing@obrien.ie
➤ Phone 01-4923333

The O'Brien Press, 20 Victoria Road, Rathgar, Dublin 6.
Tel: + 353 1 4923333; Fax: +353 1 4922777
E-mail: books@obrien.ie

# LAMBERT PUPPET THEATRE & MUSEUM

**30th Anniversary**

"Ireland's only purpose-built puppet theatre

Performances each weekend
For booking Tel (01) 280 0974

# South Dublin

## Things to do

### 476 Act One School of Acting

14 Rathgar Rd, Rathmines, Dublin 6; Tel: 4961018;
Fax: 4969632; E-mail: actone@eircom.net
**Open:** Oct–end May; weekly 90-minute–2-hour workshops ■
**Charge:** €590 per year ■ **Suitable for ages:** 6–16 ■ **Bus routes:**
14, 15, 15A/B/D/E/F, 65B/C/X.
This school hosts yearly programmes for ages 6–16, including
voice work, characters, mime, puppetry, storytelling, dance and
theatre trips. The courses progress to acting techniques, TV
presenting, contemporary dance, stunts, stage combat and
working with scripts. Performances are given at the end of the
course.

### 477 Airfield Trust

Upr Kilmacud Rd, Dundrum, Dublin 14 (from City Centre via
Goatstown, turn right from the Goatstown Rd onto Taney Rd at
the Goat Grill. Take the first left (Birches Lane), go up to the
T-junction and turn left onto the Upr Kilmacud Rd. Entrance is at
the first gate on your right); Tel: 2984301; Fax: 2962832;
E-mail: webmaster@airfield.ie; Website: www.airfield.ie/
**Open:** All year, Tue–Sun 11am–4pm (tea rooms and gardens
only); 2 Apr–29 Sep, Tue–Sun 11am–5pm ■ **Charge:** Child €2;
Adult €4; Concessions €3; Season tickets €40 ■ **Suitable for ages:**
All ■ **Car parking:** Free ■ **Bus routes:** 75, 86.
Airfield estate was left in trust by the Overend sisters, daughters of
a successful Dublin solicitor. Airfield runs a fully operational farm,
with cattle, sheep, pigs, horses, donkeys and poultry. There are
magnificent gardens with a Victorian greenhouse, a walled garden
with herbs, a rose garden, an orchard, yew borders and a laurel
walk. The tea rooms are inside the house itself, with a dining room
also open. Airfield regularly hosts cultural and artistic events,
including literary readings and music recitals in the library. There
are also some vintage cars to see, including the sisters' Rolls
Royce.
✱ TOP CHOICES: FOR AGES 0–2 ✱ TOP CHOICES: FOR AGES 2–5 ✱
TOP CHOICES: FOR ENERGETIC KIDS ✱

## 478 Allen, Debbie, School Of Dance, Dundrum

Dundrum Business Park, Dundrum Rd, Dublin 14; Tel: 2954610.
**Open:** All year; classes held at various times from Mon–Sat,
according to age and level ■ **Charge:** Fees given on request ■
**Suitable for ages:** 4+ ■ **Car parking:** On-street parking ■ **Bus
routes:** 17, 44, 44A/B/C, 48A.
This school gives ballet, modern and jazz dance classes to boys
and girls aged 4+.

## 479 Allen, Debbie, School of Dance, Rathfarnham

War Memorial Hall, Rathfarnham Rd, Terenure, Dublin 6W
(Terenure end of Rathfarnham Rd); Tel: 2954610.
**Open:** All year; classes held Mon–Sat ■ **Charge:** Prices given on
request ■ **Suitable for ages:** 4+ ■ **Car parking:** On-street parking
■ **Bus routes:** 15, 15A/B/D/E/F, 16, 16A, 17.
Ballet, modern and jazz classes for boys and girls aged 4+.

## 480 Annamoe Trout Farm ♿ ⛓

Annamoe, Co. Wicklow (on the road between Laragh and
Roundwood); Tel: (0404) 45470;
Website: www.annamoetroutfishery.com
**Open:** May–Sep; Mon–Sun 9.30am–5.30pm ■ **Charge:** €5 to fish
in bait pond, including rent of a rod and bait; Extra for whatever
fish you catch ■ **Suitable for ages:** 3+ ■ **Car parking:** Free ■ **Bus
routes:** St. Kevin's Bus from St. Stephen's Green.
**Sports:** Fishing
Annamoe is a nine-acre fish farm on the banks of the Annamoe
river. It is open all year to adults and the over-12s. In the summer,
the bait pond is opened, and little ones are guaranteed to catch a
fish. There is a toddlers' bait pond and a picnic area, and you can
bring your fish home for tea or cook it right away. You must be 12
years old to go fly fishing unaccompanied.
✱ **TOP CHOICES: FOR AGES 10+** ✱

## 481 Artzone ♿ ◩

Ballyroan Community Centre, Marian Rd, Rathfarnham, Dublin
16; Taney Parish Centre, Dundrum, Dublin 14; Contact: Gillian;
Tel: 4990614, 086 8159073.

**Open:** Sep–Jun, 4 terms a year; Summer camps in July in both venues; Ballyroan Community Centre: Mon 4–5pm; Sat 10–11am, 11.15am–12.15pm; Taney Parish Centre: Thur 4.15–5.15pm ▪ **Charge:** €55– €60 per 8-week term of 1 hour a week; €90 for a week's holiday camp ▪ **Suitable for ages:** Up to 12.

This is a highly recommended art school, running weekly art classes during the school term and camps during the Easter and summer holidays. The teachers are graduates of the Faculty of Education from the National College of Art and Design. Courses cover painting, drawing, print, collage and 3-D work. Holiday camps include a children's art-related day trip. All materials are included in all courses. Children with special needs can be accommodated.

★ **TOP CHOICES: HOBBIES/ARTS AND CRAFTS** ★ **TOP CHOICES: SUMMER CAMPS** ★ **TOP CHOICES: FOR IMAGINATIVE KIDS** ★

## 482 Ashbrook Lawn Tennis Club

Rear Grosvenor Rd, Rathgar, Dublin 6; Contact: Muriel Carney; Tel: 4964421.
**Open:** All year; Mon–Fri 10am–2pm for weekly courses ▪ **Charge:** €50 a week for summer camps ▪ **Suitable for ages:** 5+ ▪ **Car parking:** On-street parking ▪ **Bus routes:** 15, 15A/B/C, 83. **Sports:** tennis

A small tennis club, which can arrange junior coaching. It runs weekly tennis camps in the summer. You can use the facilities during the rest of the year, but you need to arrange to get keys.

## 483 Ball, Michael (Music Teacher)

Dún Laoghaire, Co. Dublin; Tel: 2350747.
**Open:** All year; class times on request ▪ **Charge:** Fees on request ▪ **Suitable for ages:** 8+.

Michael Ball gives classical piano tuition, including theory, composition, aural training, musicianship and piano accompaniment, as well as preparation for ABRSM exams.

## 484 Ballybrack Boys Association Football Club

Clubhouse, Coolevin, Ballybrack, Co. Dublin; Tel: 2825074.
**Open:** Sep–May ▪ **Suitable for ages:** 7+ ▪ **Bus routes:** 7, 45, 46, 111.
**Sports:** soccer

## 485 Ballyroan Karate Club

Ballyroan Community Centre, Marian Rd, Rathfarnham; Contact: Brendan Perry; Tel: 4946675.

**Open:** All year; Wed 7.30–8.30; Sun mornings – call for times ■ **Charge:** Child €3.50 ■ **Suitable for ages:** 6+ ■ **Bus routes:** 15B.

**Sports:** martial arts

Karate classes for over-6s are held on Wed evenings and Sun mornings.

**✱ TOP CHOICES: HOBBIES/ARTS AND CRAFTS ✱**

## 486 Ballyroan Library 🛒 ♿ ✏ 🖥

Orchardstown Ave, Rathfarnham, Dublin 14; Tel: 4941900; Fax: 4947083; E-mail: libraries@sdcc.ie; Website: www.sdcc.ie/library

**Open:** All year; Mon–Thur 9.45am–8pm; Fri–Sat 9.45am–4.40pm; closed bank holidays ■ **Charge:** Free ■ **Suitable for ages:** All ■ **Car parking:** Free ■ **Bus routes:** 15B, 75.

Activities include a Parent-and-Toddler Group (Mon and Fri 10.30am–12pm), Story Time (3–6-yr-olds, Wed 3–3.30pm) and Junior Chess Club (Sat 10.30am–12pm). There is also a Teenage Reading Group – check for dates and times. Other seasonal arts-and-crafts and reading events for children are organised throughout the year.

**✱ TOP CHOICES: FOR AGES 2–5 ✱ TOP CHOICES: FOR AGES 5–10 ✱ TOP CHOICES: FOR AGES 10+ ✱**

## 487 Basketball

Irish Basketball Association, National Basketball Arena, Tymon, Dublin 24; Tel: 4590211; Fax: 4590212; Website: www.iba.ie

**Open:** Oct–Mar; Call for individual clubs' meeting days and times ■ **Charge:** Annual fees range from €45 to €200; Basketball strip approx. €50 ■ **Suitable for ages:** 10+.

Most of the clubs listed below run junior teams and leagues; call for details. Where available, the venues have been listed, but these can change, so always check. The association also runs a primary school programme. Competitive teams start at under-11. Most teams require that you buy a strip to begin with, which can cost around €50.

**✱ TOP CHOICES: HOBBIES/ARTS AND CRAFTS ✱**

## 488 Ballyboden Basketball Club

St. Laurence's School, Ballybrack, Co. Dublin; Contact: Susan Cassidy; Tel: 2825019.

**Open:** All year; call for meeting days and times ▪ **Charge:** Membership fees and basketball strip price on request ▪ **Suitable for ages:** 10+ ▪ **Bus routes:** 7, 45A, 46, 111.

## 489 Cluny Raiders Basketball Club

St. Joseph's of Cluny, Killiney, Co. Dublin; or Cabinteely Community School, Cabinteely, Co. Dublin; Contact: Peter Bourke; Tel: 2856164.

**Open:** All year; call for meeting days and times ▪ **Charge:** Membership fees and basketball strip price on request ▪ **Suitable for ages:** 11+ ▪ **Bus routes:** 45, 46, 46C/D, 59, 84, 86 ▪ **DART station:** Killiney.

## 490 Comets Basketball Club

St. Thomas, Bray, Co. Wicklow; Contact: Marie O'Toole; Tel: 2867384.

**Open:** Oct–Mar; call for club meeting days and times ▪ **Charge:** Membership fees and basketball strip price on request ▪ **Suitable for ages:** 10+ ▪ **Bus routes:** 45, 45A, 84, 145, 146, 184, 185 ▪ **Rail station:** Bray ▪ **DART station:** Bray.

## 491 Dalkey Basketball Club

Cuala GAA, Hyde Pk, Hyde Rd, Dalkey, Co. Dublin; Contact: Stephen Cahill; Tel: 8491511.

**Open:** All year; call for meeting days and times ▪ **Charge:** Membership fees and basketball strip price on request ▪ **Suitable for ages:** 11+ ▪ **Bus routes:** 7D, 59, 59A ▪ **DART station:** Dalkey.

## 492 Meteors Basketball Club

Naomh Olaf GAA Club, Sandyford, Co. Dublin; St. Benildus College, Kilmacud, Co. Dublin; Contact: Lisa Timmons; Tel: 2956130.

**Open:** All year; call for meeting days and times ▪ **Charge:** Membership fees and basketball strip price on request ▪ **Suitable for ages:** 10+ ▪ **Bus routes:** 5, 11, 11A, 44, 46B, 75, 86.

## 493 Templeogue Basketball Club

Presentation College, Terenure, Dublin 6W; Contact: Phillip

Whitmoth; Tel: 4907529.

**Open:** All year; call for meeting days and times ▪ **Charge:** Membership fees and basketball strip price on request ▪ **Suitable for ages:** 10+ ▪ **Bus routes:** 15, 15A/B/D/E, 16, 16A, 17, 49, 49A, 65.

## 494 Bective Rangers Rugby Football Club

Donnybrook Rd, Dublin 4; Tel: 2838254, 2693894.

**Open:** Sep–Apr ▪ **Suitable for ages:** 5+ ▪ **Car parking:** Free ▪ **Bus routes:** 7B, 10, 10A, 46, 46A, 58C, 84X, 118, 746.

**Sports:** rugby

## 495 Big Sugar Loaf

Kilmacanoge, Co. Wicklow.

**Open:** All year; 24 hrs a day ▪ **Charge:** Free ▪ **Suitable for ages:** 5+ ▪ **Car parking:** On-street parking close to the Church in Kilmacanoge ▪ **Bus routes:** Bus Éireann or St. Kevin's Bus to Kilmacanoge.

Walk down the side road opposite the church. Turn right at a house called Redridge, following the path to a gate between two houses. Continue up the path past the houses. After the stone walls is a good spot for a picnic. Turn left at a track higher up, and then take the right fork higher up again. Continue onwards, keeping the fields on your right, until you get to a sand pit. Then just pick any path upwards until a very steep bit at the end. Come back down this same steep bit, but this time turn right into the wide track just below, and follow it all the way down to the fields.

✱ **TOP CHOICES: WALKS** ✱

## 496 Blackrock College Rugby Football Club

Stradbrook Rd, Blackrock, Co. Dublin; Tel: 2805967.

**Open:** Sep–Apr ▪ **Suitable for ages:** 5+ ▪ **Car parking:** Free ▪ **Bus routes:** 7, 7A, 17, 45, 114, 115.

**Sports:** rugby

✱ **TOP CHOICES: HOBBIES/ARTS AND CRAFTS** ✱

## 497 Blackrock College Summer School

Rock Road, Blackrock, Co. Dublin; Tel: 2888681.

**Open:** Summer; Mon–Fri 9:30am–5pm ▪ **Charge:** Approx. €90 per week ▪ **Suitable for ages:** 3–14.

**Sports:** gaelic football, hurling, soccer, swimming, athletics, gymnastics

This operates during the summer months and caters for 3–14-yr-olds, with a wide range of activities. There's swimming every day at Willow Park, as well as sports, athletics, gymnastics and computers. A very popular summer school.

**★ TOP CHOICES: SUMMER CAMPS ★**

## 498 Blackrock Library

Main St, Blackrock, Co. Dublin; Tel: 2888117; Fax: 2888117; E-mail: libraries@dlrcoco.ie; Website: www.dlrcoco.ie/library
**Open:** All year; Mon/Wed/Fri–Sat 10am–1pm, 2–5pm; Tue/Thur 2–8pm; open alternate Mons and Sats, closed bank holidays ■
**Charge:** Free ■ **Suitable for ages:** All ■ **Car parking:** Free ■ **Bus routes:** 7, 7A, 8, 17, 45, 114 ■ **Rail station:** Blackrock ■ **DART station:** Blackrock.
The children's section here organises holiday and seasonal activities throughout the year – book well in advance.

## 499 Blackrock Park

Rock Rd, Blackrock, Co. Dublin (off Rock Rd); Tel: 2054700 ext. 4448; E-mail: environ@dlrcoco.ie; Website: www.dlrcoco.ie
**Open:** All year; Winter: Mon–Sun 10am–4.30pm; Summer: Mon–Sun 8am–8.30pm ■ **Charge:** Free ■ **Suitable for ages:** All ■ **Car parking:** On-street parking or in the local shopping centres ■ **Bus routes:** 7, 7A, 17, 45, 46E, 114, 115 ■ **DART station:** Blackrock.
**Sports:** cycling
This is a linear park, bounded by the sea and railway on one side, and by Rock Road on the other. All you have to do is cross the railway and you are sitting on rocks looking at the sea. A new cycleway has been added, which has proved popular, as well as a new adventure-style playground. The fountain in the middle of the pond is very unusual and feeding the ducks here is greeted enthusiastically by most younger children. Parking can be difficult.

**★ TOP CHOICES: PLAYGROUNDS ★ TOP CHOICES: FOR AGES 0–2 ★
TOP CHOICES: FOR AGES 2–5 ★ TOP CHOICES: FOR AGES 5–10 ★**

## 500 Blackrock Shopping Centre

Blackrock, Co. Dublin (opposite the Frascati Centre, on the main road going in to Blackrock village); Tel: 2831670, 2831511 ext. 44 (Superquinn crèche).
**Open:** All year; Mon–Wed 9am–6pm; Thur–Fri 9am–9pm; Sat

9am–6pm; Sun 12–6pm ▪ **Charge:** Crêche €2 per hour for max 90 minutes ▪ **Suitable for ages:** All ▪ **Car parking:** Free ▪ **Bus routes:** 5, 7, 7A, 45 ▪ **DART station:** Blackrock.

A small shopping centre, mostly taken up with fashion boutiques. There's a crêche in the Superquinn here, which is open to all shoppers during the centre's opening hours (opening half-an-hour later, and closing half-an-hour earlier, than the times given). It tends to be less busy in the mornings and late afternoons.

## 501 Blessington Activity Centre

Burgage, Blessington, Co. Wicklow (take the N81 south from Blessington, take the first left out of the town and carry on until you reach the club on the lakeshore); Tel: (045) 865024.

**Open:** Apr–Oct; Sat–Sun for lessons; Call for times; Call for dates of this year's summer camps ▪ **Charge:** Lessons for two hours start at around €20 ▪ **Suitable for ages:** 8+ ▪ **Bus routes:** 65.

**Sports:** sailing, windsurfing

This centre concentrates on sailing and windsurfing. The club is on the lake in Blessington, which a very safe sailing environment. Lessons are held at the weekends, and they also run summer camps for learning to sail a dinghy. The activity centre, also a school, is located beside Blessington Sailing Club, but is a separate entity – you do not have to be a member of the sailing club to take lessons here.

## 502 Blessington Sailing Club 🚻

Blessington, Co. Wicklow (take the N81 south from Blessington, take the first left out of the town and carry on until you reach the club on the lakeshore); Tel: 4945790 (Declan Scallon), 4567130 (Joe Smith); E-mail: blsc@eircom.net; Website: www.blessingtonsailingclub.com

**Open:** Apr–Oct; Sun 1–5pm; Wed 6–9pm ▪ **Charge:** Membership is approx. €230 for a family or €170 for an individual; Classes and camps are extra ▪ **Suitable for ages:** 7+ ▪ **Car parking:** Free ▪ **Bus routes:** 65.

**Sports:** sailing

This is a family-oriented sailing club. Racing is organised on Sunday afternoons and Wednesday evenings. All equipment is supplied – all you need is a pair of runners. The juniors have their own 'Junior Shack', which allows them to be independent from the main clubhouse if they desire. There are also picnic areas and BBQs around the lakeshore, with charcoal supplied on a Sunday.

Non-members can do the courses, but you must be a member to sail without a class.

★ TOP CHOICES: HOBBIES/ARTS AND CRAFTS ★

## 503 Bloomfields Shopping Centre 🛒 🎲 ☕ ♿ 🎈

Lwr George's St, Dún Laoghaire, Co. Dublin (opposite St. Michael's Hospital); Tel: 2300551 (centre), 2304628 (crêche); E-mail: bloom@iol.ie

**Open:** All year; Centre: Mon–Wed 8.30am–8.30pm; Thur–Fri 8.30am–10pm; Sat 8.30am–8.30pm; Crêche–drop in times only: Mon–Wed 12.30–5pm; Thur–Fri 12.30–8pm; Sat 10am–6pm ■ **Charge:** Crêche 1 hour €4.20 per child for max 2-hour stay; Parties €8.50 per child ■ **Suitable for ages:** All ■ **Car parking:** Paying car park from €1.80 per hour ■ **Bus routes:** 7, 7A, 8, 45A, 46A, 59, 75, 111.

A nice but small shopping centre. Tweeny Town crêche run a drop-in facility for 2–8-yr-olds, and also a playgroup on weekday mornings. You can have a birthday party there, with food supplied, for €8.50 per child – you supply the cake.

★ TOP CHOICES: BIRTHDAY PARTY IDEAS ★

## 504 Boxing

Irish Amateur Boxing Association, National Stadium, South Circular Rd, Dublin 8; Tel: 4733192; E-mail: iaba@eircom.net

**Open:** All year ■ **Charge:** Most clubs charge €1 or €2 per week ■ **Suitable for ages:** 11+.

Boxing clubs usually take children from 11 years old. Parents must sign for permission for them to join, and all children must undergo a medical examination and wear protective headgear. All boxing clubs listed have Leinster Council IABA affiliation for 2002/2003. Call for locations, as these can change.

## 505 Avona Boxing Club

Call for locations as these can change; Contact: John Roche; Tel: 4571241.

**Open:** All year; call for current meeting times ■ **Suitable for ages:** 11+.

## 506 CIE Boxing Club

Inchicore area; Contact: Peter Perry; Tel: 4544476.

**Open:** All year; call for current meeting times ■ **Suitable for ages:**

11+ ▪ **Bus routes:** 51, 51B, 68, 69.

## 507 Crumlin Boxing Club

Call for locations as these can change; Tel: 2836261 (Vincent Kelly), 087 9873046 (Phillip Sutcliffe).
**Open:** All year; call for current meeting times ▪ **Suitable for ages:** 11+.

## 508 Donore Boxing Club

Call for locations as these can change.; Contact: Robert McEvoy; Tel: 4558418.
**Open:** All year; call for current meeting times ▪ **Suitable for ages:** 11+.

## 509 Ferrini Boxing Club

Call for locations as these can change; Contact: Amanda Martin; Tel: 4651021.
**Open:** All year; call for current meeting times ▪ **Suitable for ages:** 11+.

## 510 Mount Tallant Boxing Club

Call for locations as these can change; Contact: Michael Kavanagh; Tel: 4562596.
**Open:** All year; call for current meeting times ▪ **Suitable for ages:** 11+.

## 511 St. Joseph's Boxing Club, Ballyboden

Call for locations as these can change; Contact: Tony Delaney; Tel: 4943927.
**Open:** All year; call for current meeting times ▪ **Suitable for ages:** 11+.

## 512 Bray Cinema ♿ €

Quinsboro Rd, Bray, Co. Wicklow (near Bray DART station); Tel: 2868686; E-mail: Bray-Cineplex@Cinemas-Online.co.uk; Website: www.braycineplex.com
**Open:** All year; Mon–Sun, children's programmes before 7pm ▪ **Charge:** Matinee child/adult €4; early eves €5 ▪ **Suitable for ages:** 3+ ▪ **Car parking:** Free ▪ **Bus routes:** 45A, 84, 84X, 145, 146, 184, 185 ▪ **Rail station:** Bray ▪ **DART station:** Bray.
A local multiplex cinema, but with no special kids' club.
**✱ TOP CHOICES: FOR AGES 5–10 ✱ TOP CHOICES: FOR AGES 10+ ✱**

## 513 Bray Strand/Bray Head 🚆 ①

Bray, Co. Wicklow; Tel: 2054700 (ext. 4021).
**Open:** All year; Mon–Sun 24 hours ▪ **Charge:** Free ▪ **Suitable for ages:** All ▪ **Car parking:** On-street parking ▪ **Bus routes:** 45, 45A, 84, 145, 146, 184, 185 ▪ **Rail station:** Bray ▪ **DART station:** Bray.
**Sports:** swimming

Bray strand is basic and stony. It had a blue flag until 2001. At one end is Bray Head – a fairly easy climb with great views to Wicklow, and sometimes Wales! The cliff walk to Greystones is also lovely, but at four miles is not for young children. Most children will enjoy a little time at the slots and dodgems just across the road from the strand.

✱ **TOP CHOICES: FOR ENERGETIC KIDS** ✱

## 514 Bray Wheelers Cycling Club

Bray, Co. Wicklow; Contact: Gillian Martin; Tel: 2864461, 2856382 (Urban Monks).
**Open:** Mar–Sep; Sat/Sun mornings usually ▪ **Charge:** €16.50 per year ▪ **Suitable for ages:** 14+.
**Sports:** cycling

The junior cyclists usually meet outside Bray on Sat and Sun mornings. Racing starts in March and club activities in April – call for details.

## 515 Brickfield Park 🤾 ♿ 🧗

Iveagh Grounds, off Crumlin Rd, Dublin 12 (between Crumlin and Mourne roads and just north of the Iveagh Grounds);
Tel: 4542555; E-mail: parks.parks@dublincity.ie;
Website: www.dublincity.ie/parks
**Open:** All year; Mon–Fri 8.30am–dusk; Sat–Sun 9.30am–dusk ▪ **Charge:** Free ▪ **Suitable for ages:** All ▪ **Car parking:** On-street parking ▪ **Bus routes:** 50, 56A, 77, 77A, 150, 210.
**Sports:** soccer

Brickfield Park is a public park used mainly as a sports ground, particularly for soccer. It has grass areas as well as an all-weather pitch, and a playground for younger kids. The pitches can be booked, or you can just turn up and play if one is free.

## 516 Brittas Bay 🚆 🌊 ①

Brittas Bay, Co. Wicklow (between Wicklow and Arklow on the coast road).

**Open:** All year; Mon–Sun 24 hours ▪ **Charge:** Free ▪ **Suitable for ages:** All ▪ **Car parking:** Free.

**Sports:** swimming

Brittas Bay is probably the most popular beach within day-tripping distance south of Dublin. It has miles of sandy dunes and gently sloping sands, which make it an ideal place for a family day out. Indeed, large numbers of south Dubliners decamp to here in the summer, staying in the many private caravan parks. Brittas can get overcrowded on sunny days, particularly on Sundays, but if you walk far enough along the strand it is usually possible to get a good amount of space. Both the north and south beaches have blue flags.

**✱ TOP CHOICES: BEACHES ✱**

## 517 Brookfield Lawn Tennis Club

Palmerston Park, Rathmines, Dublin 6; Contact: Rachel McDonagh; Tel: 4974168.

**Open:** All year; Mon–Sun 8am–9pm; 5pm closing for children ▪ **Charge:** Junior membership €155 ▪ **Suitable for ages:** 7+ ▪ **Bus routes:** 13B, 14, 14A.

**Sports:** tennis

Brookfield is a members-only club with an active children's section, particularly during the summer holidays when weekly camps are run for an additional cost.

## 518 Broxson, Aoife (Music Teacher)

Bray, Co. Wicklow; Tel: 2761297.

**Open:** All year; class times on request ▪ **Charge:** Fees on request ▪ **Suitable for ages:** 6+.

Aoife Broxson provides tuition in classical piano and violin, and prepares students for RIAM exams.

## 519 Bushy Park

Templeogue Rd, Terenure, Dublin 6W (the two main entrances are at Rathdown Ave and over the stepping stones or footbridge on Springfield just past the bridge at Rathfarnham Rd); Tel: 6684364, 4900320; E-mail: parks.parks@dublincity.ie; Website: www.dublincity.ie/parks

**Open:** All year; Mon–Fri 8.30am–dusk; Sat–Sun 9.30am–dusk ▪ **Charge:** Free ▪ **Suitable for ages:** All ▪ **Car parking:** On-street parking ▪ **Bus routes:** 15, 15A/B/D/E/F, 16, 16A, 49, 49A, 65, 65B.

**Sports:** gaelic football, hurling, soccer, tennis

Bushy Park is one of the best all-round parks in south Dublin. A 20.5-hectare park on the Dodder Walk, it boasts a busy playground, woodland walks, an ornamental pond, tennis courts and sports pitches, with a variety of football and GAA clubs. Older kids love climbing the steep banks in the woodland area, while the tiny maze in the playground is a hit with younger ones. You can feed the ducks and the wildfowl on the pond. The hill down towards the pond is great for tobogganing in the snow. The 16 tennis courts can be rented by the hour, or you can buy a season ticket, and they are part of the Dublin Public Parks Tennis league. The small shop in the tennis clubhouse is open during the summer months. There are also occasional music performances in the park.

✱ TOP CHOICES: PARKS ✱ TOP CHOICES: PLAYGROUNDS ✱ TOP CHOICES: WALKS ✱ TOP CHOICES: FOR AGES 0–2 ✱ TOP CHOICES: FOR AGES 2–5 ✱ TOP CHOICES: FOR AGES 5–10 ✱ TOP CHOICES: FOR ENERGETIC KIDS ✱

## 520 The Busy Bee Summer School of Cooking

54 Ballinclea Heights, Killiney, Co. Dublin (turn just before Killiney Castle; the main entrance is on the other side of the road); Contact: 2858674; Tel: 2858674.

**Open:** End Jun–end Aug; Mon–Fri 10.30am–1pm ▪ **Charge:** Child €175; A deposit of €75 is needed; if your week course falls during a bank holiday there is a reduction of €35 ▪ **Suitable for ages:** 11–16 ▪ **Car parking:** On-street parking ▪ **Bus routes:** 59 ▪ **DART station:** Dalkey.

The Busy Bee school has been running for over 20 years, and is now something of an institution. Students first watch a demonstration of how to cook a three-course meal, then cook two of the dishes, which they take home. It is an informal course, and the emphasis is on presentation and cooking for enjoyment. The school provides all equipment and basic ingredients, as well as a booklet with all the recipes. Students are asked to dress neatly. Pick-up from the DART station can be arranged. Teenagers who can cook? Surely that's money well spent!

✱ TOP CHOICES: SUMMER CAMPS ✱ TOP CHOICES: FOR AGES 10+ ✱ TOP CHOICES: FOR SHY KIDS ✱

## 521 Cabinteely Library ✍

Old Bray Rd, Cabinteely, Dublin 18; Tel: 2855363;
Fax: 2353000; E-mail: libraries@dlrcoco.ie;
Website: www.dlrcoco.ie/library
**Open:** All year; Mon*/Wed/Fri/Sat* 10am–1pm, 2–5pm;
Tue/Thur 2–8pm. *Open alternate Mons and Sats, subject to
change around bank holidays ▪ **Charge:** Free ▪ **Suitable for ages:**
All ▪ **Car parking:** Free ▪ **Bus routes:** 45, 84, 86.
Storytelling for 3–6-yr-olds is at 3.30–4pm on Fridays. Other
seasonal arts-and-crafts and reading events for children are
organised throughout the year.
✱ **TOP CHOICES: FOR AGES 2–5** ✱

## 522 Cabinteely Park ♿ 🚻

Brennanstown Rd, Cabinteely, Co. Dublin (bounded by the Bray
Rd and Brennanstown Rd, main entrance off Lambourne Wood);
Tel: 2850118 (ext. 4448); E-mail: environ@dlrcoco.ie;
Website: www.dlrcoco.ie
**Open:** All year; Winter: 10am–5pm; Summer: 10am–10.30pm ▪
**Charge:** Free ▪ **Suitable for ages:** All ▪ **Car parking:** On-street
parking ▪ **Bus routes:** 45, 46, 46C/D, 84, 86.
**Sports:** cycling, soccer
Cabinteely is a great park for cycling and walking for all ages.
There are streams, woods and gardens. You can have great fun on
mountain bikes here, and there are also sports pitches that you
can book or just turn up to play on. The buildings and courtyards
of Cabinteely House are being preserved to be converted into a
museum. FÁS runs a horticulture training course here, and a
former cow byre with a grain loft has been converted to the
Grainstore Youth Arts Centre.
✱ **TOP CHOICES: PARKS** ✱ **TOP CHOICES: FOR AGES 0–2** ✱ **TOP
CHOICES: FOR AGES 2–5** ✱ **TOP CHOICES: FOR AGES 5–10** ✱

## 523 Cabinteely School for Speech and Drama

Cabinteely Community School, Johnstown Rd, Cabinteely, Dublin
18; Contact: Daphne/Fiona; Tel: 2856942, 2876861.
**Open:** Sep–Dec and Jan–May; Tue/Thur 4.30–6.30pm ▪ **Charge:**
€100 for Sep–Dec term; €90 for Jan–May term (extra €10 levy for
stage props, etc.) ▪ **Suitable for ages:** 4+ ▪ **Car parking:** Free ▪
**Bus routes:** 7A/7B, 46, 86.

Speech and drama classes for 4–12-yr-olds are held on Tue and Thur afternoons, and there is also a youth theatre run, for 12–20-yr-olds. The courses encourage self-confidence through the medium of drama, and cover all aspects of stagecraft and improvisation. Children from ages 8+ can be prepared for exams in speech and drama. The youth theatre has workshops on stagecraft, improvisation, etc. There are performances during the year and theatre visits.

★ TOP CHOICES: FOR IMAGINATIVE KIDS ★

## 524 Calliaghstown Riding Centre ♿

Rathcoole, Co. Dublin; Tel: 4589236, 4588322 (office); Fax: 4588171; E-mail: calliagh@iol.ie; Website: www.calliaghstownridingcentre.com
**Open:** All year; Mon–Thur 9am–9pm; Fri–Sun 9am–6pm; call for dates of this year's summer camps ▪ **Charge:** €15 per hourly lesson; Prices on request for summer camps and other courses ▪ **Suitable for ages:** 5+ ▪ **Bus routes:** 69.
**Sports:** horse-riding
This school offers cross-country riding, trekking and livery classes. Experienced riders can go on a trial ride through the mountains and along the Wicklow Way. Calliaghstown also runs a pony camp during the summer. It has indoor and outdoor arenas, and classes for disabled riders are also on offer.

## 525 Carrickmines Croquet and Lawn Tennis Club

Carrickmines, Foxrock, Co. Dublin; Contact: Pat Crowe; Tel: 2894631, 2885051.
**Open:** All year; Mon–Fri 9am–11.30pm; Sat–Sun 9am–6pm; call for details of this year's summer camp dates ▪ **Charge:** €80 annual junior membership; Tennis coaching fees are extra; Summer camp fees on request ▪ **Suitable for ages:** 6+ ▪ **Car parking:** Free ▪ **Bus routes:** 63, 86, 117.
**Sports:** tennis, croquet
Carrickmines has an active junior programme which runs all year, with coaching available at an additional cost. There are also camps during most school holidays. Membership is required, and coaching costs extra.

## 526 Carrickmines Equestrian Centre

Glenamuck Rd, Foxrock, Dublin 18; Tel: 2955990;

Fax: 2955934; E-mail: info@carrickminesequestrian.ie;
Website: www.carrickminesequestrian.ie
**Open:** All year; Tue–Sun 10am–6pm ▪ **Charge:** Child €18; A
term of 12 or 13 lessons is approx. €12 per hour ▪ **Suitable for
ages:** 6+ ▪ **Car parking:** On-street parking ▪ **Bus routes:** 44, 63.
**Sports:** horse-riding
Carrickmines has an indoor arena and two large outdoor floodlit
arenas for jumping. It offers cross-country riding, as well as
polocrosse. Pony camps and showjumping competitions run
during the summer; call for this year's dates and prices.

**✽ TOP CHOICES: HOBBIES/ARTS AND CRAFTS ✽**

## 527 Cerebral Palsy Ireland Swimming Pool

Sandymount Ave, Dublin 4 (on Sandymount end of Sandymount
Ave, heading towards the Green from Ballsbridge); Tel: 2695608.
**Open:** All year; Mon–Sat 5–7pm; Sun 9.30am–5pm ▪ **Charge:**
Child €1.80; Adult €3 ▪ **Suitable for ages:** All ▪ **Car parking:** Free
▪ **Bus routes:** 1, 2, 3, 18 ▪ **DART station:** Sandymount.
**Sports:** swimming
This pool was designed for children with physical disabilities and
so has steps, rather than a ladder, into the water. The water comes
up to the top of the pool, making it easier to get in and out. The
hoist is fixed in place, so there is no need to call to arrange it in
advance. However, there are usually queues, and it is better to
arrive 15–20 minutes before your swim time. The pool is open to
the public in the evenings and on Sunday. Children must be
accompanied by an adult. Call for exact times for start of swims.

## 528 Cheeverstown House Leisure Centre

Kilvare, Templeogue Rd, Dublin 6W (on left of main road just
before the turn off to the M50); Tel: 4904681, 4905988 (pool);
Fax: 4905753.
**Open:** All year; Sat–Sun 10am–5.30pm ▪ **Charge:** Child €2; Adult
€3.20; Fee is for entrance to swimming pool; Swimming lesson
fees on request ▪ **Suitable for ages:** All ▪ **Bus routes:** 15B, 49,
65, 65B.
**Sports:** swimming
A home for special-needs children, with a public swimming pool. The
pool can only take 25 people at a time. You can book in advance,
but in person only. Swimming classes are available every afternoon;
call to see which ones would suit your child's age and ability.

## 529 Churchtown Keyboard School

58 Landscape Pk, Churchtown, Dublin 14; Tel: 2960430.
**Open:** All year; Mon–Fri afternoons ▪ **Charge:** Prices given on request ▪ **Suitable for ages:** 7+ ▪ **Bus routes:** 14.
Churchtown Keyboard School provides keyboard classes, which are just for fun, in groups of a maximum of six students.
★ TOP CHOICES: HOBBIES/ARTS AND CRAFTS ★ TOP CHOICES: FOR IMAGINATIVE KIDS ★

## 531 Clara Lara

The Vale of Clara, Rathdrum, Co. Wicklow (on the road between Santas and Roundwood); Tel: (0404) 46161;
E-mail: claralara@eircom.net;
Website: www.claralarafunpark.com
**Open:** May–Sep; Mon–Sun 10.30am–6pm ▪ **Charge:** Child €8; Adult €10; Prices include access to all rides; Children under 1 metre and OAPs are free; Radio-controlled cars are extra ▪
**Suitable for ages:** All ▪ **Car parking:** Free.
**Sports:** golf, rowing/canoeing, swimming, mini golf
Clara Lara Fun Park is a 100-acre water-based fun park for children. It has a huge range of rides, from rafts to tree houses and climbing frames, as well as go-carts and row boats. The Aqua Shuttle – the highest slide in Ireland – is also here. There are swings and slippery poles, both on and into the water. Clara Lara has a shop and café, picnic areas and BBQ spots, so bring some charcoal and burgers. Remember to bring a towel and change of clothes, including old trainers to wear in the water. This is a great birthday venue if you can arrange the transport, and group discounts are available. You will need to sort out your own food. There are also miles of suitable terrain for hill walking in the vicinity.
★ TOP CHOICES: PICNIC SPOTS ★ TOP CHOICES: BIRTHDAY PARTY IDEAS ★ TOP CHOICES: PLAYGROUNDS ★ TOP CHOICES: FOR AGES 5–10 ★ TOP CHOICES: FOR AGES 10+ ★ TOP CHOICES: FOR ENERGETIC KIDS ★

## 532 Comhaltas Ceoltóirí Éireann (Craobh Chualann)

32 Belgrave Sq, Monkstown, Co. Dublin; Tel: 2875610;
Fax: 2803759; E-mail: info@craobhchualann.com;
Website: www.craobhchualann.com

**Open:** All year; Junior *Grúpaí Ceoil* Sun 7–9pm ▪ **Charge:**
Membership fees: Junior €6; Adult €12; Family €20; Classes from
€62 ▪ **Suitable for ages:** All ▪ **Bus routes:** 7, 7A, 8 ▪ **Rail station:**
Seapoint ▪ **DART station:** Seapoint.
An organisation promoting Irish music, language and culture.
Craobh Chulann branch offers classes in banjo, bodhrán, button
accordion, fiddle, tin whistle, step dancing and Irish language.
Classes are held from 7–10pm. Children and adults take part in
classes together at beginner, intermediate and advanced levels.
Junior *Grúpaí Ceoil* is held on Sundays from 7–9pm.

## 533 Comhaltas Ceoltóirí Éireann (Craobhnaithi) ♿

2 Belgrave Sq, Monkstown, Co. Dublin (activities held at Ballinteer
Community School, Broadford Road, Ballinteer, Dublin 16);
Tel: 2800295; Fax: 2803759; E-mail: craobhnaithi@lycos.com;
Website: www.homepage.eircom.net/~craobhnaithi/
**Open:** All year; Music classes: Thur 5pm; Irish dancing: Wed
6.30–8.30pm ▪ **Charge:** Membership fees: Junior €6; Family €20;
Adult €12; Classes from €62 ▪ **Suitable for ages:** 5+ ▪ **Bus
routes:** 48A, 75, 116.
An organisation promoting Irish music, language and culture.
Traditional music classes are held, from beginners onwards, in
concertina, fiddle, tin whistle, flute, accordion, banjo and *sean nós*
singing, every Thur from 5pm onwards in Ballinteer Community
School. There are also Irish dancing classes on Wed nights,
6.30–8.30pm.

## 534 Cornelscourt Shopping Centre 🛒 🎲 ☕ ♿

Cornelscourt, Dublin 18 (off the Cabinteely bypass);
Tel: 2892677.
**Open:** All year; Centre: Mon–Fri 8.30am–10pm; Sat
8.30am–9pm; Sun 10am–6pm; Crèche: Mon–Wed 9am–5.30pm;
Thur–Fri 9am–7pm; Sat–Sun 9am–5.30pm ▪ **Charge:** Crèche €3
per hour (max 2-hour stay per day) ▪ **Suitable for ages:** All ▪ **Car
parking:** Free ▪ **Bus routes:** 45, 46, 46C, 84, 84X, 86, 117.
There's a massive Dunnes Stores here. Their crèche takes
2–7-yr-olds, for two hours maximum per day, at €3 per hour.

## 535 Courtney, Ted (Music Teacher)

Sandycove, Co. Dublin; Tel: 2804519;
Website: www.tedcourtney.com
**Open:** All year; class times on request ▪ **Charge:** Fees on request
▪ **Suitable for ages:** 13+.
Ted Courtney gives tuition in clarinet, voice and musicianship, and
prepares students for RIAM, ABRSM, LCM and DIT exams.

## 536 Dalkey Castle and Heritage Centre
♿ €

Castle St, Dalkey, Co. Dublin (south on the N11 from the city
centre. Dalkey is along the coast); Tel: 2858366; Fax: 2843141;
E-mail: diht@indigo.ie
**Open:** All year; Sat–Sun/bank holidays 11am–5pm; Apr–Oct:
Mon–Fri 9.30am–5pm ▪ **Charge:** Child €4; Adult €7; Concessions
€5; Family ticket €18 ▪ **Suitable for ages:** 3+ ▪ **Car parking:** Free
▪ **Bus routes:** 8 ▪ **DART station:** Dalkey.
Dalkey was once Dublin's main port, and this is one of seven
original tower houses in the vicinity, dating from 1429. The
exhibition here includes models of Dalkey's transport system, as
well as texts and photographs of James Joyce – part of *Ulysses* was
set in Dalkey. There's a 'murder hole' to see, and spectacular
views of the town, sea and mountains.

## 537 Dalkey Island 🏰

Dalkey, Co. Dublin (ferry from Colliemore Harbour in Dalkey
village).
**Open:** Easter to Sep; Mon–Sun during daylight hours ▪ **Charge:**
Free ▪ **Suitable for ages:** 7+ ▪ **Car parking:** On-street parking ▪
**Bus routes:** 7D, 59, 59A ▪ **DART station:** Dalkey.
**Sports:** diving, rowing/canoeing, swimming, fishing, snorkeling
You can get a ferry to the island from Colliemore Harbour in
Dalkey. There are rowing boats for hire, but this not
recommended, as the current is tricky and the island is further
away than it looks. The island is deserted apart from a population
of wild goats, a ruined fort, a bird sanctuary and a Martello tower.
There is a tiny sandy beach to the left of where the boat pulls in,
and it is beside here that you need to wave to the boatman to
bring you back. You can go swimming with the seals off the island
and they are often friendly, but remember they are big and the
currents around here are dangerous, so this is only for older

children. Snorkelling here is also great, with very clear water and lovely seaweed to look at. However, the island is full of rabbit holes, and surrounded by cliffs, so it is not recommended for under-7s.

✱ TOP CHOICES: BEACHES ✱ TOP CHOICES: WALKS ✱ TOP CHOICES: FOR AGES 10+ ✱ TOP CHOICES: FOR ENERGETIC KIDS ✱

## 538 Dalkey Library

Castle St, Dalkey, Co. Dublin; Tel: 2855317; Fax: 2855789; E-mail: libraries@dlrcoco.ie; Website: www.dlrcoco.ie/library
**Open:** All year; Mon/Wed/Fri/Sat 10am–1pm, 2–5pm; Tue/Thur 2–8pm; closed Sat–Mon on bank holiday weekends ■ **Charge:** Free ■ **Suitable for ages:** All ■ **Car parking:** Free ■ **Bus routes:** 8 ■ **DART station:** Dalkey.

Dalkey library has two dedicated music rooms, for practising the harp and the piano. Storytelling for 3–6-yr-olds is at 3.30–4pm on Thursdays. Seasonal arts-and-crafts activities, plus reading events, are organised throughout the year.

✱ TOP CHOICES: FOR AGES 2–5 ✱ TOP CHOICES: FOR AGES 5–10 ✱

## 539 David Lloyd Riverview Racquet and Fitness Club

Beech Hill, Clonskeagh, Dublin 14 (on Beech Hill, between Donnybrook Bus Station and Clonskeagh Rd); Contact: Michael Moss; Tel: 2830322.
**Open:** All year; Mon–Fri 6.30am–10.30pm; Sat–Sun 8am–10pm; children under 12 must be out by 8pm ■ **Charge:** Junior membership €153 plus €63 a month; Full family membership €1,525 plus €176 a month; Non-tennis membership €1,150 plus €140 a month; Summer camp prices on request ■ **Suitable for ages:** All ■ **Car parking:** Free ■ **Bus routes:** 11, 11A.
**Sports:** martial arts, rugby, squash, swimming, tennis

A private tennis club with squash courts. There is a large swimming pool and a paddling pool for younger children. A crêche is available for tots, but must usually be booked about a week in advance. Tennis coaching is expensive, but very popular. Swimming and martial arts lessons are also available. Fit Club is a club for kids with after-school and evening activities, and also summer camps. Tennis camps are run during the school holidays.

## 540 Deansgrange Library

Clonkeen Drive, Deansgrange, Dublin 18 (at the Deansgrange

crossroads); Tel: 2850860; Fax: 2898359;
E-mail: libraries@dlrcoco.ie; Website: www.dlrcoco.ie/library
**Open:** All year; Mon/Wed/Fri/Sat 10am–1pm, 2–5pm; Tue/Thur
2–8pm; closed Sat–Mon on bank holiday weekends ▪ **Charge:**
Free ▪ **Suitable for ages:** All ▪ **Car parking:** Free ▪ **Bus routes:**
45, 46A, 75.

A chess club for 7–14-yr-olds is held on Thursdays, 6.30–7.30pm
(booking is necessary). Storytelling for 3–6-yr-olds is on Thursdays,
3.30–4pm. Other seasonal arts-and-crafts and reading events for
children are organised throughout the year.
**★ TOP CHOICES: FOR AGES 2–5 ★ TOP CHOICES: FOR AGES 5–10 ★
TOP CHOICES: FOR AGES 10+ ★**

## 541 Deerpark

Mount Merrion, Co. Dublin (bounded by North Ave and Mount
Merrion Rd); Tel: 2054700 (ext. 4448);
E-mail: environ@dlrcoco.ie; Website: www.dlrcoco.ie
**Open:** All year; 10am–dusk ▪ **Charge:** Free ▪ **Suitable for ages:**
All ▪ **Car parking:** On-street parking.
**Sports:** cycling, tennis

Deerpark has acres of woodland, lawns and walkways. It also
houses Mount Merrion Tennis Club. Dublin Public Parks Tennis
league runs here during the summer months.

## 542 De La Salle Palmerstown Football Club

Kilternan, Co. Dublin; Tel: 2952235.
**Open:** Sep–May ▪ **Suitable for ages:** 7+ ▪ **Bus routes:** 44, 63,
118.
**Sports:** soccer

## 543 Devil's Glen

Ashford, Co. Wicklow (turn right off the N11 at Ashford House
Hotel, signposts to woods two miles on).
**Open:** All year; Mon–Sun 24 hours ▪ **Charge:** Free ▪ **Suitable for
ages:** All ▪ **Car parking:** Free.

A lovely glen on the Vartry River. The wood houses a sculpture
park, with sculptures scattered around, all made from different
woods. It can get very muddy after rain, and is sometimes almost
impassable. The scenery is beautiful, particularly in the snow
when icicles can often be seen in sheltered areas.
**★ TOP CHOICES: WALKS ★**

## 544 Dexter, John, Harmony Choir

22 Delbrook Manor, Dublin 16; Contact: John Dexter;
Tel: 2987781, 087 7989560;
Website: www.johndexterharmony.com
**Open:** call for rehearsal times and audition dates ▪ **Charge:**
Tuition is €610 per year ▪ **Suitable for ages:** 7–14.
A boys' treble choir, who do backing on many pop and rock
recordings. Entrance is by audition only.

## 545 Djouce Woods 🚻

Long Hill Rd, Valclusa, Co. Dublin (ignore sign for Powerscourt
Waterfall from Enniskerry; take the right fork onto Long Hill Rd.
Park in first carpark).
**Open:** All year; Mon–Sun 24 hours ▪ **Charge:** Free ▪ **Suitable for
ages:** All ▪ **Car parking:** Free.
This is a two-hour walk, but you can cut it short and skip Earl's
Drive if you have young children. Most of the tracks near Djouce
Woods are suitable for buggies. Take the wide track through the
woods. Go straight through the crossroads and down as far as a
sharp bend, where you turn left. There are great views here of the
waterfall and deer park. Follow the path uphill and take a
right-hand track down to a ford across the river. Note: Do not
cross if the river is flooding. Follow Earl's Drive around lots of
hairpin bends, taking in the beautiful smell of the cypress trees,
until you reach the Paddock Ponds, which are now marshes. Now
walk around and follow the path back down the forest paths to
the car park.
**✱ TOP CHOICES: WALKS ✱ TOP CHOICES: FOR AGES 10+ ✱ TOP
CHOICES: FOR ENERGETIC KIDS ✱**

## 546 Dodder Park

Dodder Park, Dropping Well, Milltown, Dublin 6 (at junction of
Churchtown Rd and Milltown Rd); Tel: 6684364;
E-mail: parks.parks@dublincity.ie;
Website: www.dublincity.ie/parks
**Open:** All year; Mon–Fri 8.30am–dusk; Sat–Sun 9.30am–dusk ▪
**Charge:** Free ▪ **Suitable for ages:** All ▪ **Car parking:** Free ▪ **Bus
routes:** 14, 14A.
**Sports:** soccer, fishing
The linear Dodder Park is often thought to start at the Dropping
Well pub, just below the weir. It continues past the old laundry,

and then down the hill at the top of Milltown Road. You can walk on as far as the footbridge on Lower Dodder Rd, then continue along a narrow path beside the river until you reach the bridge at Rathfarnham Rd. The park continues across the stepping stones or over a footbridge to Bushy Park. This stretch is very popular with anglers and with dog walkers. There are no playgrounds, but children will enjoy exploring the weirs, and the long path is great for those learning to cycle. There are sports grounds for soccer, but you need to book to get access to the goals.

★ TOP CHOICES: FOR AGES 5–10 ★

## 547 Dolphin Activity Holidays

Church Buildings, Church Lane, Main St, Rathfarnham, Dublin 14;
Tel: 4924084, 4907522, 4907960; Fax: 4920950;
E-mail: delphidu@iol.ie;
Website: www.delphiaadventureholidays.ie
**Open:** Jul–Aug; camps run weekly; call for dates and times ■
**Charge:** €325 per child for one week ■ **Suitable for ages:** 8+ ■
**Bus routes:** Weekly bus service from Dublin provided.
**Sports:** archery, badminton, horse-riding, rowing/canoeing, sailing, swimming, tennis, windsurfing, abseiling, rock climbing, raft building, orienteering, hillwalking
Dolphin is an activity/adventure holiday for 8–17-yr-olds, held in the Delphi Activity Centre in Clew Bay. Activities range from surfing and windsurfing to archery, abseiling and tennis and much more. Accommodation is in centrally heated dormitories, and a bus service is provided from Dublin weekly. School groups are also accommodated.

★ TOP CHOICES: SUMMER CAMPS ★

## 548 Dolphin's Barn Library

Parnell Rd, Dublin 12 (beside the canal, near the fire station);
Tel: 4540681; Website: www.iol.ie/dublincitylibrary
**Open:** All year; Mon/Wed 1–8pm; Tue/Thur/Fri–Sat 10am–5pm; closed Sat–Mon on bank holiday weekends ■ **Charge:** Free ■
**Suitable for ages:** All ■ **Car parking:** Free ■ **Bus routes:** 17, 22, 50, 50A/B, 56A, 77, 77A/B, 150, 210.
Special reading events and seasonal arts and crafts are organised for children throughout the year.

## 549 Donnybrook Lawn Tennis Club

Brookvale Rd, Dublin 4; Tel: 2692838.

**Open:** All year; Mon–Fri 5.30–11pm; Sat–Sun 10am–10pm; Summer camps: Mon–Fri 10am–3pm; Call for this year's dates ■ **Charge:** Approx. €150 annual fee for junior membership; Tennis coaching fees are extra; Summer camp fees on request ■ **Suitable for ages:** 5+ ■ **Car parking:** Free ■ **Bus routes:** 10, 10A, 118, 46, 46A/B/C, 58C, 746, 7B, 84X.
**Sports:** tennis

A tennis club with grass courts. Coaching for juniors is available all year, and training camps are run during the summer. The club caters for players at all levels, from beginner to junior open tennis. Membership is required, and coaching costs extra.

## 550 Duane, Caoimhe Ashley (Music Teacher)

Bray, Co. Wicklow; Tel: 2866979.
**Open:** All year; class times on request ■ **Charge:** Fees on request ■ **Suitable for ages:** 5+.

Caoimhe Ashley Duane gives tuition in piano, electric keyboards, acoustic guitar, classical guitar, electric guitar, bass guitar, alto saxophone, concert flute, clarinet, recorder, tin whistle and drums. She teaches classical, jazz, traditional and world music. Preparation is given for RIAM exams and *feiseanna*.

## 551 Duane, David Patrick (Music Teacher)

Bray, Co. Wicklow; Tel: 2866979.
**Open:** All year; class times on request ■ **Charge:** Fees on request ■ **Suitable for ages:** 8+.

David Patrick Duane gives tuition in piano, electric keyboards, acoustic guitar, electric guitar, steel guitar, concert flute, clarinet, tin whistle, drums and voice. He teaches classical, jazz, traditional and popular genres, and also voice for musicals. Preparation is given for RIAM exams.

## 552 Dublin Bay Sea Thrill

Carlisle Terminal, East Pier, Dún Laoghaire, Co. Dublin (the Sea Thrill base is opposite the old ferry terminal, to the left of the National Yacht Club at the East Pier in Dún Laoghaire, 1 minute's walk from the DART station); Tel: 2600949; Fax: 2301232; E-mail: info@seathrill.ie; Website: www.seathrill.ie
**Open:** All year; Mon–Sun sunrise–sunset ■ **Charge:** Booked on a per-boat basis, with each boat taking up to 10 people; A 40-minute ride is €340 and a 50-minute ride €380; BBQ after is additional ■ **Suitable for ages:** 12+ ■ **Car parking:** On-street

parking ▪ **Bus routes:** 45A, 46A, 59, 59A, 75, 111, 746 ▪ **DART station:** Dún Laoghaire.

This is a high-speed adventure around Dublin Bay in marine rescue boats. The trip departs from the East Pier steps in Dún Laoghaire and heads out towards Dalkey Island, the Muglins and Killiney Bay. You sit on the sides of the boat and need to be quite strong to hang on! It is very fast-paced, and pregnant women and under-12s are not allowed on board. Waterproof sailing suits and lifejackets are supplied. Trips last about 40 or 50 minutes. A BBQ can be organised in private waterfront gardens at the end of the trip, at an additional cost. This is quite a popular, though expensive, activity for a teenage birthday. Most will go on to McDonalds after the trip rather than the BBQ. Wear comfortable clothing and boat-friendly shoes, like runners. Bring a change of clothes, as they may get wet.

✱ **TOP CHOICES: BIRTHDAY PARTY IDEAS ✱ TOP CHOICES: FOR ENERGETIC KIDS ✱ TOP CHOICES: FOR IMAGINATIVE KIDS ✱**

## 553 Dublin Folk Dance Group

Holy Cross Church Hall, Dundrum, Dublin 16 (classes are held in the hall, which is down the steps underneath the church); Tel: 2987929.

**Open:** Sep–Jun; Mon 7.30–10pm ▪ **Charge:** €4/ €5 per person for group classes ▪ **Suitable for ages:** 13–18 ▪ **Car parking:** On-street parking ▪ **Bus routes:** 17, 48A, 75.

An 18-year-old school for Irish and folk dancing, for children aged 13–18. There's no participation in competitions, but the group put on performances in parks in the summer, and even perform abroad.

✱ **TOP CHOICES: HOBBIES/ARTS AND CRAFTS ✱**

## 554 Dublin Girls Singers

Church of Ireland, Kill o' the Grange, Deansgrange, Co. Dublin; Contact: Fiona Lee; Tel: 2824446.

**Open:** All year; Mon evenings ▪ **Charge:** €300 per year ▪ **Suitable for ages:** 8–17.

The Dublin Girls Singers meet each Mon evening, and are professionally directed. The tuition fee is payable in two instalments.

## 555 Dundrum Library ✏️ 🖥️

Dundrum, Dublin 14 (near the graveyard and Churchtown Rd);

Tel: 2985000; Fax: 2985000; Website: www.dlrcoco.ie/library
**Open:** All year; Mon/Wed/Fri–Sat 10am–1pm, 2–5pm; Tue/Thur
2–8pm; Closed Sat–Mon on bank holiday weekends ▪ **Charge:**
Free ▪ **Suitable for ages:** All ▪ **Car parking:** Free ▪ **Bus routes:**
17, 44, 48A, 75, 86.
The Parent-and-Toddler Group here meets on Wed at 11am.
Seasonal arts-and-crafts and reading events for children are
organised throughout the year. There is no wheelchair access to
the children's library.
✱ **TOP CHOICES: FOR AGES 2–5** ✱

## 556 Dún Laoghaire Archers

Indoor: National Rehabilitation Hospital, Rochestown Avenue,
Dún Laoghaire, Co. Dublin; Outdoor: St. Michael's College,
Nutley Avenue, Merrion Rd, Dublin 4; Contact: Joe Malone;
Tel: 2802361.
**Open:** All year; Fri 8–10pm ▪ **Suitable for ages:** 10+ ▪ **Bus
routes:** 7A, 45A, 46A, 58C, 59, 59A, 75, 111 ▪ **Rail station:** Dún
Laoghaire ▪ **DART station:** Dún Laoghaire.
**Sports:** archery

## 557 Dún Laoghaire Library 🚼 ♿ ✍

Lwr George's St, Dún Laoghaire, Co. Dublin; Tel: 2801147;
Fax: 2846141; E-mail: libraries@dlrcoco.ie;
Website: www.dlrcoco.ie/library
**Open:** All year; Mon/Sat 10am–1pm, 2–5pm; Tue/Thur
1.15–8pm; Wed/Fri 10am–5pm; Closed Sat–Mon on bank holiday
weekends ▪ **Charge:** Free ▪ **Suitable for ages:** All ▪ **Car parking:**
Disc parking on street, or use Bloomfields Shopping Centre car
park ▪ **Bus routes:** 7, 7A, 8, 46A, 59, 75, 111 ▪ **Rail station:** Dún
Laoghaire ▪ **DART station:** Dún Laoghaire.
There is a children's section here, with holiday and seasonal
activities organised throughout the year – book well in advance.

## 558 Dún Laoghaire Music Centre ✍

130 Lwr George's St, Dún Laoghaire, Co. Dublin; Tel: 2844178;
E-mail: dlmc@eircom.net; Website: www.dlmc@eircom.net
**Open:** All year; Call for details of course dates and times; Summer
projects run every week in Jul ▪ **Charge:** Children's World of
Music €135 per 12-week term; Individual tuition from €225 per
12-week term; Group tuition from €155 per 12-week term; Music
Technology €390 (group), €485 (individual) per term; Choir €45

per term; Other courses and summer course prices on request ■
**Suitable for ages:** 2+ ■ **Bus routes:** 7, 7A, 8, 46A ■ **Rail station:**
Dún Laoghaire ■ **DART station:** Dún Laoghaire.

Dún Laoghaire Music Centre provides lessons in traditional and
classical instruments for all age groups. Their Children's World of
Music classes, for 2–6-yr-olds, offer an introduction to music and
instruments. There are also classes in the following: Music Theatre
Workshops (for 7–9-yr-olds); Singing for Fun (for teens); Acting
Through Song; ensemble; choir; theory; and music technology.
There are summer projects for ages 5–12, with music, drama,
dance, arts and crafts.

✱ TOP CHOICES: HOBBIES/ARTS AND CRAFTS ✱ TOP CHOICES: FOR
AGES 2–5 ✱ TOP CHOICES: FOR AGES 5–10 ✱ TOP CHOICES: FOR AGES
10+ ✱ TOP CHOICES: FOR SHY KIDS ✱ TOP CHOICES: FOR IMAGINATIVE
KIDS ✱

## 559 Dún Laoghaire Shopping Centre

Marine Rd, Dún Laoghaire, Co. Dublin (Marine Rd is a side street
opposite Dún Laoghaire DART station); Tel: 2802981 (centre),
2301248 (crèche); Fax: 2809938.
**Open:** All year 2. Crèche; Centre: Mon–Thur 9am–7pm; Fri–Sat
8am–9pm; Crèche: Mon–Sat 10am–5.30pm, last child taken at
5pm ■ **Charge:** Crèche €4 per hour, for max 2 hours per day ■
**Suitable for ages:** All ■ **Car parking:** Paying car park from €2 per
hour ■ **Bus routes:** 7, 7A/7B, 11, 45A, 46A/X, 59, 111, 746.
An old shopping centre compared to Bloomfields, but still
popular. The Over the Rainbow crèche will look after 3–7-yr-olds
for €4 per hour, for a maximum 2 hours per day.

## 560 Dún Laoghaire Youth Dance Theatre

Bloomfield Shopping Centre, Lwr George's St, Dún Laoghaire, Co.
Dublin; Tel: 2803455; Fax: 2803466; E-mail: danceire@iol.ie;
Website: www.dancetheatreireland.com
**Open:** All year; 8–12-yr-olds: Modern/hip hop classes Sat
11.15am–12.15pm, 12.15–1.15pm; 13–17-yr-olds: Modern/hip
hop classes Sat 1.15–2.15pm, 2.15–3.15pm, 3.15–4.15pm; Also
summer courses for ages 8–12 and 13–17 ■ **Charge:** €70 per
10-week term of group classes; Summer courses €115 for a week
of all-day dance classes ■ **Suitable for ages:** 8–12, 13–17 ■ **Car
parking:** Free ■ **Bus routes:** 7, 7A, 8, 45A, 46A, 59, 75, 111 ■
**Rail station:** Dún Laoghaire ■ **DART station:** Dún Laoghaire.

Dún Laoghaire Youth Dance Theatre offers classes in modern and hip hop dance to the over-8s. Classes are held in a purpose-built dance studio. Week-long summer courses, 'Dance All Day', run during July. There is also an outreach service for children with disabilities. Loose, light, comfortable clothes and soft shoes are to be worn.

✱ TOP CHOICES: HOBBIES/ARTS AND CRAFTS ✱ TOP CHOICES: SUMMER CAMPS ✱

## 561 Dunne, Maedhbh (Music Teacher)

Goatstown, Dublin 14; Tel: 2960491.
**Open:** All year; class times on request ■ **Charge:** Fees on request ■ **Suitable for ages:** 6+.
Maedhbh Dunne gives classical piano tuition, and prepares students for RIAM and ABRSM exams.

## 562 ESB Sportsco

South Lotts Rd, Dublin 4 (approach from Haddington Rd or Shelbourne Rd; South Lotts Rd is close to the greyhound track and just before Grand Canal Dock); Tel: 6687022; Fax: 6604187.
**Open:** All year; Mon–Sun 9am–9pm ■ **Charge:** Membership €260 a year ■ **Suitable for ages:** All ■ **Car parking:** Free ■ **Bus routes:** 1, 2, 3 ■ **DART station:** Lansdowne Rd.
**Sports:** badminton, basketball, skateboarding, soccer, swimming, volleyball
A private sports club, open to non-ESB workers, with a waiting list of between two and six months. The pool is particularly popular, and the swimming club and lessons usually have a waiting list to join. A skateboarding arena is a big hit with older boys and girls. There's a hall for volleyball, soccer and basketball, as well as four AstroTurf pitches. Members can rent halls by the hour for indoor soccer and other sports. This is great for birthday parties. You organise food yourself, but the kids can eat it in the bar. Summer camps involve a mixture of most of the sports on offer.

✱ TOP CHOICES: BIRTHDAY PARTY IDEAS ✱ TOP CHOICES: SUMMER CAMPS ✱ TOP CHOICES: FOR ENERGETIC KIDS ✱

## 563 Faughs Hurling Club

Wellington Lane, Templeogue, Dublin 6W; Tel: 4903566; Fax: 4902098; Website: www.faughs.ie
**Open:** All year ■ **Charge:** Children free; Small weekly fee ■ **Suitable for ages:** 5+ ■ **Bus routes:** 54, 54A, 65, 65B.
**Sports:** gaelic football, hurling

## 564 Frascati Shopping Centre

Frascati Rd, Blackrock, Co. Dublin; Tel: 2883444; Fax: 2881697.
**Open:** All year; Centre: Mon–Wed 9am–6pm; Thur–Fri
9am–9pm; Sat 9am–6pm; Sun 12–6pm; Crêche opens
half-an-hour later than centre opening hours and closes
half-an-hour earlier ▪ **Charge:** Free crêche at Roches Stores ▪
**Suitable for ages:** All ▪ **Car parking:** Free ▪ **Bus routes:** 5, 7, 7A,
45 ▪ **DART station:** Blackrock.
There's a big Roches Stores here, with a free crêche for
2–6-yr-olds.

## 565 Funderland

Merrion Rd, Ballsbridge, Dublin 4 (from the city centre, head
south towards Ballsbridge; the RDS is signposted and is off
Merrion Rd, between Simmonscourt Rd and Anglesea Rd);
Tel: 6680866 (RDS); Fax: 6604014; E-mail: info@rds.ie;
Website: www.rds.ie
**Open:** Christmas only – 26 Dec–5 Jan; Mon–Sun 12–10pm ▪
**Charge:** Child €1; Adult €1; Pay per ride, approx. €3 ▪ **Suitable
for ages:** 5+ ▪ **Car parking:** Anglesea Rd, or Simmonscourt Rd –
€4 per hour ▪ **Bus routes:** 5, 7, 7A, 18, 45 ▪ **DART station:**
Sandymount.
Funderland is an Irish institution. Every year, hordes of kids –
teenagers particularly – queue for hours to get the wits scared out
of them. There are rides to suit all, from the bumper cars and the
ghost train to the Giant Wheel and Space Shuttle. If you want a
gut-churning experience, this is the place to come, though the
noise and the queues are a bit much for toddlers.
✱ **TOP CHOICES: CHRISTMAS VISITS** ✱ **TOP CHOICES: FOR AGES 5–10**
✱ **TOP CHOICES: FOR AGES 10+** ✱ **TOP CHOICES: FOR TRENDY KIDS**
✱ **TOP CHOICES: FOR ENERGETIC KIDS** ✱ **TOP CHOICES: FOR
IMAGINATIVE KIDS** ✱

## 566 Futurekids, Dún Laoghaire

1 Killiney View, Albert Rd, Glenageary, Co. Dublin; Tel: 6280301;
E-mail: gerry@futurekids.ie; Website: www.futurekids.ie
**Open:** 7-week terms and summer camp; call for class times ▪
**Charge:** Prices start at €90 per 7-week term, with discount for
members of the same family ▪ **Suitable for ages:** 4+ ▪ **Bus
routes:** 59 ▪ **DART station:** Glenageary.
Basic computer literacy classes for children from aged 4–16, in

SOUTH DUBLIN

classes of one hour per week. Computer skills are taught using themes and projects, making learning relevant and fun. Subjects include word processing, spreadsheets, databases, graphics, multimedia, desktop publishing, telecommunications, operating environments, applied technologies and programming. There are also one-week summer camps.

✱ TOP CHOICES: HOBBIES/ARTS AND CRAFTS ✱

## 567 Futurekids, Rathfarnham 🖥

Rathfarnham Shopping Centre, Rathfarnham, Dublin 16; Tel: 4939622; E-mail: rathfarnham@futurekids.ie; Website: www.futurekids.ie
**Open:** 7-week terms and summer camp; call for class times ■ **Charge:** Prices start at €90 per 7-week term, with discount for members of the same family ■ **Suitable for ages:** 4+ ■ **Bus routes:** 15C/X, 16, 16A, 17.
See review for Futurekids, Dún Laoghaire, above.

## 568 Futurekids, Rathmines 🖥

The Swan Centre, Rathmines, Dublin 6; Tel: 4912379; E-mail: atwomey@indigo.ie; Website: www.futurekids.ie
**Open:** 7-week terms and summer camp; call for class times ■ **Charge:** Prices start at €90 per 7-week term, with discount for members of the same family ■ **Suitable for ages:** 4+ ■ **Bus routes:** 14, 14A,15, 15A/B/C/D/E/T/X, 65, 65B/C/X, 83.
See review for Futurekids, Dún Laoghaire, above.

## 569 Futurekids, Stillorgan 🖥

The Old Church, Lwr Kilmacud Rd, Stillorgan, Co. Dublin; Tel: 2781064; E-mail: stillorgan@futurekids.ie; Website: www.futurekids.ie
**Open:** 7-week terms and summer camp; call for class times ■ **Charge:** Prices start at €90 per 7-week term, with discount for members of the same family ■ **Suitable for ages:** 4+ ■ **Bus routes:** 11, 46B, 86.
See review for Futurekids, Dún Laoghaire, above.

✱ TOP CHOICES: FOR AGES 10+ ✱

## 570 Cumann Luthchleas Gael/GAA

Croke Park, Dublin 3; Tel: 8363222; Fax: 8366420; E-mail: info@gaa.ie; Website: www.gaa.ie

**Open:** All year ■ **Charge:** Weekly charge ■ **Suitable for ages:** 5+.
**Sports:** gaelic football, hurling, camogie, handball
Clubs in south Dublin are listed below. See the Organisations
chapter for more information on the GAA.
★ **TOP CHOICES: HOBBIES/ARTS AND CRAFTS** ★ **TOP CHOICES: FOR
ENERGETIC KIDS** ★

## 571 Clan na Gael Fontenoy GAA Club

Sean Moore Rd, Sandymount, Dublin 4; Tel: 6604064.
**Open:** All year ■ **Suitable for ages:** 5+ ■ **Bus routes:** 3, 18.
**Sports:** gaelic football, hurling

## 572 Crumlin GAA Club

Lorcan O'Toole Pk, Crumlin, Dublin 12; Contact: Michael Curran;
Tel: 4551897.
**Open:** All year ■ **Suitable for ages:** 5+ ■ **Bus routes:** 150, 17,
18.
**Sports:** gaelic football, hurling

## 573 Cuala GAA Club

Hyde Rd, Dalkey, Co. Dublin; Tel: 2850783.
**Open:** All year ■ **Suitable for ages:** 5+ ■ **Bus routes:** 59, 59A.
**Sports:** gaelic football, hurling

## 574 St. Jude's GAA Club

Wellington Lane, Dublin 12; Contact: Colum Grogan;
Tel: 4905255.
**Open:** All year ■ **Suitable for ages:** 5+ ■ **Bus routes:** 54A, 150.
**Sports:** gaelic football, hurling

## 575 Gaffney (Ní Ghamhna), Sr Cora (Music Teacher)

Bray, Co. Wicklow; Tel: 2763155.
**Open:** All year; class times on request ■ **Charge:** Fees on request
■ **Suitable for ages:** 7+.
Sr Cora Gaffney is the only teacher we have come across who
trains voice in liturgical and Gregorian chant. She also teaches
piano, recorder, tin whistle, classical voice and traditional voice.
Kodály, Orff and traditional methods are taught and preparation
can be given for RIAM, ABRSM and TCL exams.

## 576 Gaiety School of Acting

The Pavilion Theatre, Marine Rd, Dún Laoghaire, Co. Dublin;
Tel: 6799277; Fax: 6799568; E-mail: gaiety.school@indigo.ie;
Website: www.gaietyschool.com
**Open:** All year; Course 1: Oct–Dec; Course 2: Jan–Mar; Course
3: Apr–Jun; Classes run on Sat, times vary according to age and
experience; Easter Course: 4 days over Easter, 10am–5pm;
Summer Drama Course: Jul, Mon–Fri 10am–1pm ▪ **Charge:**
3-term drama course, 90 minutes per week: 6–7-yr-olds €120, all
other age groups €150; Easter Course: Make-A-Movie €190;
Summer 1-week drama course: €190 ▪ **Suitable for ages:** 6–19 ▪
**Bus routes:** 7, 7A/B, 11, 45B, 46A/X, 59, 111, 746 ▪ **Rail station:**
Dún Laoghaire.
The Young Gaiety School of Acting offers a three-course
programme to introduce children to drama. Classes are grouped
according to age and experience, and are staffed by trained
theatre professionals. The classes aim to build confidence, and to
develop imagination and self-expression. A production is given by
students who have completed the second and third courses at the
end of course three. At Easter, the school runs the Make-a-Movie
course, for 11–15-yr-olds. The students make and act in their own
film, and receive a copy each to take home. There are one-week
drama summer schools for 8–10-yr-olds, 11–13-yr-olds and
14–16-yr-olds run in July.

## 577 Glenageary Lawn Tennis Club

Silchester Rd, Glenageary, Co. Dublin; Contact: Michele
McGrath; Tel: 2808565 (Bernie Lloyd – coaching).
**Open:** All year; 9am–6pm for children ▪ **Charge:** Annual €175;
membership €155; Fees for summer camps and coaching on
request ▪ **Suitable for ages:** 8+ ▪ **Bus routes:** 7, 59 ▪ **DART
station:** Glenageary.
**Sports:** tennis
A private tennis club, with five savannah (sand surface) and four
hard courts. Tennis camps and tournaments are organised during
school holidays. Coaching is also available, at an additional
charge. Activities are for members only.

## 578 Kilmacud Glenalbyn Sports Club

Glenalbyn House, Stillorgan, Co. Dublin (opposite Stillorgan

Shopping Centre); Tel: 2880857, 2881502 (pool);
Website: www.glenalbynsportsclub.com
**Open:** All year; Mon–Sun 7am–9pm ▪ **Charge:** €160 annual
membership for a junior, which includes all activities but lessons
are extra ▪ **Suitable for ages:** All ▪ **Car parking:** Free ▪ **Bus
routes:** 10A, 11, 11A, 46, 46A/C, 63, 75, 84, 86, 115, 116, 118.
**Sports:** gaelic football, hurling, swimming, tennis
A large, private sports club, run in association with Dún
Laoghaire–Rathdown County Council, in central Stillorgan,
opposite the shopping centre. A good range of sports is available,
with a particularly good pool, which is open to non-members.
The summer camps and swimming lessons are highly
recommended; call for this year's prices and dates. You can hire
the pool for a group of children for a birthday party, but you
need to arrange something else for food, or go to Glenalbyn
House for a mineral.
✱ **TOP CHOICES: SPORTS FACILITIES** ✱ **TOP CHOICES: SUMMER
CAMPS** ✱

## 579 Glencullen Library Centre 📝

Glencullen, Co. Dublin (across the road from Johnny Fox's pub);
Tel: 086 2562450; E-mail: libraries@dlrcoco.ie;
Website: www.dlrcoco.ie/library
**Open:** All year; Mon/Wed/Fri 7–9pm; Tue/Thur 3–5pm; Closed
on bank holidays ▪ **Charge:** Free ▪ **Suitable for ages:** All ▪ **Car
parking:** Very limited ▪ **Bus routes:** 44B.
Glencullen is a part-time library with a children's section. The
library runs occasional special events for children. It has no
computer facilities for children, and there are steps up to the front
of the building.

## 580 Glendalough 🚼 ☕ ♿ € 🚉

Glendalough, Co. Wicklow (signposted from Kilmacanogue, on
Dublin–Wexford road; park in the upper car park); Tel: (0404)
45325, (0404) 45425.
**Open:** All year; Mid-Mar–mid-Oct: Mon–Sun 9.30am–6pm;
Mid-Oct–mid-Mar: Mon–Sun 9.30am–5.15pm ▪ **Charge:** Child
€2; Adult €3; The entry fee is for the monastery ▪ **Suitable for
ages:** All ▪ **Car parking:** Free ▪ **Bus routes:** St. Kevin's Bus from
St. Stephen's Green.
Glendalough is an ancient complex of tiny monastic buildings and
a round tower, set around two glacial lakes. The visitor centre has

a 20-minute audio-visual show. You can visit this and the monastery for a nominal charge, but walks along the lake are free and the scenery is spectacular. There is wheelchair access to the north lake, which has picnic areas and BBQs. The Glendalough Hotel, which is close to the entrance, has a shop and café, useful if the rain starts to come down. There are two quite hard walks on the mountains overlooking Glendalough, or you can take an easier stroll along the slopes. Walk to the upper lake and then, keeping the lake on your left, go past some old mine buildings. Climb a zigzag path until you come to a trail along the river, where there are lovely rocky pools and small waterfalls, which children will love to explore. You may spot deer and wild goats up here, and there are good picnic spots. Glendalough is often best avoided on a Sunday, when it can be very crowded.

**✶ TOP CHOICES: PICNIC SPOTS ✶ TOP CHOICES: WALKS ✶**

## 581 Golden Eagle Kenpo and Self Defense Schools

Bishop Shanahan School, Orwell Pk, Templeogue, Dublin 6W; Tel: 4602296; E-mail: maughan@indigo.ie
**Open:** All year; Wed 7.30pm ▪ **Charge:** €2.50 per class ▪ **Suitable for ages:** 8+ ▪ **Bus routes:** 15, 15B, 65, 65B.
**Sports:** martial arts
Children's Kenpo classes are held on Wed evenings at 7.30pm.

## 582 Goodwin, Xavier, Drama School

St. Patrick's Primary School, Ballyroan, Dublin 14; Tel: 4946747.
**Open:** Feb–May; Sat 7–8.30pm; Tue 7–8.30pm ▪ **Charge:** Prices given on request ▪ **Suitable for ages:** 9+ ▪ **Bus routes:** 15, 15B/X, 49, 49X, 75.
Drama classes are held here for ages 9+, leading towards a musical production.

## 583 The Grainstore Youth Arts Centre ♿ ✎

Cabinteely House, Cabinteely Park, Cabinteely, Co. Dublin (in Cabinteely Park, off the N11); Tel: 2850175;
E-mail: youthart@gofree.indigo.ie
**Open:** All year; call for course times or programmes ▪ **Charge:** Prices for performances, exhibitions or courses vary; call for details
▪ **Suitable for ages:** 10+ ▪ **Bus routes:** 46, 84, 84X, 86.
This is a local community initiative, providing arts activities for people aged 10–25. Activities include lessons in dance, drama,

music, video production and arts and crafts. The Grainstore also houses a music rehearsal room, a recording studio and a darkroom for photography.

**★ TOP CHOICES: CHRISTMAS VISITS ★ TOP CHOICES: FOR AGES 10+ ★ TOP CHOICES: FOR IMAGINATIVE KIDS ★**

## 584 Greystones Beach

Greystones, Co. Wicklow (turn left from main road and follow signs to the seafront).
**Open:** All year; Mon–Sun 24 hours ▪ **Charge:** Free ▪ **Suitable for ages:** 5+ ▪ **Bus routes:** 84, 184 ▪ **Rail station:** Greystones ▪ **DART station:** Greystones.
**Sports:** diving, swimming
Greystones is a shingle beach, with quite a deep shelf before you hit sand, making it more suitable for good swimmers. Between the harbour and the long beach there are steps down to a fabulous diving place, which strong swimmers usually find great fun. The south beach won a blue flag in 1997 and has kept it since.

**★ TOP CHOICES: BEACHES ★ TOP CHOICES: FOR AGES 0–2 ★ TOP CHOICES: FOR AGES 2–5 ★**

## 585 Greystones Lawn Tennis Club

Mill Rd, Delgany, Co. Dublin; Contact: Wendy Bourne; Tel: 2876505.
**Open:** All year; Mon–Sun 9am–11pm ▪ **Charge:** Family membership €350 ▪ **Suitable for ages:** 3+ ▪ **Bus routes:** 184 ▪ **Rail station:** Greystones ▪ **DART station:** Greystones.
**Sports:** tennis
Greystones has a two-year waiting list for membership. Kids must be off the courts by 6.30pm.

## 586 Greystones Rugby Football Club

Greystones, Co. Dublin; Contact: Michael Curtis; Tel: 2877285 (home), 2874640 (office).
**Open:** Sep–Apr ▪ **Suitable for ages:** 6+ ▪ **Bus routes:** 84, 184 ▪ **DART station:** Greystones.
**Sports:** rugby

## 587 Guinness Rugby Football Club

Crumlin Rd, Dublin 12; Contact: Thomas Dunne; Tel: 4548099.

**Open:** Sep–Apr ▪ **Suitable for ages:** 6+ ▪ **Bus routes:** 50, 56A, 77, 77A, 150, 210.
**Sports:** rugby

## 588 Gunzl, Camilla (Music Teacher)

Goatstown, Dublin 14; Tel: 2982731, 086 3596301.
**Open:** All year; lass times on request ▪ **Charge:** Fees on request ▪
**Suitable for ages:** 7+.
Camilla Gunzl gives lessons in classical and baroque violin to individuals and small groups, and prepares students for RIAM, ABRSM, GSMD, LCM and TLC exams.

## 589 Gymboree Music on the Go 🛒 🎈

Memorial Hall, Rathfarnham Rd, Terenure, Dublin 6; Perrystown Community Centre, Perrystown, Dublin 12; St. Kilian's Family Centre, La Touche Rd, Greystones, Co. Wicklow; Tel: 2789069 (info), 4905880 (parties at home); Website: www.playandmusic.ie
**Open:** All year; Terenure: Fri 10am/11am; Perrystown: Fri 10am/11am; Greystones: 1pm/2pm ▪ **Charge:** €5– €7.50 per class (with reduction for booking a block session) ▪ **Suitable for ages:** 0–5 ▪ **Car parking:** Parking in the venues except Terenure – disc parking on street.
Gymboree Music On The Go is a range of creative programmes for children from birth to 5 years old. The children can play percussion instruments, sing and dance with an instructor. The musical themes vary from reggae to polka. Parents are involved in sessions and must be present. There are also Gymboree party plans (see Gymboree main entry).
✱ TOP CHOICES: FOR AGES 0–2 ✱ TOP CHOICES: FOR AGES 2–5 ✱

## 590 Gymboree Play and Music 🛒 🎈 🤸

Lwr Kilmacud Rd, Stillorgan, Co. Dublin (Stillorgan Plaza, next to the Ormonde Cinema); Tel: 2789069, 4905880 (parties at home); Website: www.playandmusic.ie
**Open:** All year; Mon–Sat; Class times vary, but in general the centre is open from 12.30pm until early evening – check in advance ▪ **Charge:** enrolment fee of €25; €156 for a 12-week session – includes one play or music class per week plus use of the children's gym facilities six days per week; Music €156 for a 12-week session; Party Plan from €12.00 per child (min 7 children) to €300 (max 25 children), with cake supplied at an extra cost ▪ **Suitable for ages:** 0–5 years ▪ **Car parking:** Free ▪

**Bus routes:** 46, 46A, 63, 75, 84, 84X, 86.

Gymboree Play and Music Centre runs creative programmes for children from birth to 5 years. There's a purpose-built children's gym, where they can play percussion instruments, sing and dance. The musical themes vary from reggae to polka. Parents are involved in sessions, and must be present. There are also Gymboree party plans, for children up to 5 years old: 1. Semi-private in the centre: One hour in the gym with a half-hour of party food and goodie bags to follow. Costs from €10.50 per child (min. 7 children). 2. Private party: This is for exclusive use of the centre, including an entertainer, food and goody bags, and a special Gymboree gift for the birthday child. Costs €300 for max. 25 children (90 minutes duration). 3. A party in your own home with a certified Gymboree instructor. One hour of interactive singing, dancing and instrument play. Costs €100– €120, and you supply your own food.

✱ TOP CHOICES: BIRTHDAY PARTY IDEAS ✱ TOP CHOICES: PLAYGROUNDS ✱ TOP CHOICES: FOR AGES 0–2 ✱ TOP CHOICES: FOR AGES 2–5 ✱

## 591 Halpin, Aedín (Music Teacher)

Ballsbridge, Dublin 4; Tel: 6608146, 087 7994722.
**Open:** All year; class times on request ▪ **Charge:** Fees on request ▪ **Suitable for ages:** 6+.
Aedín Halpin is a Royal Irish Academy of Music teacher, who provides flute, recorder and piano lessons. She can prepare students for RIAM, ABRSM and LCM exams.

## 592 Harold's Cross Park 🚼 ♿ 🧒

Harolds Cross Rd, Dublin 6W; Tel: 4979124;
E-mail: parks.parks@dublincity.ie;
Website: www.dublincity.ie/parks
**Open:** All year; Mon–Fri 8.30am–dusk; Sat–Sun 9.30am–dusk ▪ **Charge:** Free ▪ **Suitable for ages:** All ▪ **Car parking:** On-street parking ▪ **Bus routes:** 16, 16A, 49, 49A.
This is a small park, mainly laid out in gardens. The playground is quite small, but younger children enjoy it.

## 593 Hellfire Club 🏛

Kilakee Rd, Rathfarnham, Dublin 16 (just past the Kilakee House restaurant).
**Open:** All year; Mon–Sun 24 hours ▪ **Charge:** Free ▪ **Suitable for**

**ages:** All ▪ **Car parking:** Free ▪ **Bus routes:** 15C.

The Hellfire Club is an easy climb up Montpellier Hill. It is suitable for all ages, although you may want to take the very young on your back. The club is a complete ruin, but kids love the stories surrounding it – of rich young men playing cards and gambling. One dark night it was noticed that one had a cloven hoof, and the club burst into flames.

✱ TOP CHOICES: WALKS ✱ TOP CHOICES: FOR AGES 10+ ✱ TOP CHOICES: FOR IMAGINATIVE KIDS ✱

## 594 Herbert Park 🚼 ♿ 🧗

Herbert Park, Ballsbridge, Dublin 4 (between Morehampton Rd in Donnybrook and Northumberland Rd in Ballsbridge);
Tel: 6684364; E-mail: parks.parks@dublincity.ie;
Website: www.dublincity.ie/parks
**Open:** All year; Mon–Fri 8.30am–dusk; Sat–Sun 9.30am–dusk ▪
**Charge:** Free ▪ **Suitable for ages:** All ▪ **Car parking:** On-street parking ▪ **Bus routes:** 5, 7, 7A, 45, 46.
**Sports:** gaelic football, hurling, soccer, tennis, bowling, croquet, putting, fishing

Herbert Park is divided in two, with one side mainly catering for tennis – there are 12 courts with an attendant. The other side contains a large pond and playground, and lovely walkways. The sports fields can be booked in advance, or you can chance your arm and just turn up. Dublin Public Parks Tennis league runs here in the summer, and there are occasional musical concerts.

✱ TOP CHOICES: PARKS ✱ TOP CHOICES: FOR AGES 2–5 ✱ TOP CHOICES: FOR AGES 5–10 ✱

## 595 Hockey

Irish Hockey Association, 6A Woodbine Park, Blackrock, Co. Dublin; Tel: 2600028; Fax: 2600087;
E-mail: joanmorgan@hockey.ie; Website: www.hockey.ie
**Open:** Sep–Apr; Call for meeting dates and times ▪ **Charge:** Annual membership around €45 ▪ **Suitable for ages:** 6+.

The Irish Hockey Association oversees all Irish hockey clubs. Children's teams usually start at under-8s and go up to under-16s. Coaching is often on Saturday mornings and Friday nights – call for details.

## 596 Avoca Hockey Club

St Andrew's College, Booterstown, Co. Dublin; Contact: Michelle

Orr; Tel: 4949829, 087 2557732 (Peter Agnew);
E-mail: m.orr@gaelite.ie; Website: www.avocahockeyclub.com
**Open:** Sep–Apr; call for meeting dates and times ▪ **Suitable for ages:** 6+ ▪ **Bus routes:** 5, 7, 7A, 45 ▪ **DART station:** Booterstown.

### 597 Bray Hockey Club

Loreto College, Vevay Rd, Bray, Co. Wicklow; Contact: Graham Hohn; Tel: 2723077, 086 2502307.
**Open:** Sep–Apr; call for meeting dates and times ▪ **Suitable for ages:** 6+ ▪ **Bus routes:** 45, 45A, 84 ▪ **Rail station:** Bray ▪ **DART station:** Bray.

### 598 Corinthian Hockey Club

Whitechurch Park, St. Columba's College, Kilmashogue Lane, Rathfarnham, Dublin 16; Contact: Ruth Kennedy; Tel: 4920225; E-mail: ruth–a–kennedy@accenture.com; Website: www.chc.ie
**Open:** Sep–Apr; call for meeting dates and times ▪ **Suitable for ages:** 6+ ▪ **Bus routes:** 47B.

### 599 Monkstown Hockey Club

Rathdown School, Glenageary, Co. Dublin; St. Andrew's College, 56 Booterstown Ave, Blackrock, Co. Dublin; Contact: Crawford Tipping; Tel: 2852838; E-mail: crawford.tipping@ntl.com
**Open:** Sep–Apr; call for meeting dates and times ▪ **Suitable for ages:** 6+ ▪ **Bus routes:** 7, 7A, 46A ▪ **DART station:** Glenageary.

### 600 Pembroke Wanderers Hockey Club

Serpentine Ave, Ballsbridge, Dublin 4; Contact: Peter Murphy; Tel: 6685217; E-mail: info@pembrokewanderers.ie; Website: www.pembrokewanderers.ie
**Open:** Sep–Apr; call for meeting dates and times ▪ **Suitable for ages:** 6+ ▪ **Bus routes:** 5, 7, 7A, 8, 45 ▪ **DART station:** Sandymount.

### 601 Railway Union Hockey Club

Park Ave, Sandymount, Dublin 4; Contact: John Maguire; Tel: 2800457, 086 8354881; E-mail: jmaguire@esatclear.ie
**Open:** Sep–Apr; call for meeting dates and times ▪ **Suitable for ages:** 6+ ▪ **Bus routes:** 2, 3, 7, 8 ▪ **DART station:** Sydney Parade.

SOUTH DUBLIN

## 602 St. James's Gate Hockey Club

Iveagh Grounds, Crumlin, Dublin 12; Contact: Ciaran Morgan;
Tel: 6368159, 086 8098162; E-mail: morganc@statoil.com
**Open:** Sep–Apr; call for meeting dates and times ▪ **Suitable for
ages:** 6+ ▪ **Bus routes:** 17, 77, 77A, 50, 56B, 150, 121, 122,
123.

## 603 Smithfield Hockey Club

High School, Rathgar, Dublin 6; Contact: Chris McCann;
Tel: 6265029, 086 8181803; E-mail: chrismccc@hotmail.com
**Open:** Sep–Apr; call for meeting dates and times ▪ **Suitable for
ages:** 6+ ▪ **Bus routes:** 15, 15A/B/C, 65A/B.

## 604 Three Rock Rovers Hockey Club

Grange Rd, Rathfarnham, Dublin 16; Contact: Paula Jenkins;
Tel: 2697085, 087 2389819; E-mail: pjenkins@iolfree.ie;
Website: www.threerockhc.com
**Open:** Sep–Apr; call for meeting dates and times ▪ **Suitable for
ages:** 6+ ▪ **Bus routes:** 47B.

## 605 YMCA Hockey Club

Claremont Rd, Sandymount, Dublin 4; Wesley College, Ballinteer,
Dublin 16; Contact: Sandra Gray; Tel: 4907386;
Website: www.ymcahc.ie
**Open:** Sep–Apr; call for meeting dates and times ▪ **Suitable for
ages:** 6+ ▪ **Bus routes:** 7, 8, 45, 48A ▪ **DART station:**
Sandymount.

## 606 Hughes, Pamela, LLSM Speech and Drama

28 Beechpark Rd, Foxrock, Co. Wicklow; Tel: 2899991.
**Open:** Contact the teacher to arrange times ▪ **Charge:** Fees vary
for individual circumstances ▪ **Suitable for ages:** 5+.
Speech and drama classes for ages 5+, with exams taken and a
production held yearly.

## 607 IMC Dún Laoghaire (Cinema) ♿ €

Bloomfield Shopping Centre, Lwr George's St, Dún Laoghaire, Co.
Dublin (opposite St. Michael's Hospital); Tel: 2807777.
**Open:** All year; Children's programmes: Mon–Sun before 7pm;
Kids' Club: Sat 12pm ▪ **Charge:** Child €4.50; Adult €5; Off-peak

prices given; Kids' Club €2.50 ▪ **Suitable for ages:** 3+ ▪ **Car parking:** Free ▪ **Bus routes:** 7, 7A, 8, 45A, 46A, 59, 75, 111 ▪ **Rail station:** Dún Laoghaire ▪ **DART station:** Dún Laoghaire.

A cinema multiplex featuring 12 screens spread over 3 floors, with interconnecting escalators reaching all levels. A Kids' Club on Saturday costs €2.50.

✱ TOP CHOICES: FOR AGES 5–10 ✱ TOP CHOICES: FOR AGES 10+ ✱

## 608 Independent Theatre Workshop, Mornington Rd

2 Mornington Rd, Ranelagh, Dublin 6; Tel: 4968808, 4968808.
**Open:** All year; call for local course days and times or see other entries; Call for Summer School 2003 dates ▪ **Charge:** Dance/Drama €140 per term (tots €76); Creative Drama €57; Jazz €70; Drama €70; Music Theatre €70; Call for Speech prices and summer camp fees ▪ **Suitable for ages:** 2+ ▪ **Bus routes:** 11, 11A/B, 13B, 44, 44B/C, 48A.

One of the best drama schools in Dublin, with affordable classes in drama, singing and dance for all ages from tots to teens. The school is attached to an agency representing children for stage, film, television and radio work. It runs a two-week summer course, with specialist workshops on audition technique, singing, all kinds of dance, stage fighting, character and theatre make-up, acting for the camera, radio drama and scenery painting. It also runs intensive two-week summer musical theatre courses.

✱ TOP CHOICES: HOBBIES/ARTS AND CRAFTS ✱ TOP CHOICES: SUMMER CAMPS ✱

## 609 Independent Theatre Workshop, Mountain View Rd

Beechwood Community Centre, Mountain View Rd, Ranelagh, Dublin 6; Tel: 4572012;
Website: www.independent-theatre-workshop.com
**Open:** All year; various classes available on Sun morning and Thur afternoon ▪ **Charge:** Dance/Drama €140 per term (tots €76); Creative Drama €57; Jazz €70; Drama €70; Music Theatre €70; Call for Speech prices and summer camp fees ▪ **Suitable for ages:** 4+ ▪ **Bus routes:** 11, 11A/B, 13B, 44, 44B/C, 48A.

Classes are held here in dance and drama (for 4–16-yr-olds), musical theatre (for 10–18-yr-olds), jazz (for 7–14-yr-olds), singing, speech and drama (for ages 4+), from one of the top five drama schools in Dublin. See also main entry.

SOUTH DUBLIN

## 610 Instituto Cervantes (Spanish Language Library)

58 Northumberland Rd, Dublin 4; Tel: 6682024;
Website: www.cervantes.es
**Open:** All year; Library: Mon–Fri 10.30am–2pm, 4–8.15pm;
Information Centre: Mon–Fri 9.30am–5pm; Call for language class
terms ■ **Charge:** Free ■ **Suitable for ages:** 10+ ■ **Car parking:**
On-street parking ■ **Bus routes:** 5, 7, 7A, 45, 46, 63, 84.
Instituto Cervantes is a reference library and a resource centre
for teachers and students of Spanish. There's an extensive
range of books about Spain and Latin America, in Spanish and
English, and also a media library with videos, CDs and
cassettes. The information centre also has a database, with
information on courses and universities in Spain. Spanish
language courses for children are run throughout the year; call
for details.

## 611 Irish Academy of Dramatic Arts

Dún Laoghaire Christian Institute, Upr George's St, Dún
Laoghaire, Co. Dublin; Rathdown School, Upr Glenageary Rd,
Glenageary, Co. Dublin; Tel: 2302691; Fax: 2302691.
**Open:** 3 x 10-week terms commence in Sep; Stage School: Sat
10am–1pm (ages 7–13), 2–5pm (ages 10–19); Drama/Music
workshop: Wed afternoons (ages 4–6), Thur 6–7.30pm (ages
9–13) ■ **Charge:** Sat Stage School €200; Drama/Music workshops
€85– €110 per 10-week term ■ **Suitable for ages:** 4+.
This school aims to release creativity and develop self-confidence
for 4–13-yr-olds. This is done through activities such as acting,
mime and movement, singing, poetry, voice and script work,
improvisation, mask-work, percussion and playmaking. There is
also a Saturday stage school for 7–19-yr-olds, with workshops in
drama, dance and musical theatre. The school is attached to a
casting agency.

## 612 Irish Children's Theatre Group

19 Whitebarn Rd, Churchtown, Dublin 14; Contact: Maeve
Widger; Tel: 2986636; Fax: 2986636.
**Open:** Sep–Jun; Also summer courses available, call for 2003
details; different class times according to age ■ **Charge:** €90 per
term; Summer course prices on request ■ **Suitable for ages:** 4+ ■
**Bus routes:** 14, 16, 16A, 17.

Maeve Widger has been running this school for 25 years. Subjects include drama, face painting, mime and clowning, musical theatre and puppetry. The youth theatre covers everything from Shakespeare to Tennessee Williams. Maeve also acts as an agent and has placed children in film, television and London's West End. This is one of the top five schools in Dublin, running courses for ages 4+.

★ TOP CHOICES: HOBBIES/ARTS AND CRAFTS ★ TOP CHOICES: SUMMER CAMPS ★ TOP CHOICES: FOR SHY KIDS ★ TOP CHOICES: FOR ENERGETIC KIDS ★ TOP CHOICES: FOR IMAGINATIVE KIDS ★

## 613 Irish Labour History Society Museum ♿

Beggar's Bush, Haddington Rd, Dublin 4 (from Merrion Sq N, go down Mount St Lwr to Haddington Rd); Tel: 6681071.
**Open:** All year; Winter: Mon–Fri 10am–1pm; Rest of year: Mon–Fri 10am–4pm ■ **Charge:** Free ■ **Suitable for ages:** 12+ ■ **Car parking:** Free ■ **Bus routes:** 5, 7, 7A, 8, 45.
This museum would be useful for secondary school students researching projects on trade unions and the like. It houses exhibits of historical documents relating to work and industry in Ireland since the 18th century. Wheelchair access is limited.

## 614 Irish National Sailing School

West Pier, Dún Laoghaire, Co. Dublin (pier on far left, close to Monkstown/Salthill DART station); Tel: 2844195; Fax: 2300479; E-mail: sailing@inss.ie; Website: www.inss.ie
**Open:** Mar–Nov; Classes: Mon–Fri 9am–5pm ■ **Charge:** Child €160; Maximum €160 fee for a week-long course; discounts for more than one child and also for additional weeks ■ **Suitable for ages:** 7+ ■ **Car parking:** Free ■ **Bus routes:** 7, 45, 46A, 75 ■ **DART station:** Monkstown/Salthill.
**Sports:** sailing
The INSS is the only public sailing club in Ireland or Britain. Week-long courses in dinghy sailing are held for children, during the summer and other school holidays. Levels range from beginners to advanced, using the RYA stage 1/2/3, red, white and blue badge system. Transition-year students can sign up for a 10–14-week programme during the school year. The INSS also provides instructor training for the over-15s, at Halloween, mid-term and Easter. All gear is provided and you only need to bring a towel and a packed lunch. The weekly sail to Dalkey Island is usually very popular. Remember to book

early, as courses fill up in May.

**✱ TOP CHOICES: SUMMER CAMPS ✱ TOP CHOICES: FOR ENERGETIC KIDS ✱**

## 615 James Joyce Museum and Tower €

Sandycove, Co. Dublin (8 miles south of Dublin on the coast road, beside the forty foot bathing area); Tel: 2809265, 8722077; E-mail: joycetower@dublintourism.ie; Website: www.visitdublin.ie

**Open:** All year; Apr–Oct: Mon–Sat 10am–1pm, 2–5pm; Sun, bank holidays 2–6pm; Nov–Mar: by prior arrangement ▪ **Charge:** Child €3.50; Adult €6; Child price is for ages 3–11; Concessions and under-18s €5.00; Family ticket (2 adults and 3/4 children) €16.50; Combined tickets available with Dublin Writers Museum and Shaw Birthplace ▪ **Suitable for ages:** 5+ ▪ **Car parking:** Free ▪ **Bus routes:** 7D, 59 ▪ **DART station:** Sandycove/Glasthule. Whether or not your children are aware of the significance of James Joyce, they will still enjoy visiting a Martello tower. Several of these were built along the east coast to withstand a Napoleon invasion. Joyce, who lived in the Sandycove tower briefly in 1904, made it the setting for the first chapter of his masterpiece, *Ulysses*, and one room is recreated to match the description. It contains personal items of his, as well as his death mask.

## 616 Kiddie Kuts 🚼 ♿ 🤱

U18, Blackrock Shopping Centre, Blackrock, Co. Dublin; U7, The Swan Centre, Rathmines, Dublin 6; Tel: 2836566.

**Open:** All year; Mon–Sat 9am–6pm; Sun 1–5pm ▪ **Charge:** Parties from €17/ €18 per child ▪ **Suitable for ages:** All ▪ **Bus routes:** See under shopping centres.

Brilliant! A hair salon especially for children. There are little cars for reluctant toddlers to sit in while they are getting their hair done, and a range of products and accessories to thrill any little princess. Kiddie Kuts also hold parties in the salon, popular with 7/8-yr-old girls, where food is supplied and the girls get a hairstyle with braids and accessories.

**✱ TOP CHOICES: BIRTHDAY PARTY IDEAS ✱**

## 617 Kilbogget Park 🚼 ♿ 🚻

Shrewsbury Lawn, Ballybrack, Co. Dublin (bounded by Churchview Rd and Bray Rd); Tel: 2054700 (ext. 4448); E-mail: environ@dlrcoco.ie; Website: www.dlrcoco.ie

**Open:** All year; 10am–dusk ▪ **Charge:** Free ▪ **Suitable for ages:** 2+ ▪ **Car parking:** On-street parking ▪ **Bus routes:** 45A, 46, 84, 86, 111.
**Sports:** cycling, rugby, soccer, athletics

Kilbogget Park is based on an old landfill site. It now boasts several football pitches, with pavilions, as well as an all-weather athletics track. Seapoint rugby club is also located here. The recently added cycle and pedestrian path system makes the whole park easier to navigate. The woods at the northern end are popular for exploring.

## 618 Killegar Stables

Killegar, The Scalp, Enniskerry; Tel: 2860919.
**Open:** All year; Tue–Fri 10am–5pm; Sat–Sun 10am–4pm ▪
**Charge:** €19 per hourly lesson; Prices for livery and pony camps on request ▪ **Suitable for ages:** 3+ ▪ **Car parking:** On-street parking ▪ **Bus routes:** 44.
**Sports:** horse-riding

Killegar has outdoor and indoor arenas, and offers rides out in the mountains. During the summer a jumping league is run, as well as pony camps. Killegar also offers a livery service.

## 619 Killiney Hill Park/Dalkey Hill

Vico Rd, Killiney, Co. Dublin (between Vico Rd, Killiney Hill Rd and Dalkey Ave); Tel: 2054700 (ext. 4448); Fax: 2300125; E-mail: environ@dlrcoco.ie; Website: www.dlrcoco.ie
**Open:** All year ▪ **Charge:** Free ▪ **Suitable for ages:** All ▪ **Car parking:** On-street parking ▪ **Bus routes:** 7D, 59, 59A ▪ **DART station:** Killiney/Dalkey.
**Sports:** rock climbing

Killiney and Dalkey hills run together and offer some of the best views in Dublin. They are easily reached at either end via the Killiney and Dalkey DART stations. A leisurely walk around the summits of both hills can take about four hours. Older kids will love exploring the parklands, woods and huge rocks dotted around the park. The wishing stone and the obelisk at the top of Killiney Hill are interesting. On windy days, people hang-glide off the top of Killiney Hill, while there is rock climbing in the old quarries off Dalkey Hill. The steepest slopes are on the eastern side. Slopes on the western (landward) side are more gentle, except for Dalkey Quarry, where sheer 30 to 40-metre-high cliffs enclose flat, sheltered areas at road level.

There is a café in the granite tower part of the Tea Rooms.
✻ **TOP CHOICES: PARKS** ✻ **TOP CHOICES: WALKS** ✻ **TOP CHOICES: FOR AGES 10+** ✻

## 620 Killiney Strand

Killiney, Co. Dublin (turn left off Killiney Hill Rd onto Victoria Rd and then onto Vico Rd, or drive to Vico Rd along the coast from Dalkey); Tel: 2054700 (ext. 4021).
**Open:** All year; Mon–Sun 24 hours ▪ **Charge:** Free ▪ **Suitable for ages:** All ▪ **Car parking:** Free ▪ **Bus routes:** 59 ▪ **DART station:** Killiney.
**Sports:** swimming
The main beach in Killiney is long but quite stony, and has some grassy dunes. It is a good swimming place, but lost its blue flag in 2001, following building work. So far it has not regained it. There are steps down from Vico Road to the White Rock – a great swimming place, but only for strong swimmers. There is another small bridge past the railway from here, and after this is Decco's cave – originally the opening to a lead mine. Dogs are not allowed on the strand from 1 June to 30 September, from 10.30am–7pm.
✻ **TOP CHOICES: BEACHES** ✻ **TOP CHOICES: FOR AGES 10+** ✻

## 621 Kilternan Sports Hotel

Kilternan, Co. Dublin (on the right on the main Enniskerry Rd, before the village); Tel: 2953720 (tennis), 2955559 (hotel), 2955658 (skiing); Fax: 2955670; E-mail: fitness@kilternan.ie
**Open:** All year; Mon–Fri 7am–10pm; Sat 8am–9pm; Sun 8am–7pm ▪ **Charge:** €40 per person a month for all facilities; €88 a month for family; Children can have individual membership ▪
**Suitable for ages:** All ▪ **Car parking:** Free ▪ **Bus routes:** 44, 63, 118.
**Sports:** skiing, swimming, tennis
A perennially popular sports facility, due to be renovated in early 2003. The well-known Casey brothers provide coaching for tennis. There is a swimming pool with a sauna, and Ireland's only dry ski slope. Birthday parties are possible, with a session in the swimming pool and food in the bar, but you will need to book well in advance (maximum 10 children). Summer camps are run in the tennis club only; call for this year's fees and dates.
✻ **TOP CHOICES: BIRTHDAY PARTY IDEAS** ✻ **TOP CHOICES: SPORTS FACILITIES** ✻ **TOP CHOICES: FOR AGES 10+** ✻

## 622 Kodály Society of Ireland ♿

PO Box 4569, Dublin 7 (summer courses held at Church of Ireland College of Education, Rathmines, Dublin 6); Contact: Lorraine O'Connell; Tel: email/write only; E-mail: oconnelllor@eircom.net

**Open:** Jul; 9.45am–1pm ▪ **Charge:** Fees on request ▪ **Suitable for ages:** 8–14.

The Kodály Society espouses the philosophy of Hungarian music educator Zoltán Kodály, that music is for everyone. Their summer course includes morning classes in music making and choral singing. Optional afternoon activities are available to facilitate working parents and those parents attending. They may include drama, dance and sport, as well as chamber music. Children will be given the opportunity to sing with the renowned Hungarian Radio Children's Choir.

✱ TOP CHOICES: HOBBIES/ARTS AND CRAFTS ✱ TOP CHOICES: SUMMER CAMPS ✱

## 623 LA Fitness 🚼 🎲 ☕ ⓘ

Palmerston Villas, Dartry, Dublin 6 (opposite Palmerston Park off the Miltown Rd, or at the end of Highfield Rd); Tel: 4911675; Fax: 4911682; Website: www.lafitness.co.uk

**Open:** All year; Mon–Sun 7am–10pm ▪ **Charge:** Adult membership €60 per month; Children of members pay €25 a month; Under-2s are free ▪ **Suitable for ages:** All ▪ **Bus routes:** 13B, 14, 14A.

**Sports:** swimming, gym

A new private leisure club, with a 15-metre pool and a gym. The kids' club has classes in fitness as well as games.

## 624 Lambert Puppet Theatre and Museum 🚼 ♿ 🎭

Clifton Lane, Monkstown, Co. Dublin (off Longford Tce, near the DART station); Tel: 2801863; Fax: 2804772; E-mail: eugene@lambertpuppettheatre.com; Website: www.lambertpuppettheatre.com

**Open:** All year; Sat–Sun 3.30pm, museum opens after shows; School tours available May and Jun ▪ **Charge:** Child €8.50; Adult €9.50; Price includes performance and museum visit; 3-hour party package for 15 children €250 ▪ **Suitable for ages:** All ▪ **Car parking:** Free ▪ **Bus routes:** 7, 7A ▪ **DART station:**

SOUTH DUBLIN

Salthill and Monkstown.

This puppet theatre is now 30 years old. It has a repertoire of over 30 performances to suit all ages, from fairy tales to Oscar Wilde. There is also a museum you can visit, where parents can get nostalgic over the likes of Bosco and Mr Crow from 'Wanderly Wagon'. They hold a Puppet Theatre Festival in September every year, and also puppet-making workshops; call for details. You can book an all-inclusive birthday party, including food, museum visit and a performance.

✱ TOP CHOICES: BIRTHDAY PARTY IDEAS ✱ TOP CHOICES: CHRISTMAS VISITS ✱ TOP CHOICES: FOR AGES 2–5 ✱ TOP CHOICES: FOR AGES 5–10 ✱ TOP CHOICES: FOR IMAGINATIVE KIDS ✱

## 625 Lansdowne Football Club

Lansdowne Rd, Dublin 4; Contact: John Kearney; Tel: 6689300, 6608118 (John Kearney); E-mail: snapvic@snapprinting.ie
**Open:** Sep–Apr ▪ **Suitable for ages:** 6+ ▪ **Bus routes:** 5, 7, 7A, 46 ▪ **DART station:** Lansdowne Rd.
**Sports:** rugby

## 626 Lansdowne Tennis Club

Lansdowne Rd, Dublin 4; Contact: David Roig; Tel: 6680219; Fax: 6675867; E-mail: info@landsdowneltc.com
**Open:** All year; weekday afternoons for tennis school; Sat–Sun 8am–11pm ▪ **Charge:** Approx. €150 annual junior membership; Tennis coaching fees are extra; Summer camp fees on request ▪ **Suitable for ages:** 5+ ▪ **Car parking:** Free ▪ **Bus routes:** 5, 7, 7A, 46 ▪ **DART station:** Lansdowne Rd.
**Sports:** tennis
Coaching for juniors is available all year, and training camps are run during the summer. The club caters for players at all levels, from beginner to junior open tennis. Membership is required and coaching costs extra.

✱ TOP CHOICES: SUMMER CAMPS ✱

## 627 Leeson Park School of Music 🛒

Kensington Hall, Grove Pk, Rathmines, Dublin 6; Tel: 4967890; E-mail: leesonpark@eircom.net
**Open:** All year; daily classes available ▪ **Charge:** Summer courses from €65 for a week of 30-minute classes; Other course prices on request ▪ **Suitable for ages:** All ▪ **Bus routes:** 14, 15A/B/C/X, 83. This school teaches the methods of Hungarian music educator

Zoltan Kodály (1882–1967), whose philosophy was that music is for everyone – all children, given the right opportunities (that is, the right training at the right time), can become musically literate – they can learn to read, write and enjoy music, sing in tune and, if they wish, play an instrument. Babies from three months old can do introductory music courses, which run up to age six. Over-6s can have instrumental tuition in piano, violin, viola, cello, guitar and flute, as well as instruction in choirs, orchestras, chamber music, musicianship, and Junior and Leaving certificate Music. Parents' classes are also available.

**✱ TOP CHOICES: HOBBIES/ARTS AND CRAFTS ✱ TOP CHOICES: SUMMER CAMPS ✱**

## 628 Leinster Cricket Club

Observatory Lane, Rathmines, Dublin 6; Tel: 4974673.
**Open:** May–Aug; Cricket Sun 10am–12pm; Summer camps: 14–25 Jul, Mon–Fri 10am–1pm; 11–22 Aug, Mon–Fri 10am–1pm ▪ **Charge:** Club membership €85; Summer camps (2 weeks) €90 – no need to be a member ▪ **Suitable for ages:** 8+ ▪ **Car parking:** On-street parking ▪ **Bus routes:** 14, 14A, 15, 15A/B/C/D/E/T, 65, 65B/C/X, 83.
**Sports:** cricket, tennis
Leinster Cricket Club meets on Sunday mornings for cricket, and you also get access to tennis courts. Two-week summer camps are run, and these are very popular, with tennis, squash and bowls, as well as cricket, for boys and girls.

**✱ TOP CHOICES: HOBBIES/ARTS AND CRAFTS ✱**

## 629 Leisureplex, Stillorgan

Old Bray Rd, Stillorgan, Co. Dublin (opposite Stillorgan Shopping Centre); Tel: 2881656; E-mail: stillorgan@leisureplex.ie; Website: www.leisureplex.ie
**Open:** All year; Mon–Sun 24 hours ▪ **Charge:** Activities from about €5; Birthday parties from €11 per child, including activity, food, cake, balloons, party bags and a photo ▪ **Suitable for ages:** All ▪ **Car parking:** Free ▪ **Bus routes:** 7, 7B/D, 46/A/D/E/X, 58/C/X, 63, 75, 84/X, 86, 116.
**Sports:** Snooker, pool, 10-pin bowling
Fun for all: for little ones there's The Zoo – a huge, soft play area with slides and balls, including space for under-3s. Snooker, pool and Quazar are available for ages 7/8+, as well as bowling with ball walls (there is a junior bowling club on Saturday mornings at

10am). Young teens can hang out in the games area, complete with the ever-popular dance machine. Great for birthday parties, especially for the under-8s, who have theirs hosted by Plexy the dinosaur. This branch also has Pompeii Paints – you can paint your own ceramics.

✱ TOP CHOICES: BIRTHDAY PARTY IDEAS ✱ TOP CHOICES: PLAYGROUNDS ✱ TOP CHOICES: FOR AGES 2–5 ✱ TOP CHOICES: FOR AGES 5–10 ✱ TOP CHOICES: FOR AGES 10+ ✱ TOP CHOICES: FOR ENERGETIC KIDS ✱ TOP CHOICES: FOR IMAGINATIVE KIDS ✱

## 630 Little Sugar Loaf

Kilmacanogue, Co. Wicklow (turn left at Kilmaconogue towards Glendalough, drive up almost a mile and park on the rough grassy area on the left).

**Open:** All year; Mon–Sun 24 hours ▪ **Charge:** Free ▪ **Suitable for ages:** 5+ ▪ **Car parking:** On grassy bank ▪ **Bus routes:** Bus Éireann or St. Kevin's Bus to Kilmacanoge.

This is about a two-hour walk, across rocky ground. Take the track rather than the path, and follow it until you can turn left and walk along the eastern side of the mountain, where you can see Bray Head. When it starts heading downwards, leave it and turn left, following a stone wall up. There are great spots here for picnics – the left side is more sheltered. After reaching the summit, descend parallel to old lines and follow the path down to the start.

✱ TOP CHOICES: PICNIC SPOTS ✱ TOP CHOICES: WALKS ✱

## 631 Loreto Park

Nutgrove Way, Rathfarnham, Dublin 16 (beside Nutgrove Shopping Centre); Tel: 2054700 (ext. 4448); E-mail: environ@dlrcoco.ie; Website: www.dlrcoco.ie

**Open:** All year; 10am–dusk ▪ **Charge:** Free ▪ **Suitable for ages:** All ▪ **Car parking:** On-street parking ▪ **Bus routes:** 16A, 17, 75, 161.

**Sports:** cycling, soccer

Loreto Park has a number of sports grounds, and houses the Leicester Celtic soccer club. You can book a pitch or trust to luck and just turn up and play. A new adventure-style children's playground is also very popular.

✱ TOP CHOICES: PLAYGROUNDS ✱

## 632 Loy, Jean (Music Teacher)

Dún Laoghaire, Co. Dublin; Tel: 2852270.

**Open:** All year; class times on request ▪ **Charge:** Fees on request
▪ **Suitable for ages:** 7+.
Jean Loy gives tuition in fiddle and violin. Suzuki, classical and
traditional methods are taught, and students are prepared for
RIAM exams.

## 633 Marian College 🅿

Lansdowne Rd, Dublin 4; Tel: 6689539; Fax: 6674578.
**Open:** All year; Mon–Fri 2–5pm; Sat 9am–5.45pm; Sun
10am–3.45pm ▪ **Charge:** Child €2.50; Adult €4; Entrance fee for
pool; Swimming lesson fees on request ▪ **Suitable for ages:** 2+ ▪
**Car parking:** Free ▪ **Bus routes:** 5, 7, 7A, 46 ▪ **DART station:**
Landsdowne Rd.
**Sports:** swimming, gym, scuba
A small, private pool in the school, open to the public in the
afternoons and at weekends. It is used for swimming lessons, as
well as scuba and other classes.

## 634 Marlay Park 🚼 ☕ ♿ € 👤 🚂

Grange Rd, Rathfarnham, Dublin 16 (bounded by Grange Rd,
College Rd and Whitechurch Rd); Tel: 4934059 (ext. 4448);
E-mail: environ@dlrcoco.ie; Website: www.dlrcoco.ie
**Open:** All year; Winter: Mon–Sun 10am–5pm; Summer:
Mon–Sun 10am–9pm; Model railway: Sat 3–5pm ▪ **Charge:** Free
▪ **Suitable for ages:** All ▪ **Car parking:** Free ▪ **Bus routes:** 16, 75,
116.
**Sports:** cricket, gaelic football, golf, hurling, soccer, tennis, BMX
biking
Marlay Park is a huge, open park of over 300 acres. It is set
around an old stone house with restored Regency gardens, which
are beautifully laid out. The old courtyard now houses craft and
coffee shops. There are large areas of woodland – a good place to
spot red squirrels – and a lovely stream runs through. Marlay also
boasts one of Dublin's best adventure playgrounds. This is popular
with even the most jaded kids, and features wobble bridges,
fortresses and towers, as well as a section for smaller kids. The
BMX track is great for aspiring cyclists, although safety gear must
be worn. Marlay also has a nine-hole golf course, a cricket pitch
and 14 football pitches. The model railway, run by the Dublin
Society of Model and Experimental Engineers, runs from 3–5pm
on Saturday afternoons and is free. In recent times, Marlay has
become a popular music venue. It has hosted acts such as David

Gray, Sting, Van Morrison, Westlife and Samantha Mumba. Marlay is also the start of the famous Wicklow Way walking route, with the next stop being Enniskerry.

✽ TOP CHOICES: PARKS ✽ TOP CHOICES: PLAYGROUNDS ✽ TOP CHOICES: WALKS ✽ TOP CHOICES: FOR AGES 0–2 ✽ TOP CHOICES: FOR AGES 2–5 ✽ TOP CHOICES: FOR AGES 5–10 ✽ TOP CHOICES: FOR ENERGETIC KIDS ✽

## 635 Martial Arts Centre

Masters Temple, Seaview Complex, Seafront, Bray, Co. Wicklow (behind DART station); Tel: 086 8350062, 2864085.

**Open:** All year; Tue/Thur 6.30–7.30pm; Sat 1–2pm ▪ **Charge:** €8 per session ▪ **Suitable for ages:** 5+ ▪ **Bus routes:** 45, 45A, 84, 145, 146, 184, 185 ▪ **DART station:** Bray.

**Sports:** martial arts

Karate and kickboxing classes are held here for children over 5 years old. All classes are no-contact, or only semi-contact, until the child is at green- or brown-belt level.

✽ TOP CHOICES: HOBBIES/ARTS AND CRAFTS ✽

## 636 Martin, Nora (Music Teacher)

Rathfarnham, Dublin 16; Tel: 087 2340273.

**Open:** All year; class times on request ▪ **Charge:** Fees on request ▪ **Suitable for ages:** 7+.

Nora Martin gives piano lessons for beginners and advanced students in jazz, traditional and world styles, as well as music theory. Exam preparation is provided for RIAM, Leaving Certificate and Junior Certificate.

## 637 Massey Woods 🔟

Killakee Rd, Rathfarnham, Dublin 16 (over the wall opposite Killakee House restaurant).

**Open:** All year; Mon–Sun 24 hours ▪ **Charge:** Free ▪ **Suitable for ages:** 2+ ▪ **Car parking:** On-street parking ▪ **Bus routes:** 15C.

Massey Woods are probably the closest woods to the city centre. They are open to the public, though you have to climb a small wall to get in. The woods are great for exploring and for picnics, with a great variety of trees, including beeches, oaks and chestnuts. There is a path which follows a river though a rock valley – a great place for splashing about and building dams.

✽ TOP CHOICES: PICNIC SPOTS ✽ TOP CHOICES: FOR AGES 5–10 ✽ TOP CHOICES: FOR AGES 10+ ✽ TOP CHOICES: FOR ENERGETIC KIDS ✽

## 638 Mermaid Theatre 🔲 ♿

County Wicklow Arts Centre, Main St, Bray, Co. Wicklow (behind
Bray Town Council offices); Tel: 2724030 (box office);
Fax: 2724031; Website: www.bray.ie/mermaids.htm
**Open:** All year; Gallery: Mon–Sat 10am–6pm; Theatre and
events: Times vary, call for details ▪ **Charge:** Tickets for theatre
performances from €10; Art gallery entrance is free ▪ **Suitable for
ages:** 5+ ▪ **Car parking:** Free ▪ **Bus routes:** 45, 45A, 84, 133,
145, 146, 184, 185 ▪ **Rail station:** Bray ▪ **DART station:** Bray.
Both a theatre and an art gallery, the Mermaid provides a varied
programme throughout the year, including performances from
local theatre and musical groups. There are occasional workshops
for children; call for details.
**✱ TOP CHOICES: CHRISTMAS VISITS ✱ TOP CHOICES: FOR
IMAGINATIVE KIDS ✱**

## 639 Mespil Swimming Pool

Sussex Rd, Dublin 4 (part of Mespil flats complex beside the
Mespil Hotel, about 50 metres from the gate on the right-hand
side behind Mespil House); Tel: 6684626;
E-mail: mary@mespilpool.com; Website: www.mespilpool.com
**Open:** All year; Sat–Sun 10am–1pm, 2–4pm for children ▪
**Charge:** €80 annual membership for an adult, plus €5.50 for a
swim and €4.00 for a child; Non-members: Adult €14, children €4
▪ **Suitable for ages:** All ▪ **Car parking:** Free ▪ **Bus routes:** 10,
10A, 11, 11A, 13B, 46A/B/C/D, 51D.
**Sports:** swimming
A small, private swimming pool, offering children's lessons in the
afternoons. It is used by local schools and dive clubs. It also has a
sauna and a jacuzzi. It is open to the public at weekends, but is
very expensive for non-members.

## 640 Flora Millar Dance Centres

St. Thomas's Parochial Hall, Foster's Ave, Stillorgan Rd, Stillorgan,
Co. Dublin (opposite Radisson Hotel); Tel: 2888455;
Fax: 2888309; E-mail: floramillar@ireland.com;
Website: www.floramillar.com
**Open:** All year; Children's Fun Class: Wed 4.30–5.30pm;
Teenage and Youth Latin and Ballroom Dancing: Wed
5.30–6.30pm ▪ **Charge:** Courses run for 10 weeks and must be
pre-paid; Prices given on request ▪ **Suitable for ages:** 3+ ▪

**Bus routes:** 11A, 17, 46B.

Flora Millar is one of Ireland's best-known dance teachers, and has received international recognition for her contribution to ballroom dancing. The children's fun class is a fun introduction to ballroom and Latin dancing, while the teenage and youth class covers salsa, jive, cha-cha-cha, mambo, waltz and tango. Great for those who want to impress at their 'debs'!

## 641 Monkstown Rugby Football Club

Monkstown, Co. Dublin; Contact: Gary Coughlan; Tel: 6778801.
**Open:** Sep–Apr ▪ **Suitable for ages:** 6+ ▪ **Bus routes:** 7A ▪
**DART station:** Monkstown.
**Sports:** rugby

## 642 Monkstown Swimming Pool and Fitness Centre

Monkstown Ave, Blackrock, Co. Dublin (at Monkstown village take a right at the fork in the road, and at the next church take a left. At the roundabout take a right; The complex is on the left, beside the football pitches); Tel: 2301458; Fax: 2301464; Website: www.monkstownpool.com

**Open:** All year; Mon–Fri 3.45–4.30pm, 6.45–7.30pm; Sat 10am–6pm; Sun 11am–6pm; Call for this year's summer camp details ▪ **Charge:** Child €1.30; Adult €3.55; Entrance fee for swimming pool; A block of 10 swimming lessons costs €44; Prices for summer camps and other activities on request ▪ **Suitable for ages:** All ▪ **Car parking:** Free ▪ **Bus routes:** 7, 7A, 45, 46A, 75.
**Sports:** swimming, gym

A recently refurbished pool and gym, run by Dublin City Council. The centre has two pools: the learner pool, which is 60cm deep, is suitable for boys and girls up to about 6 years old, or until they are confident in deeper water. Teenagers must be 16 to use the gym or the lanes for swimming sessions. There are Parent and Toddler swims, and swimming classes for all abilities. Summer camps are run over five weeks, for 45 minutes a day, to teach children how to swim.

## 643 Mount Pleasant Tennis and Squash Club

The Square, Ranelagh, Dublin 6; Tel: 4973733 (Sharon Robinson), 086 2363491.

**Open:** All year; Mon–Sun 9am–6pm for children ▪ **Charge:**
Annual subscription €38 for members' children; €55 for
non-members' children; Coaching and camps are extra – prices
on request ▪ **Suitable for ages:** 6+ ▪ **Car parking:** Free ▪ **Bus
routes:** 11, 11A, 13B, 18, 44, 48A, 86.
**Sports:** badminton, squash, tennis
Children up to 16 can play up to 6pm on weekdays and at
weekends, although they must be supervised. Members from 6–8
years old can play until 5pm. Badminton coaching is on a Sunday
morning. Coaching and camps cost extra.

## 644 Mount Usher Gardens 🛒 🚼 ♿ €

Ashford, Co. Wicklow (signposted from Dublin–Rosslare road
(N11)); Tel: 2810877; E-mail: mount_usher.gardens@indigo.ie;
Website: www.mount-usher-gardens.com
**Open:** Apr–Sep; Mon–Sun 10.30am–5.30pm ▪ **Charge:** Child €5;
Adult €6 ▪ **Suitable for ages:** All ▪ **Car parking:** Free ▪ **Bus
routes:** Bus Éireann to Wicklow, or Rosslare.
Mount Usher Gardens are laid out along the banks of the Vartry
river. There are trees and shrubs from all over the world here, with
rhododendrons by the riverside. Small wooden suspension bridges
usually delight children, and you can have tea in the café at the
end.
✱ **TOP CHOICES: PARKS** ✱

## 645 Murrow Strand 🚻

Murrow, Wicklow, Co. Wicklow (follow the coast road from
Wicklow harbour. Murrow is signposted from just outside town).
**Open:** All year; Mon–Sun 24 hours ▪ **Charge:** Free ▪ **Suitable for
ages:** 5+ ▪ **Rail station:** Wicklow.
**Sports:** swimming
Murrow is a long strand just beyond Wicklow Harbour. Most of
the beach is covered in big stones, so it is a beach for swimming
rather than building sandcastles.

## 646 National Performing Arts School, Barrow St

The Factory rehearsal studios, 35a Barrow St, Dublin 4 (on the
bank of the Grand Canal, beside Boland's Mill, and 100 yards
from Kitty O'Shea's pub); Tel: 6684035; E-mail: info@npas.ie;
Website: www.npas.ie
**Open:** All year; call for new term times; Summer 2003 funk/street

dance workshops: Weekly 23 Jun–18 Aug, Mon–Fri 4–6pm;
Summer 2003 summer school: Weekly 23 Jun–18 Aug, Mon–Fri
10am–4pm ▪ **Charge:** Summer school €120 per week; Summer
funk/street dance workshop €65 per week; Other course prices on
request ▪ **Suitable for ages:** 4+ ▪ **Bus routes:** 1, 3, 5, 7, 7A, 8,
45, 46, 63, 84 ▪ **DART station:** Grand Canal Dock.
One of the top five drama schools in Dublin, offering singing,
dance and drama for tiny tots; ballet (Royal Academy of Dance)
from age 4; and music theatre, street dance, tap dance, hip hop
and funk dance from age 6. Performances are staged at the
Olympia Theatre, and NPAS has its own casting agency. For
summer 2003, there's a street dance/funk workshop for
12–20-yr-olds, and summer schools for 7–11-yr-olds and
12–18-yr-olds.
✱ **TOP CHOICES: SUMMER CAMPS** ✱ **TOP CHOICES: FOR
IMAGINATIVE KIDS** ✱

## 647 National Performing Arts School, Haddington Rd

St. Mary's School, Haddington Rd, Dublin 4; Tel: 6684035;
E-mail: info@npas.ie; Website: www.npas.ie
**Open:** All year; Call for individual class times; Mini summer
school: Weekly 25 Jun–23 Jul, Mon–Fri 10am–12.30pm ▪
**Charge:** Mini summer school 2003 €65 per child; Other course
prices on request ▪ **Suitable for ages:** 4+ ▪ **Bus routes:** 1, 3, 5,
7, 7A, 8, 45, 46, 63, 84 ▪ **DART station:** Grand Canal Dock.
One of the top five drama schools in Dublin, offering singing,
dance and drama for tiny tots; ballet (Royal Academy of Dance)
from age 4; music theatre, street dance, tap dance, hip hop and
funk dance from age 6. Performances are staged at the Olympia
Theatre, and NPAS has its own casting agency. In summer 2003
the school will run a 'mini summer school' for 4–6-yr-olds,
running in June and July.
✱ **TOP CHOICES: SUMMER CAMPS** ✱ **TOP CHOICES: FOR
IMAGINATIVE KIDS** ✱

## 648 National Print Museum 🚼 🍼 ♿

Garrison Chapel, Beggar's Bush Barracks, Haddington Rd, Dublin
4 (from Merrion Sq N, go down Mount St Lwr to Haddington Rd);
Tel: 6603770; Fax: 6673545; E-mail: npmuseum@iol.ie
**Open:** All year; May–Sep: Mon–Fri 10am–12.30pm, 2.30–5pm;
Sat/Sun/bank holidays 12–5pm; Oct–Apr: Tue/Thur/Sat–Sun

2–5pm ■ **Charge:** Child €1.90; Adult €3.17; Family €6.35 ■
**Suitable for ages:** 5+ ■ **Car parking:** Free ■ **Bus routes:** 5, 7, 7A, 8, 45.

All children enjoy printing, whether it is potato blocks and rubber stamps, or design software on a computer. The National Print Museum is the place to learn about the world of commercial printing, from assembling letters by hand for newspapers, to modern methods used today. You can see examples of 'Linotype' machines, and also how children's ruled copybooks are made. The museum is surrounded by the old military barracks, where the revolutionary Erskine Childers was executed in 1922, during the Civil War.

✱ TOP CHOICES: FOR AGES 5–10 ✱ TOP CHOICES: FOR INQUISITIVE KIDS ✱

## 649 National Sealife Centre 🛒 ♿ €

Strand Rd, Bray, Co. Wicklow (on the seafront); Tel: 2861299, 2866939; Fax: 2860562.

**Open:** All year 2. Mar–Dec; Jan–Feb: Sat–Sun 10am–5pm; Mar–Dec: Mon–Sun 10am–5pm ■ **Charge:** Child €5.50; Adult €8 ■ **Suitable for ages:** All ■ **Car parking:** Park on the seafront ■ **Bus routes:** 45, 45A, 84, 145, 146, 184, 185 ■ **DART station:** Bray.

The National Sealife Centre has over 20 displays and more than 100 different marine species, from shrimps and small sharks to eels. Feeding is at 3pm every day, and there are demonstrations, talks and special presentations. Young children love the touch pools, and older ones can watch the audio-visual show and use the touch-screen computers. FinZone, which involves wearing 3-D glasses, is due back in summer 2003.

✱ TOP CHOICES: BIRTHDAY PARTY IDEAS ✱ TOP CHOICES: FOR AGES 2–5 ✱ TOP CHOICES: FOR AGES 5–10 ✱ TOP CHOICES: FOR INQUISITIVE KIDS ✱

## 650 Newpark Music Centre

Newtownpark Ave, Blackrock, Co. Dublin; Tel: 2883740; Fax: 2883989; E-mail: newparkmusic@eircom.net; Website: www.newparkmusic.com

**Open:** All year; Classes Mon–Sat, some evening classes available ■ **Charge:** Various course fees and tuition fees; call for details ■ **Suitable for ages:** 4+ ■ **Bus routes:** 7A, 8, 45, 46, 46A, 63, 84, 114 ■ **Rail station:** Seapoint ■ **DART station:** Seapoint.

A long-established music school, which offers a 'gateway' to music for 4–7-yr-olds. Activities include singing, rhythm training, percussion playing, listening, note reading and writing, and introductions to various instruments. There is tuition available in piano, strings and woodwind, and students are encouraged to take part in Newpark concerts, festivals, chamber music, master classes and orchestral activities. The centre also has an instrument 'Try Before You Buy' scheme. Vocal training is available for over-25s, and there is a two-year 'Let's All Sing' course for 7–10-yr-olds, with public performances, and a youth choir for over-10s. Call for details of courses available in the 2003 summer school.

✱ TOP CHOICES: HOBBIES/ARTS AND CRAFTS ✱

## 651 Newpark School Sports Centre

Newtownpark Ave, Blackrock, Co. Dublin (halfway down Newtownpark Ave, between Blackrock and Leopardstown. Turn in close to Texaco station; The sports centre is at the back of the school); Tel: 2883720, 2833037; Fax: 2881250;
E-mail: newparksports@oceanfree.net;
Website: www.newparksportscentre.ie
**Open:** All year; Swimming pool: Mon–Fri 7am–8pm; Gymnastics: Fri–Sat, call for times; Call for details of this year's summer camps
▪ **Charge:** Child €3; Adult €3.50; Entry fee is for the swimming pool; Fees for classes and summer camps available on request ▪
**Suitable for ages:** All ▪ **Car parking:** Free ▪ **Bus routes:** 45, 46, 46A, 63, 75, 84, 114 ▪ **DART station:** Seapoint.
**Sports:** badminton, basketball, soccer, swimming, tennis, gymnastics
This sports centre is attached to Newpark Community School. There are public swims most evenings and at weekends. Parent-and-toddler sessions are held in the pool three mornings a week, and children's swimming lessons are held most days for ages 3+. There's a junior sports club for boys and girls aged 3–6, which combines swimming and gymnastics. Gymnastics classes for boys and girls aged 5+ are held on Fri and Sat. Summer camps combining swimming, gymnastics and basketball are held during the holidays.

✱ TOP CHOICES: SUMMER CAMPS ✱

## 652 Ní Dhubhghaill, Caitríona (Music Teacher)

Rathgar/Rathmines/Ranelagh, Dublin 6; Tel: 087 2211256.

**Open:** All year; Class times on request ▪ **Charge:** €25 per 30-minute class ▪ **Suitable for ages:** 7+.
Caitríona Ní Dhubhghaill provides musicianship, music theory and aural training, as well as classical piano tuition. Students can be prepared for RIAM and ABRSM exams.

## 653 Nolan School Of Music

2 Silver Acres, Grange Rd, Dublin 14; Tel: 4933730.
**Open:** All year; class times arranged to suit the individual ▪ **Charge:** Prices given on request ▪ **Suitable for ages:** 8+ ▪ **Bus routes:** 16, 116, 161.
Classes in keyboards, accordion, recorder, clarinet and saxophone are held here, for over-8s.

## 654 Norton, Betty Ann, Theatre School, Bray

The Mermaid Theatre, Wicklow County Arts Centre, Bray, Co. Wicklow (behind Bray Town Council offices); Tel: 4751913; Fax: 4751140; E-mail: bettyann.norton@iegateway.net; Website: www.bettyann-nortontheatreschool.com
**Open:** Sep–Jun, 3 x 10 week terms; Also summer course; Courses vary from 1 hour to 90 minutes weekly ▪ **Charge:** Summer courses from €115; Other course prices on request ▪ **Suitable for ages:** 4+ ▪ **Bus routes:** 45, 45A, 84, 133, 145, 146, 184, 185 ▪ **Rail station:** Bray ▪ **DART station:** Bray.
One of the best theatre schools in Dublin, it offers speech and drama for the very young, as well as music, mime, movement, puppetry and storytelling. Older children participate in *feiseanna* and are auditioned for radio, television, theatre and films when suitable parts appear. Teenagers can join the drama workshop, designed as an aid to personality development and confidence building. There are also introduction to stage craft and theatre studies courses. The school runs classes and courses in speech therapy, aiming to build confidence and creativity.
**✱ TOP CHOICES: SUMMER CAMPS ✱**

## 655 Norton, Betty Ann, Theatre School, Clonskeagh

David Lloyd Riverview Club, Beech Hill, Clonskeagh, Dublin 14; Tel: 4751913; Fax: 4751140;
E-mail: bettyann.norton@iegateway.net;
Website: www.bettyann-nortontheatreschool.com
**Open:** Sep–Jun, 3 x 10-week terms; Also summer course; Courses

vary from 1 hour to 90 minutes weekly ▪ **Charge:** Summer
courses from €115; Other course prices on request ▪ **Suitable for
ages:** 4+ ▪ **Bus routes:** 11, 11A/B.
See review for Norton, Betty Ann, Theatre School, Bray, above.
✷ **TOP CHOICES: SUMMER CAMPS** ✷

## 656 Norton, Betty Ann, Theatre School, Dún Laoghaire

York Rd Presbyterian Church Hall, Dún Laoghaire, Co. Dublin;
Tel: 4751913; Fax: 4751140;
E-mail: bettyann.norton@iegateway.net;
Website: www.bettyann-nortontheatreschool.com
**Open:** Sep–Jun, 3 x 10-week terms; Also summer course; Courses
vary from 1 hour to 90 minutes weekly ▪ **Charge:** Summer
courses from €115; Other course prices on request ▪ **Suitable for
ages:** 4+ ▪ **Bus routes:** 7, 7A, 46, 46X.
See review for Norton, Betty Ann, Theatre School, Bray, above.
✷ **TOP CHOICES: SUMMER CAMPS** ✷

## 657 Norton, Betty Ann, Theatre School, Rathmines

St. Louis High School, Charleville Rd, Rathmines, Dublin 6;
Tel: 4751913; Fax: 4751140;
E-mail: bettyann.norton@iegateway.net;
Website: www.bettyann-nortontheatreschool.com
**Open:** Sep–Jun, 3 x 10-week terms; Also summer course; Courses
vary from 1 hour to 90 minutes weekly ▪ **Charge:** Summer courses
from €115; Other course prices on request ▪ **Suitable for ages:** 4+
▪ **Bus routes:** 14A, 15, 15A/B/C/D/E/T/X, 65, 65B/C/X, 83.
See review for Norton, Betty Ann, Theatre School, Bray, above.
✷ **TOP CHOICES: SUMMER CAMPS** ✷

## 658 Nutgrove Shopping Centre 🛒 🎲 ☕ ♿

Nutgrove Ave, Dublin 14 (beside Loreto Park); Tel: 4933289
(centre), 4069949 (crèche).
**Open:** All year; Mon–Sat 8.30am–8.30pm ▪ **Charge:** Crèche €5
per child per hour, max 2-hour stay ▪ **Suitable for ages:** All ▪ **Car
parking:** Free ▪ **Bus routes:** 16, 16A, 17, 75.
This shopping centre has a big Argos, Tesco and Roches Stores.
Tesco's crèche has a drop-in facility for 2–6-yr-olds, and runs a
playgroup on weekday mornings.

### 659 O'Connell, Isabelle (Music Teacher)

Rathgar, Dublin 6; Tel: 087 7518969.
**Open:** All year; class times on request ▪ **Charge:** €30 per
40-minute class ▪ **Suitable for ages:** 5+.
Isabelle O'Connell gives tuition in classical piano, including
preparation for RIAM, LCM and TCL exams.

### 660 O'Donoghue, Christine, Ballet School

7 Greenmount Rd, Terenure, Dublin 6; Tel: 4906704.
**Open:** Sep–Jun; Mon–Fri, classes available to suit all ages and
abilities ▪ **Charge:** Fees on request ▪ **Suitable for ages:** 4+ ▪ **Car
parking:** Disc parking on street ▪ **Bus routes:** 15, 15A/B/D/E/F.
Forty-five minute classes are available for all ages and ability.
Contact the teacher for times and further information.

### 661 Old Belvedere Rugby Football Club

Anglesea Rd, Dublin 4; Contact: David Lorrigan; Tel: 6603378
(office), 6613788.
**Open:** Sep–Apr ▪ **Suitable for ages:** 6+ ▪ **Bus routes:** 7B/D, 10,
10A, 46, 46A, 58C, 118, 746.
**Sports:** rugby

### 662 Old Wesley Rugby Football Club

Donnybrook Rd, Dublin 4; Tel: 6689149.
**Open:** Sep–Apr ▪ **Suitable for ages:** 6+ ▪ **Car parking:** Free ▪
**Bus routes:** 7B, 10, 10A, 46, 46A, 58C, 84X, 118, 746.
**Sports:** rugby

### 663 Ormonde Cinemas ♿ €

Lwr Kilmacud Rd, Stillorgan, Co. Dublin (down a lane beside the
AIB bank at the Stillorgan Plaza, opposite the Stillorgan Shopping
Centre); Tel: 7074100; Fax: 2835656;
Website: www.ormondecinemas.com
**Open:** All year; Children's programmes: Mon–Sun before 7pm;
Kids' Club: Sat 11am ▪ **Charge:** Child €4.05; Adult €4.05;
Entry price before 5pm; Kids' Club €2.50 ▪ **Suitable for ages:**
3+ ▪ **Car parking:** Free ▪ **Bus routes:** 46, 46A, 63, 75, 84,
84X, 86.
A seven-screen cinema complex, with a Saturday morning Kids'
Club. Tickets are €2.50. Booking is available online and by WAP.

## 664 Paddocks Riding Centre

Woodside Rd, Sandyford, Co. Dublin; Tel: 2954278.
**Open:** All year; Mon–Sun 9am–9pm; Call for dates of this year's
summer camps ■ **Charge:** €16 per hour-long lesson; pony camp
and livery prices on request ■ **Suitable for ages:** 3+ ■ **Bus
routes:** 44, 44B.
**Sports:** horse-riding
Paddocks offers trekking in the Dublin mountains and lessons for
all standards. Livery, where they will keep your horse for you, is
also offered. There is an outdoor, floodlit, all-weather arena for
showjumping. Pony camps are run during the summer.

## 665 Palmerston Park

Palmerston Park, Dartry, Dublin 6; Tel: 4966290;
E-mail: parks.parks@dublincity.ie;
Website: www.dublincity.ie/parks
**Open:** All year; Mon–Fri 8.30am–dusk; Sat–Sun 9.30am–dusk ■
**Charge:** Free ■ **Suitable for ages:** All ■ **Car parking:** On-street
parking ■ **Bus routes:** 13B, 14, 14A.
Palmerston Park is set out in two connected spaces. One,
including a smallish pond, is surrounded by flower gardens and is
popular with older people. The other has an open grass space,
often used for soccer (although it is not meant to be). The bushes
surrounding the park are a joy for younger children for
hide-and-seek, and there's a very popular playground, mostly
used by the under-8s.
**★ TOP CHOICES: PLAYGROUNDS ★**

## 666 Pan Pan Theatre

The Old School House, 43 Upr George's St, Dún Laoghaire, Co.
Dublin Fax: 01-2300918 (events at various venues);
Tel: 2800544; Fax: 2300918; Website: www.panpantheatre.com
**Open:** Productions during the year; Call for details of this year's
summer camp ■ **Charge:** Events and workshops are often free;
Call for summer camp details ■ **Suitable for ages:** 5+.
Pan Pan Theatre put on shows throughout the year. They also run
events and workshops, sometimes suitable for children. In
association with the National Youth Theatre of the Deaf, they also
run a two-week summer project for deaf children.

## 667 Park Singers Choir

Dept of Education, Marlborough St, Dublin 1 (rehearsals);
Contact: Sean Creamer; Tel: 2802064, 087 6656353.
**Open:** All year; call for rehearsal times ▪ **Charge:** Tuition €30 per
year ▪ **Suitable for ages:** 8–18.
A 60-member all-girls choir, for ages 8–18. Entrance is by audition
only.
★ **TOP CHOICES: HOBBIES/ARTS AND CRAFTS** ★

## 668 Pavilion Theatre 🎭 ♿

Marine Rd, Dún Laoghaire, Co. Dublin (Marine Rd is a side-street
opposite Dún Laoghaire DART station); Tel: 2312929 (box office);
Website: www.paviliontheatre.ie
**Open:** All year; Mon–Sun, performances 3pm or 7pm; Call for
details ▪ **Charge:** Child €11; Adult €19; Approx. price for theatre
performances given; Family ticket €48 (2 adults and 2 children) ▪
**Suitable for ages:** 2+ ▪ **Car parking:** Parking at a discount rate
with theatre ticket ▪ **Bus routes:** 7, 7A/B, 11, 45A, 46A/X, 59,
111, 746 ▪ **Rail station:** Dún Laoghaire ▪ **DART station:** Dún
Laoghaire.
The Pavilion shows a varied programme throughout the year,
including music, cabaret, ballet, comedy and drama, with seasonal
shows for children. You can book a pre-theatre supper, through
the theatre itself, at the Forty Foot bar and restaurant in the same
building.
★ **TOP CHOICES: CHRISTMAS VISITS** ★

## 669 Pearse Museum and St. Enda's Park 🚼 🍴 ♿

St. Enda's Park, Grange Rd, Rathfarnham, Dublin 14 (in St. Enda's
Park, opposite Marlay Park); Tel: 4933053; Fax: 4936120;
Website: www.heritageireland.ie
**Open:** All year; Nov–Jan: Mon–Sun 10am–1pm, 2–4pm;
Feb–Apr: Mon–Sun 10am–1pm; May–Aug: Mon–Sun 10am–1pm,
2–5pm; Sep–Oct: Mon–Sun 12–5pm ▪ **Charge:** Free ▪ **Suitable
for ages:** All ▪ **Car parking:** Free ▪ **Bus routes:** 16, 116, 161.
**Sports:** gaelic football, soccer
Once a school run by Patrick Pearse, the museum now houses an
audio-visual show, 'This Man Kept a School', and a nature-study
room with displays on Irish flora and fauna, which will appeal to
older children. The tea rooms are open during the summer

months, and at weekends during Oct and from Feb to Apr. The park itself is well worth visiting for its riverside walks, waterfall and walled garden. There's a nature trail that children can follow and also some playing fields. Concerts are sometimes held here in the summer.

**★ TOP CHOICES: FOR INQUISITIVE KIDS ★**

## 670 Pembroke Library 🖊️ 🖥️

Anglesea Rd, Dublin 4; Tel: 6689575;
Website: www.iol.ie/dublincitylibrary
**Open:** All year; Mon–Tue 1–8pm; Wed–Thur 10am–5pm; Fri–Sat 10am–1pm, 1.45–5pm ▪ **Charge:** Free ▪ **Suitable for ages:** All ▪ **Car parking:** Metered parking on street ▪ **Bus routes:** 5, 7, 8, 18, 45.

Activities include Happy Hour for Toddlers (Thur 10.30–11.30am) and Children's Art Class for 6–12-yr-olds (Sat 11.30am). There is wheelchair access into the library, but not upstairs, where the children's section is. Other seasonal arts-and-crafts activities, plus reading events for children, are organised throughout the year.

**★ TOP CHOICES: FOR AGES 2–5 ★**

## 671 People's Park 🚼 ♿ 🚶

George's St, Dún Laoghaire, Co. Dublin (between Glasthule and the Seafront; entrances on George's St and Queen's Rd);
Tel: 2054700 (ext. 4448); Fax: 2300125;
E-mail: environ@dlrcoco.ie; Website: www.dlrcoco.ie
**Open:** All year; 10am–dusk ▪ **Charge:** Free ▪ **Suitable for ages:** All ▪ **Car parking:** On-street parking ▪ **Bus routes:** 7, 7A, 45A, 46A, 59, 59A, 75, 111 ▪ **Rail station:** Dún Laoghaire ▪ **DART station:** Dún Laoghaire.

The People's Park is a small, Victorian-style park with gardens, enclosed by wrought-iron railings. A new adventure-style playground is very popular.

**★ TOP CHOICES: PLAYGROUNDS ★**

## 672 Pine Forest Arts Centre ♿ 🖊️ 🏭

Glencullen, Kilternan, Dublin 18; Tel: 2955595, 2941220;
Fax: 2941221; E-mail: pinefrst@iol.ie
**Open:** Mid-Jun–mid-Aug; Also a one-week course at Easter; Mon–Fri 10am–4pm ▪ **Charge:** Summer (2 weeks): €185 juniors, €210 seniors; Easter €115 juniors, €125 seniors ▪ **Suitable for ages:** 5+ ▪ **Car parking:** Free ▪ **Bus routes:** 44B.

Set in the Dublin mountains, this is an arts-and-crafts camp for kids of all ages. The centre is focused on creativity, but it is always fun and is equally popular with boys and girls. The junior course is for kids aged 5–12; the senior course is for ages 13–16. There are lots of outdoor activities, so wellies and outdoor clothing are needed. The centre runs a bus, with pick-up and set-down points in strategic locations across south Dublin, at an additional cost, though this bus does not run for the Easter course. The centre also runs schools days out and workshops.

**✱ TOP CHOICES: HOBBIES/ARTS AND CRAFTS ✱ TOP CHOICES: SUMMER CAMPS ✱ TOP CHOICES: FOR AGES 10+ ✱ TOP CHOICES: FOR IMAGINATIVE KIDS ✱**

## 673 Powerscourt House and Gardens

Powerscourt, Enniskerry, Co. Dublin (about half-a-mile south of Enniskerry village, or signposted from Bray Rd); Tel: 2046000; Website: www.powerscourt.ie

**Open:** All year; Mar–Oct: Mon–Sun 9.30am–5.30pm; Nov–Feb: Mon–Sun 9.30am–4.30pm; Closed 25–26 Dec ■ **Charge:** Child €2; Adult €4; Prices given are entrance fees to visit the gardens ■ **Suitable for ages:** All ■ **Car parking:** Free ■ **Bus routes:** 44, 85 ■ **DART station:** Bray.

Parts of Powerscourt House are open to the public, but the gardens are the real attraction. There are acres of woodland, with rivers and streams, picnic areas, a small Japanese garden and a pet cemetery. There is also a teashop, a garden centre and an Avoca Handweavers craft shop. Powerscourt also has one of the best Santas in south Dublin in the run-up to Christmas.

**✱ TOP CHOICES: PARKS ✱ TOP CHOICES: WALKS ✱**

## 674 Powerscourt Waterfall

Powerscourt, Enniskerry, Co. Wicklow (about 3 miles south of Enniskerry village, or signposted from Bray Rd); Tel: 2861717; Website: www.powerscourt.ie

**Open:** All year; Apr–Sep: Mon–Sun 9.30am–7pm; Oct–Mar: Mon–Sun 10.30am–4.30pm; Closed 2 weeks before Christmas, re-opens on St. Stephen's Day ■ **Charge:** Child €2.50; Adult €3.50; Entrance to waterfall ■ **Suitable for ages:** All ■ **Car parking:** Free.

Powerscourt Waterfall, at 130 metres, is the highest in Ireland or Britain, and is particularly impressive after heavy rain. The grounds are lovely, with lots of room for picnics. There is a great adventure playground just up from the waterfall. Children love playing beside the river at the bottom and great dams can be built. It is very dangerous to climb up the side of the waterfall – people have been killed doing this. A shop is open during the summer, selling coffee and sandwiches and so on.

**✱ TOP CHOICES: PARKS ✱ TOP CHOICES: PLAYGROUNDS ✱ TOP CHOICES: WALKS ✱**

## 675 Railway Union Sports Club

Willow Lodge, Park Ave, Dublin 4 (turn left from Sydney Parade onto Park Ave and the grounds are on the right); Tel: 2691783.
**Open:** All year; Mon–Sun 10am–6pm ▪ **Charge:** €15 to join the club and €10– €20 for each sport after that ▪ **Suitable for ages:** 6+ ▪ **Car parking:** Free ▪ **Bus routes:** 2, 3, 18 ▪ **DART station:** Sandymount.
**Sports:** cricket, hockey, soccer, tennis
A members-only outdoor sports club. There are several pitches and tennis courts, which have recently been refurbished. Various clubs run particular sports, and you must pay for each individually. Summer camps are also run separately by the different groups.

## 676 Rathcoole Boys Football Club

Forest Hill, Rathcoole, Co. Dublin; Tel: 4588593.
**Open:** Sep–May ▪ **Suitable for ages:** 7+ ▪ **Bus routes:** 69, 69X.
**Sports:** soccer

## 677 Rathdown Kenpo Club

Christ Church, Taney Rd, Dundrum, Co. Dublin (in Christ Church Taney Community Centre); Tel: 2986046;
E-mail: pdowling@hotmail.com;
Website: www.rathdownkenpo.com
**Open:** All year; Fri eves ▪ **Charge:** Child €2.50 ▪ **Suitable for ages:** 7+ ▪ **Bus routes:** 17, 44, 48A, 75 ▪ **LUAS station:** Dundrum.
**Sports:** martial arts
Friday evening Kenpo classes are available for boys and girls ages 7+.

## 678 Rathfarnham Castle 🍴 ♿

Rathfarnham, Dublin 14 (on the Rathfarnham bypass, between
Rathfarnham Rd and Grange Rd (near Rathfarnham village));
Tel: 4939462, 4939461 (tea rooms);
E-mail: rathfarnhamcastle@ealga.ie
**Open:** May–Oct; Mon–Sun 9.30am–5.30pm; last admission 1
hour before closing; Average length of visit is 45 mins; Tea rooms
are open all year round (winter times: Nov–Easter, Mon–Sun
10am–4pm) ▪ **Charge:** Child €1; Adult €2; Group/senior citizen
€1.25; Student €1; Family €5.50 ▪ **Suitable for ages:** All ▪ **Car
parking:** Free ▪ **Bus routes:** 16, 16A, 17, 47, 47A/B, 75.
An imposing castle, built around 1583, Rathfarnham Castle is
currently undergoing active conservation. Visitors can view
18th-century interiors and see the work in progress. The castle is
full of history, including a few ghosts, all of which is explained in
the guided tour. There's a very nice café here. The tea rooms
serve hot and cold lunches, and are accessible for visitors with
disabilities.

## 679 Rathmines Library 📁 🖥

157 Lwr Rathmines Rd, Dublin 6; Tel: 4973539;
Website: www.iol.ie/dublincitylibrary
**Open:** All year; Mon–Thur 10am–8pm; Fri–Sat 10am–5pm ▪
**Charge:** Free ▪ **Suitable for ages:** All ▪ **Car parking:** Metered
parking on street ▪ **Bus routes:** 14, 14A, 15, 15A, 83.
Happy Time Toddler Group is held on Thur, 10.30am–12pm, and
Tue, 10.30–11.30am. Children's Art Class, for 6–12-yr-olds, is on
Sat at 2pm. Other seasonal arts-and-crafts and reading events for
children are organised throughout the year.
**✱ TOP CHOICES: FOR AGES 0–2 ✱**

## 680 Raven's Rock 🔠

Glencree Rd, Curtlestown, Co. Dublin (three miles from
Enniskerry, on Glencree Rd to Curtlestown Woods; park in the car
park on the right).
**Open:** All year; 24 hrs a day ▪ **Charge:** Free ▪ **Suitable for ages:**
5+ ▪ **Car parking:** Free ▪ **Bus routes:** 44, 85 ▪ **DART station:**
Bray.
This is about a three-hour walk, and is not suitable for buggies.
Follow the Wicklow Way through Curtlestown Woods. After the
forest, leave the WW and turn right for the granite tor of Raven's

Rock. Continue across to the forest and go along the path between the old and new forests. When you meet fields, you can turn right and go down to the Kilmalin Pet Cemetery. You then need to walk back along the Glencree Rd to arrive back at the car park.

**★ TOP CHOICES: WALKS ★**

## 681 RDS (Royal Dublin Society)

Merrion Rd, Ballsbridge, Dublin 4 (from the city centre, head south towards Ballsbridge. The RDS is signposted and is off Merrion Rd, between Simmonscourt Rd and Anglesea Rd); Tel: 6680866; Fax: 6604014; E-mail: info@rds.ie; Website: www.rds.ie/
**Open:** All year; Mon–Sun, programme times vary for individual events; Funderland: 26 Dec–5 Jan, Mon–Sun 12–10pm ▪ **Charge:** Tickets (adult full price) approx. €25 for an exhibition; Up to €75 for a big name concert (eg Bruce Springsteen); Funderland €1 entrance and pay per ride, approx. €3 ▪ **Suitable for ages:** All ▪ **Car parking:** Anglesea Rd, or Simmonscourt Rd – €4 per hour ▪ **Bus routes:** 5, 7, 7A, 18, 45 ▪ **DART station:** Sandymount.

The Royal Dublin Society was founded in 1731 to promote and develop arts, science, agriculture and industry in Ireland. Most children are brought here at some stage, usually with their secondary school, to see some fair or exhibition. However, there are plenty of other things on offer throughout the year, including shows, recitals, concerts, seminars, lectures and competitions (such as the Young Science Writer competition, for 12–19-yr-olds). Some regular yearly events are: Fashion Week, *an Feis Ceoil*, the Dublin Horse Show, Esat BT Young Scientist and Technology Exhibition, and the Ideal Homes Show. The RDS is home to Funderland amusement park every Christmas.

## 682 Ringsend Library

Fitzwilliam St, Dublin 4; Tel: 6680063; Website: www.iol.ie/dublincitylibrary
**Open:** All year; Mon/Wed 12.45–4pm, 4.45–8pm; Tue/Thur/Sat 10am–1pm, 2–5pm ▪ **Charge:** Free ▪ **Suitable for ages:** All ▪ **Car parking:** On-street parking ▪ **Bus routes:** 3 ▪ **DART station:** Landsdowne Rd.

Happy Hour for Children is on Tue at 11am. Art classes for children are held on Sat mornings; call for details. Special events and activities are held throughout the year. Wheelchair access is proposed for 2003.

## 683 Ringsend Park ♨ ♿ 🧎

Ringsend Park, Dublin 4 (bounded by Pigeon House Rd and Irishtown Rd; Entrance also off Cambridge Rd); Tel: 6684364, 6682122; E-mail: parks.parks@dublincity.ie; Website: www.dublincity.ie/parks
**Open:** All year; Mon–Fri 8.30am–dusk; Sat–Sun 9.30am–dusk ▪ **Charge:** Free ▪ **Suitable for ages:** All ▪ **Car parking:** On-street parking ▪ **Bus routes:** 2, 3.
**Sports:** soccer, tennis
Ringsend Park is mainly used as a sports facility, for football and tennis. There is also a fairly large children's playground for younger ones. Dublin Public Parks Tennis league runs here in the summer.

## 684 Royal Irish Yacht Club

Harbour Rd, Dún Laoghaire, Co. Dublin; Tel: 2809452, 2842194 (boathouse); E-mail: riyc@indigo.ie
**Open:** Racing: all year, call for dates; Junior Sailing Course: June (call for this year's exact dates) Mon–Fri 9.30am–5pm ▪ **Charge:** Full membership per year is €1,100, as well as a one-off fee of €1,530 ▪ **Suitable for ages:** 10+ ▪ **Bus routes:** 45, 45A, 46A, 59, 59A, 75, 111, 746 ▪ **Rail station:** Dún Laoghaire ▪ **DART station:** Dún Laoghaire.
**Sports:** sailing
An eight-week junior sailing programme kicks off in June each year. It is for all levels, from beginners to the more advanced. Active dinghy sailing and racing also take place all year round. However, you must join the club, and you need to be proposed and seconded by existing members. It's expensive, and you must own your own dinghy.

## 685 Royal St. George Yacht Club

Dún Laoghaire, Co. Dublin; Tel: 2801811, 2801208 (boathouse), 2803457; Website: www.rsgyc.ie
**Open:** All year ▪ **Charge:** €1,200 membership fee and €1,100 annual subscription ▪ **Suitable for ages:** 5+ ▪ **Bus routes:** 45, 45A, 46A, 59, 59A, 75, 111, 746 ▪ **Rail station:** Dún Laoghaire ▪ **DART station:** Dún Laoghaire.
**Sports:** sailing
The St. George is a large club with a very busy junior sailing programme for members. However, it is only open to the children of members, it is very expensive, and you must be proposed and seconded by existing members. Children must own a dinghy.

SOUTH DUBLIN

## 686 St. Columba's Health and Fitness Club

College Rd, Rathfarnham, Dublin 16 (turn left at the top of Whitechurch Rd onto College Rd, which runs around the back of Marlay Park); Tel: 4938232, 2981562 (John Birch); E-mail: sccsports@eircom.net

**Open:** Children's kenpo classes run during school term times; Beginners Sat 3.30–4.30pm; Advanced Sat 4.30–5.30pm ▪ **Charge:** €30 a term for kenpo classes ▪ **Suitable for ages:** 7+ ▪ **Bus routes:** 15B, 16, 75.

**Sports:** martial arts

This is an adult's health and fitness club, with Saturday afternoon kenpo classes available for children.

## 687 St. Joseph's Boys Association Football Club

Pearse Park, Sallynoggin, Co. Dublin; Contact: Nigel Fitzpatrick; Tel: 2854394.

**Open:** Sep–May ▪ **Charge:** Small weekly fee ▪ **Suitable for ages:** 7+ ▪ **Bus routes:** 7, 7A, 45A, 55C, 111.

**Sports:** soccer

## 688 St. Mary's College Rugby Football Club

Templeville Rd, Templeogue, Dublin 6W; Contact: Gerard Delaney; Tel: 4556424, 4900440.

**Open:** Sep–Apr ▪ **Suitable for ages:** 6+ ▪ **Bus routes:** 15B/D, 49, 49A, 65.

**Sports:** rugby

## 689 Sallynoggin Library

Senior College Campus, Sallynoggin, Co. Dublin (west of Killiney and Dalkey); Tel: 2850127; Fax: 2850127; E-mail: libraries@dlrcoco.ie; Website: www.dlrcoco.ie/library

**Open:** All year; Tue/Thur 2–8pm; Wed 2–5pm; Fri 10am–1pm, 2–5pm; Closed on bank holidays ▪ **Charge:** Free ▪ **Suitable for ages:** All ▪ **Car parking:** Free ▪ **Bus routes:** 7, 7A, 111.

As well as having a regular children's library section, Sallynoggin Library also has the Ayò/Oware African board game (for children aged 7+, played Tue 6.30–7.30pm) and a Chess Club (for 7–14-yr-olds, Thur 6.30–7.30pm). Art workshops are also held throughout the year.

## 690 Samba Soccer School

RMC House, Kenilworth Sq N, Rathgar, Dublin 6; Tel: 4972455, 1890 702237; E-mail: info@sambasoccer.com;
Website: www.sambasoccer.com
**Open:** School holidays; call for this year's dates and times ▪
**Charge:** Child €85; €55 per week for Whiz Kids; €85 per week for older children ▪ **Suitable for ages:** 5+.
**Sports:** soccer

Samba Soccer School runs soccer holiday camps for boys and girls in venues all across Dublin. Each child receives a samba soccer pack, including shorts, top and a ball. Whiz kids start at age 4/5. There is one instructor for every eight children. Many venues have Brazilian coaches, who often claim to have played with, or known, some of the major stars!

**✷ TOP CHOICES: HOBBIES/ARTS AND CRAFTS ✷ TOP CHOICES: SUMMER CAMPS ✷ TOP CHOICES: FOR ENERGETIC KIDS ✷**

## 691 Sandycove/Forty Foot

Sandycove, Dún Laoghaire, Co. Dublin (turn left off Sandycove Rd for Sandycove Ave); Tel: 2054700 (ext. 4021).
**Open:** All year; Mon–Sun 24 hours ▪ **Charge:** Free ▪ **Suitable for ages:** All ▪ **Car parking:** On-street parking ▪ **Bus routes:** 7D, 59, 59A ▪ **DART station:** Sandycove.
**Sports:** diving, swimming

Sandycove is a tiny, sandy beach, and is popular with young children. It is great for paddling, being very safe and shallow, but you need to watch the dog poo. The Martello tower where Joyce lived is open to the public, and is now the James Joyce Museum. Just around the corner is the Forty Foot, a deep swimming hole which was for men only in the past, as many swam nude. Nude swimming is no longer allowed in the main area and most of the men have moved a little way down. The Forty Foot is only suitable for older children, as the water is very deep and you have to jump off rocks.

## 692 Sandycove Tennis and Squash Club

Elton Pk, Sandycove, Co. Dublin; Contact: Joan Patton; Tel: 2808769, 2809645.
**Open:** All year; Mon–Sun 9.30am–6pm (closed to juniors 1–2pm); Call for this year's camp dates ▪ **Charge:** €120 membership fee, plus €140 subscription a year; Squash is an

additional €50 per year ▪ **Suitable for ages:** 8+ ▪ **Car parking:** Free ▪ **Bus routes:** 7D, 59, 59A ▪ **DART station:** Sandycove. **Sports:** squash, tennis

Sandycove runs a busy programme for juniors all year, with leagues, tournaments and club afternoons. Camps run during school holidays.

## 693 Sandymount Strand

Sandymount, Dublin 4 (there are several car parks on Strand Rd, which can be reached from Sydney Parade or Gilford Rd). **Open:** All year; Mon–Sun 24 hours ▪ **Charge:** Free ▪ **Suitable for ages:** All ▪ **Car parking:** Free ▪ **Bus routes:** 2, 3 ▪ **DART station:** Sandymount.

Sandymount Strand is a huge sandy beach, which is great for a walk – or for a rollerblade along the coast path. Younger kids will also have fun with a bucket and spade. However, it is not good for swimming and is often visibly dirty. The tide goes out about half a mile, leaving a huge expanse of strand, which is particularly popular with dog walkers. There are ruins of old sea baths, as well as a closed Martello tower. There is quite a long walk, almost out to the famous red-and-white ESB towers at Poolbeg.

## 694 Seapoint 🚇

Blackrock, Co. Dublin (take a left onto Seafield Ave or Albany Ave from Monkstown Rd. Turn right or left at the end. It is best to park on Seapoint Ave); Tel: 2054700 (ext. 4021). **Open:** All year; Mon–Sun 24 hours ▪ **Charge:** Free ▪ **Suitable for ages:** All ▪ **Car parking:** Park on main road ▪ **Bus routes:** 4, 7A, 8 ▪ **DART station:** Seapoint. **Sports:** rowing/canoeing, swimming, windsurfing

Seapoint won a coveted Blue Flag beach award in 1999, but lost it again in 2002 due to the presence of faecal streptococci. The authorities are hoping to win the award back again. Assuming the water is clean, there is a good, deep swimming area close to the rocks. There is also plenty of opportunity for paddling along the strand. Seapoint is close to the small bird sanctuary at Booterstown, and there is usually plenty of bird life to be seen. Don't drive down the road to the beach, as it can be very difficult to get out again. It is best to park on the main road. No dogs are allowed from 1 June to 30 September, from 10.30am–7pm.

## 695 Seapoint Rugby Football Club

Churchview Rd, Killiney, Co. Dublin; Contact: Tom O'Higgins;
Tel: 2854112 (office), 2807687.
**Open:** Sep–Apr ▪ **Suitable for ages:** 6+ ▪ **Bus routes:** 59 ▪
**DART station:** Killiney.
**Sports:** rugby

## 696 Shanganagh Park 🦽

Coolevin, Shankill, Co. Dublin (off Kilbogget Park or Coolevin);
Tel: 2054700 (ext. 4448); E-mail: environ@dlrcoco.ie;
Website: www.dlrcoco.ie
**Open:** All year; Mon–Sun 10am–dusk ▪ **Charge:** Free ▪ **Suitable
for ages:** All ▪ **Car parking:** On-street parking ▪ **Bus routes:** 45A,
46, 84, 86, 111.
**Sports:** soccer, tennis, bowling
Shanganagh Park was formerly known as Tyrell's Land. The park
is divided by a railway line, although there is now a pedestrian
bridge over the line. The small space at Quinn's Rd houses a
football pitch as well as Shankill Tennis Club and Shankill
Bowling Club. Dublin Public Parks Tennis league runs here in the
summer.

## 697 Shankill Library ✎

Library Rd, Shankill, Co. Dublin; Tel: 2823081; Fax: 2824555;
E-mail: libraries@dlrcoco.ie; Website: www.dlrcoco.ie/library
**Open:** All year; Mon*/Wed/Fri/Sat* 10am–1pm, 2–5pm;
Tue/Thur 2–8pm (*Open alternate Mons and Sats, subject to
change around bank holidays) ▪ **Charge:** Free ▪ **Suitable for
ages:** All ▪ **Car parking:** Free ▪ **Bus routes:** 45, 45A, 84 ▪ **Rail
station:** Shankill ▪ **DART station:** Shankill.
The children's section here organises holiday and seasonal
activities throughout the year – book well in advance.

## 698 Shankill Tennis Club

Quinn's Rd, Shankill, Co. Dublin; Contact: Anne McEntaggart;
Tel: 2825400.
**Open:** All year; Mon–Fri 9am–1pm, 3–9pm; Sat–Sun 9am–6pm;
Kids must be off courts by 7pm ▪ **Charge:** €105 membership fee
plus €70 a year ▪ **Suitable for ages:** 6+ ▪ **Car parking:** Free ▪
**Bus routes:** 45, 45A, 84 ▪ **DART station:** Shankill.
**Sports:** tennis

The Dublin Public Parks Tennis league runs here in the summer. It has children's coaching at weekends during the rest of the year.

## 699 Sillybilly Learning Ltd 🛒 🏓

Christchurch Presbyterian Church Hall, Rathgar, Dublin 6; Foxrock Tullow Parish Hall, Brighton Rd, Foxrock, Dublin 18; Tel: 8535353; Fax: 8535953;
E-mail: enquiries@sillybillylearning.com
**Open:** All year; Thur (Rathgar); Mon (Foxrock); call for times ▪
**Charge:** Music on the Go: You are asked to pre-book 6 sessions (approx. €60) in advance; Party plan prices on request (e.g. Fairy Princess Party approx. €180 for 1 hour/ €250 for 2 hours) ▪
**Suitable for ages:** 4 months–4 years.

Sillybilly runs a programme of fun activities involving music, stories and play, for children from four months to four-and-a-half years. All the play equipment is supplied and set up in a local centre. A parent/guardian must be present and is encouraged to get involved – this is a great way of meeting other parents/minders of small children. For wheelchair access, call for details on individual venues. Sillybilly will also hold parties in your own home. You just have to provide the food. Party Plans: 1. Sillybilly party (half-an-hour): An entertainer comes to your house with puppets, games, a magic show and a bubble disco. 2. Fairy Princess Party (1 or 2 hours): Songs and stories from a costumed fairy, with games and a bubble disco. 3. Soldiers Party (half-an-hour or 2 hours): Sergeant Sillybilly comes and tells soldier stories and provides fun challenges for a half-hour. If you pass them you get a certificate. The two-hour party has a magic show, and kids get a mode balloon to take home. 4. Sports Party (2 hours): Equipment is provided – tunnels, obstacle courses, etc. 5. Disco Party (half-an-hour): Disco, games, a magic show and balloon modelling. 6. Baby party: Activity play zone provided, alongside stories, songs and bubbles.

✱ **TOP CHOICES: BIRTHDAY PARTY IDEAS** ✱ **TOP CHOICES: FOR AGES 0–2** ✱ **TOP CHOICES: FOR AGES 2–5** ✱

## 700 Silver Strand 🚽

Wicklow, Co. Wicklow (between Wicklow and Brittas Bay on the coast road).
**Open:** All year; Mon–Sun 24 hours ▪ **Charge:** Free ▪ **Suitable for ages:** All.

**Sports:** swimming

Silver Strand is a lovely, sandy stretch of beach that is often quite empty. On hot days you may have to pay a local farmer to park in a field overlooking the strand.

## 701 Smith, Ruth (Music Teacher)

Rathmines/Rathgar, Dublin 6; Tel: 086 3512718.
**Open:** All year; class times on request ▪ **Charge:** Fees on request ▪ **Suitable for ages:** 8+.
Ruth Smith teaches classical and traditional methods in piano and fiddle. RIAM exam preparation is provided.

## 702 Stagecoach Theatre, Blackrock

St. Philip and St. James Parish Centre, Cross Ave, Blackrock, Co. Dublin; Contact: Stagecoach, 3 Lwr Albert Rd, Sandycove, Co.Dublin; Tel: 2803336; Website: www.stagecoach.co.uk
**Open:** Call for term dates; 'Early Stages': Sun 2–3.30pm; Standard course: Sat 10am–1pm, 2.30–5.30pm ▪ **Charge:** 'Early Stages' (for 4–6-yr-olds) €200 per term; Standard course (3 hours per week of drama/dance/singing) €400 per term ▪ **Suitable for ages:** 4+ ▪ **Bus routes:** 7, 7A, 8 ▪ **DART station:** Booterstown.
An Irish franchise of a UK theatre school. Classes are three hours per week, consisting of an hour of jazz/modern dance, an hour of drama and an hour of singing. The classes are small – not more than fifteen children of a similar age group. Uniform and dance shoes are available from the school.

## 703 Stagecoach Theatre, Dalkey

Castle Park School, Dalkey, Co. Dublin; Contact: Stagecoach, 3 Lwr Albert Rd, Sandycove, Co.Dublin; Tel: 2803336; Website: www.stagecoach.co.uk
**Open:** Call for term dates; 'Early Stages': Sun 2–3.30pm; Standard course: Sat 10am–1pm, 2.30–5.30pm ▪ **Charge:** 'Early Stages' (for 4–6-yr-olds) €200 per term; Standard course (3 hours per week of drama/dance/singing) €400 per term ▪ **Suitable for ages:** 4+ ▪ **Bus routes:** 7D, 59, 59A ▪ **DART station:** Dalkey.
See review for Stagecoach Theatre, Blackrock, above.

## 704 Stannaway Park ♿

Kimmage, Dublin 12 (off Kylemore Rd); Tel: 4559946;
E-mail: parks.parks@dublincity.ie;

Website: www.dublincity.ie/parks
**Open:** All year; Mon–Fri 8.30am–dusk; Sat–Sun 9.30am–dusk ▪
**Charge:** Free ▪ **Suitable for ages:** 5+ ▪ **Car parking:** On-street
parking ▪ **Bus routes:** 15A, 17.
**Sports:** soccer
Stannaway is a largish park, built on a former quarry. It caters
mainly for soccer, with a number of playing fields. You can book
the fields or just turn up and try your luck.

## 705 Starstruck Stage School, Clonskeagh

David Lloyd Riverview Club, Beech Hill, Clonskeagh, Dublin 14;
Contact: Julian Benson; Tel: 6764377;
E-mail: starstruck@julian-benson.com;
Website: www.stageschool.com
**Open:** All year; 10-week terms; Sat; Usually 1 hour per week,
depending on course taken ▪ **Charge:** €100 per 10-week term for
1 hour per week; private tuition fees on request ▪ **Suitable for
ages:** 3+ ▪ **Bus routes:** 11, 11A/B.
A highly recommended performing arts school. Dance, voice and
drama coaching are offered for ages 3+. The course covers
modern, ballet, tap, jazz, Latin and hip hop dance, as well as
theatre acting and singing. The school has its own casting agency.
Call for details of this year's summer school.
✱ TOP CHOICES: HOBBIES/ARTS AND CRAFTS ✱ TOP CHOICES:
SUMMER CAMPS ✱

## 706 Starstruck Stage School, Foxrock

West Wood Club, Leopardstown Racecourse, Foxrock, Dublin 18;
Contact: Julian Benson; Tel: 6764377;
E-mail: starstruck@julian-benson.com;
Website: www.stageschool.com
**Open:** All year 10-week terms; Sat; Usually 1 hour per week,
depending on course taken ▪ **Charge:** €100 per 10-week term for
1 hour per week; Private tuition fees on request ▪ **Suitable for
ages:** 3+ ▪ **Bus routes:** 46A.
See review for Starstruck Stage School, Clonskeagh, above.
✱ TOP CHOICES: HOBBIES/ARTS AND CRAFTS ✱ TOP CHOICES:
SUMMER CAMPS ✱

## 707 Steele, Ann Marie (Music Teacher)

Stillorgan, Co. Dublin; Tel: 0863208295.
**Open:** All year; Class times on request ▪ **Charge:** €10 per

30-minute class ▪ **Suitable for ages:** 7+.
Ann Marie Steele teaches classical piano, and gives preparation for
RIAM exams.

## 708 Stillorgan Library

St. Laurence's Park, Stillorgan, Co. Dublin (opposite Stillorgan
Shopping Centre); Tel: 2889655; Fax: 2781794;
E-mail: libraries@dlrcoco.ie; Website: www.dlrcoco.ie/library
**Open:** All year; Mon/Fri–Sat 10am–1pm, 2–5pm; Tue–Thur,
10am–1pm, 2–8pm; Closed Sat–Mon on bank holiday weekends
▪ **Suitable for ages:** All ▪ **Car parking:** Free ▪ **Bus routes:** 6A,
46A, 75, 84, 86.
Regular activities include storytelling for 3–6-yr-olds (Fri
3.30–4pm). Special seasonal arts-and-crafts and reading events for
children are organised throughout the year.

## 709 Stillorgan Shopping Centre

Stillorgan, Co. Dublin (opposite Stillorgan Plaza (Ormonde
Cinemas)); Tel: 2886004, 087 6985957; Fax: 6761129;
E-mail: info@stillorgan-sc.ie;
Website: www.stillorganshoppingcentre.ie
**Open:** All year; Mon–Wed 9am–6pm; Thur–Fri 9am–9pm; Sat
9am–6pm; Sun 12–6pm; Crèche: Mon–Sat 10.30am–5.30pm ▪
**Charge:** Crèche: 1 hour €2.50, 90 minutes €3.75 ▪ **Suitable for
ages:** All ▪ **Car parking:** Free ▪ **Bus routes:** 11, 46, 46A/B, 63,
75, 84, 86.
Stillorgan Shopping Centre has a good range of children's and
babies' wear stores, including Adams, Benetton, Clark's Shoes and
Lifestyle Sports. The crèche has a drop-in facility for children from
age two-and-a-half.

## 710 Stillorgan Tae Kwon Do

St. Raphael's Primary School, Upr Kilmacud Rd, Stillorgan, Co.
Dublin; Contact: Daragh Bolton; Tel: 0872711767.
**Open:** All year; Tue/Thur evenings ▪ **Charge:** Monthly fees €30–
€40 ▪ **Suitable for ages:** 4+ ▪ **Bus routes:** 46A, 84.
**Sports:** martial arts
A new-style tae kwon do club, Little Dragons is designed for
children from age 4+, with an emphasis on character building.
Classes are held on Tuesday and Thursday evenings; call for
details.

## 711 Stratford Tennis Club

Grosvenor Sq, Rathmines, Dublin 6; Tel: 4962689, 087 2690102.
**Open:** All year; Mon–Sun 9am–9pm ▪ **Charge:** €70 per child for
a year's membership ▪ **Suitable for ages:** 5+ ▪ **Car parking:**
On-street parking ▪ **Bus routes:** 14, 14A, 15, 15A/B/C, 18, 83.
**Sports:** tennis
A small local tennis club. It holds supervised tennis for younger
children, and a few camps for 6–12-yr-olds during school holidays.
No junior inter-club tennis is held here.

## 712 Surfdock

Grand Canal Yard, South Dock Rd, Dublin 4; Tel: 6683945;
Website: www.surfdock.ie
**Open:** All year; Mon–Sun 10am–5pm; Call for dates of this year's
summer camps ▪ **Charge:** 4 3-hour sessions €200; Summer camp
prices on request ▪ **Suitable for ages:** 5+ ▪ **Car parking:**
On-street parking ▪ **Bus routes:** 3 ▪ **DART station:** Grand Canal
Dock.
**Sports:** sailing, windsurfing, kite boarding
Surfdock offers classes in windsurfing and dinghy sailing. All
equipment is provided, including wetsuits. Summer camps also
include kite boarding and other new water adventure sports, in
the Grand Canal Basin. Call for details.
✱ TOP CHOICES: HOBBIES/ARTS AND CRAFTS ✱ TOP CHOICES:
SUMMER CAMPS ✱ TOP CHOICES: FOR ENERGETIC KIDS ✱ TOP
CHOICES: FOR IMAGINATIVE KIDS ✱

## 713 Talbot, Rachel (Music Teacher)

Blackrock, Co. Dublin; Tel: 2842276.
**Open:** All year; class times on request ▪ **Charge:** Fees on request
▪ **Suitable for ages:** 6+.
Rachel Talbot gives piano tuition for children ages 6+. She also
provides recorder and classical voice tuition for children ages 8+,
and preparation for RIAM and ABRSM exams.

## 714 Templeogue College Swimming Pool ♿ 🅰

Templeville Rd, Dublin 6W (opposite St. Mary's rugby club);
Tel: 4901711; Fax: 4902854; E-mail: ftrenmond@iolfree.ie
**Open:** All year; Public swim: Mon–Fri 11am–12pm, 9.15–10pm;
Sat–Sun afternoons; Lessons: Mon–Fri 4–7pm ▪ **Charge:** Child

€2.30; Adult €3.80; Lessons cost extra ▪ **Suitable for ages:** All ▪
**Car parking:** Free ▪ **Bus routes:** 15, 15B.
**Sports:** swimming
A school swimming pool, open for limited public swims and
classes.

## 715 Templeogue Tennis Club

Templeogue Rd, Templeogue, Dublin 6W; Contact: Daragh
Murphy; Tel: 4902760.
**Open:** All year; Mon–Sun 9am–6pm ▪ **Charge:** Junior
membership €345 ▪ **Suitable for ages:** 10+ ▪ **Car parking:**
On-street parking ▪ **Bus routes:** 15B/D, 49, 49A, 65.
**Sports:** tennis
The junior section of this club is active all year, with coaching
available at an additional charge. Camps are run during the
holidays. All levels are catered for, from beginners to junior opens.

## 716 Terenure Library 🚼 ♿ 📝 🖥

Templeogue Rd, Dublin 6 (just past the junction with Terenure Rd
W, going towards Bushy Park); Tel: 4907035;
Website: www.iol.ie/dublincitylibrary
**Open:** All year; Mon/Wed 12.45–4pm, 4.45–8pm; Tue/Thur/Sat
10am–1pm, 2–5pm ▪ **Charge:** Free ▪ **Suitable for ages:** All ▪ **Car
parking:** Disc parking on street ▪ **Bus routes:** 15, 15A/B/D/E/F,
49, 49A/X, 65B.
Happy Hour for children is on Tue 11am–12pm, and a children's
book group is also held here; call for days and times. Other
seasonal arts-and-crafts and reading events for children are
organised throughout the year.

## 717 Terenure Rugby Football Club

Lakelands Park, Dublin 6W; Contact: Colette Jordan;
Tel: 4904283 (office), 087 2856441.
**Open:** Sep–Apr ▪ **Suitable for ages:** 6+ ▪ **Bus routes:** 15, 15B,
49, 65, 65B.
**Sports:** rugby

## 718 Three Rock Mountain 🚻

Woodside Rd, Barnaculla, Co. Dublin (turn right after Lamb
Doyle's pub onto Woodside Road. Continue to the Blue Light pub
in Barnaculla village and park here; walk back towards Dublin and

turn left uphill at the first side road, then take the first uphill left turn to go around the forest on the northern slopes. Take another left to ascend to the summit. After the summit turn left down a path and right at the T-junction).

**Open:** All year; Mon–Sun 24 hours ▪ **Charge:** Free ▪ **Suitable for ages:** 7+ ▪ **Car parking:** Free ▪ **Bus routes:** 44, 44B (Lamb Doyle's).

There are great views from the summit here – from Howth across the whole city and as far as the Sugar Loaf. Turn right at the edge of the forest, and then right again, and you will reach the main road. Turn left here and Lamb Doyle's pub is less than a mile away.

**✱ TOP CHOICES: WALKS ✱**

## 719 Tiggy's Art School

The Tarva, Green Rd, Dalkey, Co. Dublin; Tel: 2851514.
**Open:** Summer; Call for dates; Mon–Fri 10am–1pm ▪ **Charge:** €50 per week ▪ **Suitable for ages:** 4–10 ▪ **Bus routes:** 7D, 59, 59A ▪ **DART station:** Dalkey.

This is a summer art school, running weekly courses for 4–10-yr-olds. These include instruction in pottery, free moulding, watercolour, drawing and batik.

**✱ TOP CHOICES: HOBBIES/ARTS AND CRAFTS ✱ TOP CHOICES: SUMMER CAMPS ✱ TOP CHOICES: FOR IMAGINATIVE KIDS ✱**

## 720 Walkinstown Library

Percy French Rd, Dublin 12 (near the Esso service station); Tel: 4558159.
**Open:** All year; Mon/Wed 1–8pm; Tue/Thur 10am–5pm; Fri–Sat 10am–1pm, 2.15–5pm ▪ **Charge:** Free ▪ **Suitable for ages:** All ▪ **Car parking:** Free ▪ **Bus routes:** 19A, 150, 155.

There is a children's library here, which hosts an art class on Saturdays from 2.30–4pm. Other seasonal arts-and-crafts and reading events for children are organised throughout the year.

## 721 Walkinstown Park

Walkinstown Ave, Walkinstown, Dublin 12 (off Kylemore Rd, close to Crumlin Rd); Tel: 4503423;
E-mail: parks.parks@dublincity.ie;
Website: www.dublincity.ie/parks
**Open:** All year; Mon–Fri 8.30am–dusk; Sat–Sun 9.30am–dusk ▪ **Charge:** Free ▪ **Suitable for ages:** 2+ ▪ **Car parking:** On-street parking ▪ **Bus routes:** 18, 56A.

**Sports:** gaelic football, hurling, soccer, tennis

Walkinstown is a large park, mainly laid out for sports, including GAA, soccer and tennis. However, the overhead cables take away from its attractiveness, as well restricting development. Dublin Public Parks Tennis league runs here in the summer.

## 722 Walsh, Owen (Music Teacher)

Stillorgan, Co. Dublin; Tel: 2886134.

**Open:** All year; Class times on request ▪ **Charge:** Fees on request ▪ **Suitable for ages:** 7+.

Piano tuition is given by Owen Walsh in classical, jazz, traditional and world genres. Students are especially encouraged towards performing in public. preparation is given for TCL, ABRSM and LCM exams.

## 723 Wanderers Rugby Football Club

Lansdowne Rd, Dublin 4; Contact: Bernard McCarthy; Tel: 6606393 (office), 2605969.

**Open:** Sep–Apr ▪ **Suitable for ages:** 6+ ▪ **Bus routes:** 5, 7, 7A, 46 ▪ **DART station:** Landsdowne Rd.

**Sports:** rugby

## 724 Wei Chi Kung Fu, Blackrock

Newpark Sports Centre, Newpark School, Newtownpark Ave, Blackrock, Co. Dublin; Contact: Paul Moran; Tel: 6211640.

**Open:** All year; Mon–Fri evenings; Sat afternoons ▪ **Charge:** €55 per term ▪ **Suitable for ages:** 7+ ▪ **Bus routes:** 45, 46A/E, 63, 75, 84, 114.

**Sports:** martial arts

Kung Fu classes are available for ages 7+ on Saturday afternoons and weekday evenings; call for details.

## 725 West Wood, Leopardstown (Sports Club)

Leopardstown Racecourse, Foxrock, Dublin 18 (in the grounds of Leopardstown racecourse); Tel: 8530353, 2893208; Fax: 2892751; E-mail: info@westwood.ie; Website: www.westwood.ie

**Open:** All year; Mon–Fri 6am–11pm; Sat–Sun 8am–9pm; Call for this year's summer camp dates ▪ **Charge:** Junior membership €398 per year if parent is not a member; €300 if parent is a member; All activities are included in membership; Classes and summer camps are additional ▪ **Suitable for ages:** All ▪ **Car parking:** Free ▪ **Bus routes:** 46A.

**Sports:** badminton, martial arts, squash, swimming, tennis, gym, spinning, circuit, step, aerobics

A private members' club with two swimming pools, including a smaller children's pool. Swimming classes for children usually run for 12 weeks. Classes are held from complete beginner level to national competition level. FitZone has teen fitness classes, along with a teen gym. Other classes include spinning, circuit, step and aerobics. Younger members can also enjoy the special ball play room. Birthday parties can be booked for members and non-members.

✱ **TOP CHOICES: BIRTHDAY PARTY IDEAS** ✱ **TOP CHOICES: SPORTS FACILITIES** ✱

## 726 Whitechurch Library

Taylor's Lane, Rathfarnham, Dublin 16; Tel: 4930199; E-mail: libraries@sdcc.ie; Website: www.sdcc.ie/library

**Open:** All year except Aug; Mon 6–8pm; Wed–Thur 1–5pm; Closed on bank holidays ▪ **Charge:** Free ▪ **Suitable for ages:** All ▪ **Car parking:** Free ▪ **Bus routes:** 15C, 161.

Whitechurch includes a children's library. Some arts-and-crafts activities and reading events are organised throughout the year.

## 727 Willie Pearse Park

Windmill Rd, Crumlin, Dublin 12 (bounded by Kildare Rd, St. Mary's Rd and St. Agnes Rd); Tel: 4542555, 4561608; E-mail: parks.parks@dublincity.ie; Website: www.dublincity.ie/parks

**Open:** All year; Mon–Fri 8.30am–dusk; Sat–Sun 9.30am–dusk ▪ **Charge:** Free ▪ **Suitable for ages:** All ▪ **Car parking:** On-street parking ▪ **Bus routes:** 17, 18, 150.

**Sports:** gaelic football, hurling, soccer

This park used to be solely devoted to sports grounds, but a playground was added in the 1990s, and it is now more popular with families. Situated beside Crumlin swimming pool, it is often used by children on their way in or out of the pool.

## 728 Wind & Wave Water Sports

16A The Crescent, Monkstown, Co. Dublin (classes at back of West Pier, Salthill); Tel: 2844177.

**Open:** All year; Sat/Sun, call for times; Holiday camps: Mon–Fri
10am–5pm, call for this year's dates ▪ **Charge:** 6-hour course
€120; 8 hours €160; Holiday camp fees on request ▪ **Suitable for
ages:** 12+ ▪ **Car parking:** On-street parking ▪ **Bus routes:** 7, 7A
▪ **DART station:** Salthill.
**Sports:** sailing, windsurfing
Windsurfing classes, for over-12s, are held at weekends and
during school holidays.

## 729 Young European Strings

21 The Close, Cypress Downs, Dublin 6W; Tel: 4905263;
Fax: 4920355; E-mail: yes@iol.ie;
Website: www.youngeuropeanstrings.com
**Open:** All year; call for tuition and audition times ▪ **Charge:** Fees
on request ▪ **Suitable for ages:** 3+.
String tuition is available here for tiny tots and older children.
There are also orchestra classes for over-12s who want to aim for a
professional career (available by audition). YES tour outside the
country and stage a production every two-and-a-half years.
✱ **TOP CHOICES: HOBBIES/ARTS AND CRAFTS** ✱

# Places to eat

## 730 The Bistro Ocean Bar and Restaurant

The Millennium Tower, Charlotte's Quay Dock, Ringsend, Dublin
4 (at foot of apartment complex at the junction of Pearse St and
Ringsend Rd); Tel: 6688862; Fax: 6677435.
**Open:** All year; Mon–Sun 12.30–10pm ▪ **Charge:** €20 on average
for adults ▪ **Suitable for ages:** All ▪ **Car parking:** On-street
parking ▪ **Bus routes:** 2, 3.
The Bistro's location on the waterfront at Ringsend is great in
summer, when you can eat outside. It's really only child-friendly
for weekend brunch. High-chairs are available and the menu is
pretty child-friendly, with wedges, pizzettas, spring rolls, and so
on.

## 731 Bistro One

3 Brighton Road, Foxrock Village, Dublin 18 (turn left at end of
Westminster Rd, or right at exit of Leopardstown golf course);
Tel: 2897711; Fax: 2899858.

**Open:** All year; Tue–Sat 7–11pm ■ **Charge:** €15 on average for adult ■ **Suitable for ages:** 5+ ■ **Car parking:** On-street parking ■ **Bus routes:** 63, 86.

Older children are welcome in this Mediterranean-style restaurant. It's on the first floor, so you'll have to battle with your buggy.

## 732 Bits & Pizzas 🧺 ♿

15 Patrick St, Dún Laoghaire, Co. Dublin (between Tivoli Rd and George's St); Tel: 2842411; Fax: 2301603; E-mail: pizza@indigo.ie

**Open:** All year; Mon–Sun 12pm–12am ■ **Charge:** €10 on average for adult ■ **Suitable for ages:** All ■ **Car parking:** On-street parking ■ **Bus routes:** 45A, 46A, 59, 59A, 7, 7A, 75, 111 ■ **Rail station:** Dún Laoghaire ■ **DART station:** Dún Laoghaire.

An Italian restaurant popular with families, particularly on a Sunday. There are plenty of high chairs, but mention you need one when you book. There is no separate kids' menu, but a plain pasta and cheese pizza is available.

**★ TOP CHOICES: CHILD FRIENDLY RESTAURANTS ★**

## 733 The Dropping Well ♿

The Dropping Well, Milltown, Dublin 6 (at Classon bridge, between Milltown Rd and Churchtown Rd); Tel: 4973969; Fax: 4979882.

**Open:** All year; Mon–Sun 11am–11.30pm ■ **Charge:** €5 on average for kids; €12 on average for adult ■ **Suitable for ages:** 2+ ■ **Car parking:** Free ■ **Bus routes:** 14, 14A.

A large, well-known pub on the Dodder Walk, the Dropping Well is popular with families for traditional Sunday lunch until 7pm. A kids' menu or half portions are available, and there are a few high-chairs.

## 734 Eddie Rockets Diner 🧺 ♿ 🍴

284 Rathmines Rd Lwr, Dublin 6, Tel: 4973582; 62 Stillorgan Shopping Centre, Co. Dublin, Tel: 6703893; 17 Main St, Donnybrook, Dublin 4, Tel: 2601090; 3–4 Terenure Place, Dublin 6, Tel: 4926462; 22 Main St, Blackrock, Co. Dublin, Tel: 2835187; Nutgrove Shopping Centre, Rathfarnham, Dublin 14, Tel: 4932593; Contact: Valerie Crowley for party bookings, Tel: 6797340; Website: www.eddierockets.ie

**Open:** All year 2.; Sun–Wed 9am–1am; Thur–Sat 9am–4am; Terenure and Stillorgan open daily at 11am; Nutgrove closes at

11pm (Sat 12am) ▪ **Charge:** Kids form €5 for meal and drink; Adults €10 for burger, fries and drink ▪ **Suitable for ages:** All ▪ **Bus routes:** All city centre buses ▪ **Rail station:** Tara St ▪ **DART station:** Tara St.

Eddie Rockets is a chain of American-diner-style cafés, famous for their burgers and fries. There's a kids' menu, and kids get a free goodie bag with their meal. All of these branches have booths for sitting in, but they also have high-chairs. They do much better milkshakes and malts than the bigger fast-food chains. Kids love them.

✱ TOP CHOICES: BIRTHDAY PARTY IDEAS ✱

## 735 Forty Foot

The Pavilion, Dún Laoghaire, Co. Dublin (on the waterfront, close to the ferry terminal); Tel: 2842982.

**Open:** All year; Mon–Sun 6–10pm ▪ **Charge:** €25 on average for adult ▪ **Suitable for ages:** All ▪ **Car parking:** On-street parking ▪ **Bus routes:** 7, 7A, 45A, 46A, 59, 59A, 75, 111 ▪ **Rail station:** Dún Laoghaire ▪ **DART station:** Dún Laoghaire.

This is a brilliant location, with large windows overlooking the bay, surrounded by external decking where you can walk up and down with children if they get fed up! It is quite expensive, but there's a kids' menu for Sunday lunch. It is popular as a pre-theatre venue for the Pavilion Theatre, who can book the restaurant when you book your tickets. High-chairs are provided. There is also a bar downstairs.

## 736 FXB Restaurant 🛒 ♿

3a The Crescent, Monkstown, Co. Dublin (across from Monkstown Church); Tel: 2846187; Fax: 2845713.

**Open:** All year; Mon–Sat 6–11pm; Sun 4–11pm ▪ **Charge:** Kids' starters €1.90 and main courses €7.50; €25 on average for adult ▪ **Suitable for ages:** All ▪ **Car parking:** On-street parking ▪ **Bus routes:** 7A.

A children's menu is available until 7pm, and children are not really encouraged after this time. FXB is probably most popular with families on a Sunday, from 4–7pm. High-chairs are available.

## 737 Little Venice

Monkstown Rd, Monkstown, Co. Dublin (over Spar, opposite Goggin's pub in Monkstown); Tel: 2302491.

**Open:** All year; Mon–Sun 12–11pm ▪ **Charge:** €7.55 for kids;

€12 on average for adults ▪ **Suitable for ages:** 2+ ▪ **Car parking:**
On-street parking ▪ **Bus routes:** 7A.

This restaurant is child-friendly in the afternoons and early
evenings, with a kids' menu and high-chairs. It is popular with
families on a Sunday. The stairs can be tricky with a buggy.

## 738 Luigi Malone's Restaurant

1 Lwr Kilmacud Rd, Stillorgan, Co. Dublin (close to Stillorgan
Shopping Centre and the Ormonde Cinema, it is situated on the
first floor of the building which also contains the Millhouse pub);
Tel: 2786024; Fax: 2786028; E-mail: info@luigimalones.com;
Website: www.luigimalones.com

**Open:** All year; Mon–Sun 12–11pm ▪ **Charge:** €7.50 for kids'
menu; €15 on average for adults ▪ **Suitable for ages:** 2+ ▪ **Car
parking:** On-street parking ▪ **Bus routes:** 10A, 11, 11A, 46A/C,
63, 84, 115, 116, 118, 746.

Luigi Malone's is child-friendly up to 7pm, after which it becomes
quite boisterous, with cocktails on the go. A children's menu is
available, as are high-chairs.

✱ **TOP CHOICES: CHILD FRIENDLY RESTAURANTS** ✱

## 739 Outlaws

62 Upr George's St, Dún Laoghaire, Co. Dublin (on the right past
the shopping centre, before People's Park); Tel: 2842817.

**Open:** All year; Mon–Sun 6–11pm ▪ **Charge:** €4.10– €5.50 for
kids; €30 on average for adults ▪ **Suitable for ages:** All ▪ **Car
parking:** On-street parking ▪ **Bus routes:** 7, 7A, 45A, 46A, 59,
59A, 75, 111 ▪ **Rail station:** Dún Laoghaire ▪ **DART station:** Dún
Laoghaire.

Outlaws specialises in American/Mexican food. Children are very
welcome and there are high-chairs and a kids' menu until late.

## 740 Palmer's, Kilternan

The Golden Ball, Kilternan, Co. Dublin (on the Enniskerry road,
just outside Kilternan); Tel: 2959349; Fax: 2959349.

**Open:** All year; Tue–Sat 5–11pm; Sun 1–4pm ▪ **Charge:** kids
from €4.50; €15 on average for adults ▪ **Suitable for ages:** All ▪
**Car parking:** Free ▪ **Bus routes:** 44, 63, 118.

A good pub restaurant, popular for Sunday lunch, with a relaxed
atmosphere and lots of children running around. A kids' menu is
available, as are high-chairs.

## 741 Pierre's Bistro ♿

Terenure Place, Terenure, Dublin 6W (on Terenure crossroads, opposte Cripps footwear); Tel: 4921839.

**Open:** All year; Breakfast 7.30am–12pm; Lunch 12–5.30pm; Dinner Wed–Sat 5.30–10pm; Sunday brunch 10am–5.30pm ▪ **Charge:** €12 on average for adult ▪ **Suitable for ages:** 5+ ▪ **Car parking:** On-street parking ▪ **Bus routes:** 15, 15A/B/D/E/F, 16, 16A, 17, 49A, 65B.

A small local restaurant, serving half portions for children and quite good for Sunday brunch for the over-5s. There is a garden which can take up to ten people and is lovely on a sunny afternoon. No high-chairs are available.

## 742 Roly's Bistro ♿

7 Ballsbridge Tce, Dublin 4 (between the RDS and Herbert Park); Tel: 6682611; Fax: 6608535.

**Open:** All year; Mon–Sun 12–3pm, 6–10pm ▪ **Charge:** Over €30 on average for adults ▪ **Suitable for ages:** 5+ ▪ **Car parking:** On-street parking ▪ **Bus routes:** 5, 7, 7A, 18, 45, 46 ▪ **DART station:** Landsdowne Rd.

Roly's is one of Dublin's busiest restaurants. It is popular with families, particularly for a special Sunday lunch, but it is quite pricey. You need to book at least a week in advance. There are no child menus or half portions, although two children can share a main course. High chairs are not provided.

## 743 Tribeca Restaurant ♿

65 Ranelagh, Dublin 6 (on the main road, past the triangle and close to Ulster Bank); Tel: 4974174; Fax: 4911584.

**Open:** All year; Lunch: Mon–Fri 12–3.30pm; Dinner: Mon–Sun 6.30–10.30pm; Late opening Fri until 11pm; Brunch Sat–Sun 11am–4pm ▪ **Charge:** €30 on average for adult ▪ **Suitable for ages:** 5+ ▪ **Car parking:** On-street parking ▪ **Bus routes:** 11, 11A, 13B, 18, 44, 48A, 86.

Children are welcome in this busy restaurant in the afternoon and early evening. There are two high-chairs, but no kids' menu or half portions available. Tribeca is popular for Sunday brunch, but you have to take your chances on getting a table as there's no booking in advance.

## 744 Valparaiso

99 Monkstown Rd, Monkstown, Co. Dublin (over Goggin's pub);
Tel: 2801992.
**Open:** All year; Mon–Sun 6–11pm ▪ **Charge:** €15 on average for
adults ▪ **Suitable for ages:** 5+ ▪ **Car parking:** On-street parking ▪
**Bus routes:** 7A.
A Spanish restaurant which welcomes children and serves half
portions, though there is no children's menu. They don't have any
high-chairs.

# Party Services

## 745 Abbey Bouncing Castles 🎈

Tel: 6271938, 087 2433704.
**Open:** All year ▪ **Charge:** €90 for a day's hire ▪ **Suitable for ages:** 4+.
Abbey have a 12 feet x 12 feet bouncy castle available, with rain cover.

## 746 ABC Bouncing Castles 🎈

Tel: 2828927, 087 2060223.
**Open:** All year ▪ **Charge:** Bouncy castles from €85 per day ▪ **Suitable for ages:** 4+.
ABC have two castles available: 12 feet x 12 feet, suitable for 4–10-yr-olds; and 12 feet x 14 feet, suitable for children up to 14 years old. Rain covers are also available.

## 747 Ace One Stop Party Shop 🎈

Neilson Centre, Monastery Rd, Clondalkin, Dublin 22/24 (can hire goods to any area); Tel: 4640220;
Website: www.aceonestoppartyshop.com
**Open:** All year; Mon–Tue 10.30am–5.30pm; Wed 10.30am–2pm; Thur 10.30am–7pm; Fri 10.30am–8.30pm; Sat 10.30am–6.30pm ▪ **Charge:** Prices on request. ▪ **Suitable for ages:** All.
This shop has a wide range of helium balloons, decorations, etc., which you can buy over the counter. They will also come and decorate a venue for you. They carry a wider range of themed party ware than you will find in supermarkets. The shop hires costumes out to adults only, but they do have wigs, face paints and accessories, especially at Halloween. They can also supply bouncy castles, and will recommend a DJ for a disco.

## 748 Adams Bouncing Castles 🎈

All areas; Tel: 086 6033595, 8347963.
**Open:** All year ▪ **Charge:** Prices from €75 for a day's hire ▪ **Suitable for ages:** 4+.
Adams have a 12-feet x 12-feet bouncy castle available, suitable for 4–10-yr-olds.

## 749 Big Foot Bouncing Castles 👷

Tel: 1890 770077 (Lo-call), 087 2541032;
Website: www.bigfootbouncingcastles.com
**Open:** All year ■ **Charge:** Bouncy castles prices start at €75 per day, and go up to €350 for the Gladiator Jousting Bed ■ **Suitable for ages:** 4+.
Big Foot have loads of castles available, including some that have slides or can be filled with balls. There are also big (18-feet x 18-feet) ones for teenagers.

## 750 Bounce For Fun Party Services 👷

Tel: 086 8444970.
**Open:** All year ■ **Charge:** Bouncy castles from €80 per day; face painting from €70; catering prices on request ■ **Suitable for ages:** 4+.
Two bouncy castles are available: a 12-feet x 12-feet one, suitable for 4–10-yr-olds; and a 15-feet x 15-feet one, for children up to 14 years old. There is also an inflatable slide, for €150 per day. Face painting is available, from €70 for 15 children (a bargain!). This company also does catering for parties – prices and menus on request.

## 751 Clown Zone 👷

Covers all the Dublin area; Contact: Rachel; Tel: 086 8484853, 8684201.
**Open:** All year ■ **Charge:** Prices on request ■ **Suitable for ages:** 2+.
Clowns can come to your home and do face painting, balloon modelling and all sorts of fun and games. Clown Zone also runs clown workshops, suitable for all ages.
**✱ TOP CHOICES: BIRTHDAY PARTY VENUES ✱**

## 752 GC Bouncing Castles 👷

Tel: 086 8104215.
**Open:** All year ■ **Charge:** Prices on request ■ **Suitable for ages:** 4+.
GC have a 12-feet x 12-feet bouncy castle available all year, and also a larger castle with a slide.

## 753 Hire All Party Hire 📷

Delivers to anywhere in the Dublin area; Tel: 2953821;
Fax: 2953011; E-mail: hireall@partyhire.ie;
Website: www.partyhire.ie
**Open:** All year; Hire terms are for 48 hours ■ **Charge:** Prices on
request ■ **Suitable for ages:** 2+.
This company hires out tableware and furniture, including
children's furniture for family occasions, weddings, birthdays,
communions, confirmations, etc. For children's parties there are
kiddies' chairs in either blue or pink (€1.40 each to hire), and
adult benches which, placed side-by-side, make perfect kiddies'
tables (from €4.19 each). Baby high chairs are also supplied
(€23.50). Hire terms are for 48 hours; VAT, delivery and collection
are additional.

## 754 Jenny's Bouncing Castles 📷

Tel: 087 2899596.
■ **Charge:** €100 for a day's hire ■ **Suitable for ages:** 4+.
Jenny's have a 12-feet x 12-feet bouncy castle, available all year.

## 755 Leinster Bounce 📷

Covers the Dublin area; Tel: 4588369, 4589000;
Website: www.leinsterbounce.com
**Open:** All year ■ **Charge:** Prices on request ■ **Suitable for ages:**
4+.
Leinster Bounce have all sorts of bouncy castles available, from big
to small. For small children there are inflatable castles you can fill
with balls (supplied), and for older kids there's mad stuff like
bungee pulls and sumo wrestling rings (ring to check what ages
they're suitable for). They can also supply party ware and
balloons.
**★ TOP CHOICES: BIRTHDAY PARTY VENUES ★**

## 756 Party Animals ✎ 📷

Covers the Dublin area; Contact: Saoirse; Tel: 087 9838503.
**Open:** All year ■ **Charge:** €120 per party ■ **Suitable for ages:**
2–10 years.
Party Animals provide three types of party entertainment in your
own home. Parties last from one hour to 90 minutes. 1. Clown
Party: Good for under-6s, a clown will come and have fun and
games with the children, including a magic show, balloon

modelling and face painting. 2. Princess Party: A costumed princess will do a glitter makeover on the party girls, and then have mini-karaoke and a disco. 3. Arts-and-Crafts Party: Popular with children up to 9/10 years old. Fun and games, as well as arts and crafts, including modelling with air-drying clay.

## 757 Party Castles

Tel: 086 8742491, 4517707.
**Open:** All year ▪ **Charge:** Prices from €75 for a day's hire ▪
**Suitable for ages:** 4+.
Two castles are available: a 12-feet x 12-feet one, suitable for 4–10-yr-olds; and a 15-feet x 15-feet one, suitable for children up to 14 years old. Rain covers are also available.

## 758 Táshí Party Services 🎈

Parties in your own home or partywear delivered to your door;
Contact: Sacha/June; Tel: 6210603, 086 8583321;
Website: www.tashi.ie
**Open:** All year; Slumber parties 6.30–9pm; Other parties arranged to suit ▪ **Charge:** €48 for a themed party box; Prices for parties on request ▪ **Suitable for ages:** 3-16.
Táshí Party Services is especially for girls. There are two types of junior party available for 3–7-yr-olds: the Princess Party and the Fairy Party. These include themed partywear, and a mini-makeover with costume jewellery and hair accessories. Táshí Teens parties are for 13–16-yr-olds. These also include mini-makeovers, with Táshí stencil tattoos, or you can have a slumber party. Táshí can supply tableware, including plates, cups, napkins, cutlery, straws, lootbags, candles, invitations, helium balloons, streamers, party hats, masks, etc. A themed box, eg. the Barbie Box, is €48 (with eight place settings).
**\* TOP CHOICES: BIRTHDAY PARTY VENUES \* TOP CHOICES: FOR AGES 10+ \***

# Organisations

## 759 An Óige - Irish Youth Hostel Association

61 Mountjoy St, Dublin 7; Tel: 8304555; Fax: 8305808;
E-mail: mailbox@anoige.ie; Website: www.irelandyha.org
- **Suitable for ages:** All.

An Óige aims to help all, but especially young people, to love and appreciate the countryside, mainly by providing simple youth-hostel accommodation. There are 34 youth hostels located throughout Ireland. You must be 16+ to join An Óige, but kids of any age can stay at the hostels, if accompanied by an adult.

## 760 Association of Irish Riding Establishments (AIRE)

11 Moyre Park, Newbridge, Co. Kildare; Tel: 045431584;
Website: www.aire.ie
**Open:** All year ■ **Charge:** Group lessons from €15 to €20 per hour on average; Individual lessons are more expensive but there is a discount for booking blocks of lessons ■ **Suitable for ages:** 3+.
**Sports:** horse-riding

AIRE is responsible for the inspection and registration of horse-riding schools and establishments in Ireland. All riding schools listed here have been inspected and approved by the association. Most of the schools offer a wide choice of riding facilities, and many have indoor and outdoor arenas. All have ponies available for lessons, and many also offer trekking and riding out. Many of the schools take children from 5 years and up, while 3–4-yr-olds are normally started on private lessons to get confidence on a lead reign before joining a class. Most of the riding schools then offer a combination of fun rides, riding out in the forest or hills, or even jumping and showing. Dressage is also popular in some of the clubs. Most also offer pony clubs in the summer and other school holidays, where children attend every day for a week or two. Prices quoted are for hourly lessons, and blocks of lessons usually come at a discount – call individual clubs for details.

## 761 Birdwatch Ireland

Ruttledge House, 8 Longford Pl, Monkstown, Co. Dublin;
Contact: Cormac Crowley (cormaccrowley@eircom.net);
Tel: 8436431, 8144878; Fax: 2804477;

E-mail: info@birdwatchireland.org

**Open:** All year; weekend walks organised ▪ **Charge:** Donations welcome ▪ **Suitable for ages:** 5+.

An independent body devoted to the conservation and protection of Ireland's birds and their habitats. Weekend walks and wildlife talks are organised in the Dublin area. Children under 14 must be accompanied by an adult.

## 762 Irish Amateur Boxing Association

National Stadium, South Circular Rd, Dublin 8; Tel: 4733192; E-mail: iaba@eircom.net

**Open:** All year ▪ **Charge:** Most clubs charge €1 or €2 per week ▪ **Suitable for ages:** 11+.

**Sports:** boxing

Boxing clubs usually take children from 11 years old. Parents must sign for permission for them to join, and all children must undergo a medical examination and wear protective headgear. All boxing clubs listed have Leinster Council IABA affiliation for 2002/2003. Call for locations, as these can change.

## 763 Cairde na Cruite

Tel: 2856345; Fax: 6768007; E-mail: cruit@harp.net; Website: www.harp.net/cnac/CnaC.htm

**Open:** Summer school, 30 Jun–5 Jul ▪ **Charge:** Call for summer 2003 camp fees ▪ **Suitable for ages:** 7+.

An organisation to promote and revive the interest in the Irish Harp, Cairde na Cruite holds regular sessions and concerts for harpers of all standards, and runs a harp-hire scheme. Children can start at age 7–8. Contact Cairde na Cruite for a list of teachers. A summer school is run during the Festival for Irish Harp (30 Jun–5 Jul, An Grianán, Termonfeckin, Co. Louth).

## 764 Catholic Guides of Ireland ✍

12 Clanwilliam Tce, Grand Canal Quay, Dublin 2; Tel: 6619566; Fax: 6765691; E-mail: nat.office@girlguidesireland.ie; Website: www.girlguidesireland.ie

**Open:** All year; Groups usually meet once per week, with outings and weekends away organised in school holidays ▪ **Charge:** Costs will include uniform and membership fee ▪ **Suitable for ages:** 5+.

A youth movement for girls and young women, providing 'training for life' through fun activities, adventures and challenges. Activities for 5–6-year-olds include crafts, collecting, drawing, games, drama, singing, storytelling, nature study and cooking. For older girls there are outdoor activities – including canoeing, lightweight camping, mountaineering and orienteering – as well as indoor activities – such as photography, gymnastics, drama, radio and debating – and service to the community. Contact them for details of your local group and for information on membership for children with disabilities.

**✱ TOP CHOICES: FOR SHY KIDS ✱**

## 765 Comhchoiste Náisiúnta na gColáistí Samhraidh

46 Kildare St, Dublin 2; Tel: 6790213; Fax: 066 9156348.
**Open:** Summer; Mon–Fri ▪ **Charge:** Fees include food, accommodation and lessons; Trips may be extra ▪ **Suitable for ages:** 11+.
CONCOS is a federation of over 46 Irish summer colleges, in gaeltacht as well as non-gaeltacht areas. Children from age 11/12 years learn Irish through classes, song, dance and activities, while staying in groups with a family. Children usually attend lessons in the mornings, and activities are arranged in the afternoons. There are *céilís* in the evenings, and at weekends.

## 766 Confederation of Peace Corps

52 Lower Rathmines rd, Dublin 6; Tel: 4964399; Fax: 4964399;
E-mail: peacecor@iol.ie;
Website: www.homepage.eircom.net/~peacecorps
▪ **Charge:** Membership fee and uniform cost ▪ **Suitable for ages:** 12+.
Peace corps involve young people in the community, with activities ranging from gardening to fundraising, and uniform to be worn. There are branches in Ballyfermot, North Wall, Brackenstown, Cabra, Rivervalley and Smithfield. Contact them for details of your local group and for information on membership for children with disabilities.

## 767 Cycling Ireland

619 North Circular Rd, Dublin 1; Tel: 8551522; Fax: 8551771;
E-mail: cyclingireland@eircom.net;
Website: www.cyclingireland.org
**Open:** Mar–Sep; Check individual clubs for meeting days and times ▪ **Charge:** Scale of fees ranging from €10 to €20 a year ▪ **Suitable for ages:** 10+.

**Sports:** cycling

Cycling Ireland oversees all Irish cycling clubs. A few take junior members, from about 10 years of age. Kids need to have their own bikes and helmets. The clubs also race competitively. Some of the clubs are sponsored, with gear provided for free. Ring the club secretaries for details of meeting places. The season runs from March to September, but many clubs run skills programmes on a Saturday morning throughout the year.

## 768 Dublin Parks Tennis League (KitKat)

142 Vernon Ave, Clontarf, Dublin 3; Tel: 8338711.
**Open:** Summer; Mon–Fri 10am–1pm; Rest of year Sat 10am–12pm ▪ **Charge:** Child €1; €10– €15 for five weeks in summer; €1 a week during year ▪ **Suitable for ages:** 6+.
**Sports:** tennis

The Dublin Public Parks Tennis League is run in conjunction with local authorities, and is sponsored by KitKat. It is run in nearly all large public parks with tennis courts – there are 69 parks in the scheme in Dublin. Run throughout the summer, most children will get about four hours a week of classes, though it varies depending on demand. Courses are also run on Saturdays throughout the year, in a more limited number of parks. The charge is usually nominal and sometimes racquets can be provided.

## 769 Football Association of Ireland

80 Merrion Sq S, Dublin 2; Tel: 6766864, 8731747 (Leinster), 8550922 (Brenfer north Dublin), 4571188 (south Dublin), 8721440 (Dublin district), 1890 653653 (summer camps); Fax: 6610931; Website: www.fai.ie
**Open:** All year ▪ **Charge:** €55 a week for the 7UP sponsored summer courses; Usually €2 a week for soccer during the year ▪
**Suitable for ages:** 8+.
**Sports:** soccer

There are three different leagues for Dublin School Boys' Football – a misnomer, as they all take girls too. The Leinster office should have the details. Most clubs have training on one night during the week and on a Saturday morning. During the summer the FAI runs a large number of summer camps, which are sponsored by 7UP. The courses are open to boys and girls aged 8–16, and generally run from 10am–4pm, Mon–Fri. The emphasis is on fun and recreation. Each child receives a full kit, football and boot bag, as well as free 7UP.

## 770 Foróige

Irish Farm Centre, Bluebell, Dublin 12; Tel: 4501122;
Fax: 4501941; E-mail: foroige@eircom.net;
Website: www.foroige.ie
▪ **Suitable for ages:** 10+.
Foróige provides a comprehensive range of youth work services
through the operation of Foróige clubs, local youth services, local
youth development projects and youth information centres. It
focuses on the 10–20 age group, and particularly on vulnerable
young people. Foróige deals with issues arising from poverty,
marginalisation and social exclusion, under-achievement at
school, early school leaving, youth crime, substance abuse and
family difficulties.

## 771 Cumann Luthchleas Gael/GAA

Croke Park, Dublin 3; Tel: 8363222; Fax: 8366420;
E-mail: info@gaa.ie; Website: www.gaa.ie
**Open:** All year ▪ **Charge:** Child €1; Small weekly charge ▪
**Suitable for ages:** 5+.
**Sports:** gaelic football, hurling, camogie, handball
The GAA is an umbrella organization covering hurling, Gaelic
football, camogie and handball. Most GAA clubs are open on
Saturday mornings. Some also have weekday evening coaching,
and most run summer courses. Charges are usually nominal, at
around €1/ €2 a week – call for individual club details.

## 772 Gael Linn

35 Dame St, Dublin 2; Tel: 6767283; Fax: 6767030;
E-mail: gaellinn@eircom.net
**Open:** All year; call for details of activities ▪ **Charge:** Fees for
courses on request ▪ **Suitable for ages:** 12+.
Gael Linn promotes the use of the Irish language through
education and music. It offers Irish-language courses for teenagers,
as well as arts and sports events, competitions and Irish language
days.

## 773 The Girls' Brigade Ireland 🖊

Brigade House, 5 Upr Sherrard St, Dublin 1 (there are 19
branches in the Greater Dublin region – call for your local
branch); Tel: 8365488; Fax: 8365803;
E-mail: gbirelnd@gofree.indigo.ie;

Website: www.gofree.indigo.ie/~gbirelnd

**Open:** All year; Activities and meetings are arranged after school hours and at weekends – usually once a week ▪ **Charge:** Annual membership is €10; Uniform from €40 for Explorers to €90 for full Brigaders; Cost of activities is obtained through fundraising and grants ▪ **Suitable for ages:** 3+.

An international, interdenominational Christian organisation, which runs activities designed to help girls (from tots to teens) to attain physical, mental and spiritual maturity. The Girls' Brigade encourages girls to express what they learn, through practical service to home, community and Church. Activities include bible study, games, music and dance. Older girls can participate in public speaking and first aid, and learn childcare. Contact them for details of your local group, and for information on membership for children with disabilities.

## 774 Introart

27 Great Strand St, Dublin 1; Tel: 8727930; Fax: 8727065.
▪ **Suitable for ages:** All.

An organisation which promotes and develops programmes in the arts for people with disabilities, including children.

## 775 Irish Hockey Association

6A Woodbine Park, Blackrock, Co. Dublin; Tel: 2600028;
Fax: 2600087; E-mail: joanmorgan@hockey.ie;
Website: www.hockey.ie

**Open:** Sep–Apr; Call for meeting dates and times ▪ **Charge:** Annual membership around €45 ▪ **Suitable for ages:** 6+.
**Sports:** hockey

The Irish Hockey Association oversees all Irish hockey clubs. Children's teams usually start at under-8s and go up to under-16s. Coaching is often on Saturday mornings and Friday nights – call for details.

## 776 Irish Amateur Archery Association

68 Old Kilmainham, Inchicore, Dublin 8; Tel: 4591212;
Fax: 4733186; E-mail: kit_kinsella@yahoo.com;
Website: www.toxophilyireland.com

**Open:** All year; Outdoor: May–Sep; Indoor: Oct–Apr ▪ **Charge:** Registration fees are €45; Beginners courses are between €20 and €25 ▪ **Suitable for ages:** 10+.
**Sports:** archery

Children have to be 10 years old to take up archery in the Republic of Ireland. Most clubs will take the cost of the beginners' course out of the registration fee if you decide to become a member. After a few months you will need to buy a kit, which consists of bow, arrows, quiver and chest-guard, and can cost up to €200.

## 777 Irish Amateur Gymnastics Association

House of Sport, Long Mile Rd, Dublin 12; Tel: 4501805.
**Open:** All year ▪ **Charge:** Around €50 for 10 weeks or per term ▪ **Suitable for ages:** 5+.
**Sports:** Gymnastics
Clubs are suitable for boys and girls from ages 5 and older. Activities may include freestyle floor work, beam, horse, parallel bars and trampoline. Exams can be taken, but are not compulsory, and do not start until the age of 7. Call the association for details of your local club.

## 778 Irish Association of Youth Orchestras

City Music College, 4 Drinan St, Cork; Tel: (021) 4317738;
Fax: 214317738; E-mail: iayo@eircom.net;
Website: www.homepage.eircom.net/~iayo
▪ **Suitable for ages:** 7+.
A national network for advice and information on youth orchestras, the Irish Association of Youth Orchestras represents more than 60 member youth orchestras throughout Ireland, and provides an instrument bank and music library.

## 779 Irish Basketball Association

National Basketball Arena, Tymon, Dublin 24; Tel: 4590211;
Fax: 4590212; Website: www.iba.ie
**Open:** Oct–Mar; Call for individual clubs' meeting days and times ▪ **Charge:** Annual fees range from €45 to €200; Basketball strip €50 ▪ **Suitable for ages:** 10+.
**Sports:** basketball
Most of the clubs listed below run junior teams and leagues; call for details. Where available, the venues have been listed, but these can change, so always check. The association also runs a primary school programme. Competitive teams start at under-11. Most teams require that you buy a strip to begin with, which can cost around €50.

## 780 Irish Girl Guides

27 Pembroke Park, Dublin 4; Tel: 6683898; Fax: 6602779;
E-mail: trefoil@igg.iol.ie; Website: www.irishgirlguides.ie
**Open:** All year; Activities and meetings are arranged after school
hours and at weekends–usually once a week ▪ **Charge:** Costs
include purchase of a uniform, membership fee and trips ▪
**Suitable for ages:** 5+.
The Irish Girl Guides organisation is dedicated to encouraging girls
from any background to learn new skills and develop
self-confidence as part of a group. The girls usually meet weekly
and are divided by age into Ladybirds, Brownies, Guides and
Rangers. They wear a uniform which varies between the four
stages. There is a membership fee payable, and there may also be
a small weekly fee, towards rental of the premises and for badges,
books, outings, etc. This is a great group to join for learning about
the outdoors – activities include camping, hiking and woodcraft.
Contact them for details of your local group, and for information
on membership for children with disabilities.

## 781 Irish Red Cross Youth

16 Merrion Sq, Dublin 2; Tel: 6765135, 6765136, 6765137;
Fax: 6614461; E-mail: redcross@iol.ie; Website: www.redcross.ie
**Open:** All year; Weekly meetings ▪ **Charge:** Costs include
membership fee and uniform ▪ **Suitable for ages:** 10+.
The Irish Red Cross offers young people a wide range of activities,
including training in first aid, health and safety education,
babysitting (for over-14s) and fundraising activities. It encourages
young people to use their skills to further extend the work of the
Red Cross, which many people around the world rely on. Contact
them for details of your local group, and for information on
membership for children with disabilities.

## 782 Irish Rugby Football Union

62 Lansdowne Rd, Ballsbridge, Dublin 4 (there are branches/clubs
in all areas); Tel: 6684601; Fax: 6605640; E-mail: info@irfu.ie;
Website: www.irishrugby.ie
**Open:** Sep–Apr ▪ **Charge:** Season usually about €20 ▪ **Suitable
for ages:** 6+.
**Sports:** rugby
The IRFU is the umbrella organisation of all the state's rugby clubs.
Most rugby clubs run mini rugby, or touch rugby, for over-6s on a

Sunday morning. This is designed to be gentler than the full-blown game, and does not involve tackling. Many clubs also run summer camps. Rugby boots are usually required. Prices are usually nominal. Contact individual clubs for details.

## 783 Irish Sailing Association

3 Park Road, Dún Laoghaire, Co Dublin; Tel: 2800239; Fax: 2807558; E-mail: info@sailing.ie; Website: www.sailing.ie
**Open:** All year ▪ **Suitable for ages:** 7+.
**Sports:** sailing, windsurfing
Most sailing clubs run courses during school holidays (mainly summer) to teach children from age 7+ to sail dinghies and/or windsurf. Some clubs are private, and members must own a dinghy. Others provide all the gear, or allow you to rent it. Prices also vary greatly, but start at around €150 for a week-long course – call individual clubs for details.

## 784 Jeunesses Musicales Ireland

19 Ludford Park, Ballinteer, Dublin 16; Tel: 2987596; Fax: 2960109; E-mail: joanna@iol.ie; Website: www.jmireland.org/
▪ **Suitable for ages:** 4+.
JMI helps young people to develop musically across all boundaries within Ireland, and within the network of member countries of JM International. The organisation values all forms of music equally. Key activities include auditions for the JM International World Youth Orchestra and the JMI World Youth Choir. Annual concerts are held for children.

## 785 The National Association for Youth Drama

34 Upr Gardiner St, Dublin 1; Contact: Sarah Fitzgibbon (Development Officer); Tel: 8781301; Fax: 8781302; E-mail: nayd@indigo.ie
▪ **Suitable for ages:** 5+.
The NAYD is the umbrella organisation for youth drama and youth theatre in Ireland. Contact them to get details of your local youth theatre group.

## 786 Order of Malta Ambulance Corps

32 Clyde Rd, Ballsbridge, Dublin 4; Tel: 6684891; Fax: 6685288;

E-mail: cadets@orderofmalta.ie; Website: www.orderofmalta.ie
**Open:** All year; Weekly meetings ▪ **Charge:** Costs include membership fee and uniform ▪ **Suitable for ages:** 10+.
The Cadets are the junior section of the Ambulance Corps, for children aged between 10 and 16. Weekly meetings are held in the unit training centre in Crumlin, with training in basic life-saving skills, first aid, artificial resuscitation, nursing skills and rescue skills. Outdoor activities, discos, various sports, crafts and hobbies, competitions and social activities are also part of the Order of Malta Cadet programme. Contact them for details of your local group, and for information on membership for children with disabilities.

## 787 Orff Society

Contact: Olive Mulcahy (Director); Tel: 8331721;
E-mail: ab@iol.ie
**Open:** All year; Call for details of activities ▪ **Charge:** Call for details of performances, camps and workshops ▪ **Suitable for ages:** 3+.
This is a system devised by Carl Orff, the German composer and teacher, in 1930s Bavaria to promote 'Music for Children'. It aims to help young children to develop as people through the medium of music. The Orff Society organises classes involving music, dance and speech and drama. It runs summer camps and stages class performances.

## 788 Pavee Point

46 North Great Charles St, Dublin 1; Tel: 8780255;
Fax: 8742626; E-mail: pavee@iol.ie
▪ **Suitable for ages:** Youth work programme: 12–17.
Pavee Point aims to improve the quality of life and living circumstances of Irish Travellers, by developing processes which create solidarity and promote social justice and human rights. This includes a youth work programme.

## 789 Republic of Ireland Billiards and Snooker Association

House of Sports, Long Mile Rd, Dublin 12; Tel: 4509850;
E-mail: ribsa@clubi.ie; Website: http://www.ribsa.net/
▪ **Suitable for ages:** 10+.
**Sports:** billiards, snooker, pool
This association runs a championship in each of the under-14,

under-16 and under-18 age groups. Contact them to get details of where your local club plays. Some venues are licensed family bars or restaurants.

## 790 Irish Amateur Rowing Union

House of Sport, Long Mile Rd, Dublin 12; Tel: 4509831;
E-mail: info@iarv.ie; Website: www.iarv.ie
**Open:** All year ■ **Charge:** Small weekly fee ■ **Suitable for ages:** 12+.
**Sports:** rowing/canoeing
Rowing is suitable for children from 12 years old. All three Dublin clubs are located beside each other at Islandbridge, and use the same 1,000 metres of river. Some rowing is also available on the lake in Blessington. Most classes are on Saturday and Sunday, although some afternoon and evening training is also organised. The municipal centre concentrates on summer camps and schools training. Contact clubs for details, or turn up on a Saturday morning and ask for the captain.

## 791 Scouting Ireland

Larch Hill, Tibradden, Dublin 16; Tel: 4956300; Fax: 4956301;
E-mail: reception@scoutingirelandcsi.com;
Website: www.scoutingireland.com
**Open:** All year; Weekly meetings and trips organised during the year ■ **Charge:** Costs include uniform and membership fee; Fundraising helps cover the cost of trips and activities ■ **Suitable for ages:** 6–19.
**Sports:** sailing, swimming
The Scouting Ireland programme is designed to cater for all four sections of a scout unit, ie. beavers (6–8-yr-olds), cubs (8–11-yr-olds), scouts (11–15-yr-olds) and ventures (15–19-yr-olds). It is open to boys and girls. The programme provides a mixture of physical and mental achievement, measured by the completion of challenges and rewarded with badges. Activities are carried out in groups or individually, with the assistance of adult leaders. There is also the Sea Scouts organisation (for over-8s), which begins with regular training in scoutcraft – camping, map-reading, first aid, hiking and mountain walking are important parts of the programme. The sea training side starts with basic water safety, swimming, learning to row and then to sail. Contact them for details of your local group, and for information on membership for children with disabilities.

## 792 Swim Ireland

House of Sport, Long Mile Rd, Dublin 12; Tel: 4501739.
**Open:** All year ▪ **Charge:** Around €20– €30 a month ▪ **Suitable for ages:** 7+.
**Sports:** swimming

Contact Swim Ireland for details of your local swim club. Children often start as young as 7 years old. Classes range from learning to swim, taken at a relaxed pace, to competitive racing. The more competitive clubs require early morning swims four and five days a week before school.

## 793 Tennis Ireland

DCU, Glasnevin, Dublin 9; Tel: 8844010; Fax: 8844013.
▪ **Charge:** Membership ranges from around €75 to €200 a year ▪ **Suitable for ages:** 5+.
**Sports:** tennis

All of the tennis clubs listed have junior sections. Most of these clubs have coaching, from beginner level to competitive league tennis, but a couple of the smaller ones may simply run introductory summer camps for younger children. You need to be a member to take part in summer camps or regular coaching in most of the clubs. Call individual clubs for details, or call Tennis Ireland for details of other clubs attached to schools and so on. Tennis racquets are needed for most of the clubs and a few require whites. Prices vary enormously.

# Festivals

## 794 Baboró – Galway International Arts Festival for Children

Galway (events are held in various theatres and venues in Galway city); Tel: (091) 563636, (091) 563635; E-mail: baboro@gaf.iol.ie; Website: www.baboro.ie
**Open:** Oct; Daytime events ▪ **Charge:** Activities €4/ €5 per child ▪ **Suitable for ages:** 3–12 ▪ **Bus routes:** Bus Éireann, Tel: (091) 562000 ▪ **Rail station:** Galway.
This is an arts festival specially for children. Events include theatre, music, dance, puppetry and literary events. There are also outreach projects, hands-on workshops and a fancy dress parade.

## 795 Children's Book Festival

Festival Office, Children's Books Ireland, 17 Lwr Camden St, Dublin 2 (events are held all over Ireland); Contact: Irma McLoughlin; Tel: 4763715; Fax: 4763716; E-mail: festival@childrensbooksireland.com
**Open:** Oct; Daytime events ▪ **Charge:** Free ▪ **Suitable for ages:** 5+.
Check your local library for special reading events during this festival. There are also book signings and talks from well-loved children's authors in bookshops and city-centre libraries.

## 796 County Wexford Strawberry Fair 📝

Enniscorthy, Co. Wexford; Contact: Jim Murphy; Tel: (054) 33256.
**Open:** Last week of June; Day and evening events ▪ **Charge:** Outdoor street events are free ▪ **Suitable for ages:** All ▪ **Bus routes:** Bus Éireann, Tel: (091) 562000 ▪ **Rail station:** Enniscorthy.
A nine-day, fun-packed festival. There's music, art, children's entertainment, pub events, historical lectures, outdoor free entertainment and, of course, strawberries and cream.

## 797 Diversions Festival

Temple Bar, Dublin 2 (activities usually take place in Meeting House Square and Cow's Lane); Tel: 6772255; Website: www.temple-bar.ie

**Open:** May–Aug; Day and evening events ▪ **Charge:** Outdoor street events are free ▪ **Suitable for ages:** All ▪ **Bus routes:** All city centre buses ▪ **Rail station:** Tara St ▪ **DART station:** Tara St.

An annual free outdoor festival, which runs throughout the summer, celebrating all forms of contemporary culture. There are on-street entertainers as well as outdoor film shows and many other events.

## 798 The Earagail Arts Festival

Letterkenny Arts Centre, Central Library, Plunkett Rd, Letterkenny, Co. Donegal (events held at various locations in towns and villages throughout north Donegal); Tel: 07429186, 07421968; Fax: 07420777; Website: www.donegalculture.com

**Open:** Jul; Day and evening events ▪ **Charge:** Some events are free; There is a charge for some children's workshops ▪ **Suitable for ages:** All ▪ **Bus routes:** Bus Eireann, Tel: (091) 562000.

This festival features a two-week programme of events suitable for all the family. There are workshops for children including circus school, printmaking, and arts and crafts. Other events include carnival, music, dance, theatre, comedy and fireworks displays.

## 799 Festival of World Cultures, Dún Laoghaire

Dún Laoghaire, Co. Dublin; Tel: 2054719;
E-mail: arts@dlrcoco.ie; Website: www.dlrcoco.ie/arts/festivals

**Open:** End of Aug; Day and evening events ▪ **Charge:** There is a charge for some events ▪ **Suitable for ages:** All ▪ **Bus routes:** 7, 7A, 8, 45A, 46A, 59, 75, 111 ▪ **Rail station:** Dún Laoghaire ▪ **DART station:** Dún Laoghaire.

A weekend festival featuring a wide variety of international performers. In the past there has been a Caribbean carnival, a French circus and Indian brass bands. Half of the events are free, and there are special activities for children organised.

## 800 Galway Arts Festival

c/o Galway Arts Festival, Black Box Theatre, Dyke Rd. Galway;
Tel: 091509700; Fax: 91562655;
E-mail: info@galwayartsfestival.ie;
Website: www.galwayartsfestival.com

**Open:** Last 2 weeks of July; Day and evening events. ▪ **Charge:** Fees for events vary but there are special family ticket prices on request. ▪ **Suitable for ages:** All ▪ **Bus routes:** Bus Eireann, Tel:

(091) 562000 ▪ **Rail station:** Galway.

On of the biggest summer Arts festival in Ireland which has been running for 25 years. The 2 week festival has a varied programme of theatre, dance, music, comedy, exhibitions and talks. There's a special programme for children with events to suit all ages.

## 801 Kells Heritage Festival

c/o The Courthouse, Kells, Co. Meath; Contact: Eamonn Cooke; Tel: (046) 21581, (046) 40986; Fax: (046) 21463; E-mail: kellsheritagecentre@eircom.net; Website: www.meathtourism.ie

**Open:** Early Jul; Day and evening events ▪ **Charge:** Entry fee payable to some events, though many are free ▪ **Suitable for ages:** All ▪ **Bus routes:** Bus Eireann, Tel: (091) 562000.

An annual festival featuring art exhibitions, music, drama and street events. Special events for children include a fancy dress competition and a disco.

## 802 Kilkenny Arts Festival

Kilkenny; Tel: (056) 52175 (box office); E-mail: info@kilkennyarts.ie; Website: www.kilkennyarts.ie

**Open:** Middle of Aug; Day and evening events ▪ **Charge:** Some events are free; fees may be payable for workshops ▪ **Suitable for ages:** All ▪ **Bus routes:** Bus Éireann, Tel: (091) 562000 ▪ **Rail station:** Kilkenny.

An annual festival incorporating music, film, theatre, literature, special and visual arts. There is a great children's programme for all ages, including performances, workshops, and arts and crafts.

## 803 St. Patrick's Day Festival

Dublin (parade starts at Christ Church Cathedral and ends at Parnell Sq. Other events around the city centre); Tel: 6763205; Website: www.stpatricksday.ie

**Open:** 11–17 Mar; Day and evening events; parade starts at about midday on 17 Mar ▪ **Charge:** Most events are free ▪ **Suitable for ages:** All ▪ **Bus routes:** All city centre buses ▪ **Rail station:** Tara St/Connolly ▪ **DART station:** Tara St/Connolly.

Week-long festivities celebrating St. Patrick's Day. The main event on St. Patrick's Day itself is the parade through the city centre. O'Connell St and around Trinity College are the most congested parts of the route – with small children you're better off at the tail ends of the parade where you've a chance of a good view, or else bring your stepladder. Throughout the week there are plenty of other events, including a fireworks display, *céilí mór* and a treasure hunt at various city centre parks and venues. There is usually a busy funfair along the Liffey quays in front of the Custom House.

## 804 Samhain Halloween Festival

Dublin; Tel: 8557154.
**Open:** One evening in the last week of Oct ▪ **Charge:** Free ▪ **Suitable for ages:** 5+ ▪ **Bus routes:** All city centre buses ▪ **Rail station:** Tara St/Connolly/Pearse St ▪ **DART station:** Tara St/Connolly/Pearse St.
A one-day event around Halloween in the city centre. There's a carnival with music, dance and street theatre.

## 805 Santa's Kingdom 🚼 ♿ €

Usually Punchestown, Co. Kildare, but call for this year's venue; Tel: 1890 925100 (24-hour booking line);
Website: www.santaskingdom.ie
**Open:** Christmas; Call for 2003 dates and times ▪ **Charge:** Child €25; Adult €25 ▪ **Suitable for ages:** 0–10 years.
In the old days, Clery's department store did this on a smaller scale for pocket money. The whole experience now lasts about two hours, so compared to a pantomime it is pretty good value for money. You are guided through a series of scenes, including Ice Mountain, Elf Street and Santa's House. You are entertained along the way by singing and dancing elves, and there are real reindeer to meet. You can stop off for a break in the Snow Zone – the food is supplied by the usual fast-food franchises (you have to pay for it). Finally, you get to meet Santa himself, and receive a pretty average gift. Kids love it, although parents can hate the queues.
**✱ TOP CHOICES: CHRISTMAS VISITS ✱**

# Emergencies

The following are numbers that you will hopefully never need to ring:

## 806 Childline

Tel: 1800 666666.
**Suitable for ages:** All.
A confidential support line for children under stress.

## 807 National Children's Hospital, Tallaght

Tallaght, Dublin 24; Tel: 4142000.

## 808 Our Lady's Hospital For Sick Children

Crumlin, Dublin 12; Tel: 4096100.

## 809 Parentline

Carmichael House, North Brunswick St, Dublin 7; Tel: 1890 927277.
An organisation for parents under stress.

## 810 Samaritans

Tel: 8727700, 1850 609090.
A confidential support line for traumatised, stressed or suicidal people.

## 811 Temple St. Children's Hospital

Temple St, Dublin 1; Tel: 8748763.

# Car Parks

When car parks are listed under an entry, we are recommending the ones nearest to the venue, and that are open during the venue's opening hours. The following are all private, pay-per-hour car parks.

## Arnott's Car Park

Entry via North Prince's St.

**Open:** Mon–Wed 8am–7.30pm; Thur 8am–10pm; Fri–Sat 8am–7.30pm; Sun 11am–7pm.

## Brown Thomas Car Park

Entry via Wicklow St.

**Open:** Mon–Sat 7am–1am; Sun 10am–10pm.

## Christ Church Car Park

Entry via Werburgh St.

**Open:** Mon–Sun 7am–12am.

## Dawson St Car Park

Entry via Kildare St.

Open: Mon–Sat 8am–8pm; Sun 10am–6pm.

## Drury St Car Park

Entry via Drury St.

**Open:** Mon–Sat 7.30am–1am; Sun 11am–6pm.

## ILAC Centre Car Park

Entry via Parnell St.

**Open:** Mon–Sat 8am–7pm (Thur 9.30pm); Sun 12–6.30pm.

## Irish Life Centre Car Park

Entry via Lwr Abbey St.

**Open:** Mon–Sat 24 hours.

## IFSC Car Park

Entry via Memorial Rd, off the north quays.

**Open:** Mon–Fri 7am–7pm; Sat 7am–8pm; Sun 7am–6pm.

## Jervis Centre Car Park

Entry via Ormond Quay.

**Open:** Mon–Wed 8am–7.30pm; Thur 8am–10pm; Fri 8am–9pm; Sat 8am–8pm; Sun 11am–7pm.

## Marlborough St Car Park

Entry via O'Connell St or Seán MacDermott St.

**Open:** Mon–Sun 24 hours.

## Royal College of Surgeons Car Park

Entry via Mercer St.

**Open:** Mon–Sun 24 hours.

## St. Stephen's Green Shopping Centre Car Park

Entry Via York St, behind shopping centre.

**Open:** Mon–Sat 7.30am–12.45am; Sun 12–8pm.

## Setanta Car Park

Entry via Nassau St.

**Open:** Mon–Sun 24 hours.

## Temple Bar Car Park

Entry via Fleet St.

**Open:** Mon–Sat 24 hours.

# List of Indexes

## General

Art Galleries *page 295*
Beaches *295*
Cinemas *296*
Dance Classes and Venues *296*
Drama Classes *298*
Gardens *299*
Leisure Centres *299*
Libraries *300*
Museums *301*
Music *301*
Parks *303*
Shopping *304*
Special Activities *305*
Summer Camps *306*
Theatres *308*
Walks *308*
Other Indoor Activities *309*
Other Outdoor Activities *310*

## Sports

Archery *312*
Badminton *312*
Basketball *312*
Boxing *313*
Cricket *314*
Cycling *314*
Diving *314*
Gaelic Football *315*
Golf *315*
Hockey *316*
Horse Riding *316*
Hurling *316*
IceSkating *317*
MartialArts *317*
Rowing *318*
Rugby *318*
Sailing *318*
Skateboarding *319*
Skiing *319*
Soccer *319*
Squash *320*
Swimming *320*
Tennis *320*
Windsurfing *321*

## Top Choices

Beaches *322*
Birthday Party Ideas *322*
Child-friendly Restaurants/Cafés *323*
Christmas Visits *323*
Hobbies/Arts and Crafts *323*
Parks *324*
Picnics *325*
Playgrounds (Indoor & Outdoor) *325*
Sports Facilities *325*
Summer Camps *326*
Walks *327*
For Ages 0–2 *327*
For Ages 2–5 *328*
For Ages 5–10 *328*
For Ages 10+ *329*
For Energetic Kids *330*
For Imaginative Kids *331*
For Inquisitive Kids *331*
For Shy Kids *332*
For Trendy Kids *332*

# Indexes

## General

### Art Galleries

Dublin art galleries have plenty going on for kids, and many are even baby-friendly. There's always loads of space to push a buggy around, and even the smallest child will have an opinion on works by the great masters (especially the 'disgusting' nudes). In Dublin's main galleries – the National Gallery, the Irish Museum of Modern Art and the Hugh Lane Gallery – there are very good activity sheets for children to complete as they go around. There are also many special workshops or talks held for children at weekends, but these must usually be booked in plenty of time. We have also listed venues which occasionally hold art exhibitions. All in all, great stuff for kids!

**CITY CENTRE**

*4 Alliance Française* ■ *5 Ark, The: Children's Cultural Centre* ■ *9 Bank of Ireland Arts Centre* ■ *20 Chester Beatty Library, The* ■ *50 Gallery of Photography* ■ *57 Guinness Storehouse* ■ *59 Hugh Lane Gallery* ■ *68 Irish Museum of Modern Art* ■ *86 National Gallery of Ireland* ■ *91 National Photographic Archive* ■ *101 Project Arts Centre*

**NORTH DUBLIN**

*243 Helix, The (Theatre)* ■ *313 Skerries Mills*

**WEST DUBLIN**

*381 Civic Theatre* ■ *393 Draíocht*

**SOUTH DUBLIN**

*543 Devil's Glen* ■ *638 Mermaid Theatre*

**FESTIVALS**

*800 Galway Arts Festival* ■ *801 Kells Heritage Festival*

### Beaches

We have listed the most popular beaches along the Dublin coast that have lifeguards operating during the summer months, and indicated the few that have Blue Flags. Dogs must be kept on a lead at all times on the beach, and dogs that are listed under the Dangerous Dogs Act must wear a muzzle. Dogs are not allowed on some beaches during the summer months.

### NORTH DUBLIN

*143* Balbriggan Beach ▪ *199* Donabate/Portrane Beach ▪ *263* Loughshinny Beach ▪ *275* Muldowney Beach (Malahide) ▪ *282* North Bull Island and Dollymount Strand ▪ *292* Portmarnock Beach ▪ *300* Rush Beach ▪ *323* Sutton Beach

### SOUTH DUBLIN

*513* Bray Strand/Bray Head ▪ *516* Brittas Bay ▪ *537* Dalkey Island ▪ *584* Greystones Beach ▪ *620* Killiney Strand ▪ *645* Murrow Strand ▪ *691* Sandycove/Forty Foot ▪ *693* Sandymount Strand ▪ *694* Seapoint ▪ *700* Silver Strand

## Cinemas

We have listed all the cinemas in Dublin that show children's programmes. Most of these run Saturday morning film clubs, showing children's films that have been previously released, at a bargain entry price.

### CITY CENTRE

*66* Irish Film Centre ▪ *110* Savoy Cinema ▪ *111* Screen Cinema ▪ *118* UGC Cinemas

### NORTH DUBLIN

*287* Omniplex Cinemas ▪ *332* UCI Coolock

### WEST DUBLIN

*460* Ster Century Multiplex Cinemas ▪ *465* UCI Blanchardstown ▪ *466* UCI Tallaght

### SOUTH DUBLIN

*512* Bray Cinema ▪ *607* IMC Dún Laoghaire (Cinema) ▪ *663* Ormonde Cinemas

### FESTIVALS

*797* Diversions Festival

## Dance Classes and Venues

All children enjoy movement to music, and there are many dance classes available in Dublin for children, ranging from tap dance to belly dance to folk dance. For most forms of dance, you can start as a toddler. Ballet and Irish dancing are usually graded from age five, with exams taken. There is a growing interest in informal dancing, such as hip hop and street dance, and classes in these are quite easily found. For most classes, children are expected to wear loose clothing and soft shoes, but some forms require specialist shoes and dance wear – teachers will advise you on this. The cost of classes remains relatively low, with most well under €10 per hour as part of a group. Venues used by individual teachers may be subject to change, so always ring to book a place.

## CITY CENTRE

*7* A Start in the Arts ▪ *8* Aughrim St Dance Classes ▪ *12* Behan, Sylvia, School of Ballet ▪ *41* Dublin School of Classical & Contemporary Dance ▪ *47* Flamenco y Más ▪ *62* Independent Theatre Workshop, North Frederick St ▪ *69* Irish National Youth Ballet Company ▪ *82* Millar Flora Dance Centres ▪ *95* Norton, Betty Ann, Theatre School, Harcourt St ▪ *97* Olympia Theatre ▪ *100* Point Theatre ▪ *101* Project Arts Centre

## NORTH DUBLIN

*142* Axis Arts Centre ▪ *146* Ballet School Raheny, The ▪ *150* Barry, Billie, Stage School ▪ *162* Birmingham, Audrey, Irish Dancing ▪ *188* Cadwell, Cora, School Of Dancing ▪ *194* Coláiste Íde Sports Complex ▪ *204* Dublin Ballet School Ltd ▪ *215* Freestyle Disco ▪ *243* Helix, The (Theatre) ▪ *245* Hip Hop Dance Classes ▪ *284* Norton, Betty Ann, Theatre School, Swords ▪ *321* Starstruck Stage School, Clontarf

## WEST DUBLIN

*359* Belly Dance Ireland ▪ *373* Brady School of Dance ▪ *378* Causey Farm ▪ *381* Civic Theatre ▪ *393* Draíocht ▪ *438* Lucan Youth Dance/Drama Group ▪ *448* Worth, Orla, School of Irish Dance ▪ *459* Stageright

## SOUTH DUBLIN

*476* Act One School of Acting Act One School of Acting ▪ *478* Allen, Debbie, School Of Dance, Dundrum ▪ *479* Allen, Debbie, School of Dance, Rathfarnham ▪ *532* Comhaltas Ceoltóirí Éireann (Craobh Chualann) ▪ *533* Comhaltas Ceoltóirí Éireann (Craobhnaithi) ▪ *553* Dublin Folk Dance Group ▪ *558* Dún Laoghaire Music Centre ▪ *560* Dún Laoghaire Youth Dance Theatre ▪ *583* Grainstore Youth Arts Centre The ▪ *608* Independent Theatre Workshop, Mornington Rd ▪ *609* Independent Theatre Workshop, Mountain View Rd ▪ *611* Irish Academy of Dramatic Arts ▪ *612* Irish Children's Theatre Group ▪ *640* Millar Flora Dance Centres ▪ *646* National Performing Arts School, Barrow St ▪ *647* National Performing Arts School, Haddington Rd ▪ *654* Norton, Betty Ann, Theatre School, Bray ▪ *655* Norton, Betty Ann, Theatre School, Clonskeagh ▪ *656* Norton, Betty Ann, Theatre School, Dún Laoghaire ▪ *657* Norton, Betty Ann, Theatre School, Rathmines ▪ *660* O'Donoghue, Christine, Ballet School ▪ *668* Pavilion Theatre ▪ *681* RDS (Royal Dublin Society) ▪ *702* Stagecoach Theatre, Blackrock ▪ *703* Stagecoach Theatre, Dalkey ▪ *705* Starstruck Stage School, Clonskeagh ▪ *706* Starstruck Stage School, Foxrock

## FESTIVALS

*794* Baboró – Galway International Arts Festival for Children ▪ *796* County Wexford Strawberry Fair ▪ *797* Diversions Festival ▪ *798* Earagail Arts Festival, The ▪ *799* Festival of World Cultures, Dún Laoghaire ▪ *800* Galway Arts Festival ▪ *802* Kilkenny Arts Festival ▪ *804* Samhain Halloween Festival

# Drama Classes

Children love to express themselves. A drama class or course will build confidence in a shy child, and teach discipline to the opposite, in a fun environment. For children who aim towards careers in stage or broadcasting, many drama schools put on a yearly performance, and some are attached to casting agencies. Equally, there are plenty of classes which are held just for fun, for children from tots to teens. A good place to start is with your local youth drama group. Movement, dance and even singing are all part of the fun, and loose-fitting, comfortable clothes and soft shoes are usually worn.

## CITY CENTRE

*1 Abbey School of Music and Drama* ▪ *3 African Cultural Project* ▪ *7 A Start in the Arts* ▪ *48 Gaiety School of Acting* ▪ *62 Independent Theatre Workshop, North Frederick St* ▪ *74 Leinster School of Music and Drama* ▪ *95 Norton, Betty Ann, Theatre School, Harcourt St* ▪ *101 Project Arts Centre* ▪ *103 Royal Irish Academy of Music*

## NORTH DUBLIN

*142 Axis Arts Centre* ▪ *149 Barrington, Marie, Speech and Drama* ▪ *150 Barry, Billie, Stage School* ▪ *165 Botanic Art School, The* ▪ *238 Gaiety School of Acting* ▪ *284 Norton, Betty Ann, Theatre School, Swords* ▪ *321 Starstruck Stage School, Clontarf*

## WEST DUBLIN

*343 Alternative Entertainment Community Art Group* ▪ *381 Civic Theatre* ▪ *393 Draíocht* ▪ *423 Independent Theatre Workshop, Ballycullen Ave* ▪ *424 Independent Theatre Workshop, Firhouse Rd W* ▪ *438 Lucan Youth Dance/Drama Group* ▪ *459 Stageright*

## SOUTH DUBLIN

*476 Act One School of Acting Act One School of Acting* ▪ *523 Cabinteely School for Speech and Drama* ▪ *558 Dún Laoghaire Music Centre* ▪ *576 Gaiety School of Acting* ▪ *582 Goodwin, Xavier, Drama School* ▪ *583 Grainstore Youth Arts Centre The* ▪ *606 Hughes, Pamela, LLSM Speech and Drama* ▪ *608 Independent Theatre Workshop, Mornington Rd* ▪ *609 Independent Theatre Workshop, Mountain View Rd* ▪ *611 Irish Academy of Dramatic Arts* ▪ *612 Irish Children's Theatre Group* ▪ *638 Mermaid Theatre* ▪ *646 National Performing Arts School, Barrow St* ▪ *647 National Performing Arts School, Haddington Rd* ▪ *654 Norton, Betty Ann, Theatre School, Bray* ▪ *655 Norton, Betty Ann, Theatre School, Clonskeagh* ▪ *656 Norton, Betty Ann, Theatre School, Dún Laoghaire* ▪ *657 Norton, Betty Ann, Theatre School, Rathmines* ▪ *666 Pan Pan Theatre* ▪ *702 Stagecoach Theatre, Blackrock* ▪ *703 Stagecoach Theatre, Dalkey* ▪ *705 Starstruck Stage School, Clonskeagh* ▪ *706 Starstruck Stage School, Foxrock*

## ORGANISATIONS

*785 National Association for Youth Drama*

## FESTIVALS

**794** Baboró – Galway International Arts Festival for Children ▪ **796** County Wexford Strawberry Fair ▪ **797** Diversions Festival ▪ **798** Earagail Arts Festival, The ▪ **799** Festival of World Cultures, Dún Laoghaire ▪ **800** Galway Arts Festival ▪ **801** Kells Heritage Festival ▪ **802** Kilkenny Arts Festival ▪ **804** Samhain Halloween Festival

## Gardens

From small, city-centre gardens to grand gardens that are part of large country houses, there are many beautiful and interesting gardens in and around Dublin. Whether you like formal rose gardens, greenhouses, woodlands or riverside walks, there is something to please everybody. All of the gardens listed are suitable for children.

### CITY CENTRE

**35** Dublin Castle ▪ **52** Garden of Remembrance ▪ **68** Irish Museum of Modern Art ▪ **81** Merrion Square ▪ **108** St. Stephen's Green ▪ **117** Trinity College (The Dublin Experience and the Book of Kells)

### NORTH DUBLIN

**140** Ardgillan Castle ▪ **189** Casino Marino ▪ **240** Griffith Park ▪ **252** Howth Castle Gardens ▪ **265** Malahide Castle and Demesne ▪ **276** National Botanic Gardens ▪ **279** Newbridge Demesne ▪ **290** Pope John Paul II Park ▪ **302** St. Anne's Park

### WEST DUBLIN

**379** Celbridge Abbey Grounds ▪ **394** Drimnagh Castle ▪ **399** Farmleigh House ▪ **425** The Japanese Gardens and Irish National Stud ▪ **430** Larchill Arcadian Gardens ▪ **435** Lodge Park Heritage Centre and Steam Museum ▪ **440** Millennium Maze ▪ **451** Phoenix Park ▪ **469** War Memorial Gardens

### SOUTH DUBLIN

**477** Airfield Trust ▪ **522** Cabinteely Park ▪ **541** Deerpark ▪ **619** Killiney Hill Park/Dalkey Hill ▪ **634** Marlay Park ▪ **644** Mount Usher Gardens ▪ **669** Pearse Museum and St. Enda's Park ▪ **671** People's Park ▪ **673** Powerscourt House and Gardens

## Leisure Centres

There are many leisure centres throughout the city, with excellent sport facilities and swimming pools. You don't always have to join as a member. In many of these centres you can pay as you go for activities or the use of facilities – we have indicated where and when in the individual entries. We have given details of the sports facilities available in the main leisure centres suitable for children, as well as information on classes and activities held.

### CITY CENTRE

**77** Markiewicz Leisure Centre

## NORTH DUBLIN

*194 Coláiste Íde Sports Complex ▪ 198 Dean Swift Sports Club ▪ 293 Portmarnock Sports and Leisure Club ▪ 318 Sportslink Club ▪ 334 Westwood Health and Fitness Centre, Clontarf*

## WEST DUBLIN

*385 Clondalkin Sports and Leisure Centre ▪ 391 Coolmine Sports and Leisure Centre ▪ 443 National Aquatic Centre ▪ 444 National Basketball Arena ▪ 464 Tallaght Community School Sports Complex ▪ 468 Verona Sports and Leisure Club*

## SOUTH DUBLIN

*528 Cheeverstown House Leisure Centre ▪ 539 David Lloyd Riverview Racquet and Fitness Club ▪ 562 ESB Sportsco ▪ 578 Glenalbyn Sports Club ▪ 621 Kilternan Sports Hotel ▪ 623 LA Fitness ▪ 639 Mespil Swimming Pool ▪ 642 Monkstown Swimming Pool and Fitness Centre ▪ 651 Newpark School Sports Centre ▪ 686 St. Columba's Health and Fitness Club ▪ 714 Templeogue College Swimming Pool ▪ 725 West Wood, Leopardstown (Sports Club)*

## Libraries

All of the following are public libraries with children's sections. Apart from just lending books, libraries are a great source of information on local groups and activities, many of which are held in the libraries themselves, such as mother-and-baby clinics and chess clubs. Some libraries have regular weekly events, such as Story Time. Most have holiday and seasonal activities organised throughout the year. Materials are usually supplied, and usually free, but you'd be wise to book well in advance. Many libraries are upstairs in old buildings without any wheelchair or buggy access. All libraries with this symbol: ▣ have computer facilities available for children.

## CITY CENTRE

*4 Alliance Française ▪ 18 Central Library ▪ 19 Charleville Mall Library ▪ 20 Chester Beatty Library, The ▪ 25 Community & Youth Information Centre ▪ 26 Contemporary Music Centre, The ▪ 45 ENFO (Information on the Environment) ▪ 56 Goethe-Institut ▪ 73 Kevin Street Library ▪ 79 Marsh's Library ▪ 87 The National Library of Ireland ▪ 91 National Photographic Archive ▪ 117 Trinity College (The Dublin Experience and the Book of Kells)*

## NORTH DUBLIN

*144 Balbriggan Public Library ▪ 147 Ballymun Library ▪ 187 Cabra Library ▪ 196 Coolock Library ▪ 200 Donaghmede Library ▪ 202 Drumcondra Library ▪ 213 Finglas Library ▪ 254 Howth Library ▪ 266 Malahide Library ▪ 271 Marino Library ▪ 289 Phibsboro Library ▪ 294 Raheny Library ▪ 298 Rathbeale Public Library ▪ 312 Skerries Library*

## WEST DUBLIN

*348 Ballyfermot Library ▪ 360 Blanchardstown Library ▪ 377 Castletymon*

Library ■ *383* Clondalkin Library ■ *392* County Library, Tallaght ■ *422* Inchicore Library ■ *437* Lucan Library

## SOUTH DUBLIN

*486* Ballyroan Library ■ *498* Blackrock Library ■ *521* Cabinteely Library ■ *538* Dalkey Library ■ *540* Deansgrange Library ■ *548* Dolphin's Barn Library ■ *555* Dundrum Library ■ *557* Dún Laoghaire Library ■ *579* Glencullen Library Centre ■ *610* Instituto Cervantes (Spanish Language Library) ■ *670* Pembroke Library ■ *679* Rathmines Library ■ *682* Ringsend Library ■ *689* Sallynoggin Library ■ *697* Shankill Library ■ *708* Stillorgan Library ■ *716* Terenure Library ■ *720* Walkinstown Library ■ *726* Whitechurch Library

# Museums

Ireland's national museums are a real joy to visit. Three of them are in Dublin: the National Museum of Archaeology and History; the National Museum of History and Decorative Arts; and the Natural History Museum. Entrance is free to all three, and they make a great visit for a rainy day, as well as running excellent free workshops for children and families at weekends. There are many other, smaller museums in Dublin, well worth a visit for a cultural or educational experience. Why not go along and satisfy your child's natural curiosity?

## CITY CENTRE

*20* Chester Beatty Library, The ■ *38* Dublin Civic Museum ■ *43* Dublin Writers' Museum ■ *51* Garda Museum and Archives, The ■ *57* Guinness Storehouse ■ *58* Heraldic Museum ■ *67* Irish Jewish Museum ■ *71* James Joyce Centre ■ *88* National Museum of Ireland (History and Archaeology) ■ *89* National Museum of Ireland (History and Decorative Arts) ■ *90* National Museum of Ireland (Natural History) ■ *92* National Wax Museum, The

## NORTH DUBLIN

*216* Fry Model Railway Museum ■ *237* GAA Museum ■ *278* National Transport Museum ■ *281* Newgrange and Boyne Valley

## WEST DUBLIN

*425* The Japanese Gardens and Irish National Stud ■ *435* Lodge Park Heritage Centre and Steam Museum

## SOUTH DUBLIN

*613* Irish Labour History Society Museum ■ *615* James Joyce Museum and Tower ■ *624* Lambert Puppet Theatre and Museum ■ *648* National Print Museum ■ *669* Pearse Museum and St. Enda's Park

# Music

Ireland has given birth to a lot of talented musicians, singers and songwriters, and most have had some sort of formal training along the way. Any child can learn to play an instrument, but a general introduction to music is a good way to start before they choose. Most instruments are taught to ages 7+, although piano and strings are taught to the very young. Individual tuition in an instrument can cost from €15–€30 per hour, depending on the age of the student, and the tuition required – for example, whether a student is preparing for exams. Many teachers will vary rates according to individual circumstances, and some music schools have instrument hire schemes. Traditional Irish music is very popular, and for older children there are now classes in music technology and sound recording. Individual music teachers may teach from their own home or come to the student's residence.

Dublin is also home to some fabulous, modern, multi-purpose arts venues with excellent facilities. We have listed the main music venues and concert halls which run programmes for children. We have also listed some venues that host musical events outside their normal function, for example, parks, art galleries, and so on. Some of these also host special activities, such as workshops for children.

## CITY CENTRE

*1 Abbey School of Music and Drama* ■ *5 Ark, The: Children's Cultural Centre* ■ *7 A Start in the Arts* ■ *9 Bank of Ireland Arts Centre* ■ *13 Bel Canto School of Singing* ■ *18 Central Library* ■ *23 City Hall* ■ *26 Contemporary Music Centre, The* ■ *27 Corbett, Tom (Music Teacher)* ■ *37 Dublin City Quay Youth Samba Project* ■ *42 Dublin School of Guitar* ■ *49 Gaiety Theatre* ■ *59 Hugh Lane Gallery* ■ *74 Leinster School of Music and Drama* ■ *75 Liberty Hall Theatre* ■ *79 Marsh's Library* ■ *80 The Merriman School Of Singing and Music* ■ *81 Merrion Square* ■ *85 National Concert Hall* ■ *93 National Youth Orchestra of Ireland* ■ *95 Norton, Betty Ann, Theatre School, Harcourt St* ■ *97 Olympia Theatre* ■ *100 Point Theatre* ■ *103 Royal Irish Academy of Music* ■ *105 St. Mary's Pro-Cathedral* ■ *107 St. Patrick's Cathedral* ■ *108 St. Stephen's Green* ■ *119 Vicar St (Music Venue)* ■ *121 Walton's New School of Music*

## NORTH DUBLIN

*142 Axis Arts Centre* ■ *185 Browne, Lorraine (Music Teacher)* ■ *193 Clontarf School of Music* ■ *195 Conaghan, Dorothy (Music Teacher)* ■ *197 Daniels, Nicola (Music Teacher)* ■ *206 Dublin Youth Symphonia* ■ *241 Gymboree Music on the Go* ■ *243 Helix, The (Theatre)* ■ *255 Howth Rock Guitar and Songwriting School* ■ *269 Mangan Yamaha Keyboard and Guitar School of Music* ■ *306 Seamus Ennis Cultural Centre* ■ *308 Shoebridge, Kathleen (Music Teacher)* ■ *316 Songschool Ltd* ■ *321 Starstruck Stage School, Clontarf* ■ *322 Steele, Ann Marie (Music Teacher)* ■ *335 White, Marianne (Music Teacher)*

## WEST DUBLIN

*343 Alternative Entertainment Community Art Group* ■ *374 Buttner, Linda (Music Teacher)* ■ *381 Civic Theatre* ■ *382 Clancy Terence (Music Teacher)* ■ *383 Clondalkin Library* ■ *387 Conway Paul (Music Teacher)* ■

*393* Draíocht ■ *418* Gymboree Music on the Go ■ *446* Nolan, Martin (Music Teacher) ■ *447* O'Boyle, Catherine (Music Teacher) ■ *454* Piccolo Lasso Choir ■ *459* Stageright ■ *462* Stynes, Philomena (Music Teacher)

## SOUTH DUBLIN

*477* Airfield Trust ■ *483* Ball, Michael (Music Teacher) ■ *518* Broxson, Aoife (Music Teacher) ■ *519* Bushy Park ■ *529* Churchtown Keyboard School ■ *532* Comhaltas Ceoltóirí Éireann (Craobh Chualann) ■ *533* Comhaltas Ceoltóirí Éireann (Craobhnaithi) ■ *535* Courtney Ted (Music Teacher) ■ *538* Dalkey Library ■ *544* Dexter, John, Harmony Choir ■ *550* Duane, Caoimhe Ashley (Music Teacher) ■ *551* Duane, David Patrick (Music Teacher) ■ *554* Dublin Girls Singers ■ *558* Dún Laoghaire Music Centre ■ *561* Dunne, Maedhbh (Music Teacher) ■ *575* Gaffney (Ní Ghamhna), Sr Cora (Music Teacher) ■ *582* Goodwin, Xavier, Drama School ■ *583* Grainstore Youth Arts Centre The ■ *588* Gunzl, Camilla (Music Teacher) ■ *589* Gymboree Music on the Go ■ *590* Gymboree Play and Music ■ *591* Halpin, Aedín (Music Teacher) ■ *594* Herbert Park ■ *609* Independent Theatre Workshop, Mountain View Rd ■ *611* Irish Academy of Dramatic Arts ■ *622* Kodály Society of Ireland ■ *627* Leeson Park School of Music ■ *632* Loy, Jean (Music Teacher) ■ *634* Marlay Park ■ *636* Martin, Nora (Music Teacher) ■ *638* Mermaid Theatre ■ *647* National Performing Arts School, Haddington Rd ■ *650* Newpark Music Centre ■ *652* Ní Dhubhghaill, Caitríona (Music Teacher) ■ *653* Nolan School Of Music ■ *654* Norton, Betty Ann, Theatre School, Bray ■ *655* Norton, Betty Ann, Theatre School, Clonskeagh ■ *656* Norton, Betty Ann, Theatre School, Dún Laoghaire ■ *657* Norton, Betty Ann, Theatre School, Rathmines ■ *659* O'Connell, Isabelle (Music Teacher) ■ *667* Park Singers Choir ■ *668* Pavilion Theatre ■ *669* Pearse Museum and St. Enda's Park ■ *681* RDS (Royal Dublin Society) ■ *701* Smith, Ruth (Music Teacher) ■ *705* Starstruck Stage School, Clonskeagh ■ *706* Starstruck Stage School, Foxrock ■ *707* Steele, Ann Marie (Music Teacher) ■ *713* Talbot, Rachel (Music Teacher) ■ *722* Walsh, Owen (Music Teacher) ■ *729* Young European Strings

## ORGANISATIONS

*763* Cairde na Cruite ■ *778* Irish Association of Youth Orchestras ■ *784* Jeunesses Musicales Ireland ■ *787* Orff Society

## FESTIVALS

*794* Baboró – Galway International Arts Festival for Children ■ *796* County Wexford Strawberry Fair ■ *797* Diversions Festival ■ *798* Earagail Arts Festival, The ■ *799* Festival of World Cultures, Dún Laoghaire ■ *800* Galway Arts Festival ■ *801* Kells Heritage Festival ■ *802* Kilkenny Arts Festival ■ *803* St. Patrick's Day Festival ■ *804* Samhain Halloween Festival

## Parks

We have listed larger parks throughout the Dublin area, outlining their sports facilities, playground facilities and other areas of interest: walks, nature trails, sites of historic interest, and so on. All Dublin County Council parks with tennis courts participate in the summer

Dublin Public Parks Tennis league. It's worth looking outside your local area, as there are many fabulous parks that (weather permitting) make a lovely day out. Dogs must be kept on a lead at all times in public parks, and dogs that are listed under the Dangerous Dogs Act must wear a muzzle. If a park is listed as baby-friendly, we mean that there is a playground, and paths for pushchairs and prams. Finally, if you bring a picnic to the park, please remember to clear up after yourself.

### CITY CENTRE

*28* Croppies' Memorial Park ▪ *31* Diamond Park ▪ *70* Irishtown Nature Park ▪ *76* Liberty Park ▪ *81* Merrion Square ▪ *83* Mountjoy Square Park ▪ *108* St. Stephen's Green

### NORTH DUBLIN

*160* Belcamp Park ▪ *208* Edenmore Park ▪ *209* Ellenfield Park ▪ *210* Fairview Park ▪ *211* Father Collins Park ▪ *240* Griffith Park ▪ *242* Hampstead Park (Albert College Park) ▪ *257* Johnstown Park ▪ *265* Malahide Castle and Demesne ▪ *272* May Park (Doneycarney Park) ▪ *273* Mellowes Park (Casement Park) ▪ *290* Pope John Paul II Park ▪ *291* Poppintree Park ▪ *302* St. Anne's Park ▪ *309* Sillogue Park and Golf Course ▪ *320* Stardust Memorial Park ▪ *331* Tolka Valley Park ▪ *333* Ward River Valley Park

### WEST DUBLIN

*398* Eamon Ceannt Park ▪ *429* Lansdowne Valley ▪ *431* Le Fanu Park ▪ *439* Markievicz Park ▪ *451* Phoenix Park ▪ *469* War Memorial Gardens

### SOUTH DUBLIN

*480* Annamoe Trout Farm ▪ *499* Blackrock Park ▪ *515* Brickfield Park ▪ *519* Bushy Park ▪ *522* Cabinteely Park ▪ *531* Clara Lara ▪ *541* Deerpark ▪ *546* Dodder Park ▪ *580* Glendalough ▪ *592* Harold's Cross Park ▪ *594* Herbert Park ▪ *617* Kilbogget Park ▪ *619* Killiney Hill Park/Dalkey Hill ▪ *631* Loreto Park ▪ *634* Marlay Park ▪ *665* Palmerston Park ▪ *669* Pearse Museum and St. Enda's Park ▪ *671* People's Park ▪ *673* Powerscourt House and Gardens ▪ *674* Powerscourt Waterfall ▪ *683* Ringsend Park ▪ *696* Shanganagh Park ▪ *704* Stannaway Park ▪ *721* Walkinstown Park ▪ *727* Willie Pearse Park

## Shopping

We have listed the larger shopping centres around Dublin, and supplied information on their crèche facilities, parking facilities and opening hours. We have also listed the main department stores in the city centre.

### CITY CENTRE

*6* Arnott's Department Store ▪ *17* Brown Thomas/BT2 ▪ *24* Clery's Department Store ▪ *30* Debenham's Department Store ▪ *44* Dunnes Stores ▪ *61* ILAC Shopping Centre ▪ *72* Jervis St Shopping Centre ▪ *78* Marks & Spencer ▪ *99* Penney's Stores ▪ *102* Roches Stores ▪ *109* St. Stephen's Green Shopping Centre ▪ *114* Smyth's Toys & Computer Games

## NORTH DUBLIN

*201* Donaghmede Shopping Centre ▪ *259* Kiddie Kuts ▪ *283* Northside Shopping Centre ▪ *286* Omni Park, Santry ▪ *288* Pavilion Shopping Centre, The

## WEST DUBLIN

*361* Blanchardstown Shopping Centre ▪ *434* Liffey Valley Shopping Centre ▪ *441* The Mill Shopping Centre ▪ *458* The Square Shopping Centre

## SOUTH DUBLIN

*500* Blackrock Shopping Centre ▪ *503* Bloomfields Shopping Centre ▪ *534* Cornelscourt Shopping Centre ▪ *559* Dún Laoghaire Shopping Centre ▪ *564* Frascati Shopping Centre ▪ *616* Kiddie Kuts ▪ *658* Nutgrove Shopping Centre ▪ *709* Stillorgan Shopping Centre Stillorgan Shopping Centre

## PARTY SERVICES

*747* Ace One Stop Party Shop

## Special Activities

The following are places which run special activities for children outside their normal functions. These range from storytelling in libraries to arts-and-crafts workshops at weekends in museums. We advise you to book well in advance, as places go really quickly. It is well worth making enquiries before school holidays, as many places run great seasonal activities, and many of them are free!

## CITY CENTRE

*2* Abbey Theatre ▪ *4* Alliance Française ▪ *5* Ark, The: Children's Cultural Centre ▪ *9* Bank of Ireland Arts Centre ▪ *18* Central Library ▪ *19* Charleville Mall Library ▪ *20* Chester Beatty Library, The ▪ *23* City Hall ▪ *43* Dublin Writers' Museum ▪ *50* Gallery of Photography ▪ *55* Glenans Sailing ▪ *59* Hugh Lane Gallery ▪ *66* Irish Film Centre ▪ *68* Irish Museum of Modern Art ▪ *73* Kevin Street Library ▪ *85* National Concert Hall ▪ *86* National Gallery of Ireland ▪ *87* The National Library of Ireland ▪ *88* National Museum of Ireland (History and Archaeology) ▪ *89* National Museum of Ireland (History and Decorative Arts) ▪ *90* National Museum of Ireland (Natural History) ▪ *98* Peacock Theatre ▪ *101* Project Arts Centre ▪ *118* UGC Cinemas

## NORTH DUBLIN

*142* Axis Arts Centre ▪ *144* Balbriggan Public Library ▪ *147* Ballymun Library ▪ *187* Cabra Library ▪ *196* Coolock Library ▪ *200* Donaghmede Library ▪ *202* Drumcondra Library ▪ *213* Finglas Library ▪ *243* Helix, The (Theatre) ▪ *254* Howth Library ▪ *266* Malahide Library ▪ *271* Marino Library ▪ *287* Omniplex Cinemas ▪ *289* Phibsboro Library ▪ *294* Raheny Library ▪ *298* Rathbeale Public Library ▪ *310* Sillybilly Learning Ltd ▪ *312* Skerries Library ▪ *326* Sutton Lawn Tennis Club ▪ *328* Swords Lawn Tennis Club ▪ *332* UCI Coolock

## WEST DUBLIN

*343* Alternative Entertainment Community Art Group ▪ *348* Ballyfermot

Library ▪ *360* Blanchardstown Library ▪ *377* Castletymon Library ▪ *379* Celbridge Abbey Grounds ▪ *383* Clondalkin Library ▪ *392* County Library, Tallaght ▪ *393* Draíocht ▪ *422* Inchicore Library ▪ *430* Larchill Arcadian Gardens ▪ *434* Liffey Valley Shopping Centre ▪ *437* Lucan Library ▪ *460* Ster Century Multiplex Cinemas ▪ *465* UCI Blanchardstown ▪ *466* UCI Tallaght

## SOUTH DUBLIN

*477* Airfield Trust ▪ *486* Ballyroan Library ▪ *498* Blackrock Library ▪ *521* Cabinteely Library ▪ *531* Clara Lara ▪ *537* Dalkey Island ▪ *538* Dalkey Library ▪ *540* Deansgrange Library ▪ *548* Dolphin's Barn Library ▪ *555* Dundrum Library ▪ *557* Dún Laoghaire Library ▪ *579* Glencullen Library Centre ▪ *583* Grainstore Youth Arts Centre The ▪ *607* IMC Dún Laoghaire (Cinema) ▪ *610* Instituto Cervantes (Spanish Language Library) ▪ *629* Leisureplex, Stillorgan ▪ *638* Mermaid Theatre ▪ *649* National Sealife Centre ▪ *663* Ormonde Cinemas ▪ *670* Pembroke Library ▪ *672* Pine Forest Arts Centre ▪ *679* Rathmines Library ▪ *681* RDS (Royal Dublin Society) ▪ *682* Ringsend Library ▪ *689* Sallynoggin Library ▪ *692* Sandycove Tennis and Squash Club ▪ *697* Shankill Library ▪ *699* Sillybilly Learning Ltd ▪ *708* Stillorgan Library ▪ *716* Terenure Library ▪ *720* Walkinstown Library ▪ *726* Whitechurch Library

## ORGANISATIONS

*764* Catholic Guides of Ireland ▪ *765* Comhchoiste Náisiúnta na gColáistí Samhraidh ▪ *766* Confederation of Peace Corps ▪ *770* Foróige ▪ *772* Gael Linn ▪ *773* Girls' Brigade Ireland ▪ *781* Irish Red Cross Youth ▪ *786* Order of Malta Ambulance Corps ▪ *788* Pavee Point ▪ *791* Scouting Ireland

## FESTIVALS

*794* Baboró – Galway International Arts Festival for Children ▪ *795* Children's Book Festival ▪ *798* Earagail Arts Festival, The ▪ *799* Festival of World Cultures, Dún Laoghaire ▪ *801* Kells Heritage Festival ▪ *802* Kilkenny Arts Festival

## Summer Camps

We have listed well over 100 places that run summer camps. These cover a wide range of activities, from sport to arts and crafts. Most summer camps run over complete days for a week at a time, and most should be booked as early as possible. Many camps are also run during other school holidays – very useful for working parents.

## CITY CENTRE

*3* African Cultural Project ▪ *48* Gaiety School of Acting ▪ *55* Glenans Sailing ▪ *85* National Concert Hall ▪ *95* Norton, Betty Ann, Theatre School, Harcourt St ▪ *121* Walton's New School of Music

## NORTH DUBLIN

*145* Baldoyle Badminton Centre ▪ *161* Belgrove Football Club ▪ *165* Botanic Art School, The ▪ *190* Charleville Lawn Tennis Club ▪ *191* Clontarf Lawn Tennis Club ▪ *207* Dymphna's Equestrian Centre ▪ *212* Fingall Sailing School, Malahide ▪ *214* Forrest Equestrian Centre ▪ *217* GAA ▪ *227*

O'Dwyer's GAA Club ▪ **238** Gaiety School of Acting ▪ **239** Glasnevin Lawn Tennis Club ▪ **242** Hampstead Park (Albert College Park) ▪ **244** Hills Cricket Club ▪ **255** Howth Rock Guitar and Songwriting School ▪ **256** Howth Yacht Club ▪ **257** Johnstown Park ▪ **261** Kilronan Equestrian Centre ▪ **268** Malahide Yacht Club ▪ **269** Mangan Yamaha Keyboard and Guitar School of Music ▪ **284** Norton, Betty Ann, Theatre School, Swords ▪ **285** Oldtown Riding Stables ▪ **291** Poppintree Park ▪ **293** Portmarnock Sports and Leisure Club ▪ **301** Rush Cricket Club ▪ **315** Skerries Sailing Club ▪ **318** Sportslink Club ▪ **321** Starstruck Stage School, Clontarf ▪ **324** Sutton Dinghy Club ▪ **326** Sutton Lawn Tennis Club ▪ **328** Swords Lawn Tennis Club ▪ **330** Thornton Park Riding ▪ **334** Westwood Health and Fitness Centre, Clontarf

## WEST DUBLIN

**343** Alternative Entertainment Community Art Group ▪ **346** Ashtown Stables ▪ **375** Carton Equestrian Centre ▪ **376** Castleknock Lawn Tennis Club ▪ **384** Clondalkin Rugby Football Club ▪ **385** Clondalkin Sports and Leisure Centre ▪ **388** Coolmine Equestrian Centre ▪ **390** Coolmine Rugby Football Club ▪ **391** Coolmine Sports and Leisure Centre ▪ **393** Draíocht ▪ **395** Dublin Municipal Rowing Centre ▪ **402** Futurekids, Lucan ▪ **403** GAA ▪ **404** Ballyboden/St. Enda's GAA Club ▪ **426** Kill International ▪ **444** National Basketball Arena ▪ **449** Pelletstown Riding Centre ▪ **453** Phoenix Riding Stables ▪ **464** Tallaght Community School Sports Complex

## SOUTH DUBLIN

**481** Artzone ▪ **482** Ashbrook Lawn Tennis Club ▪ **484** Ballybrack Boys Association Football Club) ▪ **497** Blackrock College Summer Schoool ▪ **501** Blessington Activity Centre ▪ **502** Blessington Sailing Club ▪ **517** Brookfield Lawn Tennis Club ▪ **520** The Busy Bee Summer School of Cooking ▪ **524** Calliaghstown Riding Centre ▪ **525** Carrickmines Croquet and Lawns ▪ **526** Carrickmines Equestrian Centre ▪ **539** David Lloyd Riverview Racquet and Fitness Club ▪ **547** Dolphin Activity Holidays ▪ **549** Donnybrook Lawn Tennis Club ▪ **558** Dún Laoghaire Music Centre ▪ **560** Dún Laoghaire Youth Dance Theatre ▪ **562** ESB Sportsco ▪ **566** Futurekids, Dún Laoghaire ▪ **567** Futurekids, Rathfarnham ▪ **568** Futurekids, Rathmines ▪ **569** Futurekids, Stillorgan ▪ **570** GAA ▪ **576** Gaiety School of Acting ▪ **577** Glenageary Lawn Tennis Club ▪ **578** Glenalbyn Sports Club ▪ **585** Greystones Lawn Tennis Club ▪ **608** Independent Theatre Workshop, Mornington Rd ▪ **612** Irish Children's Theatre Group ▪ **614** Irish National Sailing School ▪ **618** Killegar Stables ▪ **621** Kilternan Sports Hotel ▪ **622** Kodály Society of Ireland ▪ **626** Lansdowne Tennis Club ▪ **627** Leeson Park School of Music ▪ **628** Leinster Cricket Club ▪ **642** Monkstown Swimming Pool and Fitness Centre ▪ **643** Mount Pleasant Tennis and Squash Club ▪ **646** National Performing Arts School, Barrow St ▪ **647** National Performing Arts School, Haddington Rd ▪ **650** Newpark Music Centre ▪ **651** Newpark School Sports Centre ▪ **654** Norton, Betty Ann, Theatre School, Bray ▪ **655** Norton, Betty Ann, Theatre School, Clonskeagh ▪ **656** Norton, Betty Ann, Theatre School, Dún Laoghaire ▪ **657** Norton, Betty Ann, Theatre School, Rathmines ▪ **664** Paddocks Riding Centre ▪ **666** Pan Pan Theatre ▪ **672** Pine Forest Arts Centre ▪ **675** Railway Union Sports Club ▪ **684** Royal Irish Yacht Club ▪ **685** Royal St. George Yacht Club ▪ **687** St. Joseph's Boys Association Football Club ▪ **690**

*Samba Soccer School* ■ *692 Sandycove Tennis and Squash Club* ■ *698 Shankill Tennis Club* ■ *705 Starstruck Stage School, Clonskeagh* ■ *706 Starstruck Stage School, Foxrock* ■ *711 Stratford Tennis Club* ■ *712 Surfdock* ■ *715 Templeogue Tennis Club* ■ *719 Tiggy's Art School* ■ *725 West Wood, Leopardstown (Sports Club)* ■ *728 Wind & Wave Water Sports*

## ORGANISATIONS

*760 Association of Irish Riding Establisments* ■ *763 Cairde na Cruite* ■ *765 Comhchoiste Náisiúnta na gColáistí Samhraidh* ■ *768 Dublin Parks Tennis League (KitKat)* ■ *769 Football Association of Ireland* ■ *771 GAA* ■ *782 Irish Rugby Football Union* ■ *783 Irish Sailing Association* ■ *787 Orff Society* ■ *790 Rowing Union* ■ *793 Tennis Ireland*

## Theatres

Dublin has a strong theatre-going tradition, although most children associate theatre with being dragged along to see a play as part of their schoolwork. Apart from at the Ark, it is still hard to find plays suitable for the under-12s outside the Christmas period, but keep your eyes peeled on theatre listings, as many drama schools stage a production during the year.

### CITY CENTRE

*2 Abbey Theatre* ■ *5 Ark, The: Children's Cultural Centre* ■ *9 Bank of Ireland Arts Centre* ■ *49 Gaiety Theatre* ■ *53 Gate Theatre* ■ *75 Liberty Hall Theatre* ■ *85 National Concert Hall* ■ *97 Olympia Theatre* ■ *98 Peacock Theatre* ■ *100 Point Theatre* ■ *101 Project Arts Centre* ■ *116 Tivoli Theatre*

### NORTH DUBLIN

*142 Axis Arts Centre* ■ *243 Helix, The (Theatre)*

### WEST DUBLIN

*381 Civic Theatre* ■ *393 Draíocht*

### SOUTH DUBLIN

*583 Grainstore Youth Arts Centre The* ■ *624 Lambert Puppet Theatre and Museum* ■ *638 Mermaid Theatre* ■ *668 Pavilion Theatre* ■ *681 RDS (Royal Dublin Society)*

## Walks

Walking is a great stress-buster after a heavy week. Most of the walks we have listed are suitable for young children and some are wheelchair/pushchair friendly. Some of the places listed below are parks or the grounds of castles or historical houses, while others are just lovely places where we have indicated the path you should take. Most of these walks could be done in less than two hours. We have indicated walks that are more challenging, and only suitable for older children.

**CITY CENTRE**

*28* Croppies' Memorial Park ■ *70* Irishtown Nature Park ■ *81* Merrion Square ■ *108* St. Stephen's Green

**NORTH DUBLIN**

*140* Ardgillan Castle ■ *160* Belcamp Park ■ *210* Fairview Park ■ *240* Griffith Park ■ *242* Hampstead Park (Albert College Park) ■ *253* Howth Head ■ *265* Malahide Castle and Demesne ■ *273* Mellowes Park (Casement Park) ■ *279* Newbridge Demesne ■ *282* North Bull Island and Dollymount Strand ■ *290* Pope John Paul II Park ■ *291* Poppintree Park ■ *302* St. Anne's Park ■ *331* Tolka Valley Park ■ *333* Ward River Valley Park

**WEST DUBLIN**

*379* Celbridge Abbey Grounds ■ *398* Eamon Ceannt Park ■ *425* The Japanese Gardens and Irish National Stud ■ *429* Lansdowne Valley ■ *430* Larchill Arcadian Gardens ■ *435* Lodge Park Heritage Centre and Steam Museum ■ *451* Phoenix Park ■ *469* War Memorial Gardens

**SOUTH DUBLIN**

*477* Airfield Trust ■ *495* Big Sugar Loaf ■ *499* Blackrock Park ■ *513* Bray Strand/Bray Head ■ *515* Brickfield Park ■ *519* Bushy Park ■ *522* Cabinteely Park ■ *531* Clara Lara ■ *537* Dalkey Island ■ *541* Deerpark ■ *543* Devil's Glen ■ *545* Djouce Woods ■ *546* Dodder Park ■ *580* Glendalough ■ *593* Hellfire Club ■ *594* Herbert Park ■ *617* Kilbogget Park ■ *619* Killiney Hill Park/Dalkey Hill ■ *630* Little Sugar Loaf ■ *634* Marlay Park ■ *637* Massey Woods ■ *644* Mount Usher Gardens ■ *669* Pearse Museum and St. Enda's Park ■ *672* Pine Forest Arts Centre ■ *673* Powerscourt House and Gardens ■ *674* Powerscourt Waterfall ■ *680* Raven's Rock ■ *696* Shanganagh Park ■ *718* Three Rock Mountain

**ORGANISATIONS**

*761* Birdwatch Ireland

## Other Indoor Activities

There is a wide variety of interesting places to visit in Dublin, including castles, period houses and churches. Some are open for the first time, the results of some great restoration projects over the past few years. Don't think of historical places as too formal and boring for children – many have fantastic gardens, working farms, playgrounds or little museums that will keep them interested, and there are other fun ways to learn about the past, such as interactive exhibitions and workshops. The churches listed all hold a special interest for children (and are not for the faint-hearted!). There are many other types of places listed, such as indoor play areas with climbing nets, slides and ball pools, and specialist activities such as go-karting. (See also Cinemas, Leisure Centres, Sports, Museums, Art Galleries, Theatres and Libraries.)

## CITY CENTRE

2 Abbey Theatre ▪ 4 Alliance Française ▪ 9 Bank of Ireland Arts Centre ▪ 21 Chimney, The ▪ 22 Christ Church Cathedral ▪ 23 City Hall ▪ 26 Contemporary Music Centre, The ▪ 29 Custom House Visitor Centre ▪ 35 Dublin Castle ▪ 40 Dublinia ▪ 45 ENFO (Information on the Environment) ▪ 50 Gallery of Photography ▪ 54 General Post Office ▪ 66 Irish Film Centre ▪ 79 Marsh's Library ▪ 84 The Moving Crib ▪ 87 The National Library of Ireland ▪ 91 National Photographic Archive ▪ 92 National Wax Museum, The ▪ 94 Newman House ▪ 96 Number Twenty Nine ▪ 104 St. Audeon's Church ▪ 105 St. Mary's Pro-Cathedral ▪ 106 St. Michan's Church ▪ 107 St. Patrick's Cathedral ▪ 113 Shaw Birthplace ▪ 114 Smyth's Toys & Computer Games ▪ 117 Trinity College (The Dublin Experience and the Book of Kells) ▪ 122 Waterways Visitor Centre

## NORTH DUBLIN

140 Ardgillan Castle ▪ 142 Axis Arts Centre ▪ 189 Casino Marino ▪ 205 Dublin Butterfly House ▪ 216 Fry Model Railway Museum ▪ 241 Gymboree Music on the Go ▪ 258 Kart City Ltd (Indoor Karting and Skate Park) ▪ 260 Kidzone Play and Party Centre ▪ 262 Leisureplex, Coolock ▪ 264 Lusk Heritage Centre ▪ 265 Malahide Castle and Demesne ▪ 280 Newbridge House ▪ 281 Newgrange and Boyne Valley ▪ 306 Seamus Ennis Cultural Centre ▪ 310 Sillybilly Learning Ltd ▪ 313 Skerries Mills ▪ 329 Tara's Palace

## WEST DUBLIN

343 Alternative Entertainment Community Art Group ▪ 344 Áras an Uachtaráin ▪ 381 Civic Theatre ▪ 393 Draíocht ▪ 394 Drimnagh Castle ▪ 397 Dunsink Observatory ▪ 399 Farmleigh House ▪ 415 Giraffe's Play Centre ▪ 418 Gymboree Music on the Go ▪ 427 Kilmainham Gaol ▪ 432 Leisureplex, Blanchardstown ▪ 433 Leisureplex, Tallaght ▪ 435 Lodge Park Heritage Centre and Steam Museum ▪ 443 National Aquatic Centre ▪ 452 Phoenix Park Visitor Centre ▪ 457 Sillybilly Learning Ltd ▪ 461 Straffan Butterfly Farm ▪ 463 Superdome

## SOUTH DUBLIN

477 Airfield Trust ▪ 481 Artzone ▪ 520 The Busy Bee Summer School of Cooking ▪ 536 Dalkey Castle and Heritage Centre ▪ 565 Funderland ▪ 589 Gymboree Music on the Go ▪ 624 Lambert Puppet Theatre and Museum ▪ 629 Leisureplex, Stillorgan ▪ 638 Mermaid Theatre ▪ 649 National Sealife Centre ▪ 672 Pine Forest Arts Centre ▪ 678 Rathfarnham Castle ▪ 725 West Wood, Leopardstown (Sports Club)

## FESTIVALS

795 Children's Book Festival

## Other Outdoor Activities

There are many great outdoor activities to be found in and around Dublin, for children of all ages. You can get hands-on experience at visitor farms, hire your own soccer pitch or even have a thrilling boat ride in the sea. The choice is getting bigger each year. Many of these activities make a great birthday treat, and some places will even decorate a room when they have it, and supply food for a birthday party. (See also Beaches, Parks, Gardens, Walks and Sports.)

## CITY CENTRE

**32** *Dublin Bus City Tour, The* ▪ **33** *The Dublin Bus Coast and Castle Tour* ▪ **34** *The Dublin Bus South Coast Tour* ▪ **35** *Dublin Castle* ▪ **36** *Dublin City on Ice* ▪ **39** *The Dublin Ghost Bus Tour* ▪ **60** *Ice@IFSC* ▪ **63** *Irish City Coast and Garden Tour* ▪ **64** *Irish City, Dublin Bay and Castle Tour* ▪ **65** *Irish City Dublin Bus Tour* ▪ **70** *Irishtown Nature Park* ▪ **81** *Merrion Square* ▪ **108** *St. Stephen's Green* ▪ **112** *Sea Safari* ▪ **117** *Trinity College (The Dublin Experience and the Book of Kells)* ▪ **120** *Viking Splash Tour*

## NORTH DUBLIN

**140** *Ardgillan Castle* ▪ **189** *Casino Marino* ▪ **205** *Dublin Butterfly House* ▪ **252** *Howth Castle Gardens* ▪ **253** *Howth Head* ▪ **265** *Malahide Castle and Demesne* ▪ **276** *National Botanic Gardens* ▪ **279** *Newbridge Demesne* ▪ **281** *Newgrange and Boyne Valley* ▪ **282** *North Bull Island and Dollymount Strand* ▪ **296** *Ramp City* ▪ **297** *Ramp N Rail Skatepark* ▪ **299** *Reynoldstown Victorian Country House and Farm* ▪ **302** *St. Anne's Park* ▪ **307** *Sea Safari* ▪ **331** *Tolka Valley Park* ▪ **333** *Ward River Valley Park*

## WEST DUBLIN

**347** *Astro Park* ▪ **378** *Causey Farm* ▪ **379** *Celbridge Abbey Grounds* ▪ **394** *Drimnagh Castle* ▪ **396** *Dublin Zoo* ▪ **400** *First Flight Balloons* ▪ **401** *Fort Lucan* ▪ **425** *The Japanese Gardens and Irish National Stud* ▪ **428** *Kylemore Karting (Outdoor Karting)* ▪ **430** *Larchill Arcadian Gardens* ▪ **440** *Millennium Maze* ▪ **442** *Morrell Farm* ▪ **451** *Phoenix Park* ▪ **461** *Straffan Butterfly Farm*

## SOUTH DUBLIN

**477** *Airfield Trust* ▪ **480** *Annamoe Trout Farm* ▪ **495** *Big Sugar Loaf* ▪ **513** *Bray Strand/Bray Head* ▪ **519** *Bushy Park* ▪ **522** *Cabinteely Park* ▪ **531** *Clara Lara* ▪ **537** *Dalkey Island* ▪ **543** *Devil's Glen* ▪ **545** *Djouce Woods* ▪ **552** *Dublin Bay Sea Thrill* ▪ **580** *Glendalough* ▪ **593** *Hellfire Club* ▪ **619** *Killiney Hill Park/Dalkey Hill* ▪ **630** *Little Sugar Loaf* ▪ **634** *Marlay Park* ▪ **637** *Massey Woods* ▪ **644** *Mount Usher Gardens* ▪ **669** *Pearse Museum and St. Enda's Park* ▪ **672** *Pine Forest Arts Centre* ▪ **673** *Powerscourt House and Gardens* ▪ **674** *Powerscourt Waterfall* ▪ **678** *Rathfarnham Castle* ▪ **680** *Raven's Rock* ▪ **718** *Three Rock Mountain*

# Sports

We have listed the most popular sports, as well as some special-ised sports and sports clubs. We have given details of official organisa-tions, when a sport is governed by one, and contact details for your local group. We have also listed group meeting times, costs, equip-ment needed and summer camp details. As these arrangements are changeable, we recommend that you contact individual clubs to con-firm these details. We have included swimming pools where children and families can swim, including private, school, hospital and public swimming pools.

## Archery

**CITY CENTRE**
*53 Gate Theatre*

**NORTH DUBLIN**
*163 Blackheath Archers* ▪ *203 Dublin Archers* ▪ *317 Sportslink Archery and Crossbow Club* ▪ *318 Sportslink Club*

**WEST DUBLIN**
*385 Clondalkin Sports and Leisure Centre* ▪ *417 Greenhills Archers* ▪ *455 Roadstone Archers*

**SOUTH DUBLIN**
*547 Dolphin Activity Holidays* ▪ *556 Dún Laoghaire Archers*

**ORGANISATIONS**
*776 Irish Amateur Archery Association*

## Badminton

**NORTH DUBLIN**
*145 Baldoyle Badminton Centre* ▪ *293 Portmarnock Sports and Leisure Club* ▪ *318 Sportslink Club* ▪ *334 Westwood Health and Fitness Centre, Clontarf*

**WEST DUBLIN**
*385 Clondalkin Sports and Leisure Centre*

**SOUTH DUBLIN**
*547 Dolphin Activity Holidays* ▪ *562 ESB Sportsco* ▪ *643 Mount Pleasant Tennis and Squash Club* ▪ *651 Newpark School Sports Centre* ▪ *725 West Wood, Leopardstown (Sports Club)*

## Basketball

**CITY CENTRE**
*10 Basketball* ▪ *11 Tridents Basketball Club*

## NORTH DUBLIN

*151* Basketball ▪ *152* ABFRC Basketball Club ▪ *153* Corinthians Basketball Club ▪ *154* Crusaders Basketball Club ▪ *155* Killester Basketball Club ▪ *156* Mercy College Basketball Club ▪ *156* Kilsaran Basketball Club ▪ *157* Rangers Basketball Club ▪ *157* Malahide Basketball Club ▪ *158* Swords/Fingal Basketball Club ▪ *159* Tolka Rovers Basketball Club ▪ *160* Belcamp Park ▪ *194* Coláiste Íde Sports Complex ▪ *198* Dean Swift Sports Club ▪ *242* Hampstead Park (Albert College Park) ▪ *291* Poppintree Park ▪ *293* Portmarnock Sports and Leisure Club ▪ *318* Sportslink Club

## WEST DUBLIN

*351* Basketball ▪ *352* Drimnagh Basketball Club ▪ *353* Firhouse Basketball Club ▪ *354* Kilcock Ladies' Basketball Club ▪ *355* Kilnamanagh Basketball Club ▪ *356* Leixlip Basketball Club ▪ *357* Moyle Park Basketball Club ▪ *358* Rathcoole Rockets Basketball Club ▪ *385* Clondalkin Sports and Leisure Centre ▪ *398* Eamon Ceannt Park ▪ *431* Le Fanu Park ▪ *444* National Basketball Arena ▪ *468* Verona Sports and Leisure Club

## SOUTH DUBLIN

*487* Basketball ▪ *488* Ballyboden Basketball Club ▪ *489* Cluny Raiders Basketball Club ▪ *490* Comets Basketball Club ▪ *491* Dalkey Basketball Club ▪ *492* Meteors Basketball Club ▪ *493* Templeogue Basketball Club ▪ *562* ESB Sportsco ▪ *651* Newpark School Sports Centre

## ORGANISATIONS

*779* Irish Basketball Association

## Boxing

## CITY CENTRE

*14* Boxing ▪ *15* Corinthians Boxing Club ▪ *16* Inner City Boxing Club

## NORTH DUBLIN

*166* Boxing ▪ *167* Arbour Hill Boxing Club ▪ *168* Baldoyle Boxing Club ▪ *169* Ballymun Boxing Club ▪ *170* Baycity Boxing Club ▪ *171* Bracken Boxing Club ▪ *172* Cabra Panthers Boxing Club ▪ *173* Darndale Boxing Club ▪ *174* Dublin City Vocational Schools Boxing Club ▪ *175* Fingal Boxing Academy ▪ *176* Glasnevin Boxing Club ▪ *177* Glin Amateur Boxing Club ▪ *178* Phibsboro Boxing Club ▪ *179* Portmarnock Boxing Club ▪ *180* St. Brigid's Boxing Club, Bettystown ▪ *181* St. Luke's Boxing Club, Coolock ▪ *182* St. Pappin's Boxing Club, Popintree ▪ *183* St. Saviour's Olympic Boxing Club, Santry ▪ *184* Swords Boxing Club

## WEST DUBLIN

*362* Boxing ▪ *363* Drimnagh Boxing Club ▪ *364* Golden Cobra Boxing Club ▪ *365* Lucan Boxing Club ▪ *366* Mulhuddart Boxing Club ▪ *367* Neilstown Boxing Club ▪ *368* Quarryvale Boxing Club ▪ *369* Sacred Heart Tallaght Boxing Club ▪ *370* St. Mary's Boxing Club, Saggart ▪ *371* St. Matthew's Boxing Club, Ballyfermot ▪ *372* West Side Tallaght Boxing Club

## SOUTH DUBLIN

*504* Boxing ▪ *505* Avona Boxing Club ▪ *506* CIE Boxing Club ▪ *507* Crumlin

Boxing Club ▪ **508** Donore Boxing Club ▪ **509** Ferrini Boxing Club ▪ **510** Mount Tallant Boxing Club ▪ **511** St. Joseph's Boxing Club, Ballyboden ▪ **672** Pine Forest Arts Centre

## ORGANISATIONS
**762** Irish Amateur Boxing Association

## Cricket

### NORTH DUBLIN
**244** Hills Cricket Club ▪ **301** Rush Cricket Club

### WEST DUBLIN
**450** Phoenix Cricket Club ▪ **451** Phoenix Park

### SOUTH DUBLIN
**628** Leinster Cricket Club ▪ **634** Marlay Park ▪ **675** Railway Union Sports Club

## Cycling

### NORTH DUBLIN
**160** Belcamp Park ▪ **208** Edenmore Park ▪ **209** Ellenfield Park ▪ **210** Fairview Park ▪ **211** Father Collins Park ▪ **240** Griffith Park ▪ **242** Hampstead Park (Albert College Park) ▪ **272** May Park (Doneycarney Park) ▪ **273** Mellowes Park (Casement Park) ▪ **290** Pope John Paul II Park ▪ **291** Poppintree Park ▪ **302** St. Anne's Park ▪ **319** Stanmullen Road Club (Cycling) ▪ **320** Stardust Memorial Park ▪ **327** Swords Cycling Club

### WEST DUBLIN
**398** Eamon Ceannt Park ▪ **451** Phoenix Park ▪ **467** Usher Irish Road Cycling Club ▪ **469** War Memorial Gardens

### SOUTH DUBLIN
**499** Blackrock Park ▪ **514** Bray Wheelers Cycling Club ▪ **522** Cabinteely Park ▪ **541** Deerpark ▪ **617** Kilbogget Park ▪ **631** Loreto Park

### ORGANISATIONS
**767** Cycling Ireland

## Diving

### NORTH DUBLIN
**277** National Diving School

### WEST DUBLIN
**443** National Aquatic Centre

### SOUTH DUBLIN
**537** Dalkey Island ▪ **584** Greystones Beach ▪ **691** Sandycove/Forty Foot

## Gaelic Football

**CITY CENTRE**

*31 Diamond Park*

**NORTH DUBLIN**

*160 Belcamp Park ▪ 208 Edenmore Park ▪ 209 Ellenfield Park ▪ 210 Fairview Park ▪ 211 Father Collins Park ▪ 217 GAA ▪ 218 Beann Eadair GAA Club ▪ 219 Clontarf GAA Club ▪ 220 Craobh Chiarain GAA Club ▪ 221 Erin's Isle GAA Club ▪ 222 Fingallians GAA Club ▪ 223 Innisfáil GAA Club ▪ 224 Naomh Barrog GAA Club ▪ 225 Naomh Fionnbarra GAA Club ▪ 226 Naomh Mearnog GAA Club ▪ 227 O'Dwyer's GAA Club ▪ 228 Parnell's GAA Club ▪ 229 Raheny GAA Club ▪ 230 St. Monica's GAA Club ▪ 231 St. Oliver Plunkett's GAA Club ▪ 232 St. Sylvester's GAA Club ▪ 233 St. Vincent's GAA Club ▪ 234 Scoil Uí Chonaill GAA Club ▪ 235 Skerries Harps GAA Club ▪ 236 Whitehall Colmcille GAA Club ▪ 237 GAA Museum ▪ 242 Hampstead Park (Albert College Park) ▪ 257 Johnstown Park ▪ 272 May Park (Doneycarney Park) ▪ 290 Pope John Paul II Park ▪ 291 Poppintree Park ▪ 302 St. Anne's Park ▪ 304 St. Maur's Gaelic Football Club ▪ 331 Tolka Valley Park ▪ 333 Ward River Valley Park*

**WEST DUBLIN**

*391 Coolmine Sports and Leisure Centre ▪ 398 Eamon Ceannt Park ▪ 403 GAA ▪ 404 Ballyboden/St. Enda's GAA Club ▪ 406 Liffey Gaels GAA Club ▪ 408 Round Tower GAA Club ▪ 409 St. Anne's GAA Club ▪ 410 St. Brigid's GAA Club ▪ 411 St. Mark's GAA Club ▪ 412 St. Mary's GAA Club ▪ 413 St. Peregrine's GAA Club ▪ 414 Thomas Davis GAA Sports Club ▪ 439 Markievicz Park ▪ 451 Phoenix Park*

**SOUTH DUBLIN**

*497 Blackrock College Summer Schoool ▪ 519 Bushy Park ▪ 563 Faughs Hurling Club ▪ 570 GAA ▪ 571 Clan na Gael Fontenoy GAA Club ▪ 572 Crumlin GAA Club ▪ 573 Cuala GAA Club ▪ 574 St. Jude's GAA Club ▪ 578 Glenalbyn Sports Club ▪ 594 Herbert Park ▪ 634 Marlay Park ▪ 669 Pearse Museum and St. Enda's Park ▪ 721 Walkinstown Park ▪ 727 Willie Pearse Park*

**ORGANISATIONS**

*771 GAA*

## Golf

**NORTH DUBLIN**

*160 Belcamp Park ▪ 198 Dean Swift Sports Club ▪ 208 Edenmore Park ▪ 265 Malahide Castle and Demesne ▪ 309 Sillogue Park and Golf Course*

**WEST DUBLIN**

*401 Fort Lucan*

**SOUTH DUBLIN**

*531 Clara Lara ▪ 634 Marlay Park*

## Hockey

**NORTH DUBLIN**

*208 Edenmore Park ▪ 246 Hockey ▪ 247 Clontarf Hockey Club ▪ 248 Portrane Hockey Club ▪ 249 Skerries Hockey Club ▪ 250 Sportslink Eastern Health Hockey Club ▪ 251 Suttonians Hockey Club ▪ 257 Johnstown Park ▪ 272 May Park (Doneycarney Park) ▪ 302 St. Anne's Park*

**WEST DUBLIN**

*419 Hockey ▪ 420 Glenanne Hockey Club ▪ 421 Weston Hockey Club*

**SOUTH DUBLIN**

*595 Hockey ▪ 596 Avoca Hockey Club ▪ 597 Bray Hockey Club ▪ 598 Corinthian Hockey Club ▪ 599 Monkstown Hockey Club ▪ 600 Pembroke Wanderers Hockey Club ▪ 601 Railway Union Hockey Club ▪ 602 St. James's Gate Hockey Club ▪ 603 Smithfield Hockey Club ▪ 604 Three Rock Rovers Hockey Club ▪ 605 YMCA Hockey Club ▪ 675 Railway Union Sports Club*

**ORGANISATIONS**

*775 Irish Hockey Association*

## Horse Riding

**NORTH DUBLIN**

*207 Dymphna's Equestrian Centre ▪ 214 Forrest Equestrian Centre ▪ 261 Kilronan Equestrian Centre ▪ 285 Oldtown Riding Stables ▪ 292 Portmarnock Beach ▪ 330 Thornton Park Riding*

**WEST DUBLIN**

*346 Ashtown Stables ▪ 375 Carton Equestrian Centre ▪ 388 Coolmine Equestrian Centre ▪ 426 Kill International ▪ 449 Pelletstown Riding Centre ▪ 451 Phoenix Park ▪ 453 Phoenix Riding Stables*

**SOUTH DUBLIN**

*524 Calliaghstown Riding Centre ▪ 526 Carrickmines Equestrian Centre ▪ 547 Dolphin Activity Holidays ▪ 618 Killegar Stables ▪ 664 Paddocks Riding Centre*

**ORGANISATIONS**

*760 Association of Irish Riding Establisments*

## Hurling

**CITY CENTRE**

*31 Diamond Park*

**NORTH DUBLIN**

*160 Belcamp Park ▪ 208 Edenmore Park ▪ 209 Ellenfield Park ▪ 210 Fairview Park ▪ 211 Father Collins Park ▪ 217 GAA ▪ 218 Beann Eadair GAA Club ▪ 219 Clontarf GAA Club ▪ 220 Craobh Chiarain GAA Club ▪ 221 Erin's Isle GAA Club ▪ 222 Fingallians GAA Club ▪ 223 Innisfáil GAA Club ▪ 224 Naomh Barrog GAA Club ▪ 225 Naomh Fionnbarra GAA Club ▪ 226*

*Naomh Mearnog GAA Club* ▪ **227** *O'Dwyer's GAA Club* ▪ **228** *Parnell's GAA Club* ▪ **229** *Raheny GAA Club* ▪ **230** *St. Monica's GAA Club* ▪ **231** *St. Oliver Plunkett's GAA Club* ▪ **232** *St. Sylvester's GAA Club* ▪ **233** *St. Vincent's GAA Club* ▪ **234** *Scoil Uí Chonaill GAA Club* ▪ **235** *Skerries Harps GAA Club* ▪ **236** *Whitehall Colmcille GAA Club* ▪ **237** *GAA Museum* ▪ **242** *Hampstead Park (Albert College Park)* ▪ **257** *Johnstown Park* ▪ **272** *May Park (Doneycarney Park)* ▪ **290** *Pope John Paul II Park* ▪ **291** *Poppintree Park* ▪ **302** *St. Anne's Park* ▪ **331** *Tolka Valley Park* ▪ **333** *Ward River Valley Park*

## WEST DUBLIN

**391** *Coolmine Sports and Leisure Centre* ▪ **398** *Eamon Ceannt Park* ▪ **403** *GAA* ▪ **404** *Ballyboden/St. Enda's GAA Club* ▪ **405** *Commercial Hurling Club* ▪ **406** *Liffey Gaels GAA Club* ▪ **407** *Lucan Sarsfields GAA Club* ▪ **408** *Round Tower GAA Club* ▪ **409** *St. Anne's GAA Club* ▪ **410** *St. Brigid's GAA Club* ▪ **411** *St. Mark's GAA Club* ▪ **412** *St. Mary's GAA Club* ▪ **413** *St. Peregrine's GAA Club* ▪ **414** *Thomas Davis GAA Sports Club* ▪ **451** *Phoenix Park*

## SOUTH DUBLIN

**497** *Blackrock College Summer Schoool* ▪ **519** *Bushy Park* ▪ **563** *Faughs Hurling Club* ▪ **570** *GAA* ▪ **571** *Clan na Gael Fontenoy GAA Club* ▪ **572** *Crumlin GAA Club* ▪ **573** *Cuala GAA Club* ▪ **574** *St. Jude's GAA Club* ▪ **578** *Glenalbyn Sports Club* ▪ **594** *Herbert Park* ▪ **634** *Marlay Park* ▪ **721** *Walkinstown Park* ▪ **727** *Willie Pearse Park*

## ORGANISATIONS

**771** *GAA*

# IceSkating

## CITY CENTRE

**36** *Dublin City on Ice* ▪ **60** *Ice@IFSC*

# MartialArts

## CITY CENTRE

**115** *Taekwon-Do Centre*

## NORTH DUBLIN

**141** *AutoDefence Wing Tchun* ▪ **334** *Westwood Health and Fitness Centre, Clontarf*

## WEST DUBLIN

**391** *Coolmine Sports and Leisure Centre*

## SOUTH DUBLIN

**485** *Ballyroan Karate Club* ▪ **539** *David Lloyd Riverview Racquet and Fitness Club* ▪ **581** *Golden Eagle Kenpo and Self Defense Schools* ▪ **635** *Martial Arts Centre* ▪ **677** *Rathdown Kenpo Club* ▪ **686** *St. Columba's Health and Fitness Club* ▪ **710** *Stillorgan Tae kwon do* ▪ **724** *Wei Chi Kung Fu, Blackrock* ▪ **725** *West Wood, Leopardstown (Sports Club)*

## Rowing

### WEST DUBLIN

*385* Clondalkin Sports and Leisure Centre ▪ *386* Commercial Rowing Club ▪ *395* Dublin Municipal Rowing Centre ▪ *445* Neptune Rowing Club

### SOUTH DUBLIN

*531* Clara Lara ▪ *537* Dalkey Island ▪ *547* Dolphin Activity Holidays ▪ *694* Seapoint

### ORGANISATIONS

*790* Rowing Union

## Rugby

### NORTH DUBLIN

*192* Clontarf Rugby Football Club ▪ *208* Edenmore Park ▪ *257* Johnstown Park ▪ *267* Malahide Rugby Football Club ▪ *314* Skerries Rugby Football Club ▪ *325* Suttonians Rugby Football Club

### WEST DUBLIN

*345* Ashbourne Rugby Football Club ▪ *350* Barnhall Rugby Football Club ▪ *384* Clondalkin Rugby Football Club ▪ *390* Coolmine Rugby Football Club

### SOUTH DUBLIN

*494* Bective Rangers Rugby Football Club ▪ *496* Blackrock College Rugby Football Club ▪ *539* David Lloyd Riverview Racquet and Fitness Club ▪ *586* Greystones Rugby Football Club ▪ *587* Guinness Rugby Football Club ▪ *617* Kilbogget Park ▪ *625* Lansdowne Football Club ▪ *641* Monkstown Rugby Football Club ▪ *661* Old Belvedere Rugby Football Club ▪ *662* Old Wesley Rugby Football Club ▪ *688* St. Mary's College Rugby Football Club ▪ *695* Seapoint Rugby Football Club ▪ *717* Terenure Rugby Football Club ▪ *723* Wanderers Rugby Football Club

### ORGANISATIONS

*782* Irish Rugby Football Union

## Sailing

### CITY CENTRE

*55* Glenans Sailing

### NORTH DUBLIN

*212* Fingall Sailing School, Malahide ▪ *256* Howth Yacht Club ▪ *268* Malahide Yacht Club ▪ *275* Muldowney Beach (Malahide) ▪ *300* Rush Beach ▪ *311* Skerries Beach ▪ *315* Skerries Sailing Club ▪ *324* Sutton Dinghy Club

### SOUTH DUBLIN

*501* Blessington Activity Centre ▪ *502* Blessington Sailing Club ▪ *547* Dolphin Activity Holidays ▪ *614* Irish National Sailing School ▪ *684* Royal Irish Yacht Club ▪ *685* Royal St. George Yacht Club ▪ *712* Surfdock ▪ *728* Wind & Wave Water Sports

**ORGANISATIONS**

*783* Irish Sailing Association ▪ *791* Scouting Ireland

## Skateboarding

**NORTH DUBLIN**

*296* Ramp City ▪ *297* Ramp N Rail Skatepark

**SOUTH DUBLIN**

*562* ESB Sportsco

## Skiing

**SOUTH DUBLIN**

*621* Kilternan Sports Hotel

## Soccer

**CITY CENTRE**

*31* Diamond Park ▪ *76* Liberty Park ▪ *83* Mountjoy Square Park

**NORTH DUBLIN**

*160* Belcamp Park ▪ *161* Belgrove Football Club ▪ *164* Bohemians Football Club ▪ *198* Dean Swift Sports Club ▪ *208* Edenmore Park ▪ *209* Ellenfield Park ▪ *210* Fairview Park ▪ *211* Father Collins Park ▪ *242* Hampstead Park (Albert College Park) ▪ *257* Johnstown Park ▪ *270* Marino Boys Soccer Club (Association Football Club) ▪ *272* May Park (Doneycarney Park) ▪ *273* Mellowes Park (Casement Park) ▪ *290* Pope John Paul II Park ▪ *291* Poppintree Park ▪ *293* Portmarnock Sports and Leisure Club ▪ *295* Raheny United Football Club ▪ *302* St. Anne's Park ▪ *318* Sportslink Club ▪ *331* Tolka Valley Park ▪ *333* Ward River Valley Park

**WEST DUBLIN**

*347* Astro Park ▪ *380* Cherry Orchard Football Club ▪ *385* Clondalkin Sports and Leisure Centre ▪ *398* Eamon Ceannt Park ▪ *431* Le Fanu Park ▪ *439* Markievicz Park ▪ *456* St. Patrick's Athletic Football Club ▪ *468* Verona Sports and Leisure Club

**SOUTH DUBLIN**

*484* Ballybrack Boys Association Football Club) ▪ *497* Blackrock College Summer Schoool ▪ *515* Brickfield Park ▪ *519* Bushy Park ▪ *522* Cabinteely Park ▪ *542* De La Salle Palmerstown Football Club ▪ *546* Dodder Park ▪ *562* ESB Sportsco ▪ *594* Herbert Park ▪ *617* Kilbogget Park ▪ *631* Loreto Park ▪ *634* Marlay Park ▪ *651* Newpark School Sports Centre ▪ *669* Pearse Museum and St. Enda's Park ▪ *675* Railway Union Sports Club ▪ *676* Rathcoole Boys Football Club ▪ *683* Ringsend Park ▪ *687* St. Joseph's Boys Association Football Club ▪ *690* Samba Soccer School ▪ *696* Shanganagh Park ▪ *704* Stannaway Park ▪ *721* Walkinstown Park ▪ *727* Willie Pearse Park

**ORGANISATIONS**

*769* Football Association of Ireland

## Squash

**NORTH DUBLIN**

*293* Portmarnock Sports and Leisure Club ▪ *326* Sutton Lawn Tennis Club ▪ *334* Westwood Health and Fitness Centre, Clontarf

**SOUTH DUBLIN**

*539* David Lloyd Riverview Racquet and Fitness Club ▪ *643* Mount Pleasant Tennis and Squash Club ▪ *692* Sandycove Tennis and Squash Club ▪ *725* West Wood, Leopardstown (Sports Club)

## Swimming

**CITY CENTRE**

*77* Markiewicz Leisure Centre

**NORTH DUBLIN**

*143* Balbriggan Beach ▪ *148* Ballymun Swimming Pool ▪ *199* Donabate/Portrane Beach ▪ *263* Loughshinny Beach ▪ *275* Muldowney Beach (Malahide) ▪ *282* North Bull Island and Dollymount Strand ▪ *292* Portmarnock Beach ▪ *293* Portmarnock Sports and Leisure Club ▪ *300* Rush Beach ▪ *303* St. Mary's Hospital Pool ▪ *305* St. Vincent's CBS Pool ▪ *311* Skerries Beach ▪ *318* Sportslink Club ▪ *323* Sutton Beach ▪ *334* Westwood Health and Fitness Centre, Clontarf

**WEST DUBLIN**

*349* Ballyfermot Swimming Pool ▪ *385* Clondalkin Sports and Leisure Centre ▪ *391* Coolmine Sports and Leisure Centre ▪ *431* Le Fanu Park ▪ *443* National Aquatic Centre ▪ *464* Tallaght Community School Sports Complex

**SOUTH DUBLIN**

*497* Blackrock College Summer Schoool ▪ *513* Bray Strand/Bray Head ▪ *516* Brittas Bay ▪ *527* Cerebral Palsy Ireland Swimming Pool ▪ *528* Cheeverstown House Leisure Centre ▪ *531* Clara Lara ▪ *537* Dalkey Island ▪ *539* David Lloyd Riverview Racquet and Fitness Club ▪ *547* Dolphin Activity Holidays ▪ *562* ESB Sportsco ▪ *578* Glenalbyn Sports Club ▪ *584* Greystones Beach ▪ *620* Killiney Strand ▪ *621* Kilternan Sports Hotel ▪ *623* LA Fitness ▪ *633* Marian College ▪ *639* Mespil Swimming Pool ▪ *642* Monkstown Swimming Pool and Fitness Centre ▪ *645* Murrow Strand ▪ *651* Newpark School Sports Centre ▪ *691* Sandycove/Forty Foot ▪ *694* Seapoint ▪ *700* Silver Strand ▪ *714* Templeogue College Swimming Pool ▪ *725* West Wood, Leopardstown (Sports Club)

**ORGANISATIONS**

*791* Scouting Ireland ▪ *792* Swim Ireland

## Tennis

**CITY CENTRE**

*83* Mountjoy Square Park

## NORTH DUBLIN

*160* Belcamp Park ▪ *190* Charleville Lawn Tennis Club ▪ *191* Clontarf Lawn Tennis Club ▪ *198* Dean Swift Sports Club ▪ *209* Ellenfield Park ▪ *239* Glasnevin Lawn Tennis Club ▪ *242* Hampstead Park (Albert College Park) ▪ *257* Johnstown Park ▪ *273* Mellowes Park (Casement Park) ▪ *291* Poppintree Park ▪ *293* Portmarnock Sports and Leisure Club ▪ *302* St. Anne's Park ▪ *318* Sportslink Club ▪ *326* Sutton Lawn Tennis Club ▪ *328* Swords Lawn Tennis Club ▪ *333* Ward River Valley Park ▪ *334* Westwood Health and Fitness Centre, Clontarf

## WEST DUBLIN

*376* Castleknock Lawn Tennis Club ▪ *398* Eamon Ceannt Park ▪ *431* Le Fanu Park

## SOUTH DUBLIN

*482* Ashbrook Lawn Tennis Club ▪ *517* Brookfield Lawn Tennis Club ▪ *519* Bushy Park ▪ *525* Carrickmines Croquet and Lawns ▪ *539* David Lloyd Riverview Racquet and Fitness Club ▪ *541* Deerpark ▪ *547* Dolphin Activity Holidays ▪ *549* Donnybrook Lawn Tennis Club ▪ *577* Glenageary Lawn Tennis Club ▪ *578* Glenalbyn Sports Club ▪ *585* Greystones Lawn Tennis Club ▪ *594* Herbert Park ▪ *621* Kilternan Sports Hotel ▪ *626* Lansdowne Tennis Club ▪ *628* Leinster Cricket Club ▪ *634* Marlay Park ▪ *643* Mount Pleasant Tennis and Squash Club ▪ *651* Newpark School Sports Centre ▪ *675* Railway Union Sports Club ▪ *683* Ringsend Park ▪ *692* Sandycove Tennis and Squash Club ▪ *696* Shanganagh Park ▪ *698* Shankill Tennis Club ▪ *711* Stratford Tennis Club ▪ *715* Templeogue Tennis Club ▪ *721* Walkinstown Park ▪ *725* West Wood, Leopardstown (Sports Club)

## ORGANISATIONS

*768* Dublin Parks Tennis League (KitKat) ▪ *793* Tennis Ireland

## Windsurfing

## NORTH DUBLIN

*212* Fingall Sailing School, Malahide ▪ *275* Muldowney Beach (Malahide) ▪ *282* North Bull Island and Dollymount Strand ▪ *300* Rush Beach ▪ *311* Skerries Beach

## SOUTH DUBLIN

*501* Blessington Activity Centre ▪ *547* Dolphin Activity Holidays ▪ *694* Seapoint ▪ *712* Surfdock ▪ *728* Wind & Wave Water Sports

## ORGANISATIONS

*783* Irish Sailing Association

# Top Choices

These are our personal favourites in each of the categories below:

## Top Choices: Beaches

### NORTH DUBLIN

*199* Donabate/Portrane Beach ■ *282* North Bull Island and Dollymount Strand ■ *292* Portmarnock Beach ■ *311* Skerries Beach

### SOUTH DUBLIN

*516* Brittas Bay ■ *537* Dalkey Island ■ *584* Greystones Beach ■ *620* Killiney Strand

## Top Choices: Birthday Party Ideas

### CITY CENTRE

*5* Ark, The: Children's Cultural Centre ■ *36* Dublin City on Ice ■ *39* The Dublin Ghost Bus Tour ■ *47* Flamenco y Más ■ *49* Gaiety Theatre ■ *92* National Wax Museum, The ■ *100* Point Theatre ■ *112* Sea Safari ■ *118* UGC Cinemas ■ *120* Viking Splash Tour ■ *130* Eddie Rockets Diner ■ *135* TGI Friday ■ *136* Thunder Road Café

### NORTH DUBLIN

*205* Dublin Butterfly House ■ *237* GAA Museum ■ *258* Kart City Ltd (Indoor Karting and Skate Park) ■ *259* Kiddie Kuts ■ *260* Kidzone Play and Party Centre ■ *287* Omniplex Cinemas ■ *296* Ramp City ■ *299* Reynoldstown Victorian Country House and Farm ■ *307* Sea Safari ■ *310* Sillybilly Learning Ltd ■ *334* Westwood Health and Fitness Centre, Clontarf ■ *338* Casa Pasta ■ *339* Eddie Rockets Diner

### WEST DUBLIN

*347* Astro Park ■ *385* Clondalkin Sports and Leisure Centre ■ *396* Dublin Zoo ■ *400* First Flight Balloons ■ *415* Giraffe's Play Centre ■ *428* Kylemore Karting (Outdoor Karting) ■ *430* Larchill Arcadian Gardens ■ *432* Leisureplex, Blanchardstown ■ *433* Leisureplex, Tallaght ■ *442* Morrell Farm ■ *443* National Aquatic Centre ■ *457* Sillybilly Learning Ltd ■ *460* Ster Century Multiplex Cinemas ■ *463* Superdome ■ *465* UCI Blanchardstown ■ *466* UCI Tallaght ■ *471* Eddie Rockets Diner ■ *472* Joel's Restaurant ■ *474* Spur Steakhouse ■ *475* TGI Friday's

### SOUTH DUBLIN

*503* Bloomfields Shopping Centre ■ *531* Clara Lara ■ *552* Dublin Bay Sea Thrill ■ *562* ESB Sportsco ■ *590* Gymboree Play and Music ■ *616* Kiddie Kuts ■ *621* Kilternan Sports Hotel ■ *624* Lambert Puppet Theatre and Museum ■ *629* Leisureplex, Stillorgan ■ *649* National Sealife Centre ■ *663* Ormonde Cinemas ■ *699* Sillybilly Learning Ltd ■ *725* West Wood, Leopardstown (Sports Club) ■ *734* Eddie Rockets Diner

### PARTY SERVICES

*751* Clown Zone ■ *755* Leinster Bounce ■ *758* Táshí Party Services

## Top Choices: Child-friendly Restaurants/Cafés

**CITY CENTRE**

*20 Chester Beatty Library, The* ▪ *24 Clery's Department Store* ▪ *30 Debenham's Department Store* ▪ *35 Dublin Castle* ▪ *43 Dublin Writers' Museum* ▪ *66 Irish Film Centre* ▪ *68 Irish Museum of Modern Art* ▪ *86 National Gallery of Ireland* ▪ *109 St. Stephen's Green Shopping Centre* ▪ *128 Captain America's* ▪ *132 Lemon Café* ▪ *133 Milano* ▪ *135 TGI Friday* ▪ *136 Thunder Road Café* ▪ *137 Trentuno* ▪ *138 Wagamama*

**NORTH DUBLIN**

*265 Malahide Castle and Demesne* ▪ *338 Casa Pasta* ▪ *339 Eddie Rockets Diner* ▪ *341 Giovanni's Restaurant* ▪ *342 Wong's (Chinese Restaurant)*

**WEST DUBLIN**

*470 Angler's Rest (Pub)* ▪ *472 Joel's Restaurant* ▪ *474 Spur Steakhouse*

**SOUTH DUBLIN**

*732 Bits & Pizzas* ▪ *738 Luigi Malone's Restaurant*

## Top Choices: Christmas Visits

Besides the list of things we've shown here, it's also worth checking libraries, museums and historic houses, which often run special events for children at Christmas.

**CITY CENTRE**

*5 Ark, The: Children's Cultural Centre* ▪ *22 Christ Church Cathedral* ▪ *23 City Hall* ▪ *36 Dublin City on Ice* ▪ *49 Gaiety Theatre* ▪ *53 Gate Theatre* ▪ *75 Liberty Hall Theatre* ▪ *84 The Moving Crib* ▪ *85 National Concert Hall* ▪ *97 Olympia Theatre* ▪ *100 Point Theatre* ▪ *107 St. Patrick's Cathedral*

**NORTH DUBLIN**

*142 Axis Arts Centre* ▪ *243 Helix, The (Theatre)*

**WEST DUBLIN**

*381 Civic Theatre* ▪ *393 Draíocht* ▪ *399 Farmleigh House* ▪ *430 Larchill Arcadian Gardens*

**SOUTH DUBLIN**

*565 Funderland* ▪ *583 Grainstore Youth Arts Centre The* ▪ *624 Lambert Puppet Theatre and Museum* ▪ *638 Mermaid Theatre* ▪ *668 Pavilion Theatre*

**FESTIVALS**

*805 Santa's Kingdom*

## Top Choices: Hobbies/Arts and Crafts

**CITY CENTRE**

*12 Behan, Sylvia, School of Ballet* ▪ *41 Dublin School of Classical & Contemporary Dance* ▪ *46 Flagship Scuba Diving* ▪ *62 Independent Theatre Work-*

shop, North Frederick St ▪ 74 Leinster School of Music and Drama ▪ 80 The Merriman School Of Singing and Music ▪ 82 Millar Flora Dance Centres ▪ 95 Norton, Betty Ann, Theatre School, Harcourt St ▪ 103 Royal Irish Academy of Music ▪ 115 Taekwon-Do Centre

## NORTH DUBLIN

163 Blackheath Archers ▪ 165 Botanic Art School, The ▪ 186 Brushstrokes Art School ▪ 188 Cadwell, Cora, School Of Dancing ▪ 190 Charleville Lawn Tennis Club ▪ 191 Clontarf Lawn Tennis Club ▪ 206 Dublin Youth Symphonia ▪ 217 GAA ▪ 244 Hills Cricket Club ▪ 255 Howth Rock Guitar and Songwriting School ▪ 268 Malahide Yacht Club ▪ 270 Marino Boys Soccer Club (Association Football Club) ▪ 277 National Diving School ▪ 284 Norton, Betty Ann, Theatre School, Swords ▪ 319 Stanmullen Road Club (Cycling) ▪ 321 Starstruck Stage School, Clontarf ▪ 324 Sutton Dinghy Club

## WEST DUBLIN

343 Alternative Entertainment Community Art Group ▪ 346 Ashtown Stables ▪ 351 Basketball ▪ 386 Commercial Rowing Club ▪ 388 Coolmine Equestrian Centre ▪ 402 Futurekids, Lucan ▪ 403 GAA ▪ 419 Hockey ▪ 420 Glenanne Hockey Club ▪ 423 Independent Theatre Workshop, Ballycullen Ave ▪ 426 Kill International ▪ 438 Lucan Youth Dance/Drama Group ▪ 445 Neptune Rowing Club ▪ 450 Phoenix Cricket Club ▪ 454 Piccolo Lasso Choir

## SOUTH DUBLIN

481 Artzone ▪ 485 Ballyroan Karate Club ▪ 487 Basketball ▪ 496 Blackrock College Rugby Football Club ▪ 502 Blessington Sailing Club ▪ 526 Carrickmines Equestrian Centre ▪ 529 Churchtown Keyboard School ▪ 553 Dublin Folk Dance Group ▪ 558 Dún Laoghaire Music Centre ▪ 560 Dún Laoghaire Youth Dance Theatre ▪ 566 Futurekids, Dún Laoghaire ▪ 570 GAA ▪ 608 Independent Theatre Workshop, Mornington Rd ▪ 612 Irish Children's Theatre Group ▪ 622 Kodály Society of Ireland ▪ 627 Leeson Park School of Music ▪ 628 Leinster Cricket Club ▪ 635 Martial Arts Centre ▪ 650 Newpark Music Centre ▪ 667 Park Singers Choir ▪ 672 Pine Forest Arts Centre ▪ 690 Samba Soccer School ▪ 705 Starstruck Stage School, Clonskeagh ▪ 706 Starstruck Stage School, Foxrock ▪ 712 Surfdock ▪ 719 Tiggy's Art School ▪ 729 Young European Strings

## Top Choices: Parks

### CITY CENTRE
108 St. Stephen's Green

### NORTH DUBLIN

140 Ardgillan Castle ▪ 265 Malahide Castle and Demesne ▪ 276 National Botanic Gardens ▪ 279 Newbridge Demesne ▪ 302 St. Anne's Park ▪ 331 Tolka Valley Park ▪ 333 Ward River Valley Park

### WEST DUBLIN

379 Celbridge Abbey Grounds ▪ 394 Drimnagh Castle ▪ 425 The Japanese Gardens and Irish National Stud ▪ 430 Larchill Arcadian Gardens ▪ 435 Lodge Park Heritage Centre and Steam Museum ▪ 440 Millennium Maze ▪

*451* Phoenix Park ▪ *469* War Memorial Gardens

## SOUTH DUBLIN

*519* Bushy Park ▪ *522* Cabinteely Park ▪ *594* Herbert Park ▪ *619* Killiney Hill Park/Dalkey Hill ▪ *634* Marlay Park ▪ *644* Mount Usher Gardens ▪ *673* Powerscourt House and Gardens ▪ *674* Powerscourt Waterfall

# Top Choices: Picnics

## CITY CENTRE

*81* Merrion Square ▪ *108* St. Stephen's Green ▪ *112* Sea Safari

## NORTH DUBLIN

*140* Ardgillan Castle ▪ *205* Dublin Butterfly House ▪ *265* Malahide Castle and Demesne ▪ *279* Newbridge Demesne ▪ *299* Reynoldstown Victorian Country House and Farm ▪ *302* St. Anne's Park ▪ *307* Sea Safari

## WEST DUBLIN

*379* Celbridge Abbey Grounds ▪ *425* The Japanese Gardens and Irish National Stud ▪ *430* Larchill Arcadian Gardens ▪ *442* Morrell Farm ▪ *451* Phoenix Park

## SOUTH DUBLIN

*531* Clara Lara ▪ *580* Glendalough ▪ *630* Little Sugar Loaf ▪ *637* Massey Woods

# Top Choices: Playgrounds (Indoor & Outdoor)

## CITY CENTRE

*108* St. Stephen's Green

## NORTH DUBLIN

*140* Ardgillan Castle ▪ *242* Hampstead Park (Albert College Park) ▪ *260* Kidzone Play and Party Centre ▪ *262* Leisureplex, Coolock ▪ *265* Malahide Castle and Demesne ▪ *279* Newbridge Demesne ▪ *302* St. Anne's Park

## WEST DUBLIN

*379* Celbridge Abbey Grounds ▪ *401* Fort Lucan ▪ *415* Giraffe's Play Centre ▪ *430* Larchill Arcadian Gardens ▪ *432* Leisureplex, Blanchardstown ▪ *433* Leisureplex, Tallaght ▪ *440* Millennium Maze ▪ *463* Superdome

## SOUTH DUBLIN

*499* Blackrock Park ▪ *519* Bushy Park ▪ *531* Clara Lara ▪ *590* Gymboree Play and Music ▪ *629* Leisureplex, Stillorgan ▪ *631* Loreto Park ▪ *634* Marlay Park ▪ *665* Palmerston Park ▪ *671* People's Park ▪ *674* Powerscourt Waterfall

# Top Choices: Sports Facilities

## CITY CENTRE

*36* Dublin City on Ice ▪ *46* Flagship Scuba Diving ▪ *55* Glenans Sailing ▪ *83* Mountjoy Square Park

## NORTH DUBLIN

*190* Charleville Lawn Tennis Club ■ *198* Dean Swift Sports Club ■ *207* Dymphna's Equestrian Centre ■ *208* Edenmore Park ■ *209* Ellenfield Park ■ *210* Fairview Park ■ *212* Fingall Sailing School, Malahide ■ *237* GAA Museum ■ *257* Johnstown Park ■ *258* Kart City Ltd (Indoor Karting and Skate Park) ■ *261* Kilronan Equestrian Centre ■ *274* Morton Stadium ■ *277* National Diving School ■ *285* Oldtown Riding Stables ■ *293* Portmarnock Sports and Leisure Club ■ *296* Ramp City ■ *297* Ramp N Rail Skatepark ■ *302* St. Anne's Park ■ *309* Silloque Park and Golf Course ■ *334* Westwood Health and Fitness Centre, Clontarf

## WEST DUBLIN

*346* Ashtown Stables ■ *347* Astro Park ■ *385* Clondalkin Sports and Leisure Centre ■ *388* Coolmine Equestrian Centre ■ *391* Coolmine Sports and Leisure Centre ■ *395* Dublin Municipal Rowing Centre ■ *398* Eamon Ceannt Park ■ *420* Glenanne Hockey Club ■ *426* Kill International ■ *428* Kylemore Karting (Outdoor Karting) ■ *443* National Aquatic Centre ■ *444* National Basketball Arena ■ *445* Neptune Rowing Club ■ *449* Pelletstown Riding Centre

## SOUTH DUBLIN

*578* Glenalbyn Sports Club ■ *621* Kilternan Sports Hotel ■ *725* West Wood, Leopardstown (Sports Club)

## Top Choices: Summer Camps

### CITY CENTRE

*3* African Cultural Project ■ *55* Glenans Sailing ■ *95* Norton, Betty Ann, Theatre School, Harcourt St ■ *121* Walton's New School of Music

### NORTH DUBLIN

*191* Clontarf Lawn Tennis Club ■ *238* Gaiety School of Acting ■ *255* Howth Rock Guitar and Songwriting School ■ *256* Howth Yacht Club ■ *284* Norton, Betty Ann, Theatre School, Swords ■ *288* Pavilion Shopping Centre, The ■ *293* Portmarnock Sports and Leisure Club ■ *321* Starstruck Stage School, Clontarf ■ *324* Sutton Dinghy Club

### WEST DUBLIN

*343* Alternative Entertainment Community Art Group ■ *346* Ashtown Stables ■ *385* Clondalkin Sports and Leisure Centre ■ *393* Draíocht ■ *395* Dublin Municipal Rowing Centre ■ *402* Futurekids, Lucan ■ *444* National Basketball Arena ■ *449* Pelletstown Riding Centre

### SOUTH DUBLIN

*481* Artzone ■ *497* Blackrock College Summer Schoool ■ *520* The Busy Bee Summer School of Cooking ■ *547* Dolphin Activity Holidays ■ *560* Dún Laoghaire Youth Dance Theatre ■ *562* ESB Sportsco ■ *578* Glenalbyn Sports Club ■ *608* Independent Theatre Workshop, Mornington Rd ■ *612* Irish Children's Theatre Group ■ *614* Irish National Sailing School ■ *622* Kodály Society of Ireland ■ *626* Lansdowne Tennis Club ■ *627* Leeson Park School of Music ■ *646* National Performing Arts School, Barrow St ■ *647* National Performing Arts School, Haddington Rd ■ *651* Newpark School Sports Centre

■ *654 Norton, Betty Ann, Theatre School, Bray* ■ *655 Norton, Betty Ann, Theatre School, Clonskeagh* ■ *656 Norton, Betty Ann, Theatre School, Dún Laoghaire* ■ *657 Norton, Betty Ann, Theatre School, Rathmines* ■ *672 Pine Forest Arts Centre* ■ *690 Samba Soccer School* ■ *705 Starstruck Stage School, Clonskeagh* ■ *706 Starstruck Stage School, Foxrock* ■ *712 Surfdock* ■ *719 Tiggy's Art School*

## Top Choices: Walks

### NORTH DUBLIN

*253 Howth Head* ■ *279 Newbridge Demesne* ■ *282 North Bull Island and Dollymount Strand*

### WEST DUBLIN

*430 Larchill Arcadian Gardens* ■ *451 Phoenix Park*

### SOUTH DUBLIN

*495 Big Sugar Loaf* ■ *519 Bushy Park* ■ *537 Dalkey Island* ■ *543 Devil's Glen* ■ *545 Djouce Woods* ■ *580 Glendalough* ■ *593 Hellfire Club* ■ *619 Killiney Hill Park/Dalkey Hill* ■ *630 Little Sugar Loaf* ■ *634 Marlay Park* ■ *673 Powerscourt House and Gardens* ■ *674 Powerscourt Waterfall* ■ *680 Raven's Rock* ■ *718 Three Rock Mountain*

## Top Choices: For Ages 0–2

### CITY CENTRE

*81 Merrion Square* ■ *108 St. Stephen's Green* ■ *114 Smyth's Toys & Computer Games* ■ *125 Bewley's Oriental Café, Mary St* ■ *133 Milano*

### NORTH DUBLIN

*140 Ardgillan Castle* ■ *187 Cabra Library* ■ *199 Donabate/Portrane Beach* ■ *210 Fairview Park* ■ *240 Griffith Park* ■ *241 Gymboree Music on the Go* ■ *242 Hampstead Park (Albert College Park)* ■ *260 Kidzone Play and Party Centre* ■ *263 Loughshinny Beach* ■ *265 Malahide Castle and Demesne* ■ *279 Newbridge Demesne* ■ *292 Portmarnock Beach* ■ *299 Reynoldstown Victorian Country House and Farm* ■ *302 St. Anne's Park* ■ *303 St. Mary's Hospital Pool* ■ *310 Sillybilly Learning Ltd* ■ *311 Skerries Beach* ■ *331 Tolka Valley Park* ■ *333 Ward River Valley Park*

### WEST DUBLIN

*379 Celbridge Abbey Grounds* ■ *396 Dublin Zoo* ■ *398 Eamon Ceannt Park* ■ *418 Gymboree Music on the Go* ■ *430 Larchill Arcadian Gardens* ■ *442 Morrell Farm* ■ *451 Phoenix Park* ■ *457 Sillybilly Learning Ltd* ■ *463 Superdome* ■ *469 War Memorial Gardens*

### SOUTH DUBLIN

*477 Airfield Trust* ■ *499 Blackrock Park* ■ *519 Bushy Park* ■ *522 Cabinteely Park* ■ *584 Greystones Beach* ■ *589 Gymboree Music on the Go* ■ *590 Gymboree Play and Music* ■ *634 Marlay Park* ■ *679 Rathmines Library* ■ *699 Sillybilly Learning Ltd*

## Top Choices: For Ages 2–5

### CITY CENTRE

*5 Ark, The: Children's Cultural Centre* ▪ *7 A Start in the Arts* ▪ *19 Charleville Mall Library* ▪ *43 Dublin Writers' Museum* ▪ *68 Irish Museum of Modern Art* ▪ *81 Merrion Square* ▪ *108 St. Stephen's Green* ▪ *114 Smyth's Toys & Computer Games* ▪ *125 Bewley's Oriental Café, Mary St* ▪ *129 Clery's Rooftop Café* ▪ *133 Milano*

### NORTH DUBLIN

*140 Ardgillan Castle* ▪ *187 Cabra Library* ▪ *196 Coolock Library* ▪ *199 Donabate/Portrane Beach* ▪ *205 Dublin Butterfly House* ▪ *210 Fairview Park* ▪ *213 Finglas Library* ▪ *216 Fry Model Railway Museum* ▪ *240 Griffith Park* ▪ *241 Gymboree Music on the Go* ▪ *242 Hampstead Park (Albert College Park)* ▪ *260 Kidzone Play and Party Centre* ▪ *262 Leisureplex, Coolock* ▪ *263 Loughshinny Beach* ▪ *265 Malahide Castle and Demesne* ▪ *276 National Botanic Gardens* ▪ *278 National Transport Museum* ▪ *279 Newbridge Demesne* ▪ *292 Portmarnock Beach* ▪ *299 Reynoldstown Victorian Country House and Farm* ▪ *302 St. Anne's Park* ▪ *303 St. Mary's Hospital Pool* ▪ *310 Sillybilly Learning Ltd* ▪ *311 Skerries Beach* ▪ *313 Skerries Mills* ▪ *331 Tolka Valley Park* ▪ *333 Ward River Valley Park*

### WEST DUBLIN

*348 Ballyfermot Library* ▪ *360 Blanchardstown Library* ▪ *379 Celbridge Abbey Grounds* ▪ *383 Clondalkin Library* ▪ *392 County Library, Tallaght* ▪ *396 Dublin Zoo* ▪ *398 Eamon Ceannt Park* ▪ *401 Fort Lucan* ▪ *415 Giraffe's Play Centre* ▪ *418 Gymboree Music on the Go* ▪ *430 Larchill Arcadian Gardens* ▪ *432 Leisureplex, Blanchardstown* ▪ *440 Millennium Maze* ▪ *442 Morrell Farm* ▪ *443 National Aquatic Centre* ▪ *451 Phoenix Park* ▪ *452 Phoenix Park Visitor Centre* ▪ *457 Sillybilly Learning Ltd* ▪ *463 Superdome* ▪ *469 War Memorial Gardens* ▪ *474 Spur Steakhouse*

### SOUTH DUBLIN

*477 Airfield Trust* ▪ *486 Ballyroan Library* ▪ *499 Blackrock Park* ▪ *519 Bushy Park* ▪ *521 Cabinteely Library* ▪ *522 Cabinteely Park* ▪ *538 Dalkey Library* ▪ *540 Deansgrange Library* ▪ *555 Dundrum Library* ▪ *558 Dún Laoghaire Music Centre* ▪ *584 Greystones Beach* ▪ *589 Gymboree Music on the Go* ▪ *590 Gymboree Play and Music* ▪ *594 Herbert Park* ▪ *624 Lambert Puppet Theatre and Museum* ▪ *629 Leisureplex, Stillorgan* ▪ *634 Marlay Park* ▪ *649 National Sealife Centre* ▪ *670 Pembroke Library* ▪ *699 Sillybilly Learning Ltd*

## Top Choices: For Ages 5–10

### CITY CENTRE

*5 Ark, The: Children's Cultural Centre* ▪ *21 Chimney, The* ▪ *23 City Hall* ▪ *40 Dublinia* ▪ *52 Garden of Remembrance* ▪ *58 Heraldic Museum* ▪ *59 Hugh Lane Gallery* ▪ *60 Ice@IFSC* ▪ *68 Irish Museum of Modern Art* ▪ *79 Marsh's Library* ▪ *85 National Concert Hall* ▪ *86 National Gallery of Ireland* ▪ *89 National Museum of Ireland (History and Decorative Arts)* ▪ *90 National Museum of Ireland (Natural History)* ▪ *92 National Wax*

Museum, The ▪ **96** Number Twenty Nine ▪ **107** St. Patrick's Cathedral ▪ **110** Savoy Cinema ▪ **120** Viking Splash Tour ▪ **123** Bad Ass Café ▪ **132** Lemon Café

### NORTH DUBLIN

**142** Axis Arts Centre ▪ **144** Balbriggan Public Library ▪ **147** Ballymun Library ▪ **189** Casino Marino ▪ **200** Donaghmede Library ▪ **213** Finglas Library ▪ **216** Fry Model Railway Museum ▪ **237** GAA Museum ▪ **258** Kart City Ltd (Indoor Karting and Skate Park) ▪ **260** Kidzone Play and Party Centre ▪ **262** Leisureplex, Coolock ▪ **265** Malahide Castle and Demesne ▪ **278** National Transport Museum ▪ **282** North Bull Island and Dollymount Strand ▪ **287** Omniplex Cinemas ▪ **292** Portmarnock Beach ▪ **296** Ramp City ▪ **297** Ramp N Rail Skatepark ▪ **299** Reynoldstown Victorian Country House and Farm ▪ **313** Skerries Mills ▪ **329** Tara's Palace

### WEST DUBLIN

**343** Alternative Entertainment Community Art Group ▪ **347** Astro Park ▪ **348** Ballyfermot Library ▪ **360** Blanchardstown Library ▪ **377** Castletymon Library ▪ **379** Celbridge Abbey Grounds ▪ **392** County Library, Tallaght ▪ **393** Draíocht ▪ **396** Dublin Zoo ▪ **398** Eamon Ceannt Park ▪ **401** Fort Lucan ▪ **430** Larchill Arcadian Gardens ▪ **432** Leisureplex, Blanchardstown ▪ **435** Lodge Park Heritage Centre and Steam Museum ▪ **437** Lucan Library ▪ **440** Millennium Maze ▪ **442** Morrell Farm ▪ **443** National Aquatic Centre ▪ **452** Phoenix Park Visitor Centre ▪ **461** Straffan Butterfly Farm ▪ **463** Superdome

### SOUTH DUBLIN

**486** Ballyroan Library ▪ **499** Blackrock Park ▪ **512** Bray Cinema ▪ **519** Bushy Park ▪ **522** Cabinteely Park ▪ **531** Clara Lara ▪ **538** Dalkey Library ▪ **540** Deansgrange Library ▪ **546** Dodder Park ▪ **558** Dún Laoghaire Music Centre ▪ **565** Funderland ▪ **594** Herbert Park ▪ **607** IMC Dún Laoghaire (Cinema) ▪ **624** Lambert Puppet Theatre and Museum ▪ **629** Leisureplex, Stillorgan ▪ **634** Marlay Park ▪ **637** Massey Woods ▪ **648** National Print Museum ▪ **649** National Sealife Centre

## Top Choices: For Ages 10+

### CITY CENTRE

**2** Abbey Theatre ▪ **22** Christ Church Cathedral ▪ **36** Dublin City on Ice ▪ **39** The Dublin Ghost Bus Tour ▪ **40** Dublinia ▪ **50** Gallery of Photography ▪ **57** Guinness Storehouse ▪ **59** Hugh Lane Gallery ▪ **60** Ice@IFSC ▪ **66** Irish Film Centre ▪ **72** Jervis St Shopping Centre ▪ **79** Marsh's Library ▪ **88** National Museum of Ireland (History and Archaeology) ▪ **100** Point Theatre ▪ **106** St. Michan's Church ▪ **110** Savoy Cinema ▪ **112** Sea Safari ▪ **119** Vicar St (Music Venue) ▪ **120** Viking Splash Tour ▪ **130** Eddie Rockets Diner ▪ **131** Epicurean Food Hall ▪ **132** Lemon Café ▪ **135** TGI Friday ▪ **136** Thunder Road Café

### NORTH DUBLIN

**237** GAA Museum ▪ **258** Kart City Ltd (Indoor Karting and Skate Park) ▪ **262** Leisureplex, Coolock ▪ **281** Newgrange and Boyne Valley ▪ **282** North Bull Island and Dollymount Strand ▪ **287** Omniplex Cinemas ▪ **297** Ramp N

Rail Skatepark ▪ *302* St. Anne's Park ▪ *307* Sea Safari ▪ *332* UCI Coolock ▪
*338* Casa Pasta ▪ *340* El Paso Restaurant ▪ *342* Wong's (Chinese Restaurant)

## WEST DUBLIN

*343* Alternative Entertainment Community Art Group ▪ *347* Astro Park ▪
*360* Blanchardstown Library ▪ *381* Civic Theatre ▪ *392* County Library,
Tallaght ▪ *393* Draíocht ▪ *396* Dublin Zoo ▪ *397* Dunsink Observatory ▪
*400* First Flight Balloons ▪ *401* Fort Lucan ▪ *402* Futurekids, Lucan ▪
*427* Kilmainham Gaol ▪ *428* Kylemore Karting (Outdoor Karting) ▪ *432*
Leisureplex, Blanchardstown ▪ *443* National Aquatic Centre ▪ *460* Ster
Century Multiplex Cinemas ▪ *463* Superdome ▪ *472* Joel's Restaurant

## SOUTH DUBLIN

*480* Annamoe Trout Farm ▪ *486* Ballyroan Library ▪ *512* Bray Cinema ▪
*520* The Busy Bee Summer School of Cooking ▪ *531* Clara Lara ▪ *537*
Dalkey Island ▪ *540* Deansgrange Library ▪ *545* Djouce Woods ▪ *558* Dún
Laoghaire Music Centre ▪ *565* Funderland ▪ *569* Futurekids, Stillorgan ▪
*583* Grainstore Youth Arts Centre The ▪ *593* Hellfire Club ▪ *607* IMC Dún
Laoghaire (Cinema) ▪ *619* Killiney Hill Park/Dalkey Hill ▪ *620* Killiney
Strand ▪ *621* Kilternan Sports Hotel ▪ *629* Leisureplex, Stillorgan ▪ *637*
Massey Woods ▪ *663* Ormonde Cinemas ▪ *672* Pine Forest Arts Centre

## PARTY SERVICES

*758* Táshí Party Services

## Top Choices: For Energetic Kids

### CITY CENTRE

*36* Dublin City on Ice ▪ *60* Ice@IFSC ▪ *108* St. Stephen's Green ▪ *120*
Viking Splash Tour

### NORTH DUBLIN

*140* Ardgillan Castle ▪ *237* GAA Museum ▪ *262* Leisureplex, Coolock ▪ *265*
Malahide Castle and Demesne ▪ *278* National Transport Museum ▪ *279*
Newbridge Demesne ▪ *282* North Bull Island and Dollymount Strand ▪ *296*
Ramp City ▪ *297* Ramp N Rail Skatepark ▪ *299* Reynoldstown Victorian
Country House and Farm ▪ *302* St. Anne's Park ▪ *307* Sea Safari ▪ *331*
Tolka Valley Park ▪ *333* Ward River Valley Park

### WEST DUBLIN

*347* Astro Park ▪ *378* Causey Farm ▪ *379* Celbridge Abbey Grounds ▪ *393*
Draíocht ▪ *396* Dublin Zoo ▪ *401* Fort Lucan ▪ *428* Kylemore Karting (Outdoor Karting) ▪ *430* Larchill Arcadian Gardens ▪ *432* Leisureplex, Blanchardstown ▪ *433* Leisureplex, Tallaght ▪ *440* Millennium Maze ▪ *442*
Morrell Farm ▪ *443* National Aquatic Centre ▪ *451* Phoenix Park ▪ *463*
Superdome

### SOUTH DUBLIN

*477* Airfield Trust ▪ *513* Bray Strand/Bray Head ▪ *519* Bushy Park ▪ *531*
Clara Lara ▪ *537* Dalkey Island ▪ *545* Djouce Woods ▪ *552* Dublin Bay Sea
Thrill ▪ *562* ESB Sportsco ▪ *565* Funderland ▪ *570* GAA ▪ *612* Irish Chil-

dren's Theatre Group ▪ *614* Irish National Sailing School ▪ *629* Leisureplex, Stillorgan ▪ *634* Marlay Park ▪ *637* Massey Woods ▪ *690* Samba Soccer School ▪ *712* Surfdock

## Top Choices: For Imaginative Kids

### CITY CENTRE

*2* Abbey Theatre ▪ *20* Chester Beatty Library, The ▪ *74* Leinster School of Music and Drama ▪ *80* The Merriman School Of Singing and Music ▪ *82* Millar Flora Dance Centres

### NORTH DUBLIN

*142* Axis Arts Centre ▪ *150* Barry, Billie, Stage School ▪ *186* Brushstrokes Art School ▪ *238* Gaiety School of Acting ▪ *255* Howth Rock Guitar and Songwriting School ▪ *316* Songschool Ltd ▪ *321* Starstruck Stage School, Clontarf

### WEST DUBLIN

*343* Alternative Entertainment Community Art Group ▪ *393* Draíocht ▪ *438* Lucan Youth Dance/Drama Group

### SOUTH DUBLIN

*481* Artzone ▪ *523* Cabinteely School for Speech and Drama ▪ *529* Churchtown Keyboard School ▪ *552* Dublin Bay Sea Thrill ▪ *558* Dún Laoghaire Music Centre ▪ *565* Funderland ▪ *583* Grainstore Youth Arts Centre The ▪ *593* Hellfire Club ▪ *612* Irish Children's Theatre Group ▪ *624* Lambert Puppet Theatre and Museum ▪ *629* Leisureplex, Stillorgan ▪ *638* Mermaid Theatre ▪ *646* National Performing Arts School, Barrow St ▪ *647* National Performing Arts School, Haddington Rd ▪ *672* Pine Forest Arts Centre ▪ *712* Surfdock ▪ *719* Tiggy's Art School

## Top Choices: For Inquisitive Kids

### CITY CENTRE

*20* Chester Beatty Library, The ▪ *22* Christ Church Cathedral ▪ *45* ENFO (Information on the Environment) ▪ *58* Heraldic Museum ▪ *59* Hugh Lane Gallery ▪ *79* Marsh's Library ▪ *86* National Gallery of Ireland ▪ *88* National Museum of Ireland (History and Archaeology) ▪ *89* National Museum of Ireland (History and Decorative Arts) ▪ *90* National Museum of Ireland (Natural History) ▪ *96* Number Twenty Nine ▪ *106* St. Michan's Church ▪ *122* Waterways Visitor Centre

### NORTH DUBLIN

*189* Casino Marino ▪ *216* Fry Model Railway Museum ▪ *237* GAA Museum ▪ *278* National Transport Museum ▪ *282* North Bull Island and Dollymount Strand ▪ *313* Skerries Mills

### WEST DUBLIN

*394* Drimnagh Castle ▪ *397* Dunsink Observatory ▪ *402* Futurekids, Lucan ▪ *427* Kilmainham Gaol ▪ *452* Phoenix Park Visitor Centre

**SOUTH DUBLIN**

*648* National Print Museum ■ *649* National Sealife Centre ■ *669* Pearse Museum and St. Enda's Park

## Top Choices: For Shy Kids

**CITY CENTRE**

*85* National Concert Hall

**NORTH DUBLIN**

*299* Reynoldstown Victorian Country House and Farm

**SOUTH DUBLIN**

*520* The Busy Bee Summer School of Cooking ■ *558* Dún Laoghaire Music Centre ■ *612* Irish Children's Theatre Group

**ORGANISATIONS**

*764* Catholic Guides of Ireland

## Top Choices: For Trendy Kids

**CITY CENTRE**

*6* Arnott's Department Store ■ *66* Irish Film Centre ■ *72* Jervis St Shopping Centre ■ *75* Liberty Hall Theatre ■ *88* National Museum of Ireland (History and Archaeology) ■ *92* National Wax Museum, The ■ *100* Point Theatre ■ *110* Savoy Cinema ■ *112* Sea Safari ■ *118* UGC Cinemas ■ *119* Vicar St (Music Venue) ■ *127* Butler's Chocolate Café ■ *131* Epicurean Food Hall ■ *136* Thunder Road Café

**NORTH DUBLIN**

*245* Hip Hop Dance Classes ■ *255* Howth Rock Guitar and Songwriting School ■ *258* Kart City Ltd (Indoor Karting and Skate Park) ■ *262* Leisureplex, Coolock ■ *297* Ramp N Rail Skatepark ■ *307* Sea Safari ■ *332* UCI Coolock

**WEST DUBLIN**

*343* Alternative Entertainment Community Art Group ■ *359* Belly Dance Ireland ■ *361* Blanchardstown Shopping Centre ■ *428* Kylemore Karting (Outdoor Karting) ■ *460* Ster Century Multiplex Cinemas ■ *463* Superdome ■ *465* UCI Blanchardstown

**SOUTH DUBLIN**

*565* Funderland